Human Rights in Latin American Prisons

Towards a More Comprehensive Understanding

Edited by

Clara Burbano Herrera and Yves Haeck

BRILL | NIJHOFF

LEIDEN | BOSTON

This project, Assessing the IMPACT of Urgent Measures in Protecting At-Risk Detainees in Latin America (IMPACTUM), has received funding from the European Research Council (ERC) under the European Union's Horizon 2021 research and innovation programme (Grant agreement No. 101044852) and the Research Fund Ghent University. The views and opinions expressed are, however, those of the author(s) only and do not necessarily reflect those of the European Union or the European Research Council Executive Agency. Neither the European Union nor the granting authority can be held responsible for them.

The Library of Congress Cataloging-in-Publication Data is available online at https://catalog.loc.gov
LC record available at https://lccn.loc.gov/2025041672

Typeface for the Latin, Greek, and Cyrillic scripts: "Brill". See and download: brill.com/brill-typeface.

ISSN 0924-4751
ISBN 978-90-04-74772-2 (hardback)
ISBN 978-90-04-74773-9 (e-book)
DOI 10.1163/9789004747739

This book is printed on acid-free paper and produced in a sustainable manner.

Contents

Preface

The conditions of incarceration in Latin America have long been of critical concern, as numerous reports and academic studies have highlighted the systemic issues that afflict the region's prison systems. These range from severe overcrowding and inadequate healthcare to the disproportionate impact of incarceration on marginalized communities, particularly women and individuals from socioeconomically disadvantaged backgrounds. The COVID-19 pandemic further exposed and exacerbated these structural deficiencies, emphasizing the urgent need for comprehensive reform. Against this backdrop, this volume seeks to contribute to the growing body of scholarly work that critically examines the underlying causes of these conditions, as well as the legal and policy responses that have been implemented in various Latin American countries.

This collection brings together distinguished scholars with expertise in law, human rights, criminology, and public policy to offer a multidimensional analysis of incarceration in Latin America. The chapters draw upon diverse theoretical frameworks, including "negative theories of punishment" and "experimental constitutionalism", to interrogate the persistent failures of the region's prison systems and to propose avenues for reform. The volume explores a wide range of topics, from the intersection of poverty and health in prisons to the gendered dimensions of punishment and the challenges posed by organized crime within correctional facilities. Moreover, it critically examines the role of alternative sentencing mechanisms, the regulation of the use of force in prisons, and the broader implications of public resistance to decarceration efforts.

A key theme that emerges throughout this volume is the pressing need to rethink incarceration not only in terms of its function as a penal institution, but also as a broader reflection of social inequality and systemic injustice. The book underscores how incarceration disproportionately affects marginalized communities, with economic, racial, and social factors shaping individuals' experiences behind bars. Women, in particular, face unique vulnerabilities, especially in relation to punitive policies surrounding drug offenses and reproductive rights. Furthermore, the volume highlights how incarcerated individuals frequently rely on family members to provide basic necessities such as food, medicine, and hygiene products – responsibilities that should fall under the purview of state authorities.

The COVID-19 pandemic serves as a focal point for some contributions within this collection. The crisis prompted various legal and policy responses aimed at reducing prison populations, ranging from judicial and executive measures to alternative sentencing initiatives. While some of these measures were successful in mitigating overcrowding in the short term, the post-pandemic period has witnessed a return to rising incarceration rates across much of the region. The volume therefore calls for sustained efforts to institutionalize humane prison policies and to expand alternatives to incarceration that prioritize rehabilitation and reintegration.

Beyond analyzing national policies, this book also explores the role of international human rights organizations in advocating for prison reform. Institutions such as the United Nations and the Inter-American Commission on Human Rights play a crucial role in monitoring prison conditions and holding states accountable for human rights violations. Their interventions are essential for fostering transparency, ensuring adherence to international standards, and promoting the adoption of best practices in prison management.

A key milestone in the development of this volume was the expert workshop, entitled 'Human Rights Behind Bars' held in December 2024, where all contributing authors had the opportunity to present their chapters. This gathering provided a valuable forum for discussion, allowing for the exchange of ideas, constructive feedback, and deeper engagement with the themes explored in this book. The workshop was instrumental in refining the contributions and enhancing the coherence of the volume as a whole.

We would like to extend our sincere gratitude to all the contributors for their invaluable work, as well as to the evaluators of the chapters for their insightful comments and rigorous review process. We are also deeply grateful to the European Research Council, the Research Council of Ghent University (BOF), and the Programme for Studies on Human Rights in Context, for their generous support which made this project possible. Special thanks go to the publisher Brill for believing in this academic endeavour and for its commitment to disseminating critical research on incarceration and human rights. Last but not least, we express our heartfelt appreciation to Research Fellow Ms Luna Lanckvrind for her outstanding editorial assistance. Her dedication, precision, and generous support were instrumental to the successful completion of this volume.

In presenting this work, it is our hope that the analysis and insights contained within will serve as a valuable resource for students, academics, policymakers, and human rights advocates. By engaging with the complex realities of incarceration in Latin America, this volume aspires to contribute to ongoing debates on criminal justice reform and to inspire more humane and effective approaches to punishment and rehabilitation. The discussions within these pages are not merely theoretical; they have direct implications for the lives of millions of incarcerated individuals and their families, as well as for the broader pursuit of justice and human rights in the region.

Clara Burbano Herrera and Yves Haeck
Ghent, Belgium
April 2025

Notes on Contributors

Clara Burbano Herrera
is Principal Investigator of the ERC-funded project IMPACTUM and Professor of International Human Rights Law at Ghent University, where she obtained her Ph.D. in Law. She has widely published on human rights law, particularly on precautionary measures and the role of regional systems in protecting vulnerable groups.

Yves Haeck
is Professor of International Human Rights Law at Ghent University and Director of the Programme for Studies on Human Rights in Context. He holds a Ph.D. in Law from Ghent University and has widely published on international human rights adjudication, with a focus on the European and Inter-American Human Rights systems.

Libardo Ariza
is Doctor of Law from the University of Deusto (Spain), Director of the Doctorate Program in Law and Associate Professor at the Faculty of Law of the Universidad de los Andes (Colombia). He is co-author of *Los muros de la infamia: prisiones en Colombia y en América Latina* (Universidad de Los Andes, 2011).

Gabriela Cruz
is a peer researcher in the project, "Women deprived of their liberty, motherhood and children's rights in Mexico. Empirical and judicial perspectives" at Autonomous University of Chiapas, Mexico. An indigenous woman from Oaxaca, Mexico and formerly incarcerated, Gabriela shares her story and collaborates on research to raise awareness and advocate for better conditions for women in prison.

Corina Giacomello
has been working since 2025 on human rights, gender and deprivation of liberty, children with incarcerated parents and adolescents in conflict with the law. She has published 20 books and more than 50 chapters and papers on these topics, in Latin America and Europe.

Luna Lanckvrind
is a Ph.D. candidate in International Human Rights Law at the Programme for Studies on Human Rights in Context, Ghent University, where she also com-

pleted her Bachelor and Master of Laws. She is also a researcher on the ERC-funded project IMPACTUM.

Carmen Cecilia Martínez López
is Associate Director of Legal Strategies for Latin America and the Caribbean at the Center for Reproductive Rights. She is a Venezuelan attorney with a Master's Degree in Law from Palermo University.

Lucía Nunovero Cisneros
is an attorney, M.P.H., M. Crim. (Catholic University of Louvain), and professor of Criminology at Pontificia Universidad Católica del Perú and University of Grenade (Spain) Ph.D.(c). She has authored numerous publications on Criminal Justice, Prisons and Organized Crime in Latin America.

José Luis Pérez Guadalupe
Ph.D. (1965). Professor at the University of the Pacific. Sociologist, theologian, and criminologist, with publications on religion, politics, criminology, and penal enforcement. Coauthor of the book *El Tren de Aragua y el crimen organizado en América Latina* (2025).

Natalia Pires de Vasconcelos
is a doctoral candidate in Sociology at the University of Georgia where she studies the impact of state violence and incarceration on health and welfare. Natalia holds a Ph.D. in Law from the University of São Paulo and an LL.M. from Yale Law School.

Maíra Rocha Machado
Ph.D. (2003), Getulio Vargas Foundation Law School, is a Professor of Empirical Legal Research, Criminal and Procedure Law and Prison Studies. She is the principal investigator of a research project on Law and State Violence funded by FAPESP (São Paulo Research Foundation). All her published work is available at fgv.academia.edu/mairamachado.

María Luisa Romero
is a lawyer specializing in human rights, current member of the UN Subcommittee on Prevention of Torture, and former Minister of Government of Panama. She is an advisor to Global Freedom of Expression and a graduate of Harvard College and Harvard Law School.

Soledad Sánchez Jeanney
is a human rights lawyer and independent legal consultant. She has extensive experience in human rights advocacy.

Mario Andrés Torres Gómez
is a Ph.D. Researcher in the Programme for Studies of Human Rights in Context at Ghent University (Belgium). He holds an LL.M. in International Law from Universidad de los Andes (Colombia). He has previously worked at Universidad de Los Andes and the Ministry of Justice of Colombia.

Coletta A. Youngers
is a Senior Fellow at the Washington Office on Latin America (WOLA) and human rights advocate who has written books, book chapters and reports on issues related to human rights, drug policy and women's incarceration in Latin America.

Figures and Tables

Figures

Tables

CHAPTER 1

Introduction: Human Rights in Latin American Prisons: Towards a More Comprehensive Understanding

Clara Burbano Herrera and Yves Haeck

In Latin America, many prisons have suffered decades of abandonment and neglect by states, turning them into facilities where human rights are violated, where criminal gangs recruit people to commit crimes, where discrimination and violence are prevalent, and where the rehabilitation of a person represents a tangible challenge.[1] Prisons have long been characterised by deficient sanitary conditions, inadequate infrastructure, recurring public health challenges, and widespread overcrowding. These issues have been reported by international and local organizations for decades.[2] For instance, the Inter-American Commission on Human Rights (IACHR) has emphasized the gravity of prison overcrowding in the Americas for over 45 years. It has noted that prison overcrowding is the foreseeable consequence of various factors, including inadequate infrastructure, the implementation of repressive social control policies that prioritize the deprivation of liberty as the primary response to

1 For instance in 2021, a total of 316 people deprived of their liberty died in Ecuador in state custody and hundreds more were injured in a series of planned violent attacks carried out by organized groups made up of the prisoners themselves. See: IACHR, *Report on the Human Rights of Persons Deprived of Liberty in Ecuador* (OAS, 2022) para 2.

2 Clara Burbano-Herrera and Yves Haeck,'The Use of Transformative Provisional Measures by the Inter-American Court of Human Rights: Toward a Tangible Impact' in Armin von Bogdandy et al. (eds), *The Impact of the Inter-American Human Rights System: Transformations on the Ground* (New York, Oxford Academic 2024) <https://doi.org/10.1093/oso/9780197744161.003.0009>; Libardo Ariza and Manuel Iturralde, 'Tales from La Catedral: The narco and the reconfiguration of prison social order in Colombia' in Máximo Sozzo (ed), *Prisons, Inmates and Governance in Latin America* (Palgrave Macmillan 2022) 63–92; Clara Burbano Herrera and Yves Haeck (eds), *Human Rights behind Bars: Tracing Vulnerability in Prison Populations across Continents from a Multidisciplinary Perspective* (Cham, Springer 2022) <https://doi.org/10.1007/978-3-031-11484-7>; Libardo Ariza, María Mauersberger and Fernando León Arboleda, 'Locked in the Home: A Critique of House Arrest as an Alternative to Imprisonment for Women Sentenced for Drug-Related Crimes' (2021) 101 *The Prison Journal* 286, 286–305 <https://doi.org/10.1177/00328855211010410> Michelle Butler, Gavin Slade and Camila Nunes Dias, 'Self-governing prisons: Prison gangs in an international perspective' (2022) 25 *Trends in Organized Crime* 1, 1–16.

public security, the excessive use of pre-trial detention, the use of deprivation of liberty as a criminal sanction, and the lack of a prompt and efficient response by court systems.[3] The World Prison Brief reported a 71 per cent increase in the use of pre-trial detention in the Americas between 2000 and 2020.[4] Furthermore, the World Female Imprisonment List has revealed that the global population of women and girls in detention has increased by 60 per cent since 2000.[5] These trends can be explained by the implementation of hard-line drug laws, which in many countries, such as Costa Rica and Mexico, force the de facto use of pre-trial detention, impose disproportionate sentences and do not allow the use of alternatives to imprisonment.[6]

The aim of this book is to contribute to the existing literature on the critical examination of the causes that have led to the appalling conditions to which persons deprived of their liberty in Latin America are subject. As such, the volume aims to engage in a scholarly analysis to provide a more comprehensive and contextualised understanding of the prison crisis within a human rights framework. The objective is realized through an examination of the prison situation in Latin America from two angles, namely using the theoretical framework of intersectionality with a special focus on women (Part 1) and paying particular attention to the break point provided by the COVID-19 pandemic in the Latin American context (Part 2). The volume is divided into an introduction, seven chapters and a conclusion, and is further divided into two parts. The first part of the book consists of three chapters addressing drugs and women deprived of liberty, detained women and sexual and reproductive health rights, and urgent measures adopted by international human rights bodies to protect at-risk detainees. The second part of the book comprises four chapters that provide reflections on the impact of the COVID-19 pandemic in Latin America. These chapters place particular emphasis on the analysis of the diverse decisions taken by the three branches of government (the

3 IACHR, *Report on the Human Rights of Persons Deprived of Liberty in the Americas* (OAS, 2011) para 451.

4 Institute for Crime & Justice Policy Research and Birkbeck College, 'Welcome' (*World Prison Brief*, Fourth Edition) <https://www.prisonstudies.org/>. The information is the latest available and dates from the end of February 2020.

5 As of April 2024, more than 10.99 million people were being held in penal institutions throughout the world, either as pre-trial detainees/remand prisoners or having been convicted and sentenced. Prison population rates vary considerably between different regions of the world, and between different parts of the same continent. For example, in the Americas the median rate for North American countries is 220.5 whereas for Central American countries it is 310.5. See Institute for Crime & Justice Policy Research and Birkbeck College, 'Welcome' (*World Prison Brief*, 2024) <https://www.prisonstudies.org/>.

6 IACHR, *Report on the Women Deprived of Liberty in the Americas* (OAS, 2023) para 1.

legislative, executive and judicial) to tackle the virus and its effects on the population deprived of liberty.

The first chapter in Part 1, entitled “Female Incarceration in Latin America and Mexico”, is authored by **Coletta Youngers, Corina Giacomello and Gabriela Cruz.** This chapter focuses on the examination of the phenomenon of the imprisonment of women in Latin America and Mexico. The authors provide an in-depth socio-legal analysis of the disproportionate impact of drug policies on women’s imprisonment, punishing the most invisible and unheard sectors of society. They explain in detail how the interplay of socio-economic inequality, gender differences and gender-based violence, alongside abundant and expanding illicit drug markets, creates the perfect conditions for women’s employment in the illicit drug trade. In short, drug-related crime becomes an option in a context of underdevelopment and limited choices. They point out that increased international attention to the impact of incarceration on women and their families has led to calls for the implementation of alternatives to incarceration at all stages of the criminal justice system: pre-trial, sentencing and post-sentencing. However, Latin American governments have largely failed to implement effective non-custodial alternatives. At the same time, while alternatives to incarceration are certainly necessary and desirable, they do not necessarily prevent people from becoming involved in criminal justice systems, nor do they guarantee full reintegration into society. The authors also refer to three states that have implemented legal reforms to use alternatives to incarceration. In 2013, Costa Rica adopted a legal reform to reduce the sentence for women who carry drugs into prison, so that alternatives to incarceration could be used. In Colombia, a law was passed in 2023 to provide alternatives to imprisonment for women who are single heads of households, live in situations of vulnerability, have sentences of eight years or less, and meet certain other conditions. This law incorporates a gender perspective into the criminal justice system and promotes women’s human rights. Finally, a third example is the federal Amnesty Law passed in Mexico in April 2020. The law allows for the release from prison of people from vulnerable groups (women, young people, indigenous people and people with disabilities) who have been accused or convicted of drug trafficking, theft, sedition or abortion. They point out that the number of amnesties granted to date has unfortunately remained limited: as of July 2023, only 376 out of 2,327 applications have been granted, of which 127 were women. They affirm that although the impact of the law has been frustrating at best, it is an innovative and permanent approach. The chapter concludes by recognising that while the visibility of women in prison has increased over the past decade, little has changed in Latin America. The authors emphasize the need for more effective alternatives to imprisonment, which could benefit women like Gaby; an Indigenous woman and one of the authors of the chapter, who was imprisoned for 7 years for cannabis trafficking.

The second contribution, entitled "Reproductive Health and Rights in Prisons: Challenges and Opportunities for Latin America", authored by **Carmen Cecilia Martínez López,** delineates the advancements and challenges concerning sexual and reproductive health rights within the Inter-American Human Rights System, particularly in the context of women deprived of liberty. The author emphasizes that developments on the topic are recent and have been included mainly in the advisory opinion OC-29/22 issued by the IACtHR and the recent report "Women Deprived of Liberty in the Americas" published by the IACHR in 2023. According to **Martínez López**, both the IACtHR and the IACHR have recognised that women deprived of liberty require reinforced protections to ensure that their reproductive rights are enjoyed. These human rights bodies have based their interpretations on the right to non-discrimination and the right of women to be free from gender-based violence. The interpretation of these two rights, in light of the rights and duties incorporated in Articles 1.1 and 24 of the ACHR, has permitted the development of essential standards. The author mentions the following five standards: i) a person should not be detained if there are reproductive rights concerns (for example, obstetric emergencies); ii) it must be ensured that pregnant persons are not victims of obstetric violence; iii) measures should be promoted to prevent incarceration of people to whom the state cannot or has failed to satisfy their reproductive rights; iv) states have a reinforced obligation to ensure access, without discrimination, to quality sexual and reproductive health care; and v) pregnant persons or persons during their postpartum should not be imprisoned and that, if necessary, alternatives should be posed in their favour. In the final section of her contribution, **Martínez López** provides a reflection on three concrete challenges or legal standards that she argues the Inter-American human rights bodies must develop. Firstly, the right to abortion. She asserts that individuals deprived of their liberty have a right to abortion and that states have a duty to provide it, regardless of their imprisonment. Secondly, the right of persons deprived of liberty to access information on topics concerning reproductive rights and, most importantly, the right to access comprehensive sexual education. This duty must be understood as reinforced in cases of children and adolescents who face any deprivation of liberty because comprehensive sexual education is key to the development of capacities and maturity concerning their right to autonomy. Finally, she asserts that in circumstances where reproductive rights are subject to any form of suspension during a public emergency, it is imperative that the well-being of women deprived of their liberty is prioritized. Therefore, in instances where the state is unable to guarantee the right to reproductive health, situations of emergency – particularly those precipitated by the global COVID-19 pandemic – should prompt the state to consider release or other alternatives to imprisonment.

The final contribution in Part 1 is entitled "Assessing State Compliance with Interim Measures Protecting Persons Deprived of Liberty in Latin America: Insights from the Case of *Polay Campos v Peru*" authored by **Clara Burbano Herrera and Luna Lanckvrind.** They provide an overview of the Human Rights Committee's use of interim measures to protect persons deprived of liberty in Latin America, examine state compliance with these measures, and reflect on the extent to which they can prevent human rights violations in practice. Additionally, the authors provide a comprehensive analysis of the case of *Polay Campos v Peru* at both the United Nations and Inter-American human rights levels. **Burbano Herrera and Lanckvrind** posit that the infringement of the rights of individuals who are deprived of their liberty represents a matter of significant concern in numerous Latin American countries. This is particularly salient given issues of overcrowding, unsanitary conditions, violations of fair trial, violence and denial of healthcare to sick detainees. Despite the formal recognition of the rights of detainees in international documents, there appears to be a persistent failure on the part of member states to uphold the right of persons deprived of their liberty to be treated with dignity. In order to safeguard the rights of individuals deprived of their liberty from irreparable harm, the Human Rights Committee has established the authority to grant interim measures. The research demonstrates that between 1977 and 2023 a total of 15 interim measures were requested to protect persons deprived of their liberty in Latin America. The analysis of the interim measures indicates that the beneficiaries were predominantly political prisoners who were either ill or held incommunicado in six states. Furthermore, compliance represents a significant concern; less than half of the cases were compliant with the aforementioned request. The case of *Polay Campos v Peru* offers a compelling illustration of the political context in Latin America from the 1970s to the end of the 1990s and the necessity of granting interim measures in such situations. This case provided the Committee with an opportunity to address two significant issues that had emerged in Peru during the Fujimori regime in a relatively short period of time. The first issue pertains to the degrading and inhumane treatment of individuals deprived of their liberty and accused of being members of the guerrilla group Shining Path. The second issue concerns the lack of a fair trial for these detainees. These issues were subsequently addressed by the IACtHR in its jurisprudence almost a decade later. The analysis of this case demonstrates that both the HRC and the IACHR acted in a prompt and decisive manner, adopting interim and precautionary measures with the objective of safeguarding Mr Polay Campos. In contrast, the IACtHR's approach was characterized by a notable formalism, which gave the impression that the Court lacked an accurate understanding of the situation in Peru at the time. The authors emphasize that an extensive review of case law reveals a significant challenge pervasive within the UN system, namely the scarcity of easily accessible information. Consequently, the total number and types of interim measures implemented remain uncertain. From the perspective of the impact of the measures adopted by the human rights bodies, they observe that it appears justifiable to hypothesize that the information gathered by both the HRC and the IACHR during the 1990s will be useful in assessing the petition currently under consideration by the IACHR. This indicates that the precautionary measures and information provided by Peru and the petitioners at that time, along with the decision on the merits of the Human Rights Committee, could have an impact on the current Inter-American process.

The second part of the book focuses on the analysis of COVID-19 and begins with an article by **María Luisa Romero and Soledad Sánchez Jeanney** entitled "The COVID-19 Pandemic and Prison Policy in Latin America". The authors provide a general overview of the prison context in Latin America before, during and after the pandemic, and offer a detailed analysis of the various measures implemented by Latin American governments in response to the pandemic in relation to their prison populations. The authors argue that COVID-19 highlighted the vulnerability of prisons to disease transmission due to confinement, poor sanitation, overcrowding and the prevalence of health vulnerabilities among inmates. They also underline the historic failure of states to address even basic sanitation needs and affirm that the pandemic showed that governments often understood the gravity of the threat and were able to implement basic measures to reduce prison overcrowding. Indeed, **María Luisa Romero and Soledad Sánchez Jeanney** acknowledge that even prior to the advent of the pandemic, Latin American prison systems were characterized by unsanitary conditions, inadequate funding, and overcrowding. These systems were deficient in their ability or willingness to implement even the most fundamental health prevention measures. They divide the policy responses adopted by states to combat COVID-19 into three groups, including: i) policy responses to address critical sanitation deficiencies. They explain that authorities issued protocols and guidelines for the prevention and management of COVID-19 emphasizing measures to improve basic hygiene; ii) policy responses to facilitate safe communication with the outside world, including by preventing prison visits and using technology to connect prisoners with the outside world and; iii) policy responses to reduce prison overcrowding. In March 2020, state authorities initiated processes aimed at reducing their prison populations through their judicial, legislative, and/or executive branches. These initiatives were implemented in various forms, including presidential pardons, executive decrees, emergency legislation, and directives from justice officials. The authors argue that it is challenging to assess the results of such measures because there is limited official information about the number of people released on humanitarian grounds due to the impact of the COVID-19. A preliminary conclusion based on the countries reviewed is that, in the early stages of the pandemic, no country – except Nicaragua, whose government never attributed its massive releases to the pandemic – released more than 10 percent of its prison population during COVID-19 and most actually released less than 5 percent. In terms of the challenges faced, **María Luisa Romero and Soledad Sánchez Jeanney** cite public opposition to prisoner releases from various groups, including defenders of victims' rights. Notably, in Brazil, this opposition was expressed not only by judges but also by the Ministry of Justice. Another challenge that has been highlighted is the situation of individuals following their time in prison. For instance, it is a cause for concern that in Chile, it was reported that one hundred prisoners rejected the offer of a general pardon in April 2020 and instead opted to continue their imprisonment, most probably due to the lack of a home to return to upon leaving prison. Others preferred to stay because leaving prison would mean losing the jobs and benefits they had while in prison, which would not be available otherwise. Under these conditions, former prisoners may have a very difficult time breaking the cycle of release and recidivism. The post-pandemic reality has demonstrated that, despite the efforts of states to reduce overcrowding during the pandemic, prison populations in countries in the region have continued to grow, with few exceptions. According to the World Prison Brief, the Latin American region had around 1.6 million people deprived of liberty in 2018. Subsequent years have witnessed a steady rise in the region's prison population, reaching an estimated 1.9 million in 2022. This analysis underscores the imperative for states to re-evaluate their approach to mitigating prison overcrowding. The authors end by stating that states need to seriously rethink the importance of reducing prison overcrowding given that overcrowding not only violates the rights of persons deprived of liberty, but is also concerning from a public health perspective.

The second article in this section is entitled "Addressing the Impact and Response to the COVID-19 Pandemic in Latin American Prisons", and was written by **José Luis Pérez Guadalupe and Lucía Nuñovero Cisneros**. The authors of this chapter present an analysis of the impact of the COVID-19 pandemic in Latin American prisons, and the responses given by state authorities in various countries, with a particular focus on Mexico, Colombia, Peru, Chile, Brazil and Argentina. In the first part, they provide a general overview of the problems within prisons and share statistics on prison populations and overcrowding, and their variations during the pandemic. They emphasize that from the beginning of the pandemic, experts had raised concerns about the dire sanitary conditions, food scarcity and overcrowding in Latin American prisons. These conditions made isolation impossible and resulted in inmates having untreated health conditions while barely having access to proper health services. Furthermore, they argue that penitentiary systems in Latin America are highly diverse, and therefore were differently impacted by the policies put in place to combat the COVID-19 pandemic. For instance, in countries such as Bolivia (+37%), Uruguay (14%), Paraguay (10%) and Panama (9%), the prison population continued to increase significantly during the pandemic in contexts where the prison population did not exceed 25,000 inmates nationwide. In contrast, very moderate increases or no increases in the number of inmates were evident in countries with the largest prison populations, such as Argentina (+7%), Mexico (+4%), and Brazil (+3%), with Colombia as an exception. It is evident that COVID-19 exacerbated the critical challenges faced by Latin American prisons in previous decades, particularly overcrowding and deficiencies in governance. These issues were identified as the primary structural impediments to the effective functioning of penitentiary systems in the region. The second section provides a comprehensive overview of the key lessons to be drawn from these critical years. They discuss aspects that could facilitate a more effective response to the challenges facing Latin American penitentiary systems. This includes access to information provided by the authorities. In the context of the pandemic, the lack of information exacerbated conflict and insecurity among inmates, families and communities. The authors also mention the relevance of paying close attention to the context. For instance, in response to the recommendations made by international organizations, states across the globe implemented a range of preventive and responsive measures. These measures, which were often identical in numerous countries, included the introduction of protocols designed to address the spread of infection. These measures called for the use of personal protective equipment such as masks, the isolation of infected individuals, restrictions on visits, staff reductions, the suspension of educational activities and labour, educational campaigns, the distribution of hygiene kits and testing materials, among others. However, the implementation of these measures was associated with significant challenges in the Latin American context, which is characterized by overcrowding and substandard conditions in many prisons throughout the region. For instance, the denial of visits had practical implications, such as restricting access to basic provisions for inmates, which further exacerbated their already dire circumstances. The study also highlights the need to regulate the use of force during riots in prisons. It is an undeniable fact that most riots during the pandemic occurred in overcrowded and understaffed prisons, resulting in injuries and deaths. The lack of clarity in protocols, transparency and restrictions on contact with the outside world caused discontent among inmates and staff. Finally, communication with relatives was one of the policies that most effectively mitigated these conflicts during the pandemic. They involved the liberalization of communications between inmates and their families through videoconferences or the controlled use of mobile phones. The authors concur with the conclusions reached by **María Luisa Romero and Soledad Sánchez Jeanney** that the implementation of executive and judicial decisions related to releases – in the form of substitution mechanisms in Colombia, commutative pardon in Chile, and the humanitarian pardon in Peru, as well as the amnesty law in Mexico – did not yield the results that had been anticipated.

The contribution written by **Maíra Rocha Machado and Natalia Pires de Vasconcelos**, "A Lost Critical Juncture: COVID-19 in Brazilian Prisons", analyses the context of Brazilian prisons within the context of the COVID-19 pandemic. The authors explain the response of the National Council of Justice, in particular its Recommendation 62, which provided for specific measures to encourage decarceration due to the risks presented by COVID-19, and the subsequent actions of the judiciary. The National Council of Justice had recommended that state and federal courts should approve requests for early or temporary release, probation/parole, or house arrest, in cases where the incarcerated person was elderly, was part of a group with higher health risks, or had not committed a violent crime. In fact, Recommendation 62 not only strengthened provisions of criminal law that were already contained in the Criminal Code and the Code of Criminal Procedure, but also greatly expanded their scope. The results of the authors' research demonstrate that, contrary to the request of the National Council of Justice, the response of the criminal justice system showed a notable lack of consideration for the severity of the pandemic and its subsequent risks to the health and well-being of prisoners. In the numerous habeas petitions, judges predominantly rejected requests for decarceration, opting instead to prioritize what they defined as public safety. In fact, one response that was generally adopted (albeit in an uncoordinated way) was to lock down prisons, preventing access by outsiders other than essential staff and the police. Furthermore, there was a general absence of transparent information regarding cases of COVID-19 among both incarcerated individuals and prison staff, as well as regarding the measures adopted by each institution. **Rocha Machado and Pires de Vasconcelos** posit that, within the Brazilian context, the prevalence of negative theories of punishment has a significant impact on the manner in which judges approach criminal cases, influencing their decision-making processes. This, in turn, serves to explain why attempts to reform punitive practices have historically been unsuccessful. Indeed, since the eighteenth century, the concept of "negative theories of punishment" has been in place. These theories encompass a set of ideas that emphasize an obligation to punish, place value on suffering and social exclusion, establish the notion of prison as a sanction par excellence, and devalue alternatives to punishment. Through the lens of historical neo-institutionalism, the authors argue that this legal rationality is an entrenched institutional culture, a set of ideas about what elements are relevant to rectifying legal violations and punishing individuals, which excludes considerations of the humanity and suffering of those who are imprisoned. In this context, current judicial decisions are making certain people invisible, making room for 'traffickers', 'criminals', and 'dangerous people'. In conclusion, the pandemic could have represented a pivotal moment, with the potential to effect a paradigm shift away from a culture of mass violations of the rights of incarcerated individuals. This could have provided a valuable opportunity to challenge entrenched judicial practices. However, the empirical findings suggest that institutional change did not occur. The authors conclude that the pandemic and its effects on the criminal justice system were not accompanied by productive conditions for reform, representing a critical juncture for the criminal justice system given the strength of modern penal rationality.

The final article of the present volume has been contributed by **Libardo José Ariza** and **Mario Andrés Torres**, and is entitled "Two Emergency Regimes: Prison, Judicial Intervention, and the COVID-19 Pandemic in Colombia". The chapter provides a critical analysis of the responses given by the Colombian Constitutional Court and the executive branch to the prison crisis in Colombia, before and during the COVID-19 pandemic. The analysis is grounded in the theoretical framework of 'experimental constitutionalism'. The authors state that in the context of prisons, experimental constitutionalism is a process of constitutional intervention. In this process, the courts create experimental remedies to improve prison conditions. Nevertheless, in Colombia, individuals who have been deprived of their liberty often find themselves in a state of indefinite helplessness, uncertainty and fear. The remedies devised by the Constitutional Court are intended to protect the rights of persons deprived of their liberty and to defend constitutional principles within the prison system. In practice, however, this is an empty promise that has the opposite effect: to leave people who suffer human rights violations in prison. The judicial interventions described in their contribution are examples of experimental constitutionalism. In this regard, **Libardo José Ariza** and **Mario Andrés Torres** explain that the Colombian Constitutional Court employs the doctrine of unconstitutional state affairs with the aim of addressing structural problems within prisons. The prison context is characterized by the following issues: i) massive and recurrent violations of the human rights of persons deprived of their liberty; ii) these violations are the consequence of certain authorities not complying with their legal and constitutional obligations; and iii) in these circumstances, the legal tool called *tutela*, is not sufficient to overcome the massive violation of human rights. The Court has applied the doctrine of unconstitutional state affairs on three occasions: in 1998 (T-153 of 1988); in 2013 (T-388 of 2013); and in 2022 (judgment SU-122/2022). The latter ruling extends the declaration to police stations and transitory detention centres. The crisis involved overcrowding by 40%. The Court has evolved its understanding and approach to the prison crisis. Initially, remedies were focused on the construction of prisons only; however, it was subsequently recognized that other problems, including reintegration into society, healthcare and access to justice, were also relevant. Notwithstanding the judicial decisions that were made, it was evident in 2020 that the situation of individuals who were deprived of their liberty was still extremely poor.

The executive adopted several protocols to contain the spread of the virus, including the suspension of visits, which had a negative impact given that relatives provide prisoners with basic goods. In addition, in practice, measures such as hand washing, social distancing and case reporting were not possible in the prison given the conditions. The executive also declared a state of emergency through Legislative Decree 546 of 2020. This Decree "whose main measure was to replace custodial sentences and pre-trial detention with measures such as house arrest in favour of the prison population that presented a higher level of risk in case of being infected by the virus", was the subject of considerable criticism. It appeared to prioritize the potential impact of releases on crime rates over the imperative of containing the rapid spread of the pandemic within the prison and jail system. Ironically, only 825 persons deprived of their liberty were granted temporary house arrest under the special procedure, while almost 18,000 persons were released under the ordinary procedure. The executive has adopted protocols that have not improved the situation of persons deprived of their liberty. The authors argue that experimental constitutionalism allows the Court to declare that the penitentiary is not in line with the principles of the Constitution and should be corrected progressively. Prisons should be reformed, and society should spare no effort or resources in this task, so that one day the rights of prisoners will be respected. In practice, this legal doctrine leaves the prison system in a state of permanent reform. Despite the enormous symbolic power that the declaration of an unconstitutional state of affairs carries, the material conditions of the prisoner's existence will not change significantly. What they have seen in Colombia is that the prisons have remained in a state of permanent crisis.

The diverse legal perspectives, empirical studies, and real-life experiences examined in the chapters of this volume aim to foster academic discourse on the role of law, human rights, and criminal justice policies in the lived experiences of individuals deprived of liberty, their families, and society at large. It is our hope that this work will inspire scholars and policymakers to explore alternative approaches to engaging with incarcerated individuals and addressing the structural challenges inherent in the prison system, ultimately ensuring that their human rights are upheld while in custody.

Acknowledgements

This contribution was made possible thanks to funding from the European Research Council (ERC) under the European Union's Horizon Europe 2021 research and innovation programme (Grant Agreement No. 101044852). It is part of the ERC-funded project IMPACTUM: "Assessing the Impact of Urgent Measures in Protecting At-Risk Detainees in Latin America".

PART 1

Prisons: Intersectionalities and Contexts

CHAPTER 2

Female Incarceration in Latin America and Mexico

Coletta A. Youngers, Corina Giacomello and Gabriela Cruz

1 Introduction

The number of women in prison continues to grow at alarming rates around the world, and at a much higher rate than for that of men. The fifth edition of the World Female Imprisonment List[1] shows that the number of women and girls in detention world-wide increased by 60 percent since 2000, while that of men rose by around 22 percent. The same source illustrates these trends in Latin America, with egregious statistics for some countries. Excluding the United States, an estimated 95,000 women are behind bars in the Americas today, compared to 37,671 in the year 2000, an increase of more than 150 percent in little over two decades. Brazil has among the highest numbers of incarcerated women in the world, coming in third after the U.S. and China, while Mexico is in tenth place. El Salvador has the world's third highest female prison population rate, 42 out of 100,000 people; its female prison population has increased more than sevenfold over the past two decades. Guatemala's has increased sixfold, and it is one of 17 jurisdictions around the world where women and girls account for more than 10 percent of the total prison population.[2]

According to the same source, women and girls make up 6.9 percent of the global prison population; in Latin America, 5.5 percent of those in prison are women and girls. In June 2023, there were 232,808 people in Mexican 284 prisons, of whom 13,175, that is, 5.66 percent, were women.[3] Therefore, while Mexico represents one of the countries with the highest female prison popu-

1 Helen Fair and Roy Walmsley, 'World Female Imprisonment List (fifth edition)' (*Institute for Crime & Justice Policy Research*, 2022) <https://www.prisonstudies.org/sites/default/files/resources/downloads/world_female_imprisonment_list_5th_edition.pdf> accessed 1 December 2023.

2 ibid.

3 Secretaría de Seguridad y Protección Ciudadana, 'Cuaderno mensual de información estadística penitenciaria nacional. Junio 2023' (*Gobierno de México*, 2023) <https://www.gob.mx/cms/uploads/attachment/file/915855/CE_2023_06.pdf> accessed 1 December 2023.

DOI:10.1163/9789004747739_003

lation in absolute terms, as a proportion of the population, the country mirrors international trends. Since 2000, the female prison population in the country has risen by almost 100 percent, while the total prison population has increased by 40 percent.[4]

Women's processes of criminalization are deeply intertwined with economic inequality, the persistence of gender-based violence and discrimination in Latin American societies and their re-victimization by the punitive State.[5]

The objective of this chapter is to shed light on the disproportionate impact of incarceration on women, punishing the most invisible and unheard sectors of society, as well as to underscore the need for fundamental reforms to reduce women's incarceration. It aims to present a quantitative and qualitative analysis of female incarceration in Latin America, with a specific focus on Mexico. Given that punitive drug policies are a leading cause of the dramatic rise in incarceration in the region, the chapter begins with a brief analysis of US-led drug policies and their impact on Latin American countries. Subsequently, it analyses the characteristics and extent of female incarceration in Mexico and the wider region, while also examining the impact of the COVID-19 pandemic on women in prison.

The chapter is based on a review of relevant literature and available data, as well as on the authors' field work and activism with incarcerated, and formerly incarcerated, women in the region. One of the authors, Gaby, was in prison for seven years for cannabis trafficking. Her mother, Maria, was also interviewed for this chapter and both of their experiences are presented here. The other two authors, Gaby, and Maria have a relationship of trust, which is based on collaborative work to reduce female incarceration. Gaby and Maria's participation as women with lived experience and the authors' research and advocacy are framed in feminist criminology.[6] Gaby is constantly involved in academic and activist practices that aim at changing current approaches to female incarceration through her own lived experience and reflections.

The chapter concludes with a discussion of the failure of governments across Latin America to implement non-custodial measures for women

4 Information available at: Institute for Crime & Justice Policy Research and Birkbeck, 'Mexico' (*World Prison Brief*, 2023) <https://www.prisonstudies.org/country/Mexico> accessed 1 December 2023.

5 Macarena S. Torres and María Corina M. Toro, 'Políticas de género en el ámbito de la ejecución penal: una deuda pendiente' in Marie-Christine Fuchs and Leonel G. Postigo (eds), *Sistemas penitenciarios y ejecución penal en América Latina. Una mirada regional y opciones de abordaje* (Tirant Lo Blanch 2021) 75–102.

6 Kerry Carrington, 'Feminist Criminologies' in Pat Carlen and Leandro A. França (eds), *Alternative Criminologies* (New York, Routledge 2018) 110–124.

accused of lower-level offenses and the need for more effective alternatives to incarceration that could benefit women like Gaby.

2 The U.S. "War on Drugs"

As the primary source of illicit drugs aimed at satisfying the U.S. and European markets, Latin America has been on the frontline of the U.S. "War on Drugs". This has had devastating impacts, particularly for those involved in the lowest rungs of drug trafficking chains, and with a disproportionate impact on women, as explained in greater detail below. The year 2021 marked the fifty-year anniversary of the date when then President Nixon launched the U.S. war on drugs; yet the roots of that war go deeper. The United States was one of the primary architects of the present prohibitionist international drug control regime and has long intervened, often with military might, in the affairs of Latin American nations to promote its own perceived economic and political interests. As the Cold War drew to a close at the end of the 1980s and with Central America's internal conflicts winding down, the drug war became the driving rationale for a continued U.S. military presence in the region.[7] Drugs that were determined to be illicit in the international drug control treaties[8] were put forward as a threat to the United States, coming from outside of its borders, and hence an enemy against which a war must be waged. Latin American military and police forces were funded and trained by the United States to carry out counterdrug efforts, while the Defense Department was named the "single lead agency" for the detection and monitoring of illicit drug shipments to the United States.

Decades later, overwhelming evidence illustrates that these policies have dramatically failed to achieve the stated objective of reducing the flow of illicit drugs coming across U.S. borders.[9] However, for those on the frontlines, particularly in the Andean countries of Bolivia, Colombia and Peru, "the meta-

7 Adam B. Isacson, 'The U.S Military in the War on Drugs' in Coletta A. Youngers and Eileen Rosin (eds), *Drugs and Democracy in Latin America: The Impact of U.S. Policy* (Boulder, Lynne Rienner Publishers 2005) 15.

8 The three UN drug control Conventions are the Single Convention on Narcotic Drugs of 1961, as amended by the 1972 Protocol; the Convention on Psychotropic Substances of 1971; and the United Nations Convention against Illicit Traffic in Narcotic Drugs and Psychotropic Substances of 1988.

9 Ilona Szabó, 'The war on drugs has failed. Now what?' (*Instituto Igarapé*, 2016) <https://igarape.org.br/the-war-on-drugs-has-failed-now-what/> accessed 1 December 2023. For additional information, see: Global Commission on Drug Policy, 'Time to End Prohibition' (*Glo-*

phorical 'war on drugs' became all too real a battlefield".[10] The costs suffered from the militarization of counterdrug policy have been enormous.[11] This is particularly true for indigenous rural communities where, largely abandoned by the state, the cultivation of cannabis, coca and poppy (the latter two being the raw materials for the production of cocaine and heroin, respectively) or involvement in the drug trade has become a survival strategy for reducing food insecurity. In areas such as Guerrero, Oaxaca and other Mexican states, entire indigenous communities depend on the cannabis and opioid trades in order to meet their basic needs.[12]

Drug trafficking organizations – often allied with state forces – exploit both the land and the labour of these communities, where people can be forced at gunpoint or out of economic necessity to participate in the drug trade, as one author's personal testimony below dramatically illustrates. According to del Rocio Valdivia and Juan Okowí, these organizations are "able to enact a kind of sovereignty in these communities because of the historical processes of racialization that continue to define" indigenous territories and people as colonized subjects.[13]

With U.S. encouragement, the Mexican government has been giving the military an increasing role in counterdrug operations, and in the federal police and prosecutor's offices.[14]

---

bal Commission on Drugs Policy, 2021) <Time_to_end_prohibition_EN_2021_report.pdf> accessed 1 December 2023; John Walsh, 'Loosening Drug Prohibition's Lethal Grip on the Americas' (*The Washington Office on Latin America*, 2022) <https://www.wola.org/wp-content/uploads/2022/07/Lethal-Grip_WOLA_July-2022.pdf> accessed 1 December 2023.

10 Coletta A. Youngers and Eileen Rosin, 'The U.S. 'War on Drugs': Its Impact in Latin America and the Caribbean' in Coletta A. Youngers and Eileen Rosin (eds), *Drugs and Democracy in Latin America: The Impact of U.S. Policy* (Boulder, Lynne Rienner Publishers 2005) 3.

11 Coletta A. Youngers, 'Collateral Damage: The U.S. 'War on Drugs' and Its Impact on Democracy in the Andes' in Jo-Marie Burt and Philip Mauceri (eds), *Politics in the Andes: Identity, Conflict, Reform* (Pittsburgh, University of Pittsburg Press 2004) 132–145.

12 Irene Á. Rodriguez, 'Drug-trafficking and Rural Capitalism in Guerrero' (*Noria Research*, 2021) <https://noria-research.com/chapter-2-drug-trafficking-and-rural-capitalism-in-guerrero> accessed 1 December 2023.

13 Fatima del Rocio Valdivia and Juan Okowí, 'Drug Trafficking in the Tarahumara region, northern Mexico: An analysis of racism and dispossession' (2021) 142 World Development 1, 3.

14 Laurie Freeman and Jorge L. Sierra, 'Mexico: The Militarization Trap' in Coletta A. Youngers and Eileen Rosin (eds), *Drugs and Democracy in Latin America: The Impact of U.S. Policy* (Boulder, Lynne Rienner Publishers 2005) 263.

The violence generated by the militarized war on drugs and the cartels' turf wars has taken a huge toll in terms of overall levels of violence and has resulted in widespread human rights violations, including torture, extrajudicial killings, massacres, forced disappearances, rape and feminicide. Between 2006 and June 2023, more than 400,000 homicides were recorded by the government.[15] In another shocking statistic, the government documented over 111,000 cases of people who have disappeared, mostly during that same time period,[16] although the actual number of killings and disappearances is no doubt much higher.

Another clear outcome of the war on drugs is the exportation of draconian U.S. drug laws and the staggering increase in the number of people behind bars. In sheer numbers, the number of people incarcerated across the region has increased exponentially, with prison population growth far outpacing that of the general population. While in other parts of the world, prison populations have gone down or remained static, "the prison population in Latin America has tripled over the last two decades".[17] In 2017, 15 percent of the world's prison population was in Latin America, though the region has less than 9 percent of the total world population.[18] In short, according to Bergman and Fondevila, "Latin America has witnessed a stunning and spectacular rise in its prison population over the last twenty-five years".[19] As explained in the introduction, women's incarceration is growing at a faster rate than that of men.

Research carried out by the Collective for the Study of Drugs and the Law (known by its Spanish acronym, CEDD) shows that punitive drug laws are the primary cause, due to disproportionately tough sanctions, the use of mandatory minimum sentences, the obligatory or *de facto* use of pretrial detention

15 Information available at: INEGI, 'Mortalidad. Conjunto de datos: Defunciones por homicidios' (*Inegi*, 2023) <https://www.inegi.org.mx/sistemas/olap/consulta/general_ver4/MDXQueryDatos.asp?proy=> accessed 1 December 2023; Herminia Miranda, 'México registra 15 mil 122 homicidios dolosos en primer semestre de 2023, 1.68% menos respecto de 2022' (*Animal Político*, 2023) <https://www.animalpolitico.com/seguridad/mexico-homicidios-dolosos-primer-semestre-2023-junio> accessed 1 December 2023.

16 Information available at: <https://comisionacionaldebusqueda.gob.mx/rnpdno/> accessed 1 December 2023 (link is currently unavailable); Human Rights Watch, 'México. Eventos del 2022' (*HRW*, 2022) <https://www.hrw.org/es/world-report/2023/country-chapters/mexico#2c964d> accessed 1 December 2023.

17 Marcelo Bergman and Gustavo Fondevila, *Prisons and Crime in Latin America* (Cambridge, Cambridge University Press 2021) 28.

18 ibid 29.

19 ibid 32.

for drug offenses or its overuse, and the lack of use of alternatives to incarceration, among other factors.[20] As a result, Latin American prisons are bursting at the seams, filled with those accused or convicted of low-level offenses serving excessively long sentences.

People in multiple situations of vulnerability are especially at risk. Indigenous people, particularly women, brought into the criminal justice system face severe challenges. They may not be literate, yet forced to sign documents they do not understand; they may not speak Spanish, yet are forced to endure proceedings in a language that they do not understand.[21] Additionally, they face stigma and discrimination. As one local judge from northern Mexico said, "It is true that there are more indigenous people in prison, but this does not mean that indigenous people commit more crimes, but that it is easier to blame and arrest them. The prosecutor needs to meet their target, and unfortunately this is an easy way to do it".[22]

Those who become the targets of the drug war are not those profiting most from a very lucrative business or the myriad of government officials and state agents in collusion with the drug trade, but rather those who are in its lowest ranks. This includes cultivators, small-scale dealers and those who transport drugs within countries and across borders, with a disproportionate impact on disadvantaged communities, indigenous and black people, and women.[23]

3 The Disproportionate Impact of Drug Laws on Women

As has been widely reported, most women in prison in Latin America share similar characteristics: they come from backgrounds of poverty and inequal-

20 Sergio Chaparro, Catalina P. Correa and Coletta A. Youngers, 'Irrational Punishment: Drug Laws and Incarceration in Latin America' (*Colectivo de Estudios Drogas y Derecho*, 2017) 3 <https://idpc.net/publications/2017/04/irrational-punishment-drug-laws-and-incarceration-in-latin-america> accessed 1 December 2023.

21 *Differentiated approaches with respect to certain groups of persons in detention* (*Interpretation and scope of Articles 1(1), 4(1), 5, 11(2), 12, 13, 17(1), 19, 24 and 26 of the American Convention on Human Rights and other human rights instruments*), Advisory Opinion OC-29/22, IACtHR Series A No 29 (30 May 2022); Comisión Nacional de los Derechos Humanos, 'Informe diagnóstico sobre las condiciones de vida de las mujeres privadas de libertad desde un enfoque interseccional' (*CNDH México*, 2022) <https://www.cndh.org.mx/sites/default/files/documentos/2022-04/Informe_Diagnostico_Mujeres_Privadas_Libertad.pdf> accessed 1 December 2023.

22 Valdivia and Okowí, 'Drug Trafficking in the Tarahumara region, northern Mexico' (n 13) 4.

23 Chaparro, Correa and Youngers, 'Irrational Punishment: Drug Laws and Incarceration in Latin America' (n 20) 27–30.

ity, have low levels of education, and are either underemployed or unemployed, often working in the informal economy.[24] They likely have suffered from physical abuse and/or sexual violence. The vast majority are mothers – often single mothers – and may be caregivers for their children as well as the elderly or people with disabilities.[25] Many become involved in the lower echelons of the drug trade or stealing to put food on the table for their families. In short, "drug offenses thus become an option within a context of underdevelopment and limited choices".[26]

Latin America is not only the source of controlled drugs aimed at satisfying the U.S. and European markets; it is also the most unequal region in the world in social and economic terms. Women suffer particularly disadvantageous situations, due to the persistence of asymmetrical gender relationships, which impact their access to formal paid jobs, social services, health, education and political participation. The phenomenon known as "the feminization of poverty", which refers to the growing impoverishment of women in relation to men, is particularly acute in the region. Data from the United Nations Economic Commission for Latin America and the Caribbean (ECLAC) show that in 2021 there were about 116 women living in poverty for every 100 men. The countries with the highest "feminity index in poor households"[27] were the Dominican Republic and Uruguay, while Mexico had a 109.4 index.[28]

Along with having less access to economic autonomy and professional skills, women still devote more time than men to the "economy of care", that is the paid or unpaid activities carried out in the household, either as a domes-

---

24 Ana Safranoff and Antonella Tiravassi, 'Mujeres en contextos de encierro en América Latina. Características y factores de riesgo asociados a determinados comportamientos delictivos' (*Wilson Center Latin American Program*, 2018) <https://publications.iadb.org/publications/spanish/document/Mujeres-en-contextos-de-encierro-en-Am%C3%A9rica-Latina-Caracter%C3%ADsticas-y-factores-de-riesgo-asociados-a-determinados-comportamientos-delictivos.pdf> accessed 1 December 2023.

25 IACHR, 'Women Deprived of Liberty in the Americas' (*OAS*, 2023) <https://www.oas.org/en/iachr/reports/pdfs/2023/Informe-Mujeres-privadas-libertad_ENG.pdf> accessed 1 December 2023.

26 Corina Giacomello and Coletta A. Youngers, 'Women Incarcerated for Drug-related Offenses: A Latin American Perspective' in Julia Buxton, Giavana Margo and Lona Burger (eds), *The Impact of Global Drug Policy on Women: Shifting the Needle* (Bingley, Emerald Publishing Limited 2021) 107.

27 Information available at: Observatorio de Igualdad de Género de América Latina y el Caribe, 'Índice de feminidad en hogares pobres' (*OIG*, 2023) <https://oig.cepal.org/es/indicadores/indice-feminidad-hogares-pobres> accessed 1 December 2023.

28 ibid.

tic worker or in one's own home.[29] Caregiving responsibilities and domestic unpaid work are the main factors preventing women from entering the labour market. In Latin America and the Caribbean, about 60 percent of women who live in households with children less than 15 years old do not participate in the formal economy.[30] Mexico is among the countries in Latin America where women dedicate the most time to unpaid work: women aged 15 and older dedicate 42.8 percent of their time to unpaid work and only 22.1 percent to paid work. On the contrary, men dedicate 44.6 percent of their time to paid work and only 16.9 percent to unpaid work.[31] This further undermines women's autonomy and professionalization, and puts them at risk of deteriorating socioeconomic and personal situations.

Gender-based violence repeats itself cyclically in the lives of women in the region, which in 2021 alone recorded more than 4,400 cases of gender-based killings of women, also known as femicides.[32] This term was coined after the infamous deaths of thousands of Mexican women at the hands of men in the state of Chihuahua,[33] and is currently a widespread reality throughout the country.[34] In 2019, Mexico had the second highest number of femicides in Latin America.[35]

The interplay between socio-economic inequality, gender differences and gender-based violence with abundant and expanding illicit drug markets creates the conditions for women's employment in the illicit drug trade. Drug-related jobs are a source of fast income that, while representing relatively

29 ECLAC, 'La sociedad del cuidado: horizonte para una recuperación sostenible con igualdad de género' (*CEPAL*, 2022) <https://repositorio.cepal.org/handle/11362/48363> accessed 1 December 2023.

30 ECLAC, 'Panorama Social de América Latina 2020, Santiago de Chile' (*CEPAL*, 2021) <https://www.cepal.org/es/publicaciones/46687-panorama-social-america-latina-2020> accessed 1 December 2023.

31 Information available at: Observatorio de Igualdad de Género de América Latina y el Caribe, 'Inicio' (*OIG*, 2023) <https://oig.cepal.org/es> accessed 1 December 2023.

32 Information available at: ECLAC, 'ECLAC: At Least 4,473 Women Were Victims of Femicide in Latin America and the Caribbean in 2021' (*CEPAL*, 2022) <https://www.cepal.org/en/pressreleases/eclac-least-4473-women-were-victims-femicide-latin-america-and-caribbean-2021> accessed 1 December 2023.

33 *González and Others ("Campo Algodonero") v Mexico* (Preliminary Objections, Merits, Reparation and Costs) IACtHR Series C No 205 (16 November 2009).

34 Secretaría de Seguridad y Protección Ciudadana, 'Información sobre violencia contra las mujeres' (*Secretariado Ejecutivo del Sistema Nacional de Seguridad Pública*, 2021) <https://drive.google.com/file/d/1mnvTELZwrS8GV8X2fmzPu2JxpA-gN21-/view> accessed 1 December 2023.

35 Information available at: ECLAC, 'Feminicidio' (*CEPAL*, 2023) <https://oig.cepal.org/es/indicadores/feminicidio> accessed 1 December 2023.

meagre earnings from this lucrative market, offers real economic opportunity, particularly for those in situations of vulnerability. Selling small amounts of drugs, or carrying drugs, swallowing them to cross borders, or hiding them in packages inside one's vagina, creates more profit in less time than cleaning houses, selling food on the street, ironing or carrying out other unskilled, low-paid tasks. Furthermore, less time is usually required, allowing women to fulfil their roles as caregivers and to stay at home with their children, while also being the family breadwinners.[36]

Women may also become involved in drug-related activities through their own drug consumption, or through their partners, responding to the traditional gendered roles and behaviours dictated by the imagery of "the good wife" and the "good girlfriend." Alternatively, they may be coerced by partners or family members. Gender-based violence, including sexual violence, is intimately related to women's involvement in the drug trade, both in ensuring their participation and as a threat if they fail. Within this complex combination of economic opportunity, coercion and acceptance, and social norms and expectations, both agency and victimization are usually present in women's narratives and lay the foundations for their subsequent criminalization and incarceration.[37]

However, these mitigating circumstances are rarely taken into account by state agents and the criminal justice system. Moreover, women in the lower levels of the drug trade are engaged in high-risk activity with a greater chance of being caught, often *en flagrante*. As we have noted in previous work, "their detention represents an insignificant loss to trafficking organizations and an easy gain for law enforcement".[38] As discussed below, there are some interesting exceptions to this general trend in Costa Rica, where a legal reform led to the use of alternatives to incarceration for women who smuggle drugs into prison, and in Colombia, where a new law offers alternatives to incarceration for certain women who are single heads of households in situations of vulnerability.

Beginning in the 1980s and particularly since the 1990s, drug-related offenses have become the leading cause of women's incarceration in Latin America. In countries such as Panama, Costa Rica and Brazil, women incarcerated for drug offenses represent more than 60 percent of the total female

36 Corina Giacomello, *Género, drogas y prisión. Experiencias de mujeres privadas de su libertad en México* (Mexico City, Tirant Lo Blanch 2013) 262.

37 Corina Giacomello, 'The gendered impacts of drug policy on women: case studies from Mexico' (2021) 12 International Development Policy 1.

38 Giacomello and Youngers, 'Women Incarcerated for Drug-related Offenses' (n 26) 107.

population in prison.[39] While many more men are incarcerated than women, the percentage of women incarcerated for drug offenses is almost always higher than the percentage for men. For example, in Brazil, Chile, Costa Rica, Panama and Peru, the proportion of women prisoners who are incarcerated for drug offenses is at least 30 percent higher than men incarcerated for the same offense.[40] Mostly accused of non-violent, minor offenses, the causes of women's incarceration, as described above, include mandatory or *de facto* pre-trial detention, disproportionate sentences, and limited or no access to alternatives to incarceration or benefits such as conditional release, which are often, by law, not applicable to those charged with drug offenses.[41] An important exception is the Colombian law referred to above, which, for the first time, includes those convicted of drug offenses. In Colombia, those in prison for drug offenses are generally excluded from any such benefits; in fact, during the COVID-19 pandemic, women in prison for such offenses were not included in the government's effort to decrease the female prison population by granting women house arrest.

While the COVID-19 pandemic shone a spotlight on the horrific prison conditions around the world, governments largely failed to protect those behind bars. It was these groups that were in fact most at risk of serious illness and death due to overcrowded conditions of confinement, unsanitary living conditions and lack of access to basic hygiene products or health care. Those efforts to release people from prison largely focused on men, with few women benefiting. Those women who were moved into house arrest, as well as those released from prison, did not have access to economic resources to allow their basic needs to be met. Some women returned home only to face domestic violence.[42] As prisons went into lockdowns, visits were suspended,

39 Corina Giacomello, 'Niñez que cuenta. El impacto de las políticas de drogas sobre niñas, niños y adolescentes con madres y padres encarcelados en América Latina y el Caribe' (*Church World Service*, 2019) <http://www.cwslac.org/nnapes-pdd/docs/Estudio-Regional-Ninez-que-cuenta-web.pdf> accessed 1 December 2023.

40 Coletta A. Youngers, Teresa G. Castro and Maria Manzur, 'Women Behind Bars for Drug Offenses in Latin America: What the Numbers Make Clear' (*Washington Office on Latin America*, 2020) 1 <https://www.wola.org/wp-content/uploads/2020/11/Final-Women-Behind-Bars-Report.pdf> accessed 1 December 2023.

41 Chaparro, Correa and Youngers, 'Irrational Punishment: Drug Laws and Incarceration in Latin America' (n 20) 3.

42 Washington Office on Latin America and others, 'La respuesta de los sistemas penitenciarios de América Latina frente a la crisis por COVID-19 no ha tenido en cuenta a las mujeres privadas de la libertad' (*WOLA*, 19 March 2021) <https://womenanddrugs.wola.org/wp-content/uploads/2021/04/WOLA-Propuesta-de-comunicado-audiencia-CIDH-19042021.pdf> accessed 1 December 2023.

cutting family ties, as well as much-needed supplies (food, medicine, hygiene products, etc.) – conditions that often continued long after pandemic restrictions were lifted for the society at large.

4 Women behind Bars in Mexico

In recent years, Mexico has witnessed some legal improvements. In 2009, the reforms to the General Health Law were adopted, to include norms on small-scale dealing (narcomenudeo), decriminalizing drug possession for personal use and reducing sentences for small-scale dealing to 10 months to three years in prison, as compared to the maximum sentence for large-scale trafficking of 25 years. However, the thresholds for the amounts established in the law for personal use were very low, resulting in consumers being charged and convicted of small-scale dealing. In addition, the sentence for introducing drugs into prisons, commonly carried out by women, was decreased from a minimum sentence of fifteen years to six years of imprisonment.

In 2014, the National Code of Criminal Procedures was approved, expanding the range of non-custodial measures at the pre-sentencing stage which could be applied to drug offenses related to possession and retail. In 2016, Congress approved the "National Law of Penal Execution",[43] which among other points, finally opened the door for the implementation of alternatives to incarceration for those convicted of drug offenses. Before this law, people sentenced for a drug offense had to complete the full sentence in prison. Before 2009, female prisons were full of women incarcerated with a minimum sentence of 10 or 15 years for selling drugs, bringing drugs into prisons, or for national or international trafficking as drug couriers, or "mules."

Such changes, together with other legal improvements, have helped to reduce women's incarceration for drug offenses. However, the current legislation still envisages mandatory pre-trial detention (established in the Constitution) and high minimum sentences for federal drug offenses. Furthermore, the profiles of incarcerated women have not changed, thus reflecting the perpetuation of criminal legal policies that still persecute the poorest and more disadvantaged sectors of society. More than 50 percent of women in prison earned less than 320 U.S. dollars per month before being arrested and 30 percent

43 'Penal execution', *ejecución penal* in Spanish, refers to the enforcement of the penal law and the monitoring of prisons through specialized judges.

earned less than 173 U.S. dollars.[44] About 67 percent of women in prison have children who are underage and 53.4 percent have more than two children.[45] While in the case of incarcerated men, their children's mothers take care of them, women in prison are largely abandoned and their parents mainly look after their children.[46] This creates a further economic burden for families already living in vulnerable conditions and an additional pressure on women to provide for their children from inside prisons, which offer little or no economic opportunities.[47]

Incarceration is incredibly painful and erodes the person's social and personal capital, which in the cases of most of these women was already precarious. The racism, classism and gender-based violence that span across Latin American societies are heightened in the prison context. Prisons in the region are characterized by extreme overcrowding; lack of access to adequate health care, education and employment opportunities; severely inadequate living conditions and inhumane treatment; and lack of respect of human rights.[48] This falls more severely on women, and particularly trans women who face higher exposure to sexual abuse. It also has additional impacts on women who are pregnant or that live in prison with their children, indigenous women and foreigners, given the lack of basic and specialized services.[49]

However, the impacts of incarceration on women go far beyond the prison walls and the time spent in prison: It generates a "prisonization continuum" that embraces social and family relations outside prisons, particularly affecting children and women on the outside,[50] who usually take care of all of the legal, economic, emotional and caring aspects related to those behind bars.

---

44 Instituto Nacional de Estadística y Geografía, 'Encuesta nacional de población privada de la libertad 2021. Tabulados básicos' (*INEGI*, 2021) <https://www.inegi.org.mx/programas/enpol/2021/#tabulados> accessed 1 December 2023.

45 Instituto Nacional de Estadística y Geografía, 'Encuesta nacional de población privada de la libertad 2021. Principales resultados' (*INEGI*, 2021) <https://www.inegi.org.mx/contenidos/programas/enpol/2021/doc/enpol2021_presentacion_nacional.pdf> accessed 1 December 2023.

46 ibid.

47 Comisión Nacional de los Derechos Humanos, 'Informe diagnóstico sobre las condiciones de vida de las mujeres privadas de libertad desde un enfoque interseccional' (n 21).

48 IACHR, 'Medidas para reducir la prisión preventiva' (*OAS*, 2017) <http://www.oas.org/es/cidh/informes/pdfs/prisionpreventiva.pdf> accessed 1 December 2023.

49 Torres and Toro, 'Políticas de género en el ámbito de la ejecución penal: una deuda pendiente' (n 5).

50 Giacomello, 'Niñez que cuenta. El impacto de las políticas de drogas sobre niñas, niños y adolescentes con madres y padres encarcelados en América Latina y el Caribe' (n 39).

Stigma and discrimination often remain once freedom is regained, making release from prison a process which is often painful and complicated to face and endure.

The case study presented below, by the very own voice of its protagonist and one of the authors of this chapter, Gaby, vividly and painfully demonstrates the issues briefly addressed in these pages.

5 Gaby's Story

This section presents the lived experience of one of the authors of this chapter, Gaby, who turned to the drug trade out of economic desperation and paid dearly for it, spending seven years in prison while raising three children.

The authors of this chapter have known each other since the summer of 2017, when, in the framework of a working group on women, drug policies and incarceration led by the Washington Office on Latin America (WOLA), the International Drug Policy Consortium (IDPC) and the Colombian NGO Dejusticia,[51] Gaby voluntarily participated in a series of short documentaries aimed at raising awareness on the profile of women incarcerated for drug offenses.[52] At that time, she was deprived of her liberty and lived with her mother in the female prison, Tanivet, in Oaxaca, Mexico. Since then, our friendship has grown and it intertwines with advocacy-oriented activities, conferences and publications.

Gaby is now 33 years old and lives with her children. She is originally from an indigenous Zapotec-speaking town south of Oaxaca, rooted in community traditions and customs where the town leaders are elected by the people, corn and beans are cultivated, and where good Mezcal is produced. Yet despite the beautiful scenery, it is also a place where sexism exists, and women are submissive to their husbands. Long abandoned by the state, people live in poverty. Over time, the town's basic economy became dependent on drugs such as marijuana and cocaine. Though marijuana is not grown there, drug cartels hired local people to prepare, package and transport cannabis. For many, it

---

51 Information available at: WOLA, 'Homepage' (*Women and Drugs*, 2023) <https://womenanddrugs.wola.org/> accessed 1 December 2023.

52 These were produced by WOLA, Equis Justicia para las Mujeres, and Scopio. Information available at: WOLA, 'The Stories of Women in prison for Drug Related Crimes' (*Women and Drugs*, 2023) <https://womenanddrugs.wola.org/multimedia/videos/> accessed 1 December 2023.

was the only way to earn a decent living and the overall economy of the town improved as a result. Yet if caught, those involved potentially face years in prison.

> I was 8 years old when my father emigrated to the United States, in order to give me and my four siblings a better quality of life. But as time went by, he forgot about us and so my mother worked very hard and brought us up. When I was 16, I was raped, became pregnant and so I left school and became a domestic worker. Three years later, I had a romantic partner and had my second child with him. As the months went by, I realized that my boy was not growing normally and could not hold his head up. I began to worry and wanted to take him to a doctor, but we had little money and with my job we could barely survive. His father would not take responsibility, so I had to find the means to solve the problem on my own, in a town that lacks opportunities. I met someone who was involved in marijuana trafficking, who invited me to work for a few days cleaning, preparing and packaging marijuana. I scraped together a few "pesos" and took my son to a clinic, where the doctor told me that what he had was serious, but more tests were needed, including a CAT scan. I left the office confused and in tears, not knowing what to do as a single mother on my own and facing discrimination for that, as is common in villages like mine due to ignorance.
>
> Worried about my son and desperate to find a solution, I got up the courage to ask for a loan, because I knew that with the job packaging marijuana, I could pay back the money (although it was not well paid). People in need like me see those in the marijuana trade as heroes, because they give us work, even children and old people. In our town, there are no other options. What I did, at the time it was a common job; it is as if you are selling bread. When he finished listening to me, he told me that he would not lend me the money as I needed to earn an income and for that, I had to work. He offered to pay me to travel from Oaxaca to Mexico City with a package, telling me that "if something bad happened, I didn't know him.".
>
> Out of desperation, without thinking of the consequences it would have on my life and the lives of my children, I accepted his proposal. The payment was one-thousand pesos, and looking back at it now, it was very little given what happened. We met in Oaxaca at the third-class bus station, where he handed me a backpack with a package wrapped in tape inside. He gave me directions to where to take it.

After changing buses, I came to a military checkpoint. The soldiers boarded the bus, spotted my backpack, opened it and cut through the package. They took me to the Public Prosecutor's Office in Huajuapan de León where they treated me inhumanely, with contempt and discrimination against my race and my people. Violating my rights, they forced me to sign papers even though I did not know what they were about. I didn't know how to read because I only went to primary school, and I didn't know how to speak Spanish well because I am indigenous Zapotec, and they took advantage of that. My mother showed up a day later, and was also humiliated by these unscrupulous, inhuman and despicable people.

I was sent after four days to the Etla prison where I stayed for eight months. I asked to be transferred to the Tanivet women's prison in Oaxaca, as I was told it had a special area for mothers, and I wanted to be with my son because of his illness and disability. When I arrived at Tanivet, I reunited with my younger sister, who was also incarcerated for a drug offense. I learned that my son was very sick and asked the Director for permission to have him with me, but it was denied because it was a lie that there were places for mothers. They lived with their children in awful conditions, with little food and poor hygiene; however, I still wanted to be with my son, because only I could give him the attention he needed.

After the lady who was taking care of him came to visit me and told me that she would not take care of him anymore because at any moment my son could die, the Director relented. I had no money or food to offer my son. Some of my friends gave me diapers, others gave me milk and food. My son was so skinny, almost dying. I started to work in the prison to earn some money, and he stayed with me for two years. The man who was my boyfriend at the time visited me and supported me too.

One day my mother arrived – this time not as a visitor but as a prisoner. God, what was I going to do, as she was the one taking care of my seven-year-old daughter? I had to put my daughter in a children's home. I was very sad for my mother, as she was going to have to face the same situation as me and my sister.

Then I became pregnant again, and I had my second daughter while in prison. But I kept fighting and asked to be allowed to leave the prison for my son's physical therapy, so that I could learn the exercises and then do them with my son. I also asked to be put on house arrest so that I could care for him. The judge denied everything, telling me in a

> letter that, "I should have thought about that before committing the crime".
>
> Eventually, I had to make the very difficult and painful decision for my son to go to a public care facility, where he could receive specialized medical care. I felt like the world was coming down on me. My son was so used to me, sleeping in my arms on a single stone bed on a cold mattress, while my mother slept with the baby. I felt like I was stuck between a rock and a hard place. I did not want to be away from my son, but at the same time I could not keep him from being in a better place. Doubts flooded me, as I thought about how cold we were and the lack of food. Confused, I made the painful decision to send my son there and, at the same time, my one-year-old baby went to live with my uncle and his wife so that she would no longer have to be in prison.
>
> Insomnia became my companion at night. The pain and loneliness of not being with my children became my torment: Was I right or wrong? Were they hungry? Were they cold? My life changed, but I also wanted to get out of prison to join them, and so I did everything I could to show good behaviour. I had been sentenced to 10 years in prison for transporting cannabis, but I was released after seven years. The longed-for freedom finally came, and I was reunited with my children. But now I had a new challenge: the punishment and discrimination from society for being both a single mother and a formerly incarcerated woman, with no possessions as I had lost everything. Now I am facing yet another challenge in my life, but this time I am not alone, but with my children.

Gaby's story begs the question of whether or not she should have gone to prison in the first place. She was not a "threat" to society, her incarceration had a devastating impact on her children, and being locked up for seven years and having a criminal record have pushed her even deeper into poverty. But prison does not end where its walls stand, as it often becomes a life-long condition.

Gaby left prison in July 2019, but the difficulties did not end when she went through the prison door. As she explains in her testimony, she could not find a place to rent in her community, because she was discriminated against for being a single mother and formerly incarcerated. She found a job as a cleaner in a private house, only to lose it a few months later when the unforeseeable COVID-19 pandemic hit the world with a wave of lockdowns, infections, deaths, mental health problems and unemployment. Gaby's daily economic struggles consisted of making unimaginable choices: whether to buy rice to eat or diapers for her disabled son.

On top of the daily struggle for survival, she also faced an additional barrier, which is a blind spot of the Mexican legal apparatus and leads to a condition of "suspended citizenship".[53] Currently, when a person is sentenced, her or his political rights are suspended and are re-established only when the time of the sentence is completed. The correlated effect is that people with no electoral rights cannot have access to the Electoral National Identification – commonly known as "INE" in Mexico for its acronym in Spanish – which is the main form of national identification. Without an INE, it is impossible to access state support, grants for children, apply for a job, get a passport, open a bank account, etc. Gaby was given an alternative to incarceration known as "anticipated liberty", after spending 70 percent of her sentence in prison, that is, seven years. However, she had to wait until November 2022, two years and a half after her release, to have her INE back and, with it, her fully restored citizenship.

While the electoral rights of prisoners have been on the agenda in recent years in Mexico,[54] the implications of early release with no access to the national identification document has even more dire consequences: People who are granted a non-custodial measure are expected to fulfil the obligations of a free person, that is to work, look after themselves and their families, finish their studies, avoid certain people or places and comply with other conditions that may be imposed as part of the non-custodial measures. However, they are not allowed to be full citizens in equal conditions with their peers and cannot access the very services needed to rebuild their lives coming out of prison.

Fortunately, after her release Gaby was only required to appear one time before the federal prison authority. This was mainly due to the work of the federal public defender. However, as will be described later in this chapter through the case of Gaby's mother, Maria, early release can also be accompanied by strict conditions that hinder the process of reintegration.

Gaby's case is tragically typical: As explained previously, the feminization of poverty and the economy of care are a primary cause for women's involvement in drug-related offenses. Prison conditions, which violate the dignity and human rights of incarcerated people in general,[55] are particularly dire for

53 Corina Giacomello, 'The Legal Flaws and Material Implementation Gaps of Mexico's Rehabilitation Paradigm' in Maurice Vanstone and Philip Priestly (eds), *The Palgrave Handbook of Global Rehabilitation in Criminal Justice* (Cham, Palgrave Macmillan 2022).

54 Carlos R. Eguiarte Mereles, *Voto en prisión preventiva* (Mexico City, Tirant Lo Blanch 2021).

55 IACHR, 'Informe sobre los derechos humanos de las personas privadas de libertad en las Américas' (OAS, 2011) <https://www.oas.org/es/cidh/ppl/docs/pdf/ppl2011esp.pdf> accessed 1 December 2023; Marie-Christine Fuchs and Leonel G. Postigo (eds), *Sistemas*

women and their children, both when they live in mixed prisons or in women-only prisons.[56] Basic rights are not fulfilled and women have to pay for the basic goods and services that they need to take care of themselves and their children.[57] Children who live in prison with their mothers are in a condition of *de facto* incarceration and their access to basic services, food, medication, clothing and education, as well as the contact with the external world, depends on their mother's possibilities, instead of being regulated by child-centred policies.[58]

In terms of rehabilitation, women in prison have less support networks, as well as job and educational opportunities, than men in prison, which exacerbates the difficulties that they face to support themselves and their children while in prison and after release.[59] The legal impediment for Gaby's enjoyment of full citizenship's rights represents yet another barrier to her reintegration.

6 Alternatives to Incarceration

At the international level, there is a growing consensus on the need to implement non-custodial measures for women accused of minor, non-violent offenses, especially if they are pregnant, mothers or living with small children in prison. This consensus is enshrined in the United Nations Rules for the Treatment of Women Prisoners and Non-custodial Measures for Women Offenders, commonly known as the Bangkok Rules.[60] Yet such "alternatives"

penitenciarios y ejecución penal en América Latina. Una mirada regional y opciones de abordaje (Tirant Lo Blanch 2021) 500.

56 Comisión Nacional de los Derechos Humanos, 'Informe diagnóstico sobre las condiciones de vida de las mujeres privadas de libertad desde un enfoque interseccional' (n 21).

57 IACHR, 'Women Deprived of Liberty in the Americas' (n 25).

58 *Differentiated approaches with respect to certain groups of persons in detention* (n 21); Corina Giacomello, *Niñas y niños que viven en prisión con sus madres. Una perspectiva jurídica comparada* (Mexico City, Suprema Corte de Justicia de la Nación 2018) 208; Manfred Nowak, 'The United Nations Global Study on Children Deprived of their Liberty' (*OHCHR*, 2019) <https://omnibook.com/view/e0623280-5656-42f8-9edf-5872f8f08562/page/1> accessed 1 December 2023.

59 Olga Espinoza, Catalina Droppelmann and Paloma del Villar, '¿Reincidir o resistir? Mujeres en conflicto con la ley en América Latina' in Carmen Hein and Patsilí Toledo (eds), *Criminologías feministas latinoamericanas* (Rio de Janeiro, Lumen Juris 2020) 343–377.

60 United Nations Office on Drugs and Crime, 'The Bangkok Rules' (*UNODC*, 2011) <https://www.unodc.org/documents/justice-and-prison-reform/Bangkok_Rules_ENG_22032015.pdf> accessed 1 December 2023.

too often come from a punitive mindset and result in harmful consequences; in short, they can reproduce and even exacerbate state forms of punishment, control and surveillance. They can also lead to a phenomenon known as net widening, in which more women are brought into the criminal legal system than would otherwise be the case given that sanctions viewed as less punitive than prison are available.[61] A better approach is to put into place alternatives based on restitution and providing women with the life skills and resources that can keep them out of the criminal justice system in the first place.[62] Furthermore, non-custodial measures are effective only if also accompanied by legal changes, awareness-raising, and training for judicial personnel that actually move towards the use of prison as a last resort and the overall reduction in the use of the criminal legal system.[63]

A 2023 report, Women Deprived of Liberty in the Americas,[64] by the OAS's Inter-American Commission on Human Rights (IACHR) documents that the three primary gender-oriented non-custodial measures being used by governments in Latin America today are in fact quite harmful: drug courts, house arrest and electronic monitoring. It is also important to again note that drug laws often preclude the use of non-custodial sentences or other benefits for those convicted of such offenses.

Women who use drugs may become involved in the drug trade because of their interactions in drug markets or in order to support their consumption. Strongly encouraged by the U.S. and Canadian governments, drug courts, are put forward as a way of providing treatment to those who need it and decrease the number of people in prison. In practice, however, drug courts are costly and cumbersome; they have had practically no impact on reducing prison populations in Latin America and can be very detrimental to supposed beneficiaries.[65] The IACHR report points out that human rights violations often take

61 Catherine Heard, 'Alternatives to imprisonment in Europe: A handbook of good practice' (*Associazione Antigone Onlus*, 2016) <http://www.prisonobservatory.org/upload/Good%20practice%20handbook%20AS.pdf> accessed 1 December 2023.

62 Sabrina Mahtani, 'Toolkit on Gender-Responsive Non-Custodial Measures' (*UNODC*, 2020) <https://www.unodc.org/documents/justice-and-prison-reform/20-01528_Gender_Toolkit_complete.pdf> accessed 1 December 2023.

63 Dirk van Zyl Smit, *Handbook of basic principles and promising practices on Alternatives to Imprisonment* (Vienna, UNODC 2007).

64 IACHR, 'Women Deprived of Liberty in the Americas' (n 25).

65 For additional information, see: Social Science Research Council, 'Drug Courts in the Americas' (*SSRC*, 2018) <https://www.ssrc.org/publications/drug-courts-in-the-americas/> accessed 1 December 2023.

place in treatment centres, that participation in treatment programs should be voluntary, and that drug court programs are carried out from a criminal justice, rather than a public health perspective.[66] Moreover, their scope is limited since they do not address the situation of those engaged in the drug trade for other reasons, such as economic necessity, as in the case of Gaby.

The most common gender-oriented alternatives to incarceration used in Latin America are house arrest and electronic monitoring, and they are often used together. At face value, these seem like good options. Who would not choose to leave prison for their own home? For those with more resources, including a comfortable home and family members able to support them, these can indeed be good alternatives. But for those less fortunate, both options present a range of problems and difficulties.

In some countries, such as Chile and Argentina, the use of house arrest for women increased during the COVID-19 pandemic. Yet not all women in prison have a home to go back to, either because they did not have one in the first place or because they have been abandoned by their families as a result of the stigma and discrimination that result from incarceration. Moreover, the conditions are usually so strict for women under house arrest that they cannot hold down a job, fulfil their responsibilities as caregivers, or even get medical assistance when needed. House arrest also puts a burden on others in the household who must financially support the person.[67]

Another alternative that can have very bad consequences is electronic monitoring, often used in combination with house arrest, and which has become increasingly common across Latin America. As with house arrest, electronic monitoring depends on having a home base and family support, as often the conditions are so onerous that the person wearing the ankle monitor cannot work. Moreover, having a large devise around one's ankle creates even more stigma and discrimination, can prevent people from carrying out basic tasks like grocery shopping or going to the doctor and can result in huge debts, as the cost is transferred from the state to the individual. It can also lead to health-related problems and the constant surveillance raises privacy concerns.[68] For women, any form of home confinement can put them back into abusive situations where they are subject to domestic violence.

66 IACHR, 'Women Deprived of Liberty in the Americas' (n 25) 112.

67 Corina Giacomello and Teresa G. Castro, 'Imprisoned at Home: Women Under House Arrest in Latin America' (*Washington Office on Latin America*, 2020) <https://www.wola.org/wp-content/uploads/2020/07/Imprisoned-at-Home.pdf> accessed 1 December 2023.

68 James Kilgore, *Understanding E-Carceration* (New York, The New Press 2022).

Returning to Gaby's story, her family had a direct experience with electronic monitoring. Her mother, who we will call Maria,[69] also an indigenous Zapotec woman living in the same town in Oaxaca as Gaby, was sentenced to ten years in prison in 2014 for transporting cannabis within Mexico. After five years, she was granted conditional release and put on an ankle monitor. Both the 2014 Mexican National Code of Criminal Procedures and the 2016 National Law of Penal Execution allow for the use of such alternatives to incarceration.

In Maria's case, because she was an indigenous woman, the private company providing the ankle monitor waived the monthly fee of about US$275 per month; however, she did have to pay an $800 warranty, which was a fortune for her family. Maria was fortunate that her family supported her and was able to come up with the money needed for her to leave prison and to support her once she was home.

She was also lucky to live in a community with electricity, as otherwise she would have had to move. However, Gaby recounts:

> During the time that she had on the ankle monitor, the farthest that she could go was to a nearby village. Why? Because the monitor had to be recharged. She had to charge it in the morning and in the afternoon. It took about two hours to charge, and she had to sit next to the electric outlet during that time… If the electricity went out or the signal was lost, when it came back they would call and call to ask about it…or sometimes at 2 in the morning they would call to say that she needed to charge it…they called all the time.

Maria may have had family support, but she faced tremendous stigma and discrimination in her small, indigenous community. Because her indigenous dress meant that her ankles are always exposed, she wore a bandage over the ankle monitor to hide it. Maria was sentenced to six months of electronic monitoring in October 2019. However, due to the COVID-19 pandemic, courts reduced their work pace to a minimum. Furthermore, Maria's case was reallocated to another court. In practical terms, this meant that she had to wear the ankle monitor for over 14 months. During that time, her leg where it was

69 Maria's story is told in: Coletta A. Youngers and Corina Giacomello, 'Electronic Monitoring: A New Form of Punishment for Many Women' (*Washington Office on Latin America*, 2022) <https://www.wola.org/analysis/electronic-monitoring-punishment-women/> accessed 1 December 2023; and in: Giacomello, 'The Legal Flaws and Material Implementation Gaps of Mexico's Rehabilitation Paradigm' (n 53).

placed shrunk slightly and the skin around it dried up because of the long time connecting the device to electricity.

Maria should not have been forced to choose between staying in prison and surveillance via an ankle monitor. Less harmful and potentially beneficial alternatives to incarceration include: reporting requirements that still allow people to lead normal lives; suspended sentences; community programs and services; voluntary drug treatment programs; mediation; and restorative justice programs. Such measures should be implemented with an intersectional approach which takes into account gender and cultural differences and specificities.[70]

7 Promising Alternative Approaches

While the use of rights-based and effective alternatives to incarceration remains woefully inadequate across the region, some interesting exceptions have been implemented. Perhaps the earliest example is a 2013 legal reform adopted in Costa Rica to reduce the sentence for women carrying drugs into prison, such that alternatives to incarceration could be used instead of incarceration. This initiative was based on a comprehensive study carried out by the Public Defender's Office of the Judiciary which showed that the vast majority of women in prison came from situations of poverty and vulnerability, were single mothers, and that the most common cause for their incarceration was smuggling drugs into prison. As it was applied retroactively, about 150 women were released from prison, and women are now rarely incarcerated for that offense.[71]

A more recent alternative approach is being developed in Colombia. On International Women's Day, March 8, 2023, President Gustavo Petro signed a ground-breaking law to provide alternatives to incarceration for women who are single heads of households, live in situations of vulnerability, have sentences of eight years or less, and meet certain other conditions. Finding public institutions, NGOs and businesses willing to sponsor community service programs was challenging, but sufficient sponsors were secured for the Ministry of Justice and Rights to launch its implementation on September 14, 2023.

70 *Differentiated approaches with respect to certain groups of persons in detention* (n 21); Mahtani, 'Toolkit on Gender-Responsive Non-Custodial Measures' (n 62).

71 Nischa Pieris, 'Reducing Female Incarceration Through Drug Law Reform in Costa Rica' (*Washington Office on Latin America, International Drug Policy Consortium, Dejusticia and CIM/OEA*, 2020) <https://womenanddrugs.wola.org/wp-content/uploads/2020/10/DONE-2-Costa-Rica-77bis_ENG_FINAL-.pdf> accessed 1 December 2023.

The new law,[72] which can be applied retroactively, allows women to substitute unpaid community service for prison terms, for a minimum of five hours a week. Such service can include educational activities, improvement of public spaces, and providing assistance to communities in situations of vulnerability, among others. The law states that community service should not interfere with paid labour or educational activities, and should provide education or other professional formation.

The devil will be in the details of the law's implementation. The fact that the community service is not renumerated presents challenges to women already struggling to sustain themselves and their families. Moreover, the law does not eliminate criminal records, meaning that beneficiaries will continue to face major obstacles to finding meaningful employment. For those women in prison already, they need access to information on who qualifies, the process for applying, and access to the resources needed to do so. And ultimately, their fate lies in the hands of judges. Claudia Cardona, a formerly incarcerated women who leads Mujeres Libres in Colombia, points out that, "of particular concern, women who could benefit will have to show that when the offense was committed, they were living in a situation of poverty. How do you show that? Will it depend on the subjective opinion of the judge?"[73]

However, if effectively implemented, about 3,000 women in prison could benefit and the flow of women going into prison will be significantly curtailed. In directly addressing the disproportionate impact of incarceration on women, the law incorporates a gender perspective into the criminal legal system and promotes the human rights of women in contact with the law and their families. It is an important move away from purely punitive approaches and could provide an interesting model for other countries seeking to incorporate a gender perspective into their own criminal legal systems.

Finally, a third, yet disappointing, example is the federal amnesty law passed in Mexico in April 2020, as the COVID-19 pandemic was getting underway. Promoted by civil society organizations, including the Washington Office on Latin America (WOLA) and Equis Justicia para las Mujeres, the law allows for the release from prison of those coming from groups in situations of vulnerability (women, youth, indigenous people and those with disabilities) and

72 Coletta A. Youngers, 'Colombia to Implement Law on Alternatives to Incarceration for Women Heads of Household' (*Washington Office on Latin America*, 2022) <https://www.wola.org/analysis/colombia-law-alternatives-incarceration-women-heads-household/> accessed 1 December 2023.

73 Quoted in: Youngers, 'Colombia to Implement Law on Alternatives to Incarceration for Women Heads of Household' (n 72).

who are accused of or sentenced for drug trafficking, theft, sedition and abortion. A commission was set up to review petitions for amnesty; however, it encountered numerous obstacles, compounded by the shutdowns caused by the pandemic. Despite some improvements in operations, the number of amnesties granted to-date remains limited: As of July 2023, of 2,327 requests, only 376 had been granted, of whom 127 are women.[74]

While the impact of the law has to date been disappointing at best, it is permanent (unlike many measures passed during the COVID-19 pandemic) and an innovative approach. In adopting the law, the government has recognized the disproportionate impact of incarceration on historically marginalized sectors of the population. It is also a recognition of punitive drug policies that have filled the countries prisons with those who have committed low-level offenses for excessive periods of time. With more transparent and effective implementation, the federal amnesty law in Mexico has the potential to become a better tool for restoring justice and reducing prison populations.[75]

This experience in Mexico, as well as the potential roadblocks to implementing the new law in Colombia, point to the myriad of obstacles that prevent well-meaning reforms from having the desired impact, or even become counterproductive, as is so often the case with drug courts, house arrest and electronic monitoring. Lack of resources, weak institutions and overwhelmed judicial personnel all contribute to the failure of public policies. Perhaps the greatest obstacle is the continued discrimination and stigma faced by women in and coming out of prison, especially if they have been involved in the drug trade.[76]

8 Conclusion

While over the last decade, the visibility of women in prison has increased, in Latin America little has changed in terms of paths of criminalization[77] and

74 Secretaría de Gobernación de México, 'Beneficio de Amnistía' (*Mesas de Justicia*, 2023) <https://justicia.segob.gob.mx/es/UASJ/Ley_de_Amnistia> accessed 1 December 2023 (link is currently unavailable).

75 Coletta A. Youngers, 'Liberarlas es Justicia: Mujeres, políticas de drogas y encarcelamiento en América Latina' (*Washington Office on Latin America*, 2023) 56 <https://www.wola.org/wp-content/uploads/2023/11/Briefing-Paper-Liberarlas-es-justicia_Final_Web.pdf> accessed 1 December 2023.

76 Youngers, 'Liberarlas es Justicia: Mujeres, políticas de drogas y encarcelamiento en América Latina' (n 75) 66.

77 Mahtani, 'Toolkit on Gender-Responsive Non-Custodial Measures' (n 62).

prison conditions.[78] Gaby and Maria's stories – and those of countless other incarcerated and formerly incarcerated women – show the human impact of a "War on Drugs" that has had devastating consequences for millions of people around the world, and particularly for those in Latin America. It also illustrates the disproportionate impact of punitive drug policies on women, particularly women who face multiple situations of vulnerability, including indigenous women. At the same time, over many decades now, the present highly punitive international drug control paradigm has failed to make even a dent in illegal drug markets, which continue to flourish and multiply.

These stories point to the need for two fundamental areas of reform. First is the need to fundamentally transform the punitive drug policies that have resulted in hyper-incarceration, moving from policies based on repression to policies rooted in public health and human rights, and with a gender-focus. As noted in a WOLA report, "countries should move in the direction of decriminalization (removing criminal penalties for possession and small-scale cultivation of drugs and drug crops) and creating legally regulated markets, beginning with cannabis, in order to take organized crime – and the violence and corruption it generates – out of the drug trade".[79] Those communities that have been victims of prohibitionist policies should be compensated for the suffering inflicted upon them and should benefit from new legal markets.

The second is the need to fundamentally rethink who is put behind bars and for what reasons, recognizing that prisons should, indeed, become obsolete.[80] While we move towards that goal, laws need to be reformed so far fewer people go into prison and alternatives to incarceration adopted. These should include job training or other educational opportunities that can provide women – and indigenous women in particular – with the skills and resources that they need to live lives with dignity and provide for their families. Incarceration creates a vicious circle where women who are already disadvantaged come out of prison with criminal records and face tremendous stigma and discrimination, as Gaby has described. Recidivism then becomes all too common, due to lack of other economic options. Would it not be better if women were provided with opportunities instead of put behind bars?

---

78 Torres and Toro, 'Políticas de género en el ámbito de la ejecución penal: una deuda pendiente' (n 5).

79 Youngers, Castro and Manzur, 'Women Behind Bars for Drug Offenses in Latin America: What the Numbers Make Clear' (n 40) 23.

80 Angela Y. Davis, *Are Prisons Obsolete?* (New York, Seven Stories Press 2003).

Acknowledgements

The authors would like to thank Carolina Ahumada for her assistance with the translations needed to produce this chapter.

References

Bergman M and Fondevila G, *Prisons and Crime in Latin America* (Cambridge, Cambridge University Press 2021).

Carrington K, 'Feminist Criminologies' in Carlen Pat and França Leandro A. (eds), *Alternative Criminologies* (New York, Routledge 2018) 110–124.

Chaparro S, Correa CP, and Youngers CA, 'Irrational Punishment: Drug Laws and Incarceration in Latin America' (*Colectivo de Estudios Drogas y Derecho*, 2017) <https://idpc.net/publications/2017/04/irrational-punishment-drug-laws-and-incarceration-in-latin-america>.

Comisión Nacional de los Derechos Humanos, 'Informe diagnóstico sobre las condiciones de vida de las mujeres privadas de libertad desde un enfoque interseccional' (*CNDH México*, 2022) <https://www.cndh.org.mx/sites/default/files/documentos/2022-04/Informe_Diagnostico_Mujeres_Privadas_Libertad.pdf>.

Davis AY, *Are Prisons Obsolete?* (New York, Seven Stories Press 2003).

Differentiated approaches with respect to certain groups of persons in detention (*Interpretation and scope of Articles 1(1), 4(1), 5, 11(2), 12, 13, 17(1), 19, 24 and 26 of the American Convention on Human Rights and other human rights instruments*), Advisory Opinion OC-29/22, IACtHR Series A No 29 (30 May 2022).

ECLAC, 'Panorama Social de América Latina 2020, Santiago de Chile' (*CEPAL*, 2021) <https://www.cepal.org/es/publicaciones/46687-panorama-social-america-latina-2020>.

ECLAC, 'La sociedad del cuidado: horizonte para una recuperación sostenible con igualdad de género' (*CEPAL*, 2022) <https://repositorio.cepal.org/handle/11362/48363>.

ECLAC, 'ECLAC: At Least 4,473 Women Were Victims of Femicide in Latin America and the Caribbean in 2021' (*CEPAL*, 2022) <https://www.cepal.org/en/pressreleases/eclac-least-4473-women-were-victims-femicide-latin-america-and-caribbean-2021>.

ECLAC, Feminicidio' (*CEPAL*, 2023) <https://oig.cepal.org/es/indicadores/feminicidio>.

Eguiarte Mereles CR, *Voto en prisión preventiva* (Mexico City, Tirant Lo Blanch 2021).

Espinoza O, Droppelmann C, and del Villar P, "¿Reincidir o resistir? Mujeres en conflicto con la ley en América Latina' in Hein C and Toledo P (eds), *Criminologías feministas latinoamericanas* (Rio de Janeiro, Lumen Juris 2020) 343–377.

Fatima del Rocio Valdivia and Okowí Juan , 'Drug Trafficking in the Tarahumara Region, Northern Mexico: An Analysis of Racism and Dispossession' (2021) 142 *World Development* 1–10.

Fair H and Walmsley R, 'World Female Imprisonment List (fifth edition)' (*Institute for Crime & Justice Policy Research*, 2022) <https://www.prisonstudies.org/sites/default/files/resources/downloads/world_female_imprisonment_list_5th_edition.pdf>.

Freeman L and Sierra JL, 'Mexico: The Militarization Trap' in Youngers CA and Rosin E (eds), *Drugs and Democracy in Latin America: The Impact of U.S. Policy* (Boulder, Lynne Rienner Publishers 2005) 263–302.

Fuchs M-C and Postigo LG (eds), *Sistemas penitenciarios y ejecución penal en América Latina. Una mirada regional y opciones de abordaje* (Tirant Lo Blanch 2021).

Giacomello C, *Género, drogas y prisión. Experiencias de mujeres privadas de su libertad en México* (Mexico City, Tirant Lo Blanch 2013).

Giacomello C, *Niñas y niños que viven en prisión con sus madres. Una perspectiva jurídica comparada* (Mexico City, Suprema Corte de Justicia de la Nación 2018).

Giacomello C, 'Niñez que cuenta. El impacto de las políticas de drogas sobre niñas, niños y adolescentes con madres y padres encarcelados en América Latina y el Caribe' (*Church World Service*, 2019) <http://www.cwslac.org/nnapes-pdd/docs/Estudio-Regional-Ninez-que-cuenta-web.pdf>.

Giacomello C, 'The Gendered Impacts of Drug Policy on Women: Case Studies from Mexico' (2021) 12 *International Development Policy* 1–29.

Giacomello C, 'The Legal Flaws and Material Implementation Gaps of Mexico's Rehabilitation Paradigm' in Vanstone M and Priestly P (eds), *The Palgrave Handbook of Global Rehabilitation in Criminal Justice* (Cham, Palgrave Macmillan 2022).

Giacomello C and Castro TG, 'Imprisoned at Home: Women Under House Arrest in Latin America' (*Washington Office on Latin America*, 2020) <https://www.wola.org/wp-content/uploads/2020/07/Imprisoned-at-Home.pdf>.

Giacomello C and Youngers CA, 'Women Incarcerated for Drug-Related Offenses: A Latin American Perspective' in Buxton J, Margo G, and Burger L (eds), *The Impact of Global Drug Policy on Women: Shifting the Needle* (Bingley, Emerald Publishing Limited 2021).

Global Commission on Drug Policy, 'Time to End Prohibition' (*Global Commission on Drugs Policy*, 2021) <Time_to_end_prohibition_EN_2021_report.pdf>.

González and Others ("Campo Algodonero") v Mexico (Preliminary Objections, Merits, Reparation and Costs) IACtHR Series C No 205 (16 November 2009).

Heard C, 'Alternatives to imprisonment in Europe: A handbook of good practice' (*Associazione Antigone Onlus*, 2016) <http://www.prisonobservatory.org/upload/Good%20practice%20handbook%20AS.pdf>.

Human Rights Watch, 'México. Eventos del 2022' (*HRW*, 2022) <https://www.hrw.org/es/world-report/2023/country-chapters/mexico#2c964d>.

IACHR, 'Informe sobre los derechos humanos de las personas privadas de libertad en las Américas' (*OAS*, 2011) <https://www.oas.org/es/cidh/ppl/docs/pdf/ppl2011esp.pdf>.

IACHR, 'Medidas para reducir la prisión preventiva' (*OAS*, 2017) <http://www.oas.org/es/cidh/informes/pdfs/prisionpreventiva.pdf>.

IACHR, 'Women Deprived of Liberty in the Americas' (*OAS*, 2023) <https://www.oas.org/en/iachr/reports/pdfs/2023/Informe-Mujeres-privadas-libertad_ENG.pdf>.

INEGI, 'Mortalidad. Conjunto de datos: Defunciones por homicidios' (*Inegi*, 2023) <https://www.inegi.org.mx/sistemas/olap/consulta/general_ver4/MDXQueryDatos.asp?proy=>.

Institute for Crime & Justice Policy Research and Birkbeck, 'Mexico' (*World Prison Brief*, 2023) <https://www.prisonstudies.org/country/Mexico>.

Instituto Nacional de Estadística y Geografía, 'Encuesta nacional de población privada de la libertad 2021. Tabulados básicos' (*INEGI*, 2021) https://www.inegi.org.mx/programas/enpol/2021/#tabulados.

Instituto Nacional de Estadística y Geografía, 'Encuesta nacional de población privada de la libertad 2021. Principales resultados' (*INEGI*, 2021) <https://www.inegi.org.mx/contenidos/programas/enpol/2021/doc/enpol2021_presentacion_nacional.pdf>.

Isacson AB, 'The U.S Military in the War on Drugs' in Youngers Coletta A. and Rosin Eileen (eds), *Drugs and Democracy in Latin America: The Impact of US Policy* (Boulder, Lynne Rienner Publishers 2005).

Kilgore J, *Understanding E-Carceration* (New York, The New Press 2022).

Mahtani S, 'Toolkit on Gender-Responsive Non-Custodial Measures' (*UNODC*, 2020) <https://www.unodc.org/documents/justice-and-prison-reform/20-01528_Gender_Toolkit_complete.pdf>.

Miranda H, 'México registra 15 mil 122 homicidios dolosos en primer semestre de 2023, 1.68% menos respecto de 2022' (*Animal Político*, 2023) <https://www.animalpolitico.com/seguridad/mexico-homicidios-dolosos-primer-semestre-2023-junio>.

Nowak M, 'The United Nations Global Study on Children Deprived of their Liberty' (*OHCHR*, 2019) <https://omnibook.com/view/e0623280-5656-42f8-9edf-5872f8f08562/page/1>.

Observatorio de Igualdad de Género de América Latina y el Caribe, 'Índice de feminidad en hogares pobres' (*OIG*, 2023) <https://oig.cepal.org/es/indicadores/indice-feminidad-hogares-pobres>.

Pieris N, 'Reducing Female Incarceration Through Drug Law Reform in Costa Rica' (*Washington Office on Latin America, International Drug Policy Consortium, Dejusticia and CIM/OEA*, 2020) <https://womenanddrugs.wola.org/wp-content/uploads/2020/10/DONE-2-Costa-Rica-77bis_ENG_FINAL-.pdf>.

Rodriguez IA, 'Drug-trafficking and Rural Capitalism in Guerrero' (*Noria Research*, 2021) <https://noria-research.com/chapter-2-drug-trafficking-and-rural-capitalism-in-guerrero>.

Safranoff A and Tiravassi A, 'Mujeres en contextos de encierro en América Latina. Características y factores de riesgo asociados a determinados comportamientos delictivos' (*Wilson Center Latin American Program*, 2018) <https://publications.iadb.org/publications/spanish/document/Mujeres-en-contextos-de-encierro-en-Am%C3%A9rica-Latina-Caracter%C3%ADsticas-y-factores-de-riesgo-asociados-a-determinados-comportamientos-delictivos.pdf>.

Secretaría de Seguridad y Protección Ciudadana, 'Información sobre violencia contra las mujeres' (*Secretariado Ejecutivo del Sistema Nacional de Seguridad Pública*, 2021) <https://drive.google.com/file/d/1mnvTELZwrS8GV8X2fmzPu2JxpA-gN21-/view>.

Secretaría de Gobernación de México, 'Beneficio de Amnistía' (*Mesas de Justicia*, 2023) <https://justicia.segob.gob.mx/es/UASJ/Ley_de_Amnistia> (link is currently unavailable).

Secretaría de Seguridad y Protección Ciudadana, 'Cuaderno mensual de información estadística penitenciaria nacional. Junio 2023' (*Gobierno de México*, 2023) <https://www.gob.mx/cms/uploads/attachment/file/915855/CE_2023_06.pdf>.

Social Science Research Council, 'Drug Courts in the Americas' (*SSRC*, 2018) <https://www.ssrc.org/publications/drug-courts-in-the-americas/&#>.

Szabó I, 'The war on drugs has failed. Now what?' (*Instituto Igarapé*, 2016) <https://igarape.org.br/the-war-on-drugs-has-failed-now-what/>.

Torres MS and Toro MCM, 'Políticas de género en el ámbito de la ejecución penal: una deuda pendiente' in Fuchs M-C and Postigo LG (eds), *Sistemas penitenciarios y ejecución penal en América Latina. Una mirada regional y opciones de abordaje* (Valencia, Tirant Lo Blanch 2021) 75–102

United Nations Office on Drugs and Crime, 'The Bangkok Rules' (*UNODC*, 2011) <https://www.unodc.org/documents/justice-and-prison-reform/Bangkok_Rules_ENG_22032015.pdf>.

van Zyl Smit D, *Handbook of Basic Principles and Promising Practices on Alternatives to Imprisonment* (Vienna, UNODC 2007).

Walsh J, 'Loosening Drug Prohibition's Lethal Grip on the Americas' (*The Washington Office on Latin America*, 2022) <https://www.wola.org/wp-content/uploads/2022/07/Lethal-Grip_WOLA_July-2022.pdf>.

Washington Office on Latin America and others, 'La respuesta de los sistemas penitenciarios de América Latina frente a la crisis por COVID-19 no ha tenido en cuenta a las mujeres privadas de la libertad' (*WOLA*, 19 March 2021) <https://womenanddrugs.wola.org/wp-content/uploads/2021/04/WOLA-Propuesta-de-comunicado-audiencia-CIDH-19042021.pdf>.

WOLA, 'The Stories of Women in prison for Drug Related Crimes' (*Women and Drugs*, 2023) <https://womenanddrugs.wola.org/multimedia/videos/>.

Youngers CA, 'Collateral Damage: The U.S. 'War on Drugs' and Its Impact on Democracy in the Andes' in Burt J-M and Mauceri P (eds), *Politics in the Andes: Identity, Conflict, Reform* (Pittsburgh, University of Pittsburg Press 2004) 132–145.

Youngers CA, 'Colombia to Implement Law on Alternatives to Incarceration for Women Heads of Household' (*Washington Office on Latin America*, 2022) <https://www.wola.org/analysis/colombia-law-alternatives-incarceration-women-heads-household/>.

Youngers CA, 'Liberarlas es Justicia: Mujeres, políticas de drogas y encarcelamiento en América Latina' (*Washington Office on Latin America*, 2023) <https://www.wola.org/wp-content/uploads/2023/11/Briefing-Paper-Liberarlas-es-justicia_Final_Web.pdf>.

Youngers CA, Castro TG, and Manzur M, 'Women Behind Bars for Drug Offenses in Latin America: What the Numbers Make Clear' (*Washington Office on Latin America*, 2020) <https://www.wola.org/wp-content/uploads/2020/11/Final-Women-Behind-Bars-Report.pdf>.

Youngers CA and Giacomello C, 'Electronic Monitoring: A New Form of Punishment for Many Women' (*Washington Office on Latin America*, 2022) <https://www.wola.org/analysis/electronic-monitoring-punishment-women/>.

Youngers CA and Rosin E, 'The U.S. 'War on Drugs': Its Impact in Latin America and the Caribbean' in Coletta AY and Rosin E (eds), *Drugs and Democracy in Latin America: The Impact of U.S. Policy* (Boulder, Lynne Rienner Publishers 2005).

CHAPTER 3

Reproductive Health and Rights in Prisons: Challenges and Opportunities for Latin America

Carmen Cecilia Martínez López

1 Introduction

In Latin America women, in all their diversity, and pregnant people are particularly vulnerable to violence within detention and prison contexts. Within a patriarchal system, prisons are usually constructed with a one-size-fits-all model, developed without considering a gender perspective.[1] This contributes to harsh prison conditions, such as the ones that have been identified in States such as El Salvador or Honduras,[2] having disproportionate impacts to the detriment of women. Furthermore, it leads to a complete dismissal of State positive obligations towards detained and imprisoned women.

This context is substantially aggravated when it comes to reproductive rights. Although there is no dispute that reproductive rights are human rights, there is a substantial failure in the recognition and development of State duties to respect and guarantee reproductive rights within prison conditions.[3] On the other hand, reproductive rights continue to be stigmatized in many States, and in some circumstances, exercising reproductive rights may lead to even worse prison conditions.[4]

The Inter-American Court of Human Rights (IACtHR) and the Inter-American Commission on Human Rights (IACHR) have recently developed case law reflecting the issue.[5] Based on the rights to non-discrimination and

1 *Differentiated approaches with respect to certain groups of persons in detention (Interpretation and scope of Articles 1(1), 4(1), 5, 11(2), 12, 13, 17(1), 19, 24 and 26 of the American Convention on Human Rights and other human rights instruments)*, Advisory Opinion OC-29/22, IACtHR Series A No 29 (30 May 2022).

2 IACHR, 'Women deprived of liberty in the Americas' (*OAS*, 2023 <https://www.oas.org/en/iachr/reports/pdfs/2023/Informe-Mujeres-privadas-libertad_ENG.pdf> accessed 12 April 2024.

3 IACHR, 'Women deprived of liberty in the Americas' (n 2) para 117.

4 *Manuela and Others v El Salvador* (Preliminary Objections, Merits, Reparations and Costs) IACtHR Series C No 441 (2 November 2021).

5 *Differentiated approaches with respect to certain groups of persons in detention (Interpretation and scope of Articles 1(1), 4(1), 5, 11(2), 12, 13, 17(1), 19, 24 and 26 of the American Conven-*

the right to be free from violence, these bodies have recognized that people who have been detained or who are imprisoned require reinforced protections to ensure that their reproductive rights are recognised within that context.

The following chapter seeks to identify and address the main challenges and opportunities that States must act upon to ensure respect and protection of reproductive rights within prison conditions. As will be argued, reproductive rights safeguards must be prioritized within prisons. Despite useful and relevant developments within Inter-American law on the topic, the current state of international law falls short of ensuring that women and pregnant people do not suffer violence and discrimination within prisons. To achieve this goal, the chapter is structured in three parts: (1) a description of the State's duties towards women who are imprisoned, (2) a description of recent developments within the IACtHR and the IACHR concerning reproductive rights in prison conditions, and (3) a reference to opportunities that both bodies are yet to address thoroughly to advance decidedly on the topic.

2 The Legal Framework: The Right to Be Free from Discrimination and Gender-Based Violence in Prison Conditions

Articles 1.1 and 24 of the American Convention on Human Rights enshrine a right to non-discrimination. This right encompasses the need to adopt positive measures to ensure that no one suffers disproportionate impacts from norms perceived as neutral.[6] This duty extends to adopting legislative measures or measures of another nature to ensure that such affirmative protections are enshrined within positive law.

Directly articulated with the norms above, the Belém do Pará Convention recognizes the right of women, **in all their diversity**, to live free from violence. The IACtHR has held that this situation requires States to adopt reinforced measures particularly in situations where a context of gender based violence

tion on Human Rights and other human rights instruments). Advisory Opinion OC-29/22. Series A No 29.; IACHR, Women deprived of liberty in the Americas.

6 Edward J. Pérez, 'La igualdad y no discriminación en el derecho interamericano de los derechos humanos' (*Comisión Nacional de los Derechos Humanos*, 2016) <https://appweb.cndh.org.mx/biblioteca/archivos/pdfs/fas-CSIDH-Igualdad-No-Discriminacion_1.pdf> accessed 12 April 2024; *Xákmok Kásek Indigenous Community v Paraguay* (Merits, Reparations and Costs) IACtHR Series C No 214 (24 August 2010).

has been identified.[7] The Belém do Pará Convention has been understood to protect all women, including trans women.[8] Similar protections have been granted to non-binary people.[9] It has been understood that aside from trans women, members of the LGBTQ+ community as a whole also face forms of structural discrimination that require similar protections against violence and inequalities.[10]

Individuals deprived of their liberty remain in circumstances of vulnerability that require positive actions to protect their rights. As stated by the IACtHR, people who have been deprived of their liberty face a restriction on that right but should not face restrictions or the removal of any other human rights.[11] In *Chinchilla Sandoval*, for instance, the IACtHR acknowledged the duty of Guatemala to ensure access to health services for the victim, an imprisoned women who died as a consequence of the lack of provision of healthcare.[12] The IACtHR further stated that States are in a guarantor position of individuals deprived of their liberty. Hence, they are in a unique position to ensure the protection of their rights.[13]

The prison conditions in Latin America require a specific emphasis. As identified both by the IACHR and IACtHR, prison conditions in Latin America constitute a structural problem requiring structural remedies.[14] Particularly, prison overcrowding and lack of access to public services amount to general-

7 *González and Others ("Cotton Field") v Mexico* (Preliminary Objection, Merits, Reparations and Costs) IACtHR Series C No 205 (16 November 2009); *Vicky Hernández and Others v Honduras* (Merits, Reparations and Costs) IACtHR Series C No 422 (26 March 2021).

8 *Vicky Hernández and Others v Honduras* (n 7).

9 *Non-binary*: An umbrella term for *gender identities* that go beyond the *gender binary* of female and male. Non-binary people may refer to themselves as non-binary, and/or may use a range of identity terms, such as: *agender, bigender, genderqueer*, and *gender fluid*. Often abbreviated as NB or enby. See: National LGBTQIA+ Health Education Center, 'Glossary' (*LGBTQIA+ Health Education Center*, 1 January 2024) <https://www.lgbtqiahealtheducation.org/glossary/> accessed 12 April 2024.

10 *Vicky Hernández and Others v Honduras* (n 7).

11 *Chinchilla Sandoval and Others v Guatemala* (Preliminary Objection, Merits, Reparations and Costs) IACtHR Series C No 312 (29 February 2016).

12 *Chinchilla Sandoval and Others v Guatemala* (n 11).

13 *Chinchilla Sandoval and Others v Guatemala* (n 11); *Isaza Uribe and Others v Colombia* (Merits, Reparations and Costs) IACtHR Series C No 363 (20 November 2018).

14 IACHR, 'Report on the Human Rights of Persons Deprived of Liberty in the Americas' (*OAS*, 2011) <https://www.oas.org/en/iachr/pdl/docs/pdf/ppl2011eng.pdf> accessed 12 April 2014; *Differentiated approaches with respect to certain groups of persons in detention* (n 1).

ized human rights violations that lead to circumstances analogous to torture.[15] Judge Ferrer Mac-Gregor Poisot of the IACtHR has delved into the topic thoroughly, understanding the structural nature of dire prison conditions throughout the Americas.[16]

Within the described context, the case of women, in all their diversity, deprived of their liberty builds upon this case law. It recognizes that they are in an exacerbated position of vulnerability which generates an intersection of vulnerability factors that lead to the duty of States to address their specific situation to avoid constituting intersectional discrimination.[17]

However, States have hardly committed to these forms of intersectional discrimination. The IACHR has argued that "imprisoned women face serious impacts on their human rights based on the failure to provide differentiated treatment and to adopt diligent prison policies and measures that consider women's special needs".[18] The IACtHR arrives at a similar conclusion, recognising that these forms of intersectional discrimination could further lead to breaches of the right to be free from torture and cruel, inhuman, or degrading treatment.[19]

Therefore, the IACHR and IACtHR have developed a non-exhaustive list of State duties in recent reports to address the particular prison conditions of this population. These duties include (1) collecting data with a gender perspective, (2) ensuring that prison infrastructure is adequate for them – including ensuring that they can address their particular needs, (3) protecting them from violence, particularly sexual violence, within the prison, (4) ensuring essential services, in accordance to their needs, among others.[20]

Within this context, the IACHR's and IACtHR's contributions crystalize a reinforced right for women in prison to be free from discrimination and violence, in broad terms, ensuring the integration of a gender perspective in policy development measures in their favour and recognizing that their particular situations place them in a unique vulnerability of being victims of

15 *Differentiated approaches with respect to certain groups of persons in detention* (n 1).

16 ibid.

17 *Guzmán Albarracín and Others v Ecuador* (Merits, Reparations and Costs) IACtHR Series C No 405 (24 June 2020); *Differentiated approaches with respect to certain groups of persons in detention* (n 1).

18 IACHR, 'Women deprived of liberty in the Americas' (n 2) para 122.

19 *Differentiated approaches with respect to certain groups of persons in detention* (n 1).

20 IACHR, 'Report on the Human Rights of Persons Deprived of Liberty in the Americas' (n 14); *Differentiated approaches with respect to certain groups of persons in detention* (n 1).

intersectional discrimination.[21] These considerations should also be understood as applicable to trans women and non-binary people.

3 Reproductive Rights in Prison: The Recent Contributions of the IACHR and the IACtHR

The international human rights framework applicable to persons deprived of liberty has contributed to the development of specific rules concerning reproductive rights. This section describes these contributions.

3.1 *Detention and Deprivation of Liberty after Suffering Obstetric Emergencies*

A first contribution that must be presented is that deprivation of liberty due to the suffering of an obstetric emergency amounts to a breach of international human rights law. Using punitive powers to address a health emergency is incompatible with the American Convention on Human Rights.

The leading case in this context was the *Manuela* case,[22] where El Salvador was found responsible for the arbitrary criminalization of a young and impoverished woman who suffered an obstetric emergency at her home in a rural area.[23] While she was unconscious, her family took her to the nearest health facilities, which were at least three hours away from her home. She did not receive timely and appropriate healthcare because the medical personnel denounced her before police authorities for allegedly having committed an abortion, in breach of doctor-patient confidentiality. The delay in medical attention put her at a significantly increased risk of death. During her convalescence, Manuela was unjustly detained, imprisoned, and eventually – under a procedure that was characterized by many due process violations based on gender-based stereotypes – convicted and sentenced to 30 years in prison for the crime of aggravated homicide.[24] Manuela ultimately died in prison

21 ibid.

22 Litigated by the Center for Reproductive Rights and the Colectiva Feminista. *Manuela and Others v El Salvador* (n 4).

23 *Manuela and Others v El Salvador* (n 4); Morena Herrera, 'Derechos reproductivos. Corte IDH. Caso Manuela y otros v El Salvador. Excepciones preliminares, Fondo, Reparaciones y Costas. Sentencia de 2 de noviembre de 2021. Serie C No. 441' (2022) 6 Revista Debates sobre Derechos Humanos 129.

24 Center for Reproductive Rights and Colectiva Feminista, 'The Impact of Blanket Abortion Bans on Women Experiencing Obstetric Emergencies' (*Reproductive Rights*, 2021)

because of lymphatic cancer that existed before her obstetric emergency, which was deficiently treated by the Salvadorean authorities.[25]

The IACtHR considered this case to be paradigmatic of the general situation in El Salvador, where a context of criminalization of women due to obstetric emergencies exists as a consequence of the total criminalization of abortions in the country.[26] Effectively, as reported by the IACHR in its report on the human rights situation in El Salvador of 2021, this context is built upon a full ban on abortion that restricts access to this reproductive service even if the pregnancy is the result of rape or poses a grave risk to their lives and health.[27] Common practice in El Salvador, however, is that women criminalized for an alleged abortion are actually prosecuted and convicted for aggravated homicide, with prison sentences of up to 50 years.[28] According to the IACHR, 49 women died from preventable causes that could have been avoided if they had access to legal abortions,[29] and at least 74 women have been prosecuted and convicted after suffering an obstetric emergency,[30] whereby most of them were accused by medical personnel. The pattern affects mostly young women who live in impoverished circumstances.

The IACtHR was emphatic in considering that reproductive health constraints, such as an obstetric emergency, should not lead to criminalization.[31] An obstetric emergency was defined within the judgment as "situations suffered by the woman or the foetus that require immediate attention; to the contrary, she or the foetus may suffer irreparable harm to their health and even die".[32] The IACHR built upon the development of the IACtHR and expressed its concern that

> in contexts characterized by poverty and barriers to access to reproductive health services, women who suffer complications during pregnancy that lead them to lose the pregnancy face the risk of being

<https://reproductiverights.org/wp-content/uploads/2021/03/Factsheet-MANUELA_INGLES.pdf> accessed 12 April 2024.

25 *Manuela and Others v El Salvador* (n 4).

26 ibid.

27 IACHR, 'The Human Rights Situation in El Salvador' (*OAS*, 14 October 2021) <https://www.oas.org/en/iachr/reports/pdfs/2021_ElSalvador-EN.pdf> accessed 12 April 2024.

28 IACHR, 'The Human Rights Situation in El Salvador' (n 27).

29 IACHR, 'The Human Rights Situation in El Salvador' (n 27) para 196.

30 ibid para 198.

31 *Manuela and Others v El Salvador* (n 4) para 161.

32 *Manuela and Others v El Salvador* (n 4) para 41.

> imprisoned and convicted based on the suspicion that they have induced an abortion.[33]

Furthermore, as a safeguard, the IACtHR developed standards on doctor-patient confidentiality, recognizing that the right to reproductive health ensures in absolute terms that patients who suffer obstetric emergencies or request access to any type of reproductive service, including abortion, are not subjects of denunciation by the medical personnel or hospital staff.[34] Moreover, medical personnel should not be compelled to reveal this information, and it must be deemed inadmissible if the information they provided in legal proceedings breaches doctor-patient confidentiality. Finally, doctor-patient confidentiality also protects medical files and should only be accessible under very exceptional circumstances.[35]

The contribution is relevant for this research inasmuch standards applicable to persons deprived of liberty must also consider the reasons that ultimately led them to prison. The norm described should ultimately lead to structural reforms towards ensuring (1) the release of all persons detained as a consequence of obstetric emergencies, (2) the adoption of safeguards – including doctor-patient confidentiality – to ensure that anyone can access reproductive healthcare services free from fear of being accused and prosecuted for these facts. In the particular case of the *Manuela* judgment, the IACtHR ordered El Salvador to adopt specific protocols to ensure accessibility to healthcare for any person who suffered obstetric emergencies and to adopt regulations that ensure doctor-patient confidentiality to women who are accessing healthcare systems for reproductive healthcare services, including abortion.[36]

3.2 *Detention during Convalescence or Medical Attention Associated with Reproductive Healthcare*

A second contribution of the *Manuela* judgment concerned the conditions faced by anyone detained for accessing reproductive healthcare systems. Obstetric emergencies include miscarriages, unplanned out-of-hospital births, cord prolapse, ruptured ectopic pregnancies, eclampsia, postpartum haemorrhage, and many others.[37] The *Manuela* case concerned an *unplanned out-of-*

---

33 IACHR, 'Women deprived of liberty in the Americas' (n 2) 60.

34 *Manuela and Others v El Salvador* (n 4) para 229.

35 ibid para 228.

36 ibid paras 286 and 287.

37 Geoffrey Chamberlain and Philip Steer, 'Obstetric Emergencies' (1999) 318 BMJ 1342.

hospital birth, with eclampsia and postpartum haemorrhage. However, criminalization has been applied broadly to all sorts of obstetric emergencies, mostly but not exclusively to cases where the baby was not born.[38]

The IACtHR observed that, in El Salvador, women who suffered obstetric emergencies were usually handcuffed and shackled to their beds during convalescence.[39] It must be clarified that this process within the context of an obstetric emergency has exclusively punitive objectives; since the severity of the risk of death and the health constraints associated with the obstetric emergency, it is unreasonable to believe that a measure of that nature would be needed.

The IACtHR found that such shackling amounted to a violation of the right not to be subjected to torture or cruel, inhuman or degrading treatment or punishment established in Article 5(2) of the American Convention. It determined that Manuela

> had recently given birth and was being treated for severe preeclampsia. Therefore, it was unreasonable to assume that there was a real risk of flight that could not have been mitigated by other less harmful means.[40]

The reasoning implicitly reflects that

> [t]he intent and purpose of torturing and humiliating Manuela were explicit, as the state authorities shackled her consciously under the discriminatory belief that women who fail to be mothers should be punished and that Manuela's severe suffering was also clear because she had recently lost her pregnancy and required immediate treatment for severe preeclampsia.[41]

---

38 For instance, in the *Imelda Cortez* case, she was convicted for attempted aggravated murder for an obstetric emergency that did not lead to her child's death. Her conviction was considered arbitrary by the United Nations Working Group on Arbitrary Detention. See: Working Group on Arbitrary Detention, 'Opinión núm. 19/2020, relativa a Imelda Cortez Palacios (El Salvador)' (25 June 2020) A/HRC/WGAD/2020/19.

39 *Manuela and Others v El Salvador* (n 4) para 200.

40 *Manuela and Others v El Salvador* (n 4) para 200.

41 María F. Perico and María C. Castellanos, '*Manuela et al. v El Salvador*: The Pitfalls of a Landmark Case for Reproductive Justice from a Torture Perspective' (*EJIL:Talk!*, 2023) <https://www.ejiltalk.org/manuela-et-al-v-el-salvador-the-pitfalls-of-a-landmark-case-for-reproductive-justice-from-a-torture-perspective/> accessed 12 April 2024.

The IACHR built upon these findings and broadened its scope, determining that these considerations should be made extensive to pregnant persons.[42] Also, the IACHR further elaborates that best practices in the area should consist of

> i) a prohibition on coercive measures, ii) ban on their use in practice, and iii) use of such measures on a temporary and exceptional basis if a woman jeopardizes her own physical safety or that of others.[43]

Thus, people who have suffered obstetric emergencies or pregnant people that require reproductive healthcare should never be shackled or handcuffed. If there is no risk of harm, handcuffing anyone in this context shall be considered as amounting to a violation of the right not to be subjected to torture or cruel, inhuman or degrading treatment or punishment.

3.3 *Obstetric Violence*

A third significant contribution of the IACtHR to the topic is the prohibition of obstetric violence within prison contexts. The IACtHR developed the notion of obstetric violence in its advisory opinion on differentiated approaches to deprivation of liberty, recognizing for the first time as a rule that such type of gender-based violence should be entirely eradicated.[44] This topic has had and promises to continuously have increasing relevance in the Inter-American system.[45]

The IACtHR defined obstetric violence in the above-mentioned advisory opinion as violence exercised on pregnant people during pregnancy, childbirth, and after childbirth.[46] It built upon previous theoretical frameworks created by the IACHR.[47] The IACtHR has subsequently developed its definition on the topic, arguing that it "encompasses all situations of disrespectful,

42 IACHR, 'Women deprived of liberty in the Americas' (n 2) para 166.

43 ibid para 166.

44 *Differentiated approaches with respect to certain groups of persons in detention* (n 1).

45 Carmen C. Martínez, 'Violencia obstétrica. Salud Reproductiva. Corte IDH, Caso Brítez Arce y otros v Argentina' (2023) 7 Revista Debates sobre Derechos Humanos 153.

46 *Brítez Arce and Others v Argentina* (Merits, Reparations and Costs) IACtHR Series C No 474 (16 November 2022) para 81; *Differentiated approaches with respect to certain groups of persons in detention* (n 1) para 160.

47 IACHR, 'Violence and Discrimination against women and girls' (OAS, 2019) para 181 <https://www.oas.org/en/iachr/reports/pdfs/violencewomengirls.pdf> accessed 12 April 2024. The concept was built bearing in mind thematic hearings concerning Mexico (2014) and Costa Rica (2015) held before that IACHR.

abusive, neglectful treatment or denial thereof that take place during the pregnancy, childbirth or post-partum period, in private or public health facilities".[48] It further established that pregnant persons have

> the right to live a life free of obstetric violence and the States have the obligation to prevent, punish and abstain from practicing it, as well as to ensure that its agents act accordingly, taking into account the special vulnerability implied during pregnancy and the postpartum period.[49]

It concludes by crystalizing that obstetric violence is

> exercised by those in charge of health care for pregnant persons accessing services during pregnancy, childbirth and post-partum. It is expressed mostly, although not exclusively, in a dehumanizing, disrespectful, abusive or negligent treatment of pregnant women; in withholding of treatment or complete information about their health and the applicable treatments; in forced or coerced medical interventions, and in the tendency to pathologize natural reproductive processes, among other life-threatening expressions in health care during pregnancy, childbirth and post-partum.[50]

The IACtHR has found that obstetric violence amounted to breaches of the rights to life, personal integrity, health, non-discrimination, and the right to be free from gender-based violence. In the *Brítez* case, the IACtHR considered that the denial of access to specialized treatment that the victim needed, as well as the lack of information on treatments, amounted to obstetric violence.[51] In the *Rodríguez Pacheco* case, the IACtHR found Venezuela responsible for failing to investigate diligently the obstetric violence that the victim had faced in a private healthcare facility.[52]

Within the particular context of prison conditions, the IACtHR established that States must strengthen measures of prevention of obstetric violence in the obstetrical health services that they provide to this population.[53]

---

48 *Brítez Arce and Others v Argentina* (n 47) para 75; *Rodríguez Pacheco and Others v Venezuela* (Preliminary Objections, Merits, Reparations and Costs) IACtHR Series C No 504 (27 November 2023).

49 *Brítez Arce and Others v Argentina* (n 47) para 77.

50 *Brítez Arce and Others v Argentina* (n 47) para 81.

51 *Brítez Arce and Others v Argentina* (n 47).

52 *Rodríguez Pacheco and Others v Venezuela* (n 49).

53 *Differentiated approaches with respect to certain groups of persons in detention* (n 1) para 160.

Thus, the IACtHR considered that it requires:

> respectful maternal care during the entire process of pregnancy and childbirth, which implies organized care for every woman in a manner that would maintain their dignity, privacy and confidentiality; that would ensure their physical integrity and appropriate treatment, and that would allow them to make an informed decision and receive constant support during the birth process.[54]

Under these standards and given that pregnant people are subjects of special protection, States have an increased burden to prevent obstetric violence; thus, States must ensure that these persons have autonomy and information to make fully informed decisions about their pregnancy and appropriate treatment for their pregnancies and the time after that. Moreover, States must refrain from perpetrating obstetric violence, protect pregnant persons from such, and, if necessary, investigate such cases with due diligence.

3.4 *Reproductive Healthcare in Prison Conditions*

Fourthly, ensuring access to reproductive healthcare in prison conditions has been considered a cornerstone of the situation of individuals deprived of their liberty. The IACtHR deemed that deprivation of liberty historically has involved barriers to access to sexual and reproductive rights and, in that sense, the Court considers that the State has a reinforced obligation to ensure access, without discrimination, to quality sexual and reproductive health care.[55] Thus, ensuring reproductive health requires that States adopt measures to ensure accessibility, adaptability, availability and quality of reproductive healthcare even in prison contexts.[56] In response, the IACtHR developed safeguards that should be put in place to lift those barriers, which include[57]

1. Providing medical examinations at the moment of entering a prison establishment to determine their sexual and reproductive health needs.
2. Ensuring access to information concerning sexual and reproductive health;
3. Providing basic reproductive healthcare needs, including "gender-based preventive services", free provision of contraceptive methods, family

54 *Differentiated approaches with respect to certain groups of persons in detention* (n 1) para 161.
55 ibid para 152.
56 ibid para 150.
57 ibid para 152.

planning services, and access to services to prevent and treat sexually transmitted infections;
4. Giving timely healthcare services to victims of sexual violence, including prophylactic therapies, emergency contraception, and psychosocial care;
5. Providing pregnant people information on their health and well-being, the foetus, medical controls, and results.

These safeguards must be read along with the IACHR's policy considerations. For instance, the considerations above impose "the States' duty to adopt measures to guarantee access to healthcare with a gender perspective on a regular and timely basis, at least in the specialties of gynecology, mastology, and sexual and reproductive health".[58]

Thus, the standards require States to adopt actions including legislative and policy reforms, to ensure that the reproductive rights of women deprived of their liberty are effectively satisfied, meeting the above standards.

3.5 *Alternatives to Imprisonment*

Finally, a discussion on the intersection of reproductive rights with the rights of persons deprived of their liberty leads inevitably to the consideration of alternatives to imprisonment in many cases. Both the IACtHR and the IACHR have focused on the former, and coincide in considering that pregnant persons or persons during postpartum should not be imprisoned and that, if necessary, alternatives should be posed in their favour.

The IACtHR considered that:

> The Court deems that women [individuals] deprived of liberty, who are pregnant, postpartum or breastfeeding or with responsibilities of care, must be given preference for alternative or substitute measures to detention or imprisonment or for moderate forms of detention, such as house arrest or the use of electronic bracelets or anklets, depending on the degree of the offense – such as the commission of non-violent offenses – and the minimum risk that [an] offender represents to society, as well as the best interests of the children.[59]

The IACHR elaborates policy considerations for implementing this standard, recommending that States consider each person's individual circumstances to

58 IACHR, 'Women deprived of liberty in the Americas' (n 2) para 147.

59 *Differentiated approaches with respect to certain groups of persons in detention* (n 1) para 133.

determine what alternative could best fit a particular case.[60] It argues, among others, that special consideration should be given to (1) the historical disadvantage women and individuals capable of gestation have faced in society, (2) socioeconomic vulnerabilities, (3) prior victimization, (4) risks associated to the place of origin, age, or ethnic or racial origin; and (5) the disproportionate impact that imprisonment could have on that particular individual.[61]

Thus, there is a tendency towards acknowledging the right of pregnant people or people in postpartum to receive, inasmuch possible, alternatives to imprisonment as a rule. A legal consequence of this logic would require reconsidering and favouring the release of pregnant persons within prison conditions or who are currently postpartum. This should lead to a reconsideration of the imprisonment of those persons who have been criminalized for obstetric events and more importantly, it should prompt a reconsideration of the use of criminal law in many cases "related to reproductive health and rights".

4 Towards Stronger Safeguards for Reproductive Rights within Prisons

The contributions described in the previous section show the increasing importance that reproductive rights within prison contexts have had within the Inter-American legal framework. However, the topic still requires an evolution in order to ensure the full satisfaction of these rights for all persons that continue to be imprisoned. The following chapter seeks to discuss some prospective legal standards that are protected within the American Convention of Human Rights, but require development by the Inter-American human rights bodies.

4.1 *Access to Abortion as a Safeguard in Prison Conditions*

The recent developments regarding the WHO guidelines on abortion have clearly affirmed the existence of a right to abortion, and a consequent right not to be criminalized for undergoing an abortion.[62] These WHO guidelines establish the detrimental effects of the criminalization of abortion on preg-

60 IACHR, 'Women deprived of liberty in the Americas' (n 2) paras 316 and 317.

61 IACHR, 'Women deprived of liberty in the Americas' (n 2) para 317.

62 World Health Organization, 'Abortion Care Guideline' (*WHO*, 2022) <https://iris.who.int/bitstream/handle/10665/349316/9789240039483-eng.pdf?sequence=1> accessed 12 April 2024.

nant persons and public health in general. The findings of these guidelines obtain further strength from recent developments in treaty body monitoring observations[63] and domestic case law.[64]

Under these standards, individuals deprived of their liberty also have a right to abortion, and States have a duty to provide it regardless of their situation of imprisonment. As argued by the European Committee on Torture Prevention, under the laws of non-discrimination, access to healthcare, including abortion, must be ensured in the same circumstances as for those who are not imprisoned.[65] Such a safeguard is especially relevant in the context of prison conditions, where sexual violence against inmates perpetrated by other inmates or security officers tends to be common.[66] The IACHR, in this regard, calls for the removal of the full ban on abortion in States such as Honduras and El Salvador.[67] The IACtHR failed to analyse this structural problem in the *Manuela* judgment, an aspect that has been criticized.[68]

Thus, ensuring access to abortion in all circumstances should be secured in conformity with international human rights law. This requires that States adopt specific policies to ensure that everyone deprived of their liberty has information on how to request such reproductive health services and that it is made available at the request of the persons deprived of their liberty in similar circumstances as for those available to anyone outside of prison.

Moreover, this should lead to a requirement of full decriminalization of abortion. The criminalization of abortion leads to substantial barriers associated with the stigmatization of this reproductive right. Even partial decriminalization will not remove the barriers that people in more vulnerable circumstances—such as those deprived of their liberty—would face. Persons capable of gestation in detention, would only be able to have access to abortion in accordance with international law if the stigma that comes from the use of criminal law for this reproductive healthcare service is fully eliminated.

---

63 Human Rights Committee, 'Concluding observations on the sixth periodic report of Peru' (28 March 2023) CCPR/C/PER/CO/6.

64 Corte Constitutional de Colombia, *Sentencia C-055 de 2022* (21 February 2022).

65 European Committee on Prevention of Torture, '10th General Report on the CPT's activities' (*Council of Europe*, 18 August 2000) <https://rm.coe.int/1680696a74> accessed 12 April 2024.

66 *Differentiated approaches with respect to certain groups of persons in detention* (n 1); IACHR, 'Women deprived of liberty in the Americas' (n 2).

67 IACHR, 'Women deprived of liberty in the Americas' (n 2) para 60.

68 Rebecca Smyth, 'Abortion in International Human Rights Law: Missed Opportunities in Manuela v El Salvador' (2023) 32 Feminist Legal Studies 123.

4.2 *Information and Comprehensive Sexual Education*

Another major topic concerns the right to access information on topics concerning reproductive rights and, most importantly, the right to access comprehensive sexual education.[69] People deprived of liberty, on many occasions, come from vulnerable contexts where the State failed to provide adequate comprehensive sexual education. In these circumstances, girls, women and other persons with ability of gestation have fewer chances to be free from sexual violence and to exercise their right to bodily autonomy.[70]

The IACtHR has deemed access to information on bodily autonomy and comprehensive sexual education as tools for the progressive development of full capacities to exercise sexual autonomy and reproductive rights. Given the special vulnerabilities that many persons in prison face, comprehensive sexual education must be made accessible, both as a tool for the exercise of these rights and also as a method to prevent sexual violence to their detriment.[71]

This duty must be understood as reinforced in cases of children and adolescents who face any deprivation of liberty. Comprehensive sexual education is the cornerstone to the development of capacities and maturity concerning their right to autonomy. Access to comprehensive sexual education in spaces where power dynamics exist, such as prisons, becomes fundamental to protect them from forms of sexual violence.[72]

As a consequence, the need to incorporate comprehensive sexual education programs becomes fundamental in prison conditions, particularly in favour of children. This aligns very strongly with structural remedies issued by the IACtHR in recent cases, where it has found that incorporating comprehensive sexual education curricula is a mandatory policy under international law precisely to prevent the effects of these vulnerabilities.[73]

---

69 *Manuela and Others v El Salvador* (n 4); IACHR, 'Women deprived of liberty in the Americas' (n 2).

70 *Guzmán Albarracín and Others v Ecuador* (n 17).

71 *Guzmán Albarracín and Others v Ecuador* (n 17).

72 *Guzmán Albarracín and Others v Ecuador* (n 17); *Angulo Losada v Bolivia* (Preliminary Objections, Merits and Reparations) IACtHR Series C No 475 (18 November 2022); Catalina Martínez Coral and Lita Martínez, '¿Cómo evitar la repetición de más casos en Latinoamérica como el de Paola Guzmán Albarracín?' (*Agenda Estado de Derecho*, 9 December 2020) <https://agendaestadodederecho.com/como-evitar-la-repeticion-de-mas-casos-en-latinoamerica-como-el-de-paola-guzman-albarracin/> accessed 12 April 2024; Catalina Martínez Coral and Carmen C. Martínez, 'Sexual violence against girls in schools as a public health issue: a commentary on the case Paola Guzmán Albarracín v Ecuador' (2021) 29 Sexual and Reproductive Health Matters 1.

73 *Manuela and Others v El Salvador* (n 4); *Angulo Losada v Bolivia* (n 73).

4.3 *Reproductive Rights in Times of Emergency: The Response to COVID-19 in the Context of Prisons*

COVID-19 impacted directly and disproportionately all individuals within prison contexts. The historical marginalization that people within this situation continuously face was aggravated due to the prison conditions that have been denounced recurrently by international human rights mechanisms, including prison overcrowding and lack of access to water, among others.[74] Notwithstanding, COVID-19 nor any other type of public emergency should lead to any form of suspension of reproductive rights and healthcare, including in cases of women deprived of their liberty.

Accessibility to reproductive rights during the COVID-19 pandemic was substantially reduced *de facto*, to the detriment of everyone deprived of their liberty. For instance, the suspension of visiting rights removed an opportunity for people to receive sanitary products pertaining to their reproductive health, food, and other basic needs.[75] Moreover, pregnant, postpartum, or lactating persons who are deprived of their liberty require special protection due to the ongoing reproductive process, in addition to the dire prison conditions that they already face.[76]

Facing these enhanced vulnerabilities that health emergencies could cause, the State's duty to ensure reproductive rights to people deprived of their liberty also becomes more demanding. As the world is not exempt from facing similar challenges in the future, it is essential to develop a framework for reproductive rights in states of emergency. *Cincondiciones* is a significant contribution to the debate, arguing in favour of the duty to ensure access to reproductive rights free from discrimination regardless of the state of emergency.[77] *Cincondiciones* was developed as a toolkit for the protection of reproductive rights during healthcare crises such as COVID-19. It was endorsed by 16 NGOs from all over the Latin American region, including the Center for Reproduct-

74 World Health Organization, 'Preparedness, prevention and control of COVID-19 in prisons and other places of detention Interim guidance' (*WHO*, 2020) 1 <https://iris.who.int/bitstream/handle/10665/339830/WHO-EURO-2021-1405-41155-57257-eng.pdf?sequence=1> accessed 12 April 2024.

75 OHCHR, 'Principales expertas/os en derechos humanos piden la implementación atrasada de las Reglas de Bangkok de la ONU, una década después de su adopción' (*OHCHR*, 2020) <https://www.ohchr.org/sites/default/files/Documents/HRBodies/OPCAT/BangkokRules-leaders-statement_ES.pdf> accessed 12 April 2024.

76 ibid

77 Clacai, 'Cincondiciones. Herramientas para defender la salud reproductiva en tiempos de COVID-19' (*Cincondiciones*, 2020) <https://www.clacaidigital.info/bitstream/handle/123456789/1412/CinCondiciones-2020_FINAL.pdf?sequence=1&isAllowed=y> accessed 12 April 2024.

ive Rights, and frames its content in five principles: (1) abortion is an essential healthcare service that must be provided even during emergencies; (2) maternal healthcare services must be ensured in crisis times as it is an essential during pregnancy and labour; (3) contraception methods are priorities and must be ensured without interruption; (4) access to information concerning reproductive rights should not be derogated during the emergency, and (5) non-discrimination is non-derogable even during a crisis.[78] Its results align with the IACHR's report on the pandemic, which establishes the State's duty to ensure "the availability and continuity in the supply of services of this nature in the context of emergency" to all persons,[79] which would include those deprived of their liberty.

However, if the State is unable to satisfy the right to reproductive health, situations of emergency – particularly such as COVID-19 – should lead the State to consider the release of these persons or other alternatives to imprisonment.[80] Building upon the IACtHR's considerations on favouring the release of persons who are pregnant, in postpartum, or lactating mentioned in the previous section,[81] the duty to prioritize the release of persons if they do not have adequate reproductive health access should be ensured, or at the least, alternatives to their detention.

5 Conclusion

Within the already dire situation of reproductive rights in States such as El Salvador, women, pregnant people and persons capable of gestation in prisons face intersectional form of discrimination in these contexts, where the power dynamics exacerbate the historical vulnerabilities that they have faced in exercising their rights, including bodily autonomy. These individuals, thus, face important challenges in the full exercise of their reproductive rights while in prisons.

---

78 ibid.

79 IACHR, 'Pandemic and Human Rights' (*OAS*, 9 September 2022) para 274 <https://www.oas.org/en/iachr/reports/pdfs/2023/PandemiaDDHH_EN.pdf> accessed 12 April 2024.

80 World Health Organization, 'Preparedness, prevention and control of COVID-19 in prisons and other places of detention Interim guidance' (n 75); UN Office on Drugs and Crime, 'Preparación para el COVID-19 y respuestas en las cárceles' (*UNODC*, 2020) <https://www.unodc.org/documents/justice-and-prison-reform/covid-19/20-02218_Position_paper_ES.pdf> accessed 12 April 2024.

81 *Differentiated approaches with respect to certain groups of persons in detention* (n 1).

The chapter briefly described the situation of reproductive rights in Latin America concerning people deprived of their liberty. As can be seen, the developments on the topic have been very recent and respond mainly to an advisory opinion issued by the IACtHR and a recent report issued by the IACHR.

Both the IACtHR and the IACHR build upon the right to non-discrimination and the right to be free from gender based violence to make significant developments to ensure advanced protections for anyone who is deprived of their liberty. The analysis of these two rights, in light of other rights and duties established in the American Convention of Human Rights, has allowed the development of essential standards on when not to detain a person due to reproductive rights concerns (the case of obstetric emergencies), ensuring that pregnant persons are not an object of obstetric violence, and promoting measures to prevent incarceration of people for whom the State cannot or has failed to guarantee reproductive rights.

The same methodology, grounded in the rights to non-discrimination and the right to be free from gender violence, creates opportunities for the development of reproductive rights. Both the IACtHR and the IACHR are called upon to enshrine in future judgments and reports a specific State duty to ensure reproductive rights – including access to abortion – in favour of persons deprived of their liberty. Doing so will reduce the obstacles that they face to access these health services and will contribute to a more just society where persons deprived from their liberty and anyone outside of prison are able to access fully to their rights.

References

Angulo Losada v Bolivia (Preliminary Objections, Merits and Reparations) IACtHR Series C No 475 (18 November 2022).

Brítez Arce and Others v Argentina (Merits, Reparations and Costs) IACtHR Series C No 474 (16 November 2022).

Center for Reproductive Rights and Colectiva Feminista, 'The Impact of Blanket Abortion Bans on Women Experiencing Obstetric Emergencies' (*Reproductive Rights*, 2021) <https://reproductiverights.org/wp-content/uploads/2021/03/Factsheet-MANUELA_INGLES.pdf>.

Chamberlain G and Steer P, 'Obstetric Emergencies' (1999) 318 *BMJ* 1342.

Chinchilla Sandoval and Others v Guatemala (Preliminary Objection, Merits, Reparations and Costs) IACtHR Series C No 312 (29 February 2016).

Clacai, 'Cincondiciones. Herramientas para defender la salud reproductiva en tiempos de COVID-19' (*Cincondiciones*, 2020) <https://www.clacaidigital.info/bitstream/handle/123456789/1412/CinCondiciones-2020_FINAL.pdf?sequence=1&isAllowed=y>.

Corte Constitutional de Colombia, *Sentencia C-055 de 2022* (21 February 2022).

Differentiated approaches with respect to certain groups of persons in detention (*Interpretation and scope of Articles 1(1), 4(1), 5, 11(2), 12, 13, 17(1), 19, 24 and 26 of the American Convention on Human Rights and other human rights instruments*), Advisory Opinion OC-29/22, IACtHR Series A No 29 (30 May 2022).

European Committee on Prevention of Torture, '10th General Report on the CPT's activities' (*Council of Europe*, 18 August 2000) <https://rm.coe.int/1680696a74>.

González and Others ("Cotton Field") v Mexico (Preliminary Objection, Merits, Reparations and Costs) IACtHR Series C No 205 (16 November 2009).

Guzmán Albarracín and Others v Ecuador (Merits, Reparations and Costs) IACtHR Series C No 405 (24 June 2020).

Herrera M, 'Derechos reproductivos. Corte IDH. Caso Manuela y otros v El Salvador. Excepciones preliminares, Fondo, Reparaciones y Costas. Sentencia de 2 de noviembre de 2021. Serie C No. 441' (2022) 6 *Revista Debates sobre Derechos Humanos* 129–137.

Human Rights Committee, 'Concluding observations on the sixth periodic report of Peru' (28 March 2023) CCPR/C/PER/CO/6.

IACHR, 'Report on the Human Rights of Persons Deprived of Liberty in the Americas' (*OAS*, 2011) <https://www.oas.org/en/iachr/pdl/docs/pdf/ppl2011eng.pdf>.

IACHR, 'Violence and Discrimination against women and girls' (*OAS*, 2019) <https://www.oas.org/en/iachr/reports/pdfs/violencewomengirls.pdf>.

IACHR, 'The Human Rights Situation in El Salvador' (*OAS*, 14 October 2021) <https://www.oas.org/en/iachr/reports/pdfs/2021_ElSalvador-EN.pdf>.

IACHR, 'Pandemic and Human Rights' (*OAS*, 9 September 2022) <https://www.oas.org/en/iachr/reports/pdfs/2023/PandemiaDDHH_EN.pdf>.

IACHR, 'Women deprived of liberty in the Americas' (*OAS*, 2023 <https://www.oas.org/en/iachr/reports/pdfs/2023/Informe-Mujeres-privadas-libertad_ENG.pdf>.

Isaza Uribe and Others v Colombia (Merits, Reparations and Costs) IACtHR Series C No 363 (20 November 2018).

Martínez CC, 'Violencia obstétrica. Salud Reproductiva. Corte IDH, Caso Brítez Arce y otros v Argentina' (2023) 7 *Revista Debates sobre Derechos Humanos* 153–164.

Martínez CC and Martínez L, '¿Cómo evitar la repetición de más casos en Latinoamérica como el de Paola Guzmán Albarracín?' (*Agenda Estado de Derecho*, 9 December 2020) <https://agendaestadodederecho.com/como-evitar-la-repeticion-de-mas-casos-en-latinoamerica-como-el-de-paola-guzman-albarracin/>.

Martínez CC and Martínez CC, 'Sexual violence against girls in schools as a public health issue: a commentary on the case Paola Guzmán Albarracín v Ecuador' (2021) 29 *Sexual and Reproductive Health Matters* 1–5.

National LGBTQIA+ Health Education Center, 'Glossary' (*LGBTQIA+ Health Education Center*, 1 January 2024) <https://www.lgbtqiahealtheducation.org/glossary/>.

OHCHR, 'Principales expertas/os en derechos humanos piden la implementación atrasada de las Reglas de Bangkok de la ONU, una década después de su adopción' (*OHCHR*, 2020) <https://www.ohchr.org/sites/default/files/Documents/HRBodies/OPCAT/BangkokRules-leaders-statement_ES.pdf>.

Pérez EJ, 'La igualdad y no discriminación en el derecho interamericano de los derechos humanos' (*Comisión Nacional de los Derechos Humanos*, 2016) <https://appweb.cndh.org.mx/biblioteca/archivos/pdfs/fas-CSIDH-Igualdad-No-Discriminacion_1.pdf>.

Perico MF and Castellanos MC, '*Manuela et al. v El Salvador*: The Pitfalls of a Landmark Case for Reproductive Justice from a Torture Perspective' (*EJIL:Talk!*, 2023) <https://www.ejiltalk.org/manuela-et-al-v-el-salvador-the-pitfalls-of-a-landmark-case-for-reproductive-justice-from-a-torture-perspective/>.

Rodríguez Pacheco and Others v Venezuela (Preliminary Objections, Merits, Reparations and Costs) IACtHR Series C No 504 (27 November 2023).

Smyth R, 'Abortion in International Human Rights Law: Missed Opportunities in Manuela v El Salvador' (2023) 32 *Feminist Legal Studies* 123–134.

UN Office on Drugs and Crime, 'Preparación para el COVID-19 y respuestas en las cárceles' (*UNODC*, 2020) <https://www.unodc.org/documents/justice-and-prison-reform/COVID-19/20-02218_Position_paper_ES.pdf>.

Vicky Hernández and Others v Honduras (Merits, Reparations and Costs) IACtHR Series C No 422 (26 March 2021).

Working Group on Arbitrary Detention, 'Opinión núm. 19/2020, relativa a Imelda Cortez Palacios (El Salvador)' (25 June 2020) A/HRC/WGAD/2020/19.

World Health Organization, 'Preparedness, prevention and control of COVID-19 in prisons and other places of detention Interim guidance' (*WHO*, 2020). <https://iris.who.int/bitstream/handle/10665/339830/WHO-EURO-2021-1405-41155-57257-eng.pdf?sequence=1> accessed 12 April 2024.

World Health Organization, 'Abortion Care Guideline' (*WHO*, 2022) <https://iris.who.int/bitstream/handle/10665/349316/9789240039483-eng.pdf?sequence=1>.

Xákmok Kásek Indigenous Community v Paraguay (Merits, Reparations and Costs) IACtHR Series C No 214 (24 August 2010).

CHAPTER 4

Assessing State Compliance with Interim Measures Protecting Persons Deprived of Liberty in Latin America

Insights from the Case of Polay Campos v Peru

Clara Burbano Herrera and Luna Lanckvrind

1 Introduction*

The development of the United Nations human rights system has traditionally enjoyed wide support in Latin America, with many states[1] ratifying numerous

* This contribution was made possible thanks to funding from the European Research Council (ERC) under the European Union's Horizon Europe 2021 research and innovation programme (Grant Agreement No. 101044852). It is part of the ERC-funded project IMPACTUM: "Assessing the Impact of Urgent Measures in Protecting At-Risk Detainees in Latin America".

1 Argentina, Bolivia, Ecuador and Uruguay have ratified all nine core UN human rights treaties, as well as their optional protocols. Chile has ratified all nine core UN human rights treaties and their optional protocols, except for the Optional Protocol to the International Covenant on Economic, Social and Cultural Rights. The same applies for Peru, which is additionally not a part of the Second Optional Protocol to the International Covenant on Civil and Political Rights. Honduras is party to all nine core human rights treaties and their optional protocols, except for the Optional Protocol to the Convention on the Elimination of All Forms of Discrimination against Women and the Optional Protocol to the Convention on the Rights of the Child on a communications procedure. Colombia has ratified all nine core UN human rights treaties. It has ratified and signed all of the optional protocols to these treaties, except for the Optional Protocol to the Convention on the Rights of Persons with Disabilities, the Optional Protocol to the Convention on the Rights of the Child on a communications procedure, the Optional Protocol to the Convention against Torture and Other Cruel, Inhuman or Degrading Treatment or Punishment, and the Optional Protocol to the International Covenant on Economic, Social and Cultural Rights. Venezuela has signed all nine core human rights treaties, and has ratified all of them except for the International Convention for the Protection of all Persons from Enforced Disappearance. All the optional protocols were also ratified, except for the Optional Protocol to the Convention against Torture and Other Cruel, Inhuman or Degrading Treatment or Punishment and the Optional Protocol to the Convention on the Rights of the Child on a communications procedure. El Salvador, Nicaragua and Guatemala have ratified eight core UN human rights treaties, but have not signed the International Convention for the Protection of All Persons

core human rights treaties.[2] Several provisions in these documents seek to protect the rights of persons deprived of liberty. Article 9(1) of the International Covenant on Civil and Political Rights[3] (ICCPR), for example, states that "no one shall be deprived of his liberty except on such grounds and in accordance with such procedure as are established by law" and Article 9(4) states that "anyone who is deprived of his liberty by arrest or detention shall be entitled to take proceedings before a court, in order that that court may decide without delay on the lawfulness of his detention and order his release if the detention is not lawful". Article 6(1) of the ICCPR contains the prohibition on arbitrary deprivation of life and Articles 6(2), (3), (4), (5) and (6) refer to persons sentenced to death.[4]

---

from Enforced Disappearance. Paraguay has ratified all nine core UN human rights treaties and their respective optional protocols, except for the Optional Protocol to the International Covenant on Economic, Social and Cultural Rights. Panama has also signed and ratified every core UN human rights treaty and the optional protocols to these treaties, except for the Optional Protocol to the International Covenant on Economic, Social and Cultural Rights and the International Convention on the Protection of the Rights of All Migrant Workers and Members of their Families. Mexico has signed and ratified all core human rights treaties as well as their optional protocols, except for the Optional Protocol to the Convention on the Rights of the Child on a communications procedure and the Optional Protocol to the International Covenant on Economic, Social and Cultural Rights. See UN OCHCR, 'Status of Ratification Interactive Dashboard' (*OHCHR*, 2025) <https://indicators.ohchr.org/> accessed 7 January 2025.

2 Ellen L. Lutz and Kathryn Sikkink, 'International Human Rights Law and Practice in Latin America' (2000) 54 Legalization and World Politics 633, 639.

3 International Covenant on Civil and Political Rights (adopted 16 December 1966, entered into force 23 March 1976) 999 UNTS 171.

4 Article 6 ICCPR states: "1. Every human being has the inherent right to life. This right shall be protected by law. No one shall be arbitrarily deprived of his life. 2. In countries which have not abolished the death penalty, sentence of death may be imposed only for the most serious crimes in accordance with the law in force at the time of the commission of the crime and not contrary to the provisions of the present Covenant and to the Convention on the Prevention and Punishment of the Crime of Genocide. This penalty can only be carried out pursuant to a final judgement rendered by a competent court. 3. When deprivation of life constitutes the crime of genocide, it is understood that nothing in this article shall authorize any State Party to the present Covenant to derogate in any way from any obligation assumed under the provisions of the Convention on the Prevention and Punishment of the Crime of Genocide. 4. Anyone sentenced to death shall have the right to seek pardon or commutation of the sentence. Amnesty, pardon or commutation of the sentence of death may be granted in all cases. 5. Sentence of death shall not be imposed for crimes committed by persons below eighteen years of age and shall not be carried out on pregnant women. 6. Nothing in this article shall be invoked to delay or to prevent the abolition of capital punishment by any State Party to the present Covenant.".

Despite the formal recognition of these provisions, in practice, some member states in Latin America[5] have failed to fulfil their obligations to protect persons deprived of their liberty.[6] The Human Rights Committee (the Committee or the HRC), a treaty-monitoring body established by States Parties,[7] addresses communications from individuals under their jurisdiction who claim to be victims of violations of rights established in the ICCPR.[8] During such proceedings, the Committee has utilized interim measures as a tool to prevent irreparable harm to victims, particularly in cases involving detention.[9]

The aim of this article is to provide a comprehensive overview of the interim measures adopted by the Committee to safeguard at-risk detainees in Latin America. This article examines the extent to which states comply with these measures and the extent to which such compliance can facilitate the fulfilment of formal commitments to protect persons deprived of liberty and prevent human rights violations in practice. The scope of this article is limited to cases concerning Latin America because, until now, there have been no studies on this region. Additionally, this study will allow us to analyze the current (and past) use of interim measures by the HRC and to some extent, to compare its application with the Inter-American human rights bodies.

The chapter is divided into six sections. The first section discusses the Latin American context. The second section contains the relevant legal framework. The third section provides an overview of the case law on interim measures for the protection of persons deprived of their liberty in Latin America. It provides a concise analysis of the total number of interim measures found between 1977 and 2023 to protect detainees in Latin America, namely 15 requests for interim measures made by the HRC related to six states. The fourth section presents a case study, specifically the case of *Polay Campos v Peru*. It analyzes the various aspects of the case at both the United Nations and Inter-American human rights levels. It considers the context, the legal process, and the similarities and differences in the responses of the two inter-

---

5 Such as El Salvador, Ecuador, Colombia, Venezuela and Peru.

6 Such as Uruguay, Paraguay, Chile, Nicaragua, Guatemala and Bolivia.

7 Sarah Joseph and others, *The International Covenant on Civil and Political Rights: Cases, Materials, and Commentary* (Oxford, Oxford University Press 2013) 54.

8 Article 1 Optional Protocol to the ICCPR.

9 The Committee's use of interim measures extends beyond the context of detention. For example, it has frequently issued requests for interim measures in cases involving disputed legal proceedings related to deportation, expulsion or extradition orders. Joanna Harrington, 'The Legitimacy of Interim Measures from the Perspective of a State: The Example of Canada' in Eva Rieter and Karin Zwaan (eds), *Urgency and Human Rights* (The Hague, Asser Press 2021) 115–134, 115–116.

national human rights systems to requests for urgent measures. This comparison is highly relevant, as it provides an assessment of which approach is more effective in protecting persons deprived of liberty at imminent risk of harm, which is important for litigators and applicants seeking urgent protection within the context of detention. Comparing both systems also provides an opportunity to uncover shortcomings in both systems' follow-up mechanisms for interim measures. The fifth section introduces the concepts of compliance and impact in the context of urgent measures for the protection of detainees at-risk, and analyzes them in practice with reference to the case of *Polay Campos v Peru*. The sixth section contains concluding reflections on the HRC's practice concerning interim measures, the interaction between the Committee and the Inter-American human rights bodies and their significance for the safeguarding of individuals deprived of their liberty in the region. It underscores the need for the Committee to prioritize the dissemination of interim measures and their rationale. Additionally, it highlights a notable contrast between the Inter-American Commission's historically robust approach and the Inter-American Court's transition from a highly formalistic stance to a more informal one.

2 Latin America: Contextual Background

Latin America has been particularly affected by "unprecedented levels of human rights violations"[10] under authoritarian rule during the 1970s and 1980s, when many people including political opponents, journalists, and human rights defenders were imprisoned without due process and held in appalling conditions.[11] In this context, it is important to note that in the early decades of the ICCPR's existence, many states in Latin America had not yet ratified this treaty and its Optional Protocol, which allowed for the individual complaints procedure. As a result, victims of the violations committed by non-member states within the region during this period were unable to seek redress before the Committee.

10 Lutz and Sikkink, 'International Human Rights Law and Practice in Latin America' (n 2) 639–640.

11 Cynthia Milton, *Art From a Fractured Past: Memory and Truth-Telling in Post-Shining Path Peru* (Durham, Duke University Press 2014) 272–273; Clara Burbano Herrera and Yves Haeck, 'The historical and present-day role of non-governmental organisations before the inter-American human rights system in documenting serious human rights violations and protecting human rights and the rule of law through ensuring accountability' (2021) 17 Utrecht Law Review 8–25.

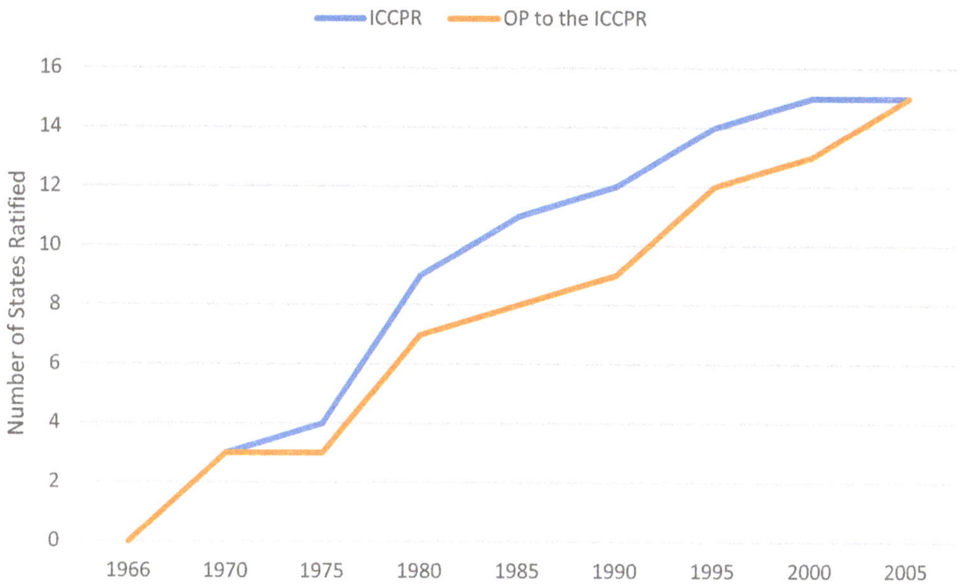

FIGURE 4.1 Ratification of the ICCPR and the OP to the ICCPR by Latin American states (1966–2005)
SOURCE: UN OCHCR STATUS OF RATIFICATION INTERACTIVE DASHBOARD (2025)

Figure 4.1 illustrates that, already since the 1960s, Colombia, Uruguay and Ecuador were supporters of the UN human rights system, consequently becoming the first countries in Latin America to sign and ratify both the ICCPR and its Optional Protocol. They were followed by Chile, Panama, Peru and Venezuela, which ratified the Covenant in the 1970s. However, Chile and El Salvador only ratified the Optional Protocol two decades later. In the 1980s, many other Latin American States joined by ratifying these two important documents, including Argentina, Bolivia, Mexico, and Nicaragua. Several States waited until the 1990s to become party to the ICCPR, such as Paraguay, Guatemala and Honduras, with the latter two taking several additional years to ratify the Optional Protocol. It was not until 2005 that all Latin American states were fully bound by the Optional Protocol to the ICCPR, thereby committing to its communications procedure.

Even though significant progress has been made since then in terms of democracy and respect for human rights,[12] detainees' rights remain a contro-

12 Sacha Darke and Maria Lúcia Karam, 'Latin American prisons' in Yvonne Jewkes and others (eds), *Handbook on Prisons* (New York, Routledge 2016) 462; European Parliamentary Research Service, 'Democracy and human rights in Latin America' (*European Parliament*, 2022) 1 <https://www.europarl.europa.eu/RegData/etudes/BRIE/2022/698868/EPRS_BRI(2022)698868_EN.pdf> accessed 22 October 2024.

TABLE 4.1 Ratification record of the ICCPR and OP to the ICCPR by Latin American states

Country	ICCPR	OP to the ICCPR
Argentina	1986	1986
Bolivia	1982	1982
Chile	1972	1992
Colombia	1969	1969
Ecuador	1969	1969
El Salvador	1979	1995
Guatemala	1992	2000
Honduras	1997	2005
Mexico	1981	2002
Nicaragua	1980	1980
Panama	1977	1977
Paraguay	1992	1995
Peru	1978	1980
Uruguay	1970	1970
Venezuela	1978	1978

SOURCE: UN OCHCR STATUS OF RATIFICATION INTERACTIVE DASHBOARD (2025)

versial and under-looked issue, with many Latin American prisons facing concerns about overcrowding, violence, unsanitary and inhumane living conditions, and allegations of due process violations during criminal proceedings.[13]

13 Mariela Morales Antoniazzi, 'The Rights of Persons Deprived of Liberty in Latin America: From the Perspective of an *ius constitutionale commune*' in Clara Burbano Herrera and Yves Haeck (eds), *Human Rights Behind Bars: Tracing Vulnerability in Prison Populations Across Continents from a Multidisciplinary Perspective* (Cham, Springer Nature 2022) 113–140, 114–115; Juan Gonzalez-Bertomeu, 'Prisons and prisoners' rights' in Juan Gonzalez-Bertomeu and Roberto Gargarella (eds), *The Latin American Casebook: Courts, Constitutions, and Rights* (New York, Routledge 2016) 604–605; UN OHCHR, 'Immediate action needed to address conditions of detention in Latin America' (*OHCHR*, 22 February 2012) <https://www.ohchr.org/en/stories/2012/02/immediate-action-needed-address-conditions-detention-latin-america#:~:text=Citing%20a%20range%20of%20structural,in%20many%20prisons%20amount%20to> accessed 22 October 2024.

The critical situation has continued to deteriorate even further due to the recent COVID-19 outbreak.[14]

3 Legal Framework

In the context of appalling prison conditions, human rights bodies have granted urgent measures to protect the human rights of persons deprived of their liberty who are at risk. These measures are either laid down in the rules of procedure of these bodies, in international human rights treaties, or in additional protocols.[15] Urgent measures can be defined as a legal tool aimed to protect persons in situations that, due to their extreme gravity, pose an imminent risk of causing irreparable harm to those persons.[16] They are designed to ensure the practical realization of rights.[17] In particular, urgent measures serve as a means of protecting human rights, preventing human rights violations and preventing irreparable damage to the rights of individuals deprived of their liberty in urgent and serious situations. Such kinds of situations exist when for example, persons are sentenced to the death penalty without a fair trial, or when persons deprived of their liberty are in serious danger arising from harsh detention conditions.[18]

14 Lina Marmolejo and others, 'Responding to COVID-19 in Latin American Prisons: The Cases of Argentina, Chile, Colombia and Mexico' (2020) Victims & Offenders 1, 3–6; Clara Burbano Herrera and Yves Haeck, *Human Rights Behind Bars: Tracing Vulnerability in Prison Populations Across Continents from a Multidisciplinary Perspective* (Cham, Springer Nature 2022) 1–10, 1.

15 Aurélie Van Baelen and Clara Burbano Herrera, 'LGBTI Persons Deprived of Liberty: Overrepresented, Extremely Vulnerable and De Jure Invisible' in Clara Burbano Herrera and Yves Haeck (eds), *Human Rights Behind Bars: Tracing Vulnerability in Prison Populations Across Continents from a Multidisciplinary Perspective* (Cham, Springer Nature 2022) 173–202, 186.

16 Clara Burbano Herrera and Yves Haeck, 'Provisional Measures: Inter-American Court of Human Rights (IACtHR)' (*Max Planck Encyclopedias of International Law*, 2019) <https://opil.ouplaw.com/display/10.1093/law-mpeipro/e3524.013.3524/law-mpeipro-e3524> accessed 22 October 2024.

17 Clara Burbano Herrera, Yves Haeck and Alessandra Cuppini, 'Transformative Provisional Measures and Prisons in the Americas: Protecting the Invisibles' in Clara Burbano Herrera and Yves Haeck (eds), *Human Rights Behind Bars: Tracing Vulnerability in Prison Populations Across Continents from a Multidisciplinary Perspective* (Cham, Springer Nature 2022) 141–172, 142; Clara Burbano Herrera, *Provisional measures in the case law of the Inter-American Court of Human Rights* (Antwerp, Intersentia 2010) 1.

18 Clara Burbano Herrera and Yves Haeck, 'The Impact of Precautionary Measures on Persons Deprived of Liberty in the Americas' in Par Engstrom (ed), *The Inter-American*

Urgent measures are notably used by regional human rights bodies, such as: the Inter-American Commission of Human Rights (IACHR or the Commission), which uses the term precautionary measures;[19] the Inter-American Court on Human Rights (IACtHR or the Court), which uses the term provisional measures;[20] the European Court of Human Rights (ECtHR), which uses the term interim measures;[21] and the African Court on Human and Peoples' Rights (ACtHPR), which uses the term provisional measures.[22] As proceedings before international human rights bodies can last several years, urgent measures also aim to ensure the realization of the final decision before actions with irreparable consequences could render its implementation impossible.[23]

3.1 *Human Rights Committee*

At the UN level, the HRC has granted interim measures to protect detainees in the Americas, who can generally be divided into two categories according to

---

Human Rights System: Impact Beyond Compliance (London, Palgrave Macmillan 2018) 89–113, 91.

19 Article 25(1) of the Rules of Procedure of the Inter-American Commission on Human Rights states: "(…) the Commission may, on its own initiative or at the request of a party, request that a State adopt precautionary measures. Such measures, whether related to a petition or not, shall concern serious and urgent situations presenting a risk of irreparable harm to persons or to the subject matter of a pending petition or case before the organs of the inter-American system".

20 Article 63(2) of the American Convention on Human Rights states: "In cases of extreme gravity and urgency, and when necessary to avoid irreparable damage to persons, the Court shall adopt such provisional measures as it deems pertinent in matters it has under consideration. With respect to a case not yet submitted to the Court, it may act at the request of the Commission".

21 Rule 39(1) of the Rules of Court of the ECtHR states: "The Chamber or, where appropriate, the President of the Section or a duty judge appointed pursuant to paragraph 4 of this Rule may, at the request of a party or of any other person concerned, or of their own motion, indicate to the parties any interim measure which they considers should be adopted in the interests of the parties or of the proper conduct of the proceedings".

22 Rule 59(1) of the Rules of the Court of the ACtHPR states: "Pursuant to Article 27(2) of the Protocol, the Court may, at the request of a party, or on its own accord, in case of extreme gravity and urgency and where necessary to avoid irreparable harm to persons, adopt such provisional measures as it deems necessary, pending determination of the main Application".

23 Zelalem M. Teferra, 'Provisional measures in international human rights law: the practice of the African Court on Human and Peoples' Rights' (2022) 6 African Human Rights Yearbook 28, 32; Antonio C. Trindade, 'The Evolution of provisional measures of protection under the case law of the Inter-American Court of Human Rights 1987–2002' (2003) 24 Human Rights Law Journal 162, 164; Alexandre Ruiz Feases, 'Sharpening the European Commission's tools: interim measures' (2020) 16 European Competition Journal 404, 417.

the nature of their risk: (1) persons deprived of liberty who are ill and/or in need of medical care and (2) persons held in incommunicado detention.[24] The Committee defines persons deprived of liberty as persons "subjected to any form of arrest, detention or imprisonment"[25] who require "special protection against torture and other ill-treatment."[26] This includes people who are in police custody, remand detention, prison, house arrest, administrative detention and involuntary hospitalization.[27]

The HRC may consider individual communications alleging violations of the rights set forth in the ICCPR by States Parties to the First Optional Protocol to the International Covenant on Civil and Political Rights. The competence to adopt interim measures was first introduced in the Committee's Rules of Procedure in 1977.[28] These measures can be taken *proprio motu* or at the request of the petitioner.[29]

During the first three decades of the HRC's existence, it frequently resorted to using informal interim measures because its individual complaints procedure was still "fresh" and regarded with more scepticism by member states than it is now.[30] This means that the Committee issued these requests under the

24 Outside of the Americas, the Committee has also granted interim measures in cases related to the death penalty, to safeguard the human rights of detainees sentenced to death and awaiting execution. See for example: *Mikhalenya and Mikhalenya v Belarus* (21 July 2021) CCPR/C/132/D/3105/2018; *Saidova v Tajikistan* (8 July 2004) CCPR/C/81/D/964/2001; *Roberts v Barbados* (19 July 1994) CCPR/C/51/D/504/1992; and *C.J. v Jamaica* (26 July 1988) A/43/40.

25 Human Rights Committee, 'General Comment No. 20 on Article 7 (Prohibition of Torture, or Other Cruel, Inhuman or Degrading Treatment or Punishment' (10 March 1992) paras 10–11.

26 Ingrid Nifosi-Sutton, *The Protection of Vulnerable Groups Under International Human Rights Law* (Abingdon, Taylor & Francis 2017) 88.

27 Human Rights Committee, 'General Comment No. 35 on Article 9 (Liberty and security of person)' (16 December 2014) CCPR/C/GC/35, para 5. See also: Subcommittee on Prevention of Torture and Other Cruel, Inhuman or Degrading Treatment or Punishment, 'General comment No. 1 (2024) on article 4 of the Optional Protocol (places of deprivation of liberty)' (4 July 2024) CAT/OP/GC/1.

28 Rosanne van Alebeek and André Nollkaemper, 'The legal status of decisions by human rights treaty bodies in national law' in Helen Keller and Geir Ulfstein (eds), *UN Human Rights Treaty Bodies: Law and Legitimacy* (Cambridge, Cambridge University Press 2012) 356–413, 387; Eva Rieter, *Preventing Irreparable Harm: Provisional Measures in International Human Rights Adjudication*, Antwerp, Intersentia, 2010, 106.

29 Eva Rieter, *Preventing Irreparable Harm: Provisional Measures in International Human Rights Adjudication* (Antwerp, Intersentia 2010) 120–121.

30 ibid 112.

rule on the transmission of cases and requests for clarification under Rule 84[31] (formerly found in Rule 91/Rule 97), instead of formally invoking Rule 94 (former Rule 86/Rule 92) on interim measures.[32] The Committee's precarious position was accentuated by the fact that it is a quasi-judicial body, which means that its views are non-binding, and that the ICCPR does not foresee the possibility of issuing such requests.[33] However, the Committee has developed the position that it is entitled to request urgent measures on the basis of the principle of object and purpose.[34] The final judgment becomes meaningless when the core of the disputed subject matter is destroyed in the course of the proceedings of the case. This means that the function of the Committee would be hindered if interim measures were not considered to be binding.[35]

At present, the competence to issue interim measures by the HRC is incorporated in Rule 94 of the HRC's Rules of Procedure. The first paragraph of this rule states:

> At any time after the registration of a communication and before a determination on the merits has been reached, the Committee may request that the State party concerned take on an urgent basis such interim measures as the Committee considers necessary to avoid possible actions which could have irreparable consequences for the rights invoked by the author.[36]

---

31 Rule 84 in the Rules of Procedure of the HRC states: "The Committee may, through the Secretary-General, request the States parties concerned, or either of them, to submit additional information or observations orally or in writing. The Committee shall indicate a time limit for the submission of such written information or observations".

32 Rieter, *Preventing Irreparable Harm: Provisional Measures in International Human Rights Adjudication* (n 28) 112.

33 Robert Kolb, 'Note on New International Case-Law Concerning the Binding Character of Provisional Measures' (2005) 74 Nordic Journal of International Law 117–130, 117.

34 Kirsten Young, *The Law and Process of the UN Human Rights Committee* (Leiden, Brill 2021) 65–67; Burbano Herrera and Haeck, 'The Impact of Precautionary Measures on Persons Deprived of Liberty in the Americas' (n 18) 91–92; Wouter Vandenhole, *The Procedures Before the UN Human Rights Treaty Bodies: Divergence Or Convergence?* (Antwerpen, Intersentia 2004) 260–231.

35 Robert Kolb, 'Note on New International Case-Law Concerning the Binding Character of Provisional Measures' (n 33) 117.

36 Rule 94(1), Rules of Procedure of the HRC (*OHCHR*, 4 January 2021) <https://tbinternet.ohchr.org/_layouts/15/treatybodyexternal/Download.aspx?symbolno=CCPR%2FC%2F3%2FRev.12&Lang=en> accessed 22 October 2024.

The Human Rights Committee uses the term "irreparable damage"[37] or "irreparable harm"[38] interchangeably to describe the concept of irreparable consequences as described in Rule 94. Generally, irreparable harm or irreparable damage means that the consequences of the state's action are irreversible, impeding applicants from securing their rights in case a violation of the ICCPR could be found at a later stage.[39] The concept of irreparable harm is described by the OHCHR as: "a harm which, due to its nature, cannot be susceptible to reparation".[40] The harm also has to be imminent (urgent) and credible (real).[41] Interim measures may not be issued if, according to the Committee, a compensation would be deemed an adequate remedy.[42]

In accordance with Rule 107(2) of the Rules of Procedure of the Committee, one or more Special Rapporteurs on New Communications and Interim Measures are appointed by the Committee. Their role is to "process new communications and requests for interim measures as they are received, as well as to deal with other procedural matters as authorized by the Committee".[43] The Committee and the Working Group of the HRC,[44] as well as the Special Rapporteur on New Communications and Interim Measures are able to issue interim measures during various stages of the proceedings. Requests for interim measures can also be reiterated several times during the examination of the case.

---

37 See for example: *Sara and Others v Finland* (23 March 1994) CCPR/C/50/D/431/1990, para 5.6.

38 See for example: *Mikhalenya and Mikhalenya v Belarus* (21 July 2021) CCPR/C/132/D/3105/2018, para 6.5.

39 Ludovic Hennebel, 'The Human Rights Committee' in Frédéric Mégret and Philip Alston (eds), *The United Nations and Human Rights: A Critical Appraisal* (Oxford, Oxford University Press 2020) 339–392, 365.

40 UN OHCHR, 'Guidance for Submitting an Individual Communication to the UN Treaty Bodies' (*OHCHR*, 2021) 2 <https://www.ohchr.org/Documents/HRBodies/Guidance-note-for-complaints-form-E.docx#:~:text=The%20communication%20should%20be%20in,petitions%40ohchr.org> accessed 22 October 2024.

41 Human Rights Committee, 'Mandate of the Special Rapporteur on New Communications and Interim Measures' (22 May 2014) CCPR/C/110/3, 2–3.

42 Sandy Ghandhi, 'The Human Rights Committee and Interim Measures of Relief' (2007) 13 Canterbury Law Review 203, 210.

43 Rule 107(2), Rules of Procedure of the Human Rights Committee.

44 The Working Group of the HRC consists of at least five Committee members, appointed by the Chairperson, with consideration given to the importance of balanced geographical representation. The composition of members may vary for each session of the HRC. See: Rule 98 Rules of Procedure of the HRC. The aim of the Working Group is to assist the Committee by making recommendations concerning applications. See: Rule 107 Rules of Procedure of the HRC.

In 1987, the mandate of the Special Rapporteur on Death Penalty Cases adopted by the Committee provided for the use of interim measures.[45] The Special Rapporteur on New Communications was first appointed in 1989 to help alleviate the increasing caseload of the Committee and this position therefore included the ability to process new requests for interim measures.[46] When taking the decision to register a communication, the Special Rapporteur is empowered to handle requests to apply interim measures, as well as requests from State Parties seeking to lift them. This means that the Special Rapporteur can decide to issue interim measures, to lift requests for interim measures, or to deny requests to adopt or lift interim measures. The Special Rapporteur is allowed to handle these requests up until the Working Group on Communications begins its examination of the admissibility of the communication. Interestingly, the Special Rapporteur's competence to adopt interim measures has not been explicitly detailed in the Committee's Rules of Procedure.[47] When the HRC is not in session, the Chairperson has the competence to grant interim measures "until the Working Group considers the substance of the case, in consultation, where necessary, with the Special Rapporteur".[48]

The complainant may initiate the procedure for interim measures by sending a request to the Committee's Secretariat asking the Committee to adopt interim measures. The author can file this request up until the Committee has issued its opinion. However, it should be submitted "as early as possible",[49] ideally before the action that the petitioner seeks to prevent occurs. If the request is made during the filing of the initial complaint, it should be clearly indicated on the front page of the initial communication to the Secretariat. In urgent situations, the petitioner may submit the request

45 Young, *The Law and Process of the UN Human Rights Committee* (n 34) 66.

46 Human Rights Committee, 'Mandate of the Special Rapporteur on New Communications and Interim Measures' (n 41) 1.

47 UN OHCHR, 'Informal guidance note by the secretariat for the States parties on procedures for the submission and consideration by treaty bodies of individual communications' (*OHCHR*, January 2017) 1 <https://www.ohchr.org/sites/default/files/Documents/HRBodies/TB/NoteStatesParties.pdf> accessed 22 October 2024; Human Rights Committee, 'Mandate of the Special Rapporteur on New Communications and Interim Measures' (n 41) 2.

48 Human Rights Committee, 'Mandate of the Special Rapporteur on New Communications and Interim Measures' (n 41) 1–3.

49 UN OHCHR, 'Guidance for Submitting an Individual Communication to the UN Treaty Bodies' (n 40) 2.

ahead of the main complaint, for example, through email, with a hard copy to follow.[50]

Typically, all requests for interim measures are referred to the Special Rapporteur, who will then take a decision under Rule 94 based on the recommendation of the Secretariat.[51] This decision is then communicated to the relevant state's authorities through various channels. In the case of *Ross v Guyana*, for example, the Chairperson issued an interim measure requesting to stay the execution of the victim, which was communicated to Guyanese authorities through all available channels, including "a fax to the Presidency, a telephone call to the Superintendent of the State Prison in Georgetown and the dictation of the request to the assistant of the Superintendent".[52] While not explicitly stated in the Rules of Procedure, the Chairperson is able to react to non-compliance of interim measures by dispatching letters to representatives of the state in question. In several instances, the Chairperson has signed letters in which concern was expressed regarding the state's non-adherence to interim measures and requesting written clarifications.[53]

The decision to issue interim measures depends on the nature of the alleged human rights violation and the risk of the state's actions "which could have irreparable consequences in respect of the rights invoked by the author".[54] Since 2019, the HRC and the Special Rapporteur have the power to decide whether decisions concerning interim measures under Rule 94 will be made public, if they "consider it appropriate".[55] This means that interim measures are no longer exempt from the rules of confidentiality,[56] which, in turn,

---

50 OMCT, *Seeking Remedies for Torture Victims: A Handbook on the Individual Complaints Procedures of the UN Treaty Bodies* (Switzerland, World Organisation Against Torture 2014) 90.

51 Helen Keller and Cedric Marti, 'Interim Relief Compared: Use of Interim Measures by the UN Human Rights Committee and the European Court of Human Rights' (2013) 73 Heidelberg Journal of International Law 325, 336.

52 Ghandhi, 'The Human Rights Committee and Interim Measures of Relief' (n 42) 210.

53 See for example: *Weiss v Austria* (24 October 2012) CCPR/C/106/D/1821/2008; *Saidova v Tajikistan* (8 July 2004) CCPR/C/81/D/964/2001; *Kovaleva and Kozyar v Belarus* (29 October 2012) CCPR/C/106/D/2120/2011; and *Tolipkhuzhaev v Uzbekistan* (22 July 2009) CCPR/C/96/D/1280/2004.

54 Human Rights Committee, 'Mandate of the Special Rapporteur on New Communications and Interim Measures' (n 41) 1–3.

55 Rule 111(6) of the Rules of Procedure states: "Decisions taken under rule 94 of the present rules by the Committee or the Special Rapporteur designated pursuant to rule 107, paragraph 2, shall be made public if the Committee or the Special Rapporteur consider it appropriate".

56 Ghandhi, 'The Human Rights Committee and Interim Measures of Relief' (n 42) 205.

could lead to a lack of transparency regarding the conditions under which they are applied. Even if they are published, the rationale behind decisions to request interim measures are not communicated to the parties involved. The same applies for states' requests to lift interim measures. Throughout the whole procedure, the state may submit arguments to the Committee which would justify the lifting of the measures. The arguments should be succinct and focused on admissibility issues instead of the merits of the complaint. The request has to be clearly stated "at the beginning of the letter addressed to the Committee",[57] whereafter it will be sent to the complainant. The latter is then given the opportunity to provide comments within a short timeframe. Taking in to account the input from both sides, a decision is then made by the Special Rapporteur or the Working Group. A request for interim measures can also be withdrawn by the Committee if the state or the complainant presents new information in favour of doing so.[58]

4 General Overview of the Latin American Case Law

Despite the existence of interim measures within the Committee since the 1970s, the number of interim measures requested and granted to protect persons deprived of liberty in Latin America remains relatively low. From 1979 to 2023, a total of 14 cases related to Latin America were identified,[59] comprising 15 interim measures requested from six different countries.[60] This number includes three cases in which the complainant's request for interim measures was expressly denied by the Committee.[61] Twelve of these fifteen interim measures were informal. This means that the Committee issued the request under the rule on the transmission of cases and requests for clarification

57 UN OHCHR, 'Informal guidance note by the secretariat for the States parties on procedures for the submission and consideration by treaty bodies of individual communications' (n 47) 2.

58 Ibid.

59 *Drescher Caldas v Uruguay* (1979); *Pietraroia v Uruguay* (1981); *Setelich v Uruguay* (1981); *Altesor v Uruguay* (1982); *Quinteros v Uruguay* (1983); *Estradet Cabreira v Uruguay* (1983); *Lafuente Peñarrieta and Others v Bolivia* (1987); *J. E. S. B. v Panama* (1994); *Polay Campos v Peru* (1997); *Spisso v Venezuela* (2017); *Dávila v Colombia* (2018); *Echeverri v Colombia* (2020); *de la Vega v Colombia* (2020) *and J.A.N.C. v Colombia* (2020).

60 It is worth noting that no interim measures were adopted between 2017 and 2023.

61 *de la Vega v Colombia* (21 July 2020) CCPR/C/129/D/2930/2017; *J.A.N.C. v Colombia* (24 July 2020) CCPR/C/129/D/2922/2016; *Dávila v Colombia* (6 April 2018) CCPR/C/122/D/2490/2014.

under Rule 84[62] (formerly found in Rule 91/Rule 97), instead of formally invoking Rule 94 (former Rule 86/Rule 92) on interim measures.[63]

Six countries were involved in these cases, namely; Uruguay (10 out of 15 interim measures), Bolivia (1 out of 15 measures), Panama (1 out of 15 measures), Peru (1 out of 15 measures), Venezuela (1 out of 15 measures) and Colombia (1 out of 15 measures).

It is important to note that the content of interim measures requested by the Committee has not always been made available to the public. From 1991 to 1996, for example, no information can be found on possible requests for interim measures in the text of the Views themselves, despite mention of their use on the cover page.[64] It is therefore difficult to ascertain what kind of interim measures were issued during that period. Moreover, there are certain states in Latin America, such as Nicaragua and Chile, which have received requests to comply with interim measures, but as the content of these measures was not published, they cannot be discussed.[65]

Similarly, during the 1990s and 2000s, several cases before the Committee dealt with persons deprived of their liberty who were in ill health and living in poor detention conditions in Peru.[66] In these cases, the Special Rapporteur issued a former Rule 91 or Rule 97 decision (not issued in document form) which could possibly have contained informal requests for interim measures to prevent irreparable harm. The content of these decisions, however, has not been made public.[67] In *Gutiérrez Vivanco v Peru*, for instance, Mr Gutiérrez was given a prison sentence of twenty years on 17 June 1994 for committing terrorist offenses as an alleged member of Shining Path. The author alleged that he was subjected to ill-treatment at the time of his arrest, which constituted a viola-

62 Rule 84 of the Rules of Procedure of the HRC states: "The Committee may, through the Secretary-General, request the States parties concerned, or either of them, to submit additional information or observations orally or in writing. The Committee shall indicate a time limit for the submission of such written information or observations".

63 Rieter, *Preventing Irreparable Harm: Provisional Measures in International Human Rights Adjudication* (n 28) 112.

64 Ibid. 126–127.

65 See for example: *Patricio Cornejo Montecino v Chile* (30 October 2008) CCPR/C/94/D/1504/2006; *Zelaya Blanco v Nicaragua* (20 July 1994) CCPR/C/51/D/328/1988.

66 See for example: *Gutiérrez Vivanco v Peru* (26 March 2002) CCPR/C/74/D/678/1996; *Laureano Atachahua v Peru* (25 March 1996) CCPR/C/56/D/540/1993; *Arredondo v Peru* (27 July 2000) CCPR/C/69/D/688/1996; *Casafranca de Gómez v Peru* (22 July 2003) CCPR/C/78/D/981/2001.

67 See for example: *Arredondo v Peru* (n 66); *Vargas Más v Peru* (26 October 2005) CCPR/C/85/D/1058/2002; *Carranza Alegre v Peru* (28 October 2005) CCPR/C/85/D/1126/2002.

tion of article 7 of the Covenant. He suffered from a chronic cardiac insufficiency, had "serious organic disabilities"[68] and could not engage in "strenuous physical exercise"[69] due to his congenital illness.[70] The application had been submitted on 20 March 1995, and more than three years later the victim was pardoned by the Supreme Court of Justice on 25 December 1998.[71] In 1996, the Special Rapporteur of the Committee issued a Rule 91 decision, which was not issued in document form. This decision could possibly have contained a request for interim measures relating to the victim's poor health.

A comparative analysis of the case law of the Committee and the inter-American human rights bodies reveals that individuals have demonstrated a clear preference for the latter in seeking protection. They have approached the IACHR and the IACtHR to issue precautionary and provisional measures, respectively, particularly in cases related to persons deprived of their liberty in appalling conditions of detention[72] and/or alleging violations of due process.[73] The proximity of the inter-American human rights organs to these states and the binding status of these measures (at least concerning provisional measures) may explain this preference.[74] As previously discussed, the ratification record of the ICCPR and its Optional Protocol by Latin American states may also provide an explanation, as it is notable that several Latin

68 *Gutiérrez Vivanco v Peru* (n 66) paras 2.6 and 2.9.

69 ibid para 2.1.

70 ibid para 2.

71 ibid para 2.9.

72 Burbano Herrera, *Provisional measures in the case law of the Inter-American Court of Human Rights* (n 17) 6; Clara Burbano Herrera and Frans Viljoen, 'Danger and fear in prison' (2015) 33 Netherlands Quarterly of Human Rights 163, 188; Clara Burbano Herrera and Yves Haeck, 'Medidas provisionales de la Corte Interamericana: algunas reflexiones' (2021) 23 Aportes Revista De La Fundación Para El Debido Proceso 31. See for example: *Mendoza and Others v Argentina* (Provisional Measures) IACtHR Series C No 260 (14 May 2013); *Miguel Castro Castro Prison v Peru* (Provisional Measures) IACtHR Series C No 160 (29 July 2020); *Alberto Pérez Jerez v El Salvador* (Precautionary Measures) No 422–12 (1 October 2014); *Saleh and Carrero v Venezuela* (Precautionary Measures) No 223–13 (2 March 2015).

73 Gonzalez-Bertomeu, 'Prisons and prisoners' rights' (n 13) 619.

74 The question of whether precautionary measures are binding remains a topic of certain debate. The United States and Ecuador have questioned the competence of the IACHR to grant them, whereas other states, including Colombia and those engaged in international advocacy, have commonly acknowledged the binding nature of these measures. See: Burbano Herrera and Haeck, 'The Impact of Precautionary Measures on Persons Deprived of Liberty in the Americas' (n 18) 91–94.

American countries, such as Guatemala[75] and El Salvador,[76] ratified the Optional Protocol to the ICCPR only after human rights violations had already occurred on a large scale.[77]

4.1 *The Beneficiaries*

As previously stated, a total of 14 cases were identified from 1979 to 2023, involving 15 requests for interim measures related to six states. This number includes three cases in which the petitioner's request for interim measures was expressly rejected by the Committee. The analysis of the interim measures reveals that the majority of such measures have been issued with the objective of safeguarding the rights of two categories of detainees: those who are in a state of ill health and those who are held incommunicado. A total of 17 beneficiaries were protected. The majority of them (16 out of 17) claimed to be ill.[78] Fourteen beneficiaries were persons in ill health and in need of medical care.[79] One beneficiary was held in incommunicado detention.[80] One beneficiary belonged to both categories,[81] which means that s/he was in ill health and was held in incommunicado detention. One beneficiary[82] was protected by a measure concerning his place of detention as a result of his deteriorating health (asking permission to remain under house arrest).

4.1.1 Ill Detainees

The HRC has adopted interim measures to protect persons deprived of their liberty in situations where detainees are suffering from illnesses for which they are not receiving the necessary medication or medical care from the state. In

---

75 Guatemala ratified the Optional Protocol to the ICCPR in 2000.

76 El Salvador ratified the Optional Protocol to the ICCPR in 1995.

77 Lutz and Sikkink, 'International Human Rights Law and Practice in Latin America' (n 2) 637–641; Milton, *Art From a Fractured Past: memory and truth-Telling in Post-Shining Path Peru* (n 11) 272.

78 *Drescher Caldas v Uruguay* (1979); *Pietraroia v Uruguay* (1981); *Setelich v Uruguay* (1981); *Altesor v Uruguay* (1982); *Estradet Cabreira v Uruguay* (1983); *Lafuente Peñarrieta and Others v Bolivia* (1987); *J. E. S. B. v Panama* (1994); *Polay Campos v Peru* (1997); *Spisso v Venezuela* (2017); *Dávila v Colombia* (2018); *Echeverri v Colombia* (2020); *de la Vega v Colombia* (2020); *J.A.N.C. v Colombia* (2020).

79 *Setelich v Uruguay* (1981); *Altesor v Uruguay* (1982); *Estradet Cabreira v Uruguay* (1983); *Lafuente Peñarrieta and Others v Bolivia* (1987); *J. E. S. B. v Panama* (1994); *Polay Campos v Peru* (1997); *Spisso v Venezuela* (2017); *Dávila v Colombia* (2018); *Echeverri v Colombia* (2020); *de la Vega v Colombia* (2020); *J.A.N.C. v Colombia* (2020).

80 *Almeida de Quinteros and Others v* Uruguay (21 July 1983) No 107/1981, CCPR/C/OP/2.

81 *Drescher Caldas v Uruguay* (21 July 1983) No 43/1979, CCPR/C/OP/2.

82 *Echeverri v Colombia* (21 July 2020) CCPR/C/129/D/2931/2017.

such instances, the HRC requests that the state provide adequate medical care to the detainees and/or information regarding their health status.

4.1.2 Detainees Being Held Incommunicado

Prolonged detention without any means to communicate with the outside world places persons deprived of their liberty at a higher risk of being ill-treated or tortured, and has detrimental effects on both their own and their families' mental health.[83] In such cases, the HRC requests that the state provide information on the whereabouts of the person deprived of his or her liberty. The term "incommunicado detention" is used to describe a situation in which an individual is deprived of their liberty and is "not permitted any contact with the outside world".[84] This implies that their "communication with other human beings is either highly restricted or non-existent".[85] According to a report of the former UN Special Rapporteur of the Commission on Human Rights Nigel Rodley, detainees should be able to access their counsel within 24 hours of detention, and their family should be informed of the place of detention and the arrest within 18 hours.[86]

4.2 *General Overview*

Notably, 16 of the 17 beneficiaries were political prisoners or political detainees.[87] Political prisoners in this context are defined as "individuals that are incarcerated as a consequence of politically biased trials".[88] This could be explained by the repressive political regime of the states during the period in

83 Amnesty International, 'Turkey: No security without human rights' (*Amnesty International*, 2021) 19 and 30–31 <https://www.amnesty.org/en/wp-content/uploads/2021/06/eur440841996en.pdf> accessed 22 October 2024.

84 Human Rights Committee, 'Promotion and protection of all human rights, civil, political, economic, social and cultural rights, including the right to development: including a joint study on global practices in relation into secret detention in the context of countering terrorism' (20 May 2010) A/HRC/13/42, 11 and 15.

85 UN OHCHR, 'Reply to Questions Raised by Member States during the Interactive Dialogue at the 66th Session of the UN General Assembly' (*OHCHR*, 18 October 2011) 1–2 <https://www.ohchr.org/sites/default/files/Documents/Issues/Torture/Reply_to_Questions_Raised_by_MStates_DialogueGA66.pdf> accessed 22 October 2024.

86 UN General Assembly, 'Report of the Special Rapporteur on the question of torture and other cruel, inhuman or degrading treatment or punishment' (3 July 2001) A/56/156, 11.

87 Political detainees are classified as "individuals deprived of their freedom without access to judicial review within a reasonable time". See, Christoph Steinert, 'Who Is a Political Prisoner?' (2021) 6 Journal of Global Security Studies 1, 3.

88 Trials are deemed politically biased if they are endorsed by the government and (a) lack a domestic legal basis, (b) violate principles of procedural justice, or (c) violate universal human rights". See: Steinert, 'Who Is a Political Prisoner?' (n 87) 11.

which these measures were taken.[89] Nine beneficiaries were part of political movements,[90] militant organisations[91] or even guerrilla groups[92] which opposed the reigning regime. For example, all six of the beneficiaries in the cases involving Uruguay were members of groups which held Marxist/communist beliefs and actively resisted the military dictatorship in Uruguay (1973–1985). In the case regarding Bolivia, seven beneficiaries were arrested and imprisoned without being given a fair trial solely because they were suspected of being guerrillas, without any evidence that they did belong to a guerrilla group.[93]

Five beneficiaries were in a special condition of vulnerability.[94] Two beneficiaries were older than 60 years old.[95] Two beneficiaries were foreign nationals,

---

89 Burbano Herrera and Haeck, 'The historical and present-day role of non-governmental organisations before the inter-American human rights system in documenting serious human rights violations and protecting human rights and the rule of law through ensuring accountability' (n 11) 9.

90 Three beneficiaries were members of the Uruguayan political party Partido Comunista del Uruguay (PCU). See: *Drescher Caldas v Uruguay* (n 81); *Pietraroia v Uruguay* (27 March 1981) No 44/1979, CCPR/C/OP/1; *Altesor v Uruguay*, 29 March 1982, No R.2/10, A/37/40. One beneficiary was a member of the Panamanian political party Partido Revolucionario Democrático, which was ousted from government as a result of the military intervention of US troops at the moment of his arrest. See: *J. E. S. B. v Panama* (17 March 1994) CCPR/C/50/D/443/1991. One beneficiary was a politician for the Cuentas Claras party, which opposed the Venezuelan government. See: *Spisso v Venezuela* (17 March 2017) CCPR/C/119/D/2481/2014.

91 One beneficiary joined the Uruguayan anarchist organisation Federación Anarquista Uruguaya (FAU). See: *Almeida de Quinteros and Others v Uruguay* (n 80).

92 Two beneficiaries were part of the Uruguayan guerrilla group Movimiento de Liberación Nacional Tupamaros (MLN-T). See: *Estradet Cabreira v Uruguay* (21 July 1983) No 105/1981, CCPR/C/OP/2; *Setelich v Uruguay* (28 October 1981) No 63/1979, CCPR/C/OP/1. One beneficiary was the former leader of the Peruvian guerrilla group Movimiento Revolucionario Túpac Amaru (MRTA). See: *Polay Campos v Peru* (6 November 1997) CCPR/C/61/D/577/1994.

93 *Lafuente Peñarrieta and Others v Bolivia* (2 November 1987) No 176/1984, CCPR/C/OP/2.

94 To determine this number, the categorization of vulnerable groups made by the UN Special Rapporteur on the right to health and Nifosi-Sutton was utilised, which includes children and adolescents; women and girls; persons with disabilities; migrants, refugees and asylum-seekers; LGBTI+ persons; and older persons (60 years and above). Nifosi-Sutton, *The Protection of Vulnerable Groups Under International Human Rights Law* (n 26) 77–78; UN OHCHR, 'Non-discrimination: groups in vulnerable situations' (*OHCHR*, 2024) <https://www.ohchr.org/en/special-procedures/sr-health/non-discrimination-groups-vulnerable-situations> accessed 22 October 2024.

95 *Pietraroia v Uruguay* (n 90); *Altesor v Uruguay* (n 90).

meaning that they were not a citizen of the state involved in the case.[96] Only one beneficiary was female.[97] However, most of the individuals who submitted applications on behalf of the beneficiaries were women. More particularly, fifteen out of nineteen applicants were female: three petitioners were the wives of the victims,[98] two petitioners were the mothers of the victim,[99] two petitioners were the daughters of the victims,[100] and eight applicants were other female relatives.[101]

4.3 *Compliance: Responses from the State Concerned*

In response to the granting of interim measures, two distinct types of responses can be identified among states. The first type pertains to requests for information directed to the HRC, which constitutes the majority of cases. The second type pertains to the implementation of specific measures. With respect to the first type of responses, an analysis of the case law reveals that in three of the eleven cases, the states provided the HRC with all the information requested. In particular, the states submitted comprehensive information to the Committee regarding the beneficiary's medical condition and the measures taken to provide medical care to the beneficiary subsequent to the Committee's request for interim measures. These cases concerned Uruguay and Colombia.[102]

In the case of *Alberto Velasquez Echeverri v Colombia*, the applicant had asked the Committee to take interim measures, citing a decline in his mental health after his transfer to a military garrison instead of house arrest. Following a request from the HRC to grant permission to let Mr Echeverri remain under house arrest, Colombia placed the beneficiary back under house arrest.[103]

In *Pietraroia v Uruguay*, the author requested that the HRC should urge Uruguay to "promptly" provide information on the beneficiary's state of health, given that he had several health conditions while serving a 12-year prison sentence, including one which could leave him blind.[104] The Commit-

96 *Lafuente Peñarrieta and Others v Bolivia* (n 93).

97 *Almeida de Quinteros and Others v Uruguay* (n 80).

98 *Drescher Caldas v Uruguay* (n 81); *Setelich v Uruguay* (n 92); *Polay Campos v Peru* (n 92).

99 *Almeida de Quinteros and Others v Uruguay* (n 80); *Estradet Cabreira v Uruguay* (n 92).

100 *Pietraroia v Uruguay* (n 90); *Altesor v Uruguay* (n 90).

101 *Lafuente Peñarrieta and Others v Bolivia* (n 93). It is unspecified in the case how exactly the petitioners were related to the victims.

102 *Pietraroia v Uruguay* (n 90); *Estradet Cabreira v Uruguay* (n 92); *Echeverri v Colombia (n 82)*.

103 *Echeverri v Colombia* (n 82) paras 1.2–1.3.

104 *Pietraroia v Uruguay* (n 90) para 4.

tee decided that the state party should observe the concerns of the applicant concerning the beneficiary's state of health and send information on this matter to the Committee.[105] Uruguay responded that the beneficiary's state of health was "good", despite the surgical removal of his left eye due to congenital glaucoma, and that he received all the necessary medical care.[106]

In *Estradet Cabreira v Uruguay*, the beneficiary endured six months of incommunicado detention and severe torture, including electric shocks, drowning, beatings, and deprivation of food, after which he was held in harsh prison conditions. The beneficiary was in a precarious state of health, since he suffered from heart disease for which he urgently needed an operation and medical attention.[107] Consequently, the Committee had asked the state to submit information on the beneficiary's health status,[108] to which Uruguay responded that he was given "regular medical examinations and that there is no reason to be concerned about his physical state of health".[109] The Committee was not satisfied with this information and requested the state to confirm whether the beneficiary suffered from a heart disease and whether he was given "appropriate medical treatment".[110] In response, Uruguay finally gave a detailed account of Luis' state of health, including the treatment and medication he received and his current condition.[111]

In five cases, the states involved provided only a fraction of the information requested by the Committee.[112] For example, the applicants in the case of *Drescher Caldas v Uruguay* had requested that the beneficiary, who was held incommunicado at the time of submission of the application, receive a medical examination by doctors selected by his family.[113] Taking into account these concerns, the HRC asked the state to provide information about the beneficiary's health and whereabouts.[114] Uruguay disclosed the current whereabouts of the beneficiary, but did not disclose his state of health, other than to say that medical checks were carried out daily.[115]

---

105 ibid para 6.
106 ibid para 8.
107 *Estradet Cabreira v Uruguay* (n 92) para 2.5.
108 Estradet Cabreira v Uruguay (n 92) para 3.
109 ibid para 4.
110 ibid para 7(d).
111 *Estradet Cabreira v Uruguay* (n 92) para 8.1.
112 *Lafuente Peñarrieta and Others v Bolivia* (n 93).; *Polay Campos v Peru* (n 92); *Drescher Caldas v Uruguay* (n 81); *Altesor v Uruguay* (n 90); *Spisso v Venezuela (n 90).*
113 *Drescher Caldas v Uruguay* (n 81) para 2.3.
114 ibid para 3.
115 ibid para 4.

In *Altesor v Uruguay*, the beneficiary had endured beatings, electric shocks, and prolonged periods of standing exceeding 400 hours while under detention. Prior to his arrest, he had undergone a lifesaving heart operation, necessitating strict adherence to work, dietary, and medication regimens.[116] In light of the beneficiary's poor health, the Committee repeatedly asked Uruguay to provide information on the victim's state of health, urging for him to be medically examined.[117] The state provided information on the beneficiary's health status, followed by a medical report. However, it failed to specify the results of subsequent medical evaluations which the beneficiary underwent.[118]

In another case, namely *Polay Campos v Peru,* Peru provided a detailed overview of the beneficiary's health, medical examinations and treatments, but it omitted information on his detention conditions, which had also been requested by the HRC.

In the case of *Lafuente Peñarrieta and Others v Bolivia*, seven individuals were arrested on suspicion of being guerrillas, whereafter they were convicted and remained in detention. They allegedly endured severe torture, including beatings, electric shocks, and water immersion during their first 15 days of detention. They were kept in inhumane conditions, in small, humid cells, and were denied proper medical care for their deteriorating health. One of the beneficiaries had sustained a skull fracture, which was treated by a neurologist only months later.[119] In response to the Committee's request for information on the seven beneficiaries' state of health when issuing its statement to Bolivia, the state merely reported that four beneficiaries were "in good health"[120] without sharing any information on the health status of the other three beneficiaries.

The beneficiary in *Spisso v Venezuela* was held in a military prison, where he was denied adequate medical treatment for his blood pressure problems and subjected to poor detention conditions, including solitary confinement, with no view of the outdoors, ill-treatment and confiscation of his messages.[121] The Committee issued interim measures asking the Venezuelan government to "take protective measures to ensure that the author was provided with adequate conditions of detention, including access to the necessary medical care".[122] The state party replied that the beneficiary had undergone medical

116 *Altesor v Uruguay* (n 90) para 1.2.
117 *Altesor v Uruguay* (n 90) paras 2–4.
118 ibid para 10.4.
119 *Lafuente Peñarrieta and Others v Bolivia* (n 93) paras 1.1–1.3.
120 ibid para 12.
121 *Spisso v Venezuela* (*n* 90) para 3.7.
122 ibid para 1.2.

examinations which indicated that he was "in good health",[123] that his cell had "good ventilation and light",[124] that he was able to access the common areas of the detention centre, and that he was given the opportunity to contact his family and counsel according to a fixed weekly schedule.[125] However, Venezuela had not provided any information about the beneficiary's placement in solitary confinement.[126]

It is evident that the interim measures were not implemented in two cases pertaining to Uruguay.[127] In *Setelich v Uruguay*, the beneficiary had been transferred to several unknown places of detention, where he was subjected to mistreatment and torture, including solitary confinement, lack of adequate food and physical abuse. He had developed a hernia as a result of a severe beating by the guards, for which he did not receive the necessary surgical intervention, leaving him unable to walk without assistance and restricted to a liquid diet.[128] The state did not send any information or response to the Committee's repeated requests to receive information about the beneficiary's health status, whereabouts and medical treatment.[129]

In the case of *Quinteros v Uruguay*, the beneficiary was presumed to be held incommunicado after being forcibly dragged out of the Embassy of Venezuela by Uruguayan military personnel.[130] The Committee requested that the state make known the whereabouts of the beneficiary and to confirm whether she was in detention.[131] Uruguay failed to inform the Committee of the beneficiary's whereabouts, claiming that it "had no part in the events described by the author of the communication".[132]

Regrettably, in the case of *J.E.S.B. v Panama*, there is insufficient publicly available information to determine compliance.[133] The beneficiary in this case was diagnosed with prostate cancer in an advanced stage, which had not been properly treated during his imprisonment. His counsel requested the adoption of interim measures to protect his state of health, which the Committee

123 ibid para 4.10.
124 ibid para 4.10.
125 ibid para 4.10.
126 ibid para 7.7.
127 *Setelich v Uruguay* (n 92); *Almeida de Quinteros and Others v Uruguay* (n 80).
128 *Setelich v Uruguay* (n 92) para 2.2.
129 ibid para 19.
130 *Almeida de Quinteros and Others v Uruguay* (n 80) paras 1.1–1.3
131 ibid paras 1.2–1.4, 3.
132 *Almeida de Quinteros and Others v Uruguay* (n 80) paras 1.4 and 6.
133 *J. E. S. B. v Panama* (n 115).

acknowledged by asking the state to refrain from adopting or sustaining measures that would "place the author's life at risk".[134]

5 Case Study: *Polay Campos v Peru*

The following section presents a comprehensive analysis of the *Polay Campos v Peru* case. This case was selected for a number of reasons. Firstly, it provides an insight into the political context in Latin America from the 1970s to the late 1990s. Secondly, it is a case in which a significant amount of information was uncovered, which is uncommon at the UN level. Furthermore, the case has been considered by the Human Rights Committee, the Inter-American Commission on Human Rights and the Inter-American Court of Human Rights, thus offering a unique opportunity to examine their respective decisions and interactions from a comparative perspective.

5.1 *The Context*

The case of *Polay Campos v Peru* concerns the arrest of the leader of the Revolutionary Movement Túpac Amaru (MRTA), Víctor Alfredo Polay Campos, on 9 June 1992.[135] The MRTA was a Marxist guerrilla movement founded in 1982, which resisted the Peruvian government by conducting military actions such as bombings, kidnappings, and assassinations until 1997.[136] Mr Polay Campos is a political prisoner who was detained in terrible conditions and sentenced to life imprisonment for aggravated terrorism by a tribunal of faceless judges during the authoritarian regime of former President Alberto Fujimori, which lasted from 1990 to 2000. Mr Fujimori carried out a large-scale crackdown on terrorist movements and guerrilla sympathizers in the country, using armed forces that fought against the MRTA.[137] Amnesty International denounced in 2003 that for several years, a large number of people convicted of "terrorism-related crimes" had been held in high security prisons and subjected to "harsh"

134 *J. E. S. B. v Panama* (n 115) paras 5.4–5.5.

135 *Polay Campos v Peru* (n 92) para 2.1.

136 Yoon Soo Choi, 'The Peruvian hostage crisis: Brief review of MRTA' (1997) 21 International Journal of Comparative and Applied Criminal Justice 33, 33–34; Carlos A. De Izcue, 'Peru's Shining Path and MRTA Analyzed with the Manwaring Paradigm' (2006) 12 Low Intensity Conflict & Law Enforcement 52, 55.

137 Alejandro Sánchez, 'The Rebirth of Insurgency in Peru' (2003) 14 Small Wars & Insurgencies 185, 188.

conditions, which in some cases could even be considered cruel, inhuman and degrading.[138]

Three petitions were submitted at the international level in relation to the facts of the case concerning Mr Polay Campos. One communication was submitted to the HRC and two petitions were submitted within the Inter-American Human Right System. During the proceedings, the HRC adopted interim measures, the IACHR granted precautionary measures (on two occasions) and the IACtHR rejected the request for provisional measures. As will be seen, there was good communication between these human rights bodies, but their analysis of the facts of the case, and their approach to the application of interim measures varied, particularly from the perspective of the IACtHR.

5.2 *The Procedure at the UN Level: The Human Rights Committee*

It is important to acknowledge that information regarding Mr Polay has been a matter of public record for many years.[139]

5.2.1 Facts of the Case

Mr Víctor Polay Campos was detained in February 1989 and escaped on 9 July 1990 from the Miguel Castro Castro Prison. Subsequently, he was arrested on 9 June 1992, and detained at the Miguel Castro Castro prison in Yanamayo on 22 July 1992. The applicant, Mr Polay's wife, submitted a communication to the HRC on 5 March 1993, and claimed that during his stay at this prison his detention conditions were "inhuman"[140] as he was held in solitary confinement for "23 and a half hours a day, in a cell measuring 2 by 2 metres, without electricity or water"[141] in temperatures below 5 degrees. He was also "not allowed to write or to speak to anyone and was only allowed out of his cell once a day, for 30 minutes".[142] A "tribunal of faceless judges"[143] convicted

138 Amnesty International, 'Peru: The "anti-terrorism" legislation and its effects – an unfinished business in the transition to democracy' (*Amnesty International*, 2003) 12 <https://www.amnesty.org/en/wp-content/uploads/2021/06/amr460012003en.pdf> accessed 22 October 2024.

139 This information was reported in the June 1992 edition of the newspaper El Comercio. El Comercio, 'Recaptura Polay Campos' *El Comercio* (Lima, 9 June 1992) <https://lum.cultura.pe/cdi/periodico/recaptura-polay-campos> accessed 20 March 2024.

140 *Polay Campos v Peru* (n 92) para 2.1.

141 ibid para 2.1.

142 ibid para 2.1.

143 ibid para 2.2.

him of aggravated terrorism on 3 April 1993, sentencing him to life imprisonment.[144]

The applicant further alleged that during Mr Polay's transfer to another prison, namely the Callao Naval Base Prison on 26 April 1993, he was beaten and given electric shocks. In this prison, he was allegedly held "in a subterranean cell where sunlight only penetrates for 10 minutes a day, through a small opening in the ceiling"[145] and was denied contact with the outside world during his first year in prison.[146] The applicant claimed that the victim's rights to non-discrimination, not to be subjected to torture, cruel, inhuman or degrading treatment, his right to a fair trial and to recognition everywhere as a person before the law under Articles 2(1), 7, 10, 14 and 16 ICCPR were violated by his ill-treatment inflicted by the Peruvian state.[147]

5.2.2 The Procedure: Peru Denies the Allegations

Peruvian authorities consistently denied the applicant's allegations and provided the Committee with medical reports to support their claims. On 1 February 1995, the state sent a note verbale, stating that the victim had received a medical examination on 20 December 1994 by the District Attorney, as well as a court-registered doctor. According to the state, the examination revealed no evidence of mistreatment apart from a muscular contraction and emotional stress, which were deemed to be "normal symptoms of incarceration".[148]

5.2.3 Informal Request of Interim Measures

In its admissibility decision on 15 March 1996, the Committee issued an informal request for interim measures, urging Peru to provide Víctor Polay Campos "adequate medical treatment at his place of detention".[149] Additionally, the Committee requested information about his current detention conditions and further details.[150] Specifically, Peru was asked:

- To forward to the Committee copies of the relevant reports of delegates of the International Committee of the Red Cross ('ICRC') on their visits to Mr Polay Campos and of the District Attorney and the doctor who had examined him on 20 December 1994, as well as reports of subsequent visits

144 ibid para 2.2.
145 *Polay Campos v Peru* (n 92) para 2.4.
146 ibid paras 2.3–2.4.
147 ibid para 3.
148 *Polay Campos v Peru* (n 92) para 4.2.
149 ibid para 6.5.
150 ibid para 6.5.

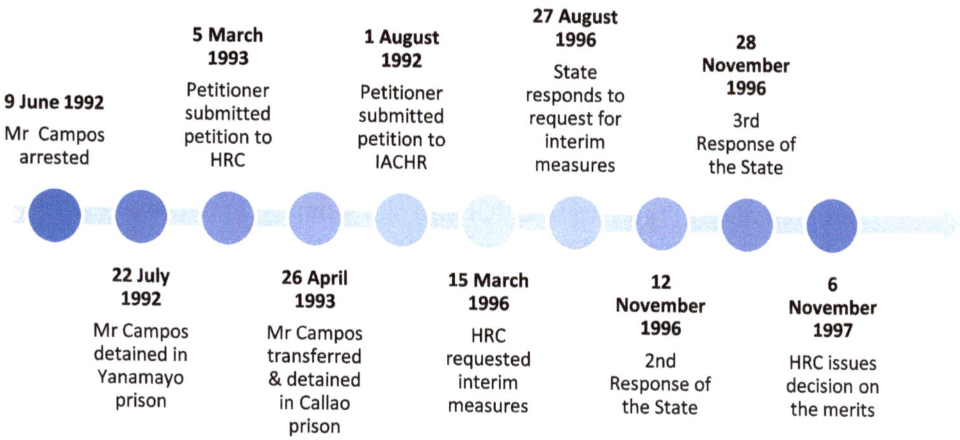

FIGURE 4.2 Timeline of the procedure at the UN level between 9 June 1992 and 28 November 1996
SOURCE: *POLAY CAMPOS V PERU* (6 NOVEMBER 1997) CCPR/C/61/D/577/1994

(these reports had been mentioned by the authorities during the procedure);[151]
- To provide detailed information about the composition and work of the special tribunals established under Peruvian anti-terrorist legislation.

As can be observed in Figure 4.2, the HRC requested information on three main aspects: the current state of health of the alleged victim, proof of his good health, and the nature of the tribunal that convicted Mr Polay. It is surprising that the Committee requested reports from the ICRC, whose reports and visits are always confidential.

5.2.4 Follow-Up

On 27 August, 12 November and 28 November 1996, the state submitted copies of three reports containing information about the beneficiary's medical treatment and detention conditions. According to these reports, the beneficiary appeared to be in good health. The first report, dated 26 April 1993, indicated that the victim's "general appearance and health were normal"[152] and that no signs of ill-treatment were found on his body. The second report was written after a visit of the District Attorney and a court-registered doctor on 20 December 1994, who found that the beneficiary was "in good health",[153] despite "suffering from muscular contraction"[154] due to psychological stress from being

151 ibid para 6.5.
152 *Polay Campos v Peru* (n 92) para 7.3.
153 Polay Campos v Peru (n 92) para 7.4.
154 ibid para 7.4.

imprisoned and experiencing pain in his left shoulder. It was also noted that his clinical tests did not show any signs of physical abuse or pressure, and that the beneficiary himself had confirmed that he was given medical attention every two weeks. A third report issued in 1996 revealed that his "health was normal",[155] contained a "summary of all medical visits and lists the medications prescribed",[156] and stressed that Mr Polay Campos continued to receive medical examinations every two weeks.

The state expressed that these three reports were not disputed by delegates of the ICRC, who had visited the beneficiary on numerous occasions. The state added that it never received any written reports from the ICRC delegates, as the visits to Mr Polay Campos were carried out on a confidential basis. According to a list furnished by the state, Mr Polay Campos was visited by ICRC delegates on 21 occasions between early December 1993 and the end of August 1996.[157]

As to the contemporaneous conditions of detention of Mr Polay Campos, the state provided the following information about his entitlements:

- 30 minutes of daily walk or sport in the prison courtyard;
- One 30-minute visit by two family members per month;
- Three hours weekly to listen to cassettes on a Walkman;
- Laundry once a week;
- One haircut every two weeks;
- Three meals per day;
- Access to reading material and books; and
- the ability to correspond with close relatives.[158]

It is notable that a considerable number of medical reports submitted by the state attest to the fact that Mr Polay was visited by medical professionals and was in good health. This information is starkly divergent from that presented in the statement by Mr Polay's wife. It is particularly concerning that the state indicated that the detainee was confined to his cell for 23.5 hours a day and was permitted only limited access to family visits. Peru did not provide any information regarding the conditions of detention at the Castro Castro prison.[159] However, it did provide information on the circumstances of the victim's detention following his incarceration at Callao.

155 ibid para 7.5.
156 ibid para 7.5.
157 *Polay Campos v Peru* (n 92) para 7.6.
158 *Polay Campos v Peru* (n 92) para 7.7.
159 ibid paras 7.1–7.6.

5.2.5 Decision of the Human Rights Committee

This case provided the Committee with an opportunity to address, in a very short space of time, two major problems that had arisen in Peru during the Fujimori regime: one related to the degrading and inhuman treatment of persons deprived of their liberty and accused of being members of the MRTA, and the other to the lack of fair trials for these detainees. These were two problems that the IACtHR would address in its jurisprudence almost ten years later.[160] It is worth mentioning that the HRC had noted that a case concerning Mr Polay Campos had been brought before the IACHR prior to the Committee.[161] However, the Committee was told that the Commission had indicated that it had no plans to prepare a report on the case within the next 12 months. In these circumstances, the HRC did not find that it was precluded from considering the communication under Article 5 paragraph 2 (a)[162] of the Optional Protocol.[163] The HRC considered the admissibility of the communication in March 1996.

In its decision on the merits on 6 November 1997, the Committee acknowledged that Peru had provided detailed information on Mr Polay Campos' medical treatment. However, it still found that his detention conditions, more specifically his isolation of over 23 hours a day and his exposure to only 10 minutes of daylight a day, constituted treatment in violation of Articles 7 and 10 (1) of the ICCPR.[164] As to Mr Polay Campos' trial and conviction by a special tribunal of "faceless judges", the Committee said that such trials by special tribunals composed of anonymous judges were incompatible with Article 14 of the Covenant, because in this type of situation, the defendants do not know who the judges trying them are. This situation brings unacceptable impediments to the preparation of their defence and communication with their lawyers. Moreover, this system fails to guarantee a cardinal aspect of a fair trial within the meaning of Article 14 of the Covenant, that the tribunal must be, and be seen to be, independent and impartial. In a system of trial by

160 *Barrios Altos v Peru* (Merits) IACtHR Series C No 75 (14 March 2001).

161 This case was registered as case No 11.048 in August 1992.

162 Article 5(2)(a) OP to the ICCPR states: "The Committee shall not consider any communication from an individual unless it has ascertained that: The same matter is not being examined under another procedure of international investigation or settlement".

163 *Polay Campos v Peru* (n 92) para 6.1.

164 *Polay Campos v Peru* (n 92) para 8.7. Article 7 ICCPR states: "No one shall be subjected to torture or to cruel, inhuman or degrading treatment or punishment. In particular, no one shall be subjected without his free consent to medical or scientific experimentation". Article 10(1) ICCPR states: "All persons deprived of their liberty shall be treated with humanity and with respect for the inherent dignity of the human person".

"faceless judges", neither the independence nor the impartiality of the judges is guaranteed, since the tribunal, being established *ad hoc*, may comprise serving members of the armed forces. In the Committee's opinion,[165] such a system also fails to safeguard the presumption of innocence, which is guaranteed by Article 14, paragraph 2 of the ICCPR. The Committee concluded that paragraphs 1, 2 and 3 (b) and (d) of Article 14 of the Covenant were violated.[166]

5.3 *The Procedure at the Regional Level*

5.3.1 The Inter-American Commission on Human Rights

On 1 August 1992, Mr Víctor Polay Campos' mother filed a petition with the IACHR regarding her son's detention. This date would suggest that the IACHR and the IACtHR were made aware of Mr Polay Campos' circumstances seven months before the HRC was approached.[167] It is also worth noting that, even before the petition was submitted by Mr Polay's mother (almost three months earlier), the President of the IACHR had already requested precautionary measures from Peru in relation to the *Case of the Miguel Castro Castro Prison v Peru*, where Mr Polay Campos was being held at the time. This is due to the fact that in the Inter-American Human Rights System, the Commission can adopt precautionary measures even if there is no petition before the system.[168] This is undoubtedly a very important power for a human rights body to have, particularly in contexts such as those in Peru and other Latin American countries,[169] where the rule of law often faces significant challenges.[170]

165 The following members of the Committee participated in the examination of this communication: Mr Nisuke Ando, Mr Prafullachandra N. Bhagwati, Mr Thomas Buergenthal, Ms Christine Chanet, Lord Colville, Mr Omran El Shafei, Ms Elizabeth Evatt, Mr Eckart Klein, Mr David Kretzmer, Mr Rajsoomer Lallah, Ms Cecilia Medina Quiroga, Mr Fausto Pocar, Mr Martin Scheinin, Mr Danilo Türk and Mr Maxwell Yalden.

166 *Polay Campos v Peru* (n 92) para 8.

167 See the section on the UN level above.

168 Felipe González, 'Urgent Measures in the Inter-American Human Rights System' (2010) 13 International Journal on Human Rights 1, 52.

169 Human Rights Watch, 'Informe Anual Sobre La Situación De Los Derechos Humanos En EL Mundo 2000: Perú' (*HRW*, 2000) <https://www.hrw.org/legacy/spanish/inf_anual/2000/americas/peru.html> accessed 20 March 2024; Human Rights Watch, 'World Report 2024: Nicaragua' (*HRW*, 2024) <https://www.hrw.org/world-report/2024/country-chapters/nicaragua> accessed 20 March 2024; Human Rights Watch, 'World Report 2024: El Salvador' (*HRW*, 2024) <https://www.hrw.org/world-report/2024/country-chapters/el-salvador> accessed 20 March 2024; Human Rights Watch, 'World Report 2024: Venezuela' (*HRW*, 2024) <https://www.hrw.org/world-report/2024/country-chapters/venezuela> accessed 20 March 2024.

170 The facts of this case are set against the backdrop of the armed conflict in Peru. Between 6 and 9 May 1992, the Peruvian government conducted an operation known as "Mudanza

5.3.1.1 *Precautionary Measures*

Eighteen days after the petition was submitted, on 18 August 1992, the President of the Commission requested (for the second time) precautionary measures to protect "persons deprived of their liberty for acts of terrorism".[171] The facts that the IACHR took into account to request precautionary measures (and subsequently provisional measures from the Court) were related to various aspects as follows:

1", with the purported objective of transferring approximately 90 women incarcerated at the "Miguel Castro Castro" prison to a women's prison. The Peruvian authorities attacked the women's pavilion at the Castro Castro prison, employing weaponry typically reserved for wartime operations. The attack continued for four days and eventually involved male inmates as well. In the aftermath of the attack, survivors were subjected to deplorable conditions, including forced nudity, sexual assault and rape. In November 2006, the IACtHR found that Peru had violated the right to life of the 41 deceased inmates, the right to humane treatment enshrined in the ACHR and in the Inter-American Convention to Prevent and Punish Torture, and the right to a fair trial and judicial protection enshrined in the ACHR in connection with Article 7(b) of the Inter-American Convention to Prevent, Punish, and Eradicate Violence Against Women. Detriment was incurred to the next of kin of the 41 deceased inmates identified, as well as to the surviving inmates. In particular, the IACtHR held that the practice of forced nudity violated the personal dignity of the victims, a violation that was especially serious in the case of female victims. The IACtHR concluded, using the wide definition of sexual violence utilized by the ICTR in the *Akayesu* case, that the fact that the naked female victims were observed at all times by armed soldiers constituted sexual violence. The IACtHR also held that, when considering the seriousness of torture and cruel, inhuman and degrading treatment, gender was "in some cases" a relevant factor. In particular, it held that the alleged act of "finger vaginal 'inspection', carried out by several hooded people at the same time, in a very abrupt manner, with the excuse of examining her" was "sexual rape". See: *Penal Castro Castro v Peru* (Merits, Reparations, and Costs) IACtHR Series C No 155 (25 November 2006). Other cases, such as that of *Loayza Tamayo v Peru*, which has similar facts and dates relating to detention conditions have also been decided by the IACtHR. In this case, Peru was held internationally responsible in 1997 for human rights violations committed against Professor Maria Elena Loayza Tamayo. She was sentenced to 20 years for the crime of terrorism in Peru. Prof Loayza did not receive a fair trial. After being convicted, she was denied the right of appeal. Throughout her time in prison, she was subjected to inhuman and degrading treatment. For an entire year, she was kept locked away for 23.5 hours a day in a damp, cold cell, measuring just 2x3m. She was not allowed to talk to anyone, listen to the radio, or to read a newspaper. When she fell ill, she was refused medical attention. *Loayza Tamayo v Peru* (Merits) IACtHR Series C No 33 (17 September 1997).

171 *Penales Peruanos v Peru* (Resolution of Urgent Measures) President of the IACtHR (14 December 1992) para 4 <https://www.corteidh.or.cr/docs/medidas/penales_se_01.pdf> accessed 20 March 2024.

- The Commission had received information that in these prisons there was a "very high incidence of illness, weight loss, overcrowding, isolation, psychological and emotional disorders of the inmates";[172]
- The inmates resided in very cold areas despite the fact that some of them were wounded and had only their "threadbare"[173] summer clothes;
- The detainees were not allowed to be visited by their families;
- There was no independent institution which was authorized or able to investigate the situation described above;
- The ICRC was not authorized to inspect the prisons.

The situation was stark. People detained and accused of terrorism. Presumably with links to the MRTA, were in a situation of extreme danger.[174] The Commission considered these facts to be strong indications of a serious situation in the Peruvian prisons of Miguel Castro Castro, Santa Monica, Cristo Rey and Yanamayo, which would lead to "an imminent danger to the right to life and personal integrity of those accused and convicted of terrorism (…)".[175] In light of this, the IACHR requested that Peru:

- Authorize an on-site visit to the facilities of Yanamayo prison, and allow the IACHR to meet with persons deprived of their liberty in these facilities;[176]
- Authorize visits by family members and lawyers to detainees in detention centres, and allow the entry of clothes, medicines, coats and toiletries;[177]

172 *Penales Peruanos v Peru* (Resolution of the Inter-American Court of Human Rights) Provisional Measures Requested by the Inter-American Commission on Human Rights Regarding Peru (27 January 1993) para 3 <https://www.corteidh.or.cr/docs/medidas/penales_se_02.pdf> accessed 20 March 2024.

173 *Penales Peruanos v Peru* (n 172) para 3.

174 Milton, *Art From a Fractured Past: Memory and Truth-Telling in Post-Shining Path Peru* (n 11) 57; Max G. Manwaring, 'Peru's Sendero Luminoso: The Shining Path Beckons' (1995) 541 Annals of the American Academy of Political and Social Science 157, 163; Angela Cornell and Kenneth Roberts, 'Democracy, Counterinsurgency, and Human Rights: the Case of Peru' (1990) 12 Human Rights Quarterly 529, 531; Peter F. Klarén, *Peru, Society and Nationhood in the Andes* (New York, Oxford University Press 2000) 415; *Penal Castro Castro v Peru* (n 170); *Espinoza Gonzáles v Peru* (Preliminary Objections, Merits, Reparations, and Costs) IACtHR Series C No 289 (20 November 2014); *Lori Berenson Mejía v Peru* (Merits, Reparations, and Costs) IACtHR Series C No 119 (25 November 2004); *Castillo Petruzzi and Others v Peru* (Merits) IACtHR Series C No 34 (3 November 1997).

175 *Penales Peruanos v Peru* (n 172) para 3.

176 *Penales Peruanos v Peru* (n 171) para 4.

177 ibid para 4

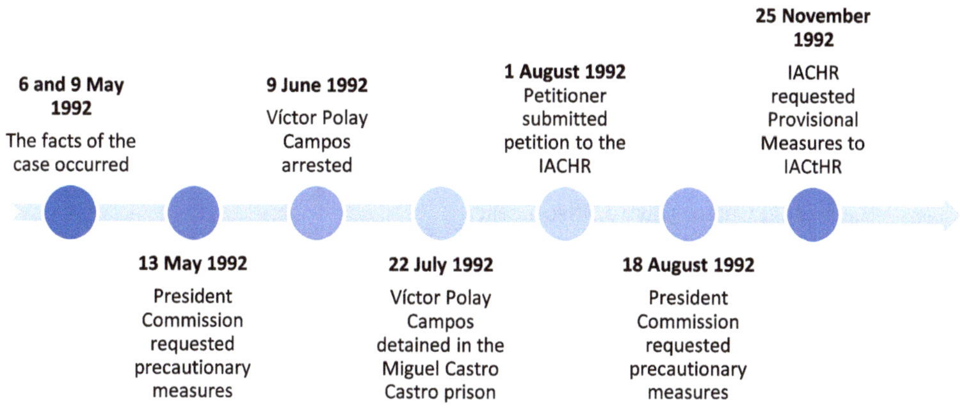

FIGURE 4.3 Timeline of the procedure at the international level between 6 May 1992 and 25 November 1992

SOURCE: *PENALES PERUANOS V PERU* (RESOLUTION OF URGENT MEASURES) PRESIDENT OF THE IACTHR (14 DECEMBER 1992); *POLAY CAMPOS V PERU* (10 MARCH 2000) REPORT NO 32/00

– Provide the medical care required by persons suffering from health conditions and transfer them to establishments where they can receive the required medical care;[178]
– Separate members of different armed groups to avoid situations of violence;[179]
– Submit to the IACHR the official list of persons who were killed and disappeared as a result of the events that took place at the Miguel Castro Castro Prison, as well as those injured, and the fate of those transferred to the centre.[180]

The President of the IACHR stated that if the measures were not adopted within 10 days, "the possibility would be contemplated of submitting a request for provisional measures to the Court".[181]

5.3.1.2 *Provisional Measures: A Different Approach to Mr Víctor Polay Campos' Detention*

On 25 November 1992, more than three months after the Commission made its second request for precautionary measures to Peru, it decided to request that the Court adopt provisional measures for the protection of the alleged victims in two cases: case No. 11.015 (Miguel Castro Castro Prison case) and

178 ibid para 4
179 ibid para 4
180 ibid para 4
181 *Penales Peruanos v Peru* (n 171) para 4.

case No. 11.048 (Polay Campos case). It is worth noting that the request for provisional measures did not mention the names of the beneficiaries, but only the case numbers. Notably, not all of the alleged victims in case 11.015 were identified at the time. This information was only revealed in the Court's 2006 judgment, which named 41 deceased prisoners as some of the victims in the Miguel Castro Castro Prison case.

The Commission requested provisional measures due to the existence of a serious situation that posed imminent danger to the personal integrity of convicted and accused persons held in various detention centres in Peru, including the Miguel Castro Castro prison where Mr Polay Campos was being held.[182] The IACHR informed the Court that the Attorney General's Office sent an official letter (No. 3135–92-MP-FN) on 16 May 1992 to Dr Oscar de la Puente Raygada, President of the Council of Ministers and Minister of Foreign Affairs.[183] This letter conveyed Peru's perception of the IACHR as an institution that supported the MRTA. This was cited by the Commission as the reason for the delay in Peru granting the requested authorizations and therefore in complying with the precautionary measures.[184]

The IACHR referred to the events that took place on 20 October 1992 at Cristo Rey prison in Ica, where two inmates died and three were injured, along with two injured police officers. The Commission also expressed a desire to visit this prison.[185] Additionally, the IACHR noted that the precautionary measures requested by its President on 13 May 1992 had not been implemented. As of that date, the state had not authorized the Commission's requested visit, nor had they provided the relevant information.[186]

The IACHR requested in the petition for provisional measures that the Court grant the IACHR authorization:

- To conduct an on-site observation of prison facilities;[187]
- To meet in private with the persons deprived of liberty in these prisons;[188]
- To grant authorization for family members to provide clothing, food, toiletries and medicines to persons deprived of their liberty;[189] and

182 *Polay Campos v Peru* (10 March 2000) Report No 32/00, para 3 <https://cidh.oas.org/annualrep/99span/Inadmisible/Peru11048.htm> accessed 20 March 2024.

183 *Penales Peruanos v Peru* (n 171) para 5.

184 ibid para 5(c).

185 *Penales Peruanos v Peru* (n 171) para 5(d).

186 ibid para 5(d).

187 ibid para 2(1).

188 ibid para 2(2).

189 ibid para 2(3).

– To grant authorization for adequate medical care to be provided through independent institutions.[190]

During the proceedings, on 4 December 1992, the Commission's secretariat sent the Court a document containing a complaint. The Commission believed that this complaint indicated a situation that could harm the rights of women prisoners in the Santa Monica Penal Centre in Chorrillos. If the facts in the complaint were true, they would accentuate the gravity and urgency of the situation considered by the judges of the Court.[191] It is noteworthy that the Commission acted promptly and it also indirectly considered gender issues, which was uncommon at the time. In this letter, the Commission was referring specifically to the situation of women deprived of their liberty.

5.3.1.3 *Rejection of Provisional Measures*

The President of the IACtHR and the Court[192] both rejected the request for provisional measures.[193] The Court's President stated that the request could not be considered provisional under Article 63(2)[194] of the American Convention, as it referred to the state's obligation to allow the Commission to conduct on-site visits to various penitentiary establishments in Peru.[195] This situation is regulated by Articles 48(2)[196] of the Convention and 44(2)[197] of

190 ibid para 2(4).

191 ibid para 6.

192 The judges were Héctor Fix-Zamudio (President), Sonia Picado Sotela (Vice President), Rafael Nieto Navia, Alejandro Montiel Argüello, Hernán Salgado Pesantes, and Asdrúbal Aguiar-Aranguren.

193 *Penales Peruanos v Peru* (n 171); *Penales Peruanos v Peru* (n 172).

194 Article 63(2) American Convention states: "In cases of extreme gravity and urgency, and when necessary to avoid irreparable damage to persons, the Court shall adopt such provisional measures as it deems pertinent in matters it has under consideration. With respect to a case not yet submitted to the Court, it may act at the request of the Commission".

195 *Penales Peruanos v Peru* (n 171); *Penales Peruanos v Peru* (n 172).

196 Article 48(2) of the American Convention states: "However, in serious and urgent cases, only the presentation of a petition or communication that fulfills all the formal requirements of admissibility shall be necessary in order for the Commission to conduct an investigation with the prior consent of the state in whose territory a violation has allegedly been committe.".

197 Article 44(2) of the Rules of Procedure of the IACHR states: "If it establishes one or more violations, it shall prepare a preliminary report with the proposals and recommendations it deems pertinent and shall transmit it to the State in question.In so doing, it shall set a deadline by which the State in question must report on the measures adopted to comply with the recommendations. The State shall not be authorized to publish the report until the Commission adopts a decision in this respect."

the Commission's Rules of Procedure. According to the President of the Court, these precepts required prior consent from the state, and this consent could not be replaced by measures ordered by the Presidency.[198] The Court's President also added that the IACHR had not provided any principle of proof as to the truth of the facts alleged, since such certainty could depend on the observations made by the IACHR during the visits it intended to make to these establishments, or on other means of conviction that had not yet been presented.[199]

While it is true that the Court's President could not order Peru (or any other state) to allow the members of the IACHR to enter its territory through provisional measures, as this constitutes a power that only states have as part of their sovereignty, the IACHR could request other measures in line with the requirements contained in Article 63(2) of the ACHR. The Court's President, for example, could order Peru to allow family members to visit persons deprived of their liberty or to request that they receive adequate medical care. The President could also request information from the state.

Following the decision of its President, in January 1995, the Court also rejected the request for provisional measures.[200] Instead, the IACtHR called upon the Commission to use its powers under the Convention, the Statute, and the Rules of Procedure to obtain the necessary evidence and to verify the facts.[201] This decision seems incongruous. It may also be misplaced. The IACHR had already attempted to obtain more information and evidence through its precautionary measures, but these were unsuccessful. The IACtHR's approach was distinctly formalistic and appeared to lack a clear understanding of the situation in Peru at the time.

5.3.1.4 *Inadmissibility*

On 3 April 1997, the IACHR received a communication from the HRC, in which it was informed that the Committee had taken cognizance of a case concerning Mr Polay,[202] which had been submitted on 5 March 1993 by Ms Roza Espinoza, Mr Polay's wife. Subsequently, the IACHR received the Committee's

198 *Penales Peruanos v Peru* (n 171) para 5.

199 ibid para 6.

200 *Penales Peruanos v Peru* (n 172).

201 ibid para 3.

202 The complaint was submitted by Ms Rosa Espinoza de Polay, the wife of Mr Polay Campos. The case was registered as No 11.048.

admissibility report and its merits opinion on 15 March 1996 and 29 October 1999 respectively.[203]

As a result, in March 2000, the IACHR decided under Article 47(d)[204] of the American Convention to declare the petition inadmissible as a repetition of a petition that has already been submitted, processed and decided upon by another international human rights protection body, such as the HRC. Both human rights bodies have similar legal prerogatives and their decisions have the same or similar scope.[205]

5.3.2 Peru's Return to Democracy: Submission of a New Petition

Following the return of democracy to the country and the restoration of the rule of law, the Peruvian Constitutional Court, in a ruling of 3 January 2003, declared unconstitutional a number of articles of the decrees used to prosecute and sentence persons accused of terrorist acts and reinterpreted many of their provisions. In this context, Mr Polay Campos got a new trial in 2006 and 2008.[206] In 1993, Mr Polay Campos was sentenced to life imprisonment by a faceless court. This sentence was overturned in 2006, and he was resentenced to 32 years in prison. In 2008, his prison sentence was increased to 35 years for the crimes of terrorism, aggravated terrorism and forgery.[207] Mr Polay Campos is currently 72 years old and is still in prison as of 2025. In an interview conducted with Mr Polay Campos' mother by the New York Times in 1997, it is mentioned that his wife, Rosa, and their three children fled to Europe.[208] In 2007, a new petition was submitted before the IACHR.

On 6 December 2007, several persons[209] including relatives of Víctor Polay Campos submitted a petition to the IACHR. They alleged that Mr Polay Cam-

203 *Polay Campos v Peru* (n 182) para 4.

204 Article 47(d) of the American Convention states: "The Commission shall consider inadmissible any petition or communication submitted under Articles 44 or 45 if: the petition or communication is substantially the same as one previously studied by the Commission or by another international organization".

205 *Polay Campos v Peru* (n 182) para 19.

206 ibid paras 13–15.

207 *Polay Campos v Peru* (20 March 2022) Report No 56/22, paras 13–15 <https://www.oas.org/es/cidh/decisiones/2022/PEAD_1548-07_ES.PDF> accessed 20 March 2024.

208 Diana J. Schemo, 'A Born Revolutionary's Path to a Living 'Tomb' in Peru' *The New York Times* (New York, 4 January 1997) <https://www.nytimes.com/1997/01/04/world/a-born-revolutionary-s-path-to-a-living-tomb-in-peru.html> accessed 20 March 2024. A version of this article appears in print on 4 January 1997, Section 1, Page 1 of the national edition with the headline: 'A Born Revolutionary's Path to a Living 'Tomb' in Peru'.

209 César Oyola, Javier Valle Riestra, Javier Mujica Petit, Otilia Campos and Otilia Clemencia Polay.

pos's health had deteriorated during his detention, given that two psychiatrists from the ICRC had concluded from examinations conducted in May 1996 and December 2000 that he was in poor health and his isolation constituted inhuman and degrading treatment.[210] The petitioners claimed that the ICRC communicated these findings to the Peruvian government without receiving any response or reaction.[211] They further alleged that officers of the Callao Naval Base provided biased medical reports on Mr Polay Campos's health, which were not supported by evidence.[212] There is no indication that a request for precautionary measures was made.

The petitioners made two main allegations. Firstly, that Mr Víctor Polay Campos was convicted of the crime of terrorism in a decision that violated his right to the principle of legality and judicial guarantees. Secondly, that the conditions of detention imposed on him affected his personal integrity. They also claimed that the Public Prosecutor's Office did not diligently investigate this matter, despite the fact that it had been reported that Mr Polay Campos had been constantly tortured since his arrest. Therefore, the petitioners considered that Article 5 (Right to Humane Treatment),[213] Article 8 (Right to a Fair Trail),[214] and Article 25 (Right to Judicial Protection)[215] of the American Convention had been violated.

With regard to the principle of legality, the petitioners argued that the criminal definition of terrorism which had been applied to convict Mr Polay did not contain a clear, precise and concrete definition of what acts constitute such an offense.[216] It was explained that, historically, the legislature had always opted for open-ended criminal definitions to punish alleged terrorist practices, in which it was very easy to include any act against persons or property. They argued that Mr Polay's actions should have been classified as rebellion, an offence provided for in Article 346 of the Criminal Code in force at the time, since his organization had the political aim of undermining the constitutional and political order, rather than causing anxiety or fear among the civilian population.[217] They alleged that the judicial authorities had taken advantage of the vagueness of the definition of terrorism in order to attribute

210 *Polay Campos v Peru* (n 207) para 1.
211 ibid para 8.
212 ibid para 23.
213 Article 5 American Convention.
214 Article 8 American Convention.
215 Article 25 American Convention.
216 *Polay Campos v Peru* (n 182) para 26.
217 ibid para 26.

to him acts which he did not commit and which did not form part of the MRTA's policy.[218]

5.3.2.1 *Peru's Response*

In response, Peru maintained that the petition should be declared inadmissible on the grounds of duplication of proceedings, in accordance with Article 47(d) of the ACHR.[219] It pointed out that, on 9 January 1998, the HRC had ruled on facts similar to those alleged in the present petition, namely on: (i) the conditions of Mr Polay Campos' detention from 22 July 1992 to 26 April 1993; (ii) his transfer from the Yanamayo prison to the Callao naval base; (iii) the conditions of his detention at the Callao naval base from 26 April 1993; and (iv) the trial to which he was subjected.[220] The state added that, on the basis of this statement, on 10 March 2000, in Report No. 32/00, the IACHR had declared inadmissible a petition filed on behalf of Mr Polay Campos on the grounds of double jeopardy.[221]

With regard to the alleged violation of Article 5 of the ACHR, the state maintained that there had been no violation of Mr Polay Campos' physical, mental or moral integrity, nor had he been subjected to torture or other inhuman or degrading treatment. On the contrary, it mentioned that since 26 April 1993 Mr Polay had been under the care of a doctor 24 hours a day.[222] Peru claimed that Mr Polay Campos had received family visits from 1994 to 2020, special visits from 1997 to 2019 and visits from his lawyers from 2001 to 2020, without any major setbacks.[223] In this regard, the state affirmed that Mr Polay Campos was not held incommunicado or isolated in his prison and that he maintained communication with the outside world.[224]

In regard to the domestic legal process, the state indicated that in 2003 the Executive had published Legislative Decree No. 926. This decree was aimed at annulling trials for terrorist offenses that were conducted before judges and prosecutors with secret identities. On the basis of this decree, the domestic authorities declared Mr Polay Campos' conviction null and initi-

218 ibid para 26.
219 ibid para 29.
220 *Polay Campos v Peru* (n 182) para 29.
221 ibid paras 29–30.
222 ibid para 31.
223 *Polay Campos v Peru* (n 182) 34.
224 ibid para 34.

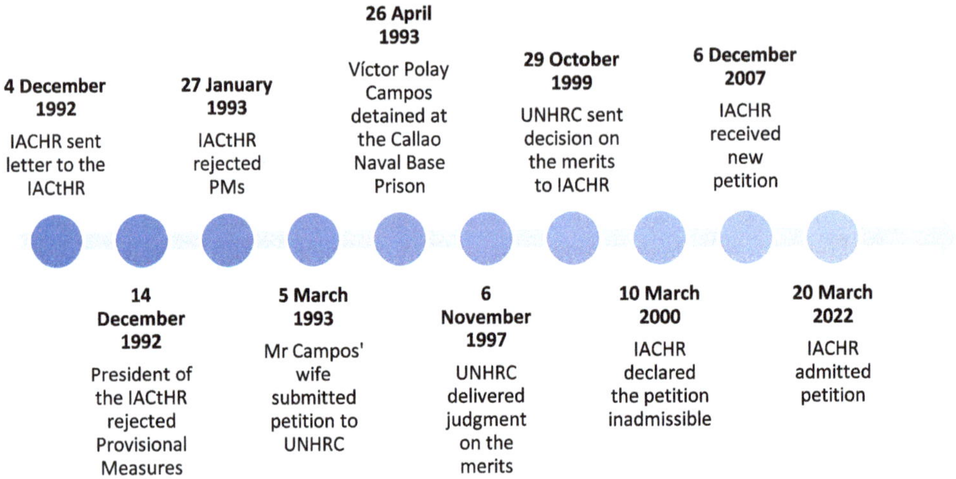

FIGURE 4.4 Timeline of the procedure at the international level between 4 December 1992 and 20 March 2022

SOURCE: *PENALES PERUANOS V PERU* (RESOLUTION OF URGENT MEASURES) PRESIDENT OF THE IACTHR (14 DECEMBER 1992); *POLAY CAMPOS V PERU* (10 MARCH 2000) REPORT NO 32/00; *POLAY CAMPOS V PERU* (6 NOVEMBER 1997) CCPR/C/61/D/577/1994; *POLAY CAMPOS V PERU* (20 MARCH 2022) REPORT NO 56/22

ated a new trial.[225] The ordinary courts concluded in two instances that he was criminally responsible for the crime of terrorism, aggravated terrorism and falsification of documents. The State emphasized that, throughout these proceedings, Mr Polay Campos had the opportunity and means to exercise his right to defence.[226] Furthermore, on 3 January 2003, the Constitutional Court reviewed the anti-terrorist legislation and confirmed the constitutionality of Article 2 of Decree Law No. 25475, which regulates the criminal offense of terrorism.[227] Finally, Peru pointed out that, in view of Mr Polay Campos' record of escape,[228] his high level of danger and national security considerations, he was being held in a maximum security prison and was therefore subject to an exceptional regime.[229]

225 ibid para 35.
226 ibid para 36.
227 ibid para 35.
228 Mr Polay Campos was detained in February 1989 and escaped on 9 July 1990 from the Miguel Castro Castro Prison. It is worth noting that this information was reported in the June 1992 edition of the newspaper El Comercio. It is also important to acknowledge that this event has been a matter of public record for many years. El Comercio, 'Recaptura Polay Campos' (n 139).
229 *Polay Campos v Peru* (n 182) para 34.

5.3.2.2 *Admissibility*

The IACHR concurred with the state's position that the HRC had ruled on several aspects related to Mr Polay Campos' detention and imprisonment. These included his conditions of detention from 22 July 1992 to 26 April 1993, his transfer to Yanamayo prison and the Callao naval base, his conditions of detention at the Callao naval base from 26 April 1993 until 1998, and the trial to which he was subjected before a court without identity. Therefore, the Commission could not consider these events for substantive examination.[230] However, the Commission stated that the petition contained additional facts and allegations beyond those initially presented. These included: i) new criminal proceedings initiated against Mr Polay Campos from 2000 to the present; ii) the rejection of two habeas corpus actions challenging the prison conditions; and iii) the alleged denial of justice following the filing of a criminal complaint on 18 January 2002, for the alleged ill-treatment and torture of Mr Polay Campos. In light of these considerations, the Commission stated that it would examine the admissibility of these facts.[231]

It was recalled that the Commission did not constitute a fourth instance and that its purpose was not to determine the innocence or guilt of Mr Polay Campos. Rather, its mandate was to define whether or not the judicial authorities had violated the obligations stipulated in the Convention, in particular the principle of presumption of innocence, the principle of legality and the right to judicial protection.[232]

As shown in Figure 4.4, after examining the conditions of admissibility, the IACHR decided to admit the petition on 20 March 2022, and as of February 2025 it remains under its consideration.

6 Compliance and Impact: Explaining Key Concepts

In order to evaluate the extent of compliance and the resulting impact of the precautionary measures, it is essential to first define the terms "compliance" and "impact" as they are used in this paper. In previous research conducted in collaboration with Prof Dr Yves Haeck, it was proposed that there is a distinction between compliance with a urgent measure and its impact.[233] Compli-

---

230 *Polay Campos v Peru* (n 182) para 42.

231 *Polay Campos v Peru* (n 182) para 43.

232 *Polay Campos v Peru* (n 182) para 50.

233 This section draws its ideas from: Burbano Herrera and Haeck, 'The Impact of Precautionary Measures on Persons Deprived of Liberty in the Americas' (n 18).

ance is associated with the action or actions undertaken by the state in question to comply with the orders issued by the international human rights body. In the context of prisons, for instance, compliance may entail the hiring of additional prison staff, the construction of a new prison, the transfer of sick detainees to a specialized hospital, or written responses to the resolutions of precautionary measures.[234] It is evident that compliance or lack of compliance affects the beneficiary of a precautionary measure directly and most prominently.

The impact of the urgent measures can be considered in two distinct ways: firstly, in terms of the effects of the actions taken by the state to comply with the order on the beneficiaries (*direct impact*); and secondly, in terms of the effects beyond the beneficiary (*indirect impact*). This includes relatives of the beneficiaries, their neighbours, other persons deprived of their liberty, national, regional and/global institutions. The impact of precautionary measures may be observed in a number of ways. These include the recovery of ill prisoners who have received adequate medical treatment (*direct impact*), a decrease in the rate of overcrowding in the prison (*indirect impact*), and a decrease in the rate of violence between detainees (*indirect impact*). Indirect impact also occurs when the precautionary measure alters the public perception of detainees, or when it creates public awareness. For example, when alliances are created to advocate for the rights of prisoners, when other social movements start to submit similar petitions to protect other detainees, or when there is increased pressure on policy makers.

The potential impact may be either *positive* or *negative*. To illustrate, a precautionary measure could lead the state to employ additional prison officials with the objective of controlling violence within the prison facility. However, these officials have not received training in accordance with human rights standards. Indeed, the recently hired staff members are attempting to control violence through the disproportionate use of force. Negative impact can also occur when a state, in response to a request from the precautionary measure, decides to denounce the American Convention on Human Rights or argues that urgent measures lack binding force.[235] Consequently, the impact of precautionary measures has a certain connection with compliance. However, the lack of compliancemay also have an impact, which can result in effects on the beneficiary (*direct impact*) and/or on society (*indirect impact*).

234 Ibid.
235 Ibid.

In order to achieve an objective analysis of compliance and impact, it is essential to examine in depth the concrete situation of risk, the broader context of the case, and the power dynamics.[236] For example, it is relevant to ascertain the circumstances that gave rise to the specific danger, the measures requested by the human rights body, the actions taken by the state, and the extent to which the beneficiary's situation has been altered following the implementation of the aforementioned measures. It is similarly pertinent to ascertain whether external factors have played a role in influencing the outcome.[237] For instance, an analysis of the potential influence of the media or social activism in specific contexts would be a valuable contribution to the field. Furthermore, the political system of member states may play a significant role in determining the manner in which urgent measures are implemented.[238]

In the context of incarceration, the assessment of the impact of such actions may also require a more comprehensive examination of a number of additional factors, including the prevalence of overcrowding within the detention facilities, as well as any observed changes over the short, medium and long term, in the mental and/or physical health of the beneficiary. In light of the limited space available here and the fact that this contribution is based on desk research, the following section will exclusively focus on compliance-related matters.

6.1 *Analysing Compliance*

6.1.1 Human Rights Committee

In examining the case of *Polay Campos v Peru*, it becomes evident that it is challenging to make a definitive assertion regarding the existence of either "compliance" or "non-compliance". Instead, it is necessary to examine each action taken by the state, analyse each, and then determine the extent of compliance, non-compliance, or even partial compliance. The following section presents an analysis of the actions taken by the state in response to the request for interim measures to protect Mr Víctor Polay Campos.

236 Clara Burbano Herrera, Yves Haeck and Alberte Hansen, 'A theoretical model for measuring the impact of urgent measures that protect at risk detainees' in Clara Burbano Herrera and Yves Haeck (eds), *Impact(s) within the Human Rights Framework* (Edward Elgar 2025) (*forthcoming*).

237 Burbano Herrera and Haeck, 'The Impact of Precautionary Measures on Persons Deprived of Liberty in the Americas' (n 18) 98.

238 Ibid. 101.

Compliance with requests for information – incomplete information: As previously outlined, the state provided documented responses to the majority of the issues requested by the Committee. In particular, the state provided information regarding the health status of Mr Polay Campos and the conditions of the beneficiary's detention following his imprisonment in Callao. However, no information was provided regarding the conditions of the beneficiary's detention at the Miguel Castro Castro prison. It seems plausible to suggest that the state may have deliberately withheld this information, particularly given the human rights violations that were occurring in this prison during the period in which Mr Polay was detained. This assertion is corroborated by the findings of the *Miguel Castro Castro Prison v Peru* case, which was decided by the Inter-American Court in 2006.[239]

Information revealing human rights violations: An analysis of the information provided by the state reveals that the beneficiary was subjected to deplorable prison conditions. For instance, the state indicated that Mr Polay Campos was kept in isolation for 23.5 hours a day and permitted only 10 minutes of daylight a day. Furthermore, it was noted that he was scarcely permitted to receive visits from family members. It would appear that the state authorities lack an understanding of international human rights standards regarding the conditions in which persons deprived of their liberty should be held. The prison conditions described by the state authorities were clearly in contravention of Articles 7 and 10(1) of the ICCPR.

Late information: While Peru did indeed provide much of the information that had been requested, as previously noted, certain aspects of the response, particularly the length of time taken by the state to respond, give cause for concern. The response from the Peruvian government was received five months after the initial request had been made. In situations of significant risk, and particularly in cases where individuals deprived of their liberty are alleged to be in poor health, this delay is highly problematic. Furthermore, the information in question was related to a specific individual, which one might assume would not be particularly challenging to obtain. In such cases, a clear reminder to the state of the deadline for the provision of information would have been beneficial, as is current standard practice for other regional bodies such as the IACHR and the IACtHR.

239 *Penal Castro Castro v Peru* (n 170).

In light of the aforementioned evidence, it can be surmised that the state has taken measures to comply with certain aspects of the Committee's request, yet has failed to do so with respect to others. Consequently, it can be argued that Peru's compliance with the Committee's interim measures was merely partial, and that this partial compliance evidenced human rights violations.

6.1.2 The Inter-American Commission on Human Rights

Non-compliance: It is regrettable that the state did not comply with the two precautionary measures requested by the Commission to safeguard the personal integrity of convicted and accused individuals held in various detention centres in Peru, including the Miguel Castro Castro prison where Mr Polay Campos was being held. The Commission was not authorized to visit Peruvian prisons, nor had it received the relevant information requested. Additionally, it was unfortunate that the Peruvian Attorney General's Office sent an official letter to Dr Oscar de la Puente Raygada, President of the Council of Ministers and Minister of Foreign Affairs, which outlined Peru's perception of the IACHR as an institution that supported the MRTA.

From a comparative perspective, it is evident that Peru reacted in a contrasting manner to the urgent measures adopted by the human rights bodies. With regard to the HRC, Peru provided information, whereas with respect to the Commission, there was a total absence of response. The Court's rejection of the provisional measures requested by the Commission did not contribute to the situation of Mr Polay Campos nor to the position of the IACHR towards Peru.

As mentioned above, the IACHR admitted a petition concerning Mr Polay Campos in 2022. It is likely that the information gathered by the Human Rights Committee and the Commission itself in the 1990s will be useful in assessing this petition. This means that the precautionary measures, the process and the recommendations made at the international level could have an impact on the current inter-American process.

7 Concluding Remarks

The infringement of the rights of individuals who are deprived of their liberty represents a matter of significant concern in numerous Latin American countries. Particularly problematic are the issues of overcrowding, unsanitary conditions, violations of fair trial and violence. Despite the formal recognition of the rights of detainees in international documents, there appears to be a persistent failure on the part of member states to uphold the right of persons deprived of their liberty to be treated with dignity.

In order to safeguard the rights of individuals deprived of their liberty from irreparable harm, the Human Rights Committee has established the authority to grant interim measures. Our research shows that between 1977 and 2023, a total of 15 interim measures were requested to protect persons deprived of their liberty in Latin-America. The analysis of the interim measures indicates that the beneficiaries were predominantly political prisoners who were either ill or held incommunicado in six countries. This context demonstrates the extensive misuse of the criminal code to silence individuals who espouse ideologies that are contrary to those of state authorities, thereby threatening the rule of law.

Furthermore, the issue of compliance represents a significant concern. A review of the cases reveals that in seven of the eleven cases, the states in question did not provide the HRC with all the information that it had requested. This indicates that less than half of the cases were compliant with the aforementioned request. In five cases, the states provided only a portion of the information requested by the Committee. Regrettably, in the case of *J.E.S. B. v Panama,* there is an insufficient amount of publicly available information to determine compliance.

The case of *Polay Campos v Peru* offers a compelling illustration of the political context in Latin America from the 1970s to the end of the 1990s and the necessity of granting interim measures in such situations. This case provided the Committee with an opportunity to address two significant issues that had emerged in Peru during the Fujimori regime in a relatively short period of time. The first issue pertains to the degrading and inhumane treatment of individuals deprived of their liberty and accused of being members of the guerrilla group Shining Path. The second issue concerns the lack of a fair trial for these detainees. These issues were subsequently addressed by the IACtHR in its jurisprudence almost a decade later.

The analysis of this case demonstrates that both the HRC and the IACHR acted in a prompt and decisive manner, adopting interim and precautionary measures with the objective of safeguarding Mr Polay Campos. Information had been received by these human rights bodies indicating that the situation in these prisons was dangerous. Those detained and accused of terrorism, presumed to have ties to the MRTA were in a vulnerable position. Moreover, it is noteworthy that the Commission addressed the particular circumstances of women deprived of their liberty, which at that time were often overlooked.

The IACtHR's approach was characterized by a marked formalism, which gave the impression that the Court lacked an accurate understanding of the situation in Peru at the time. The Court and its President rejected the request for provisional measures. It was only some years later, in a judgement from 2006, that the Court acknowledged the existence of a situation of danger during that period, as previously highlighted by the IACHR. This situation resulted in the deaths of 41 prisoners, some of whom were victims in the Miguel Castro Castro Prison case.

It is crucial to emphasize that an extensive review of case law reveals a significant challenge pervasive within the UN system, namely the scarcity of easily accessible information. It is concerning that the content of interim measures has not always been made available to the public. For example, there is no information available between the years 1991 and 1996 regarding potential requests for interim measures within the text of the Views themselves. Instead, their use is merely mentioned on the cover page. Similarly, a number of countries, including Nicaragua and Chile, have been the subject of requests for compliance with interim measures. However, as the content of these measures has not been published, it is not possible to discuss them. Consequently, the total number and types of interim measures implemented remain uncertain.

From the perspective of the impact of the measures adopted by the human rights bodies, it seems reasonable to posit that the information gathered by both the HRC and the IACHR in the 1990s will prove useful in assessing the petition currently under consideration by the IACHR. This indicates that the precautionary measures and the information provided by Peru and the petitioners at that time, along with the decision on the merits of the UN Human Rights Committee, could have an impact on the current inter-American process.

References

Alberto Pérez Jerez v El Salvador (Precautionary Measures) No 422–12 (1 October 2014).

Almeida de Quinteros and Others v Uruguay (21 July 1983) No 107/1981, CCPR/C/OP/2.

Altesor v Uruguay, 29 March 1982, No R.2/10, A/37/40.

Amnesty International, 'Peru: The "anti-terrorism" legislation and its effects – an unfinished business in the transition to democracy' (*Amnesty International*, 2003) <https://www.amnesty.org/en/wp-content/uploads/2021/06/amr460012003en.pdf>.

Amnesty International, 'Turkey: No security without human rights' (*Amnesty International*, 2021) <https://www.amnesty.org/en/wp-content/uploads/2021/06/eur440841996en.pdf>.

Arredondo v Peru (27 July 2000) CCPR/C/69/D/688/1996.

Barrios Altos v Peru (Merits) IACtHR Series C No 75 (14 March 2001) .

Burbano Herrera C, *Provisional Measures in the Case Law of the Inter-American Court of Human Rights* (Antwerp, Intersentia 2010).

Burbano Herrera C and Haeck Y, 'The Impact of Precautionary Measures on Persons Deprived of Liberty in the Americas' in Engstrom P (ed), *The Inter-American Human Rights System: Impact Beyond Compliance* (London, Palgrave Macmillan 2018) 89–113.

Burbano Herrera C and Haeck Y, 'Provisional Measures: Inter-American Court of Human Rights (IACtHR)' (*Max Planck Encyclopedias of International Law*, 2019) <https://opil.ouplaw.com/display/10.1093/law-mpeipro/e3524.013.3524/law-mpeipro-e3524>.

Burbano Herrera H and Haeck Y, 'The Historical and Present-Day Role of Non-Governmental Organisations before the Inter-American Human Rights System in Documenting Serious Human Rights Violations and Protecting Human Rights and the Rule of Law through Ensuring Accountability' (2021) 17 *Utrecht Law Review* 8–25.

Burbano Herrera C and Haeck Y, 'Medidas provisionales de la Corte Interamericana: algunas reflexiones' (2021) 23 *Aportes Revista De La Fundación Para El Debido Proceso* 31.

Burbano Herrera C and Haeck Y, *Human Rights Behind Bars: Tracing Vulnerability in Prison Populations Across Continents from a Multidisciplinary Perspective* (Cham, Springer Nature 2022) 1–10.

Burbano Herrera C, Haeck Y, and Cuppini A, 'Transformative Provisional Measures and Prisons in the Americas: Protecting the Invisibles' in Burbano Herrera C and Haeck Y (eds), *Human Rights Behind Bars: Tracing Vulnerability in Prison Populations Across Continents from a Multidisciplinary Perspective* (Cham, Springer Nature 2022) 141–172.

Burbano Herrera C, Haeck Y, and Hansen A, 'A Theoretical Model for Measuring the Impact of Urgent Measures that Protect at Risk Detainees' in Burbano Herrera C and Haeck Y (eds), *Impact(s) within the Human Rights Framework* (Edward Elgar 2025) (*forthcoming*).

Burbano Herrera C and Viljoen F, 'Danger and Fear in Prison' (2015) 33 Netherlands Quarterly of Human Rights 163.

Carranza Alegre v Peru (28 October 2005) CCPR/C/85/D/1126/2002.

Casafranca de Gómez v Peru (22 July 2003) CCPR/C/78/D/981/2001.

Castillo Petruzzi and Others v Peru (Merits) IACtHR Series C No 34 (3 November 1997).

C.J. v Jamaica (26 July 1988) A/43/40.

Cornell A and Roberts K, 'Democracy, Counterinsurgency, and Human Rights: the Case of Peru' (1990) 12 *Human Rights Quarterly* 529.

Darke S and Lúcia Karam M, 'Latin American prisons' in Jewkes Y and others (eds), *Handbook on Prisons* (New York, Routledge 2016).

Dávila v Colombia (6 April 2018) CCPR/C/122/D/2490/2014.

De Izcue CA, 'Peru's Shining Path and MRTA Analyzed with the Manwaring Paradigm' (2006) 12 *Low Intensity Conflict & Law Enforcement* 52.

de la Vega v Colombia (21 July 2020) CCPR/C/129/D/2930/2017.

Drescher Caldas v Uruguay (21 July 1983) No 43/1979, CCPR/C/OP/2.

Echeverri v Colombia (21 July 2020) CCPR/C/129/D/2931/2017.

El Comercio, 'Recaptura Polay Campos' *El Comercio* (Lima, 9 June 1992) <https://lum.cultura.pe/cdi/periodico/recaptura-polay-campos>.

Espinoza Gonzáles v Peru (Preliminary Objections, Merits, Reparations, and Costs) IACtHR Series C No 289 (20 November 2014).

Estradet Cabreira v Uruguay (21 July 1983) No 105/1981, CCPR/C/OP/2.

European Parliamentary Research Service, 'Democracy and human rights in Latin America' (*European Parliament*, 2022) <https://www.europarl.europa.eu/RegData/etudes/BRIE/2022/698868/EPRS_BRI(2022)698868_EN.pdf>.

Ghandhi S, 'The Human Rights Committee and Interim Measures of Relief' (2007) 13 *Canterbury Law Review* 203.

González F, 'Urgent Measures in the Inter-American Human Rights System' (2010) 13 *International Journal on Human Rights* 1.

Gonzalez-Bertomeu J, 'Prisons and Prisoners' Rights' in Gonzalez-Bertomeu J and Gargarella R (eds), *The Latin American Casebook: Courts, Constitutions, and Rights* (New York, Routledge 2016).

Gutiérrez Vivanco v Peru (26 March 2002) CCPR/C/74/D/678/1996.

Harrington J, 'The Legitimacy of Interim Measures from the Perspective of a State: the Example of Canada' in Rieter E and Zwaan K (eds), *Urgency and Human Rights* (The Hague, Asser Press 2021) 115–134.

Hennebel L, 'The Human Rights Committee' in Mégret F and Alston P (eds), *The United Nations and Human Rights: A Critical Appraisal* (Oxford, Oxford University Press 2020) 339–392.

Human Rights Committee, 'General Comment No. 20 on Article 7 (Prohibition of Torture, or Other Cruel, Inhuman or Degrading Treatment or Punishment' (10 March 1992).

Human Rights Committee, 'Promotion and protection of all human rights, civil, political, economic, social and cultural rights, including the right to development: including a joint study on global practices in relation into secret detention in the context of countering terrorism' (20 May 2010) A/HRC/13/42.

Human Rights Committee, 'Mandate of the Special Rapporteur on New Communications and Interim Measures' (22 May 2014) CCPR/C/110/3.

Human Rights Committee, 'General Comment No. 35 on Article 9 (Liberty and security of person)' (16 December 2014) CCPR/C/GC/35.

Human Rights Watch, 'Informe Anual Sobre La Situación De Los Derechos Humanos En EL Mundo 2000: Perú' (*HRW*, 2000) <https://www.hrw.org/legacy/spanish/inf_anual/2000/americas/peru.html>.

Human Rights Watch, 'World Report 2024: El Salvador' (*HRW*, 2024) <https://www.hrw.org/world-report/2024/country-chapters/el-salvador>.

Human Rights Watch, 'World Report 2024: Nicaragua' (*HRW*, 2024) <https://www.hrw.org/world-report/2024/country-chapters/nicaragua>.

Human Rights Watch, 'World Report 2024: Venezuela' (*HRW*, 2024) <https://www.hrw.org/world-report/2024/country-chapters/venezuela>.

International Covenant on Civil and Political Rights (adopted 16 December 1966, entered into force 23 March 1976) 999 UNTS 171.

J.A.N.C. v Colombia (24 July 2020) CCPR/C/129/D/2922/2016.

J. E. S. B. v Panama (17 March 1994) CCPR/C/50/D/443/1991.

Joseph S and others, *The International Covenant on Civil and Political Rights: Cases, Materials, and Commentary* (Oxford, Oxford University Press 2013).

Keller H and Marti C, 'Interim Relief Compared: Use of Interim Measures by the UN Human Rights Committee and the European Court of Human Rights' (2013) 73 Heidelberg Journal of International Law 325.

Klarén PF, *Peru, Society and Nationhood in the Andes* (New York, Oxford University Press 2000).

Kolb R, 'Note on New International Case-Law Concerning the Binding Character of Provisional Measures' (2005) 74 Nordic journal of international law 117–130.

Kovaleva and Kozyar v Belarus (29 October 2012) CCPR/C/106/D/2120/2011.

Lafuente Peñarrieta and Others v Bolivia (2 November 1987) No 176/1984, CCPR/C/OP/2.

Laureano Atachahua v Peru (25 March 1996) CCPR/C/56/D/540/1993.

Loayza Tamayo v Peru (Merits) IACtHR Series C No 33 (17 September 1997).

Lori Berenson Mejía v Peru (Merits, Reparations, and Costs) IACtHR Series C No 119 (25 November 2004).

Lutz EL and Sikkink K, 'International Human Rights Law and Practice in Latin America' (2000) 54 *Legalization and World Politics* 633.

Manwaring MG, 'Peru's Sendero Luminoso: The Shining Path Beckons' (1995) 541 *Annals of the American Academy of Political and Social Science* 157.

Marmolejo L and others, 'Responding to COVID-19 in Latin American Prisons: The Cases of Argentina, Chile, Colombia and Mexico' (2020) *Victims & Offenders* 1.

Mendoza and Others v Argentina (Provisional Measures) IACtHR Series C No 260 (14 May 2013).

Miguel Castro Castro Prison v Peru (Provisional Measures) IACtHR Series C No 160 (29 July 2020).

Mikhalenya and Mikhalenya v Belarus (21 July 2021) CCPR/C/132/D/3105/2018.

Milton C, *Art From a Fractured Past: Memory and Truth-Telling in Post-Shining Path Peru* (Durham, Duke University Press 2014).

Morales Antoniazzi M, 'The Rights of Persons Deprived of Liberty in Latin America: From the Perspective of an Ius Constitutionale Commune' in Burbano Herrera C and Haeck Y (eds), *Human Rights Behind Bars: Tracing Vulnerability in Prison Populations Across Continents from a Multidisciplinary Perspective* (Cham, Springer Nature 2022) 113–140.

Nifosi-Sutton I, *The Protection of Vulnerable Groups Under International Human Rights Law* (Abingdon, Taylor & Francis 2017.

OMCT, *Seeking Remedies for Torture Victims: A Handbook on the Individual Complaints Procedures of the UN Treaty Bodies* (Switzerland, World Organisation Against Torture 2014).

Patricio Cornejo Montecino v Chile (30 October 2008) CCPR/C/94/D/1504/2006.

Penal Castro Castro v Peru (Merits, Reparations, and Costs) IACtHR Series C No 155 (25 November 2006).

Penales Peruanos v Peru (Resolution of Urgent Measures) President of the IACtHR (14 December 1992) <https://www.corteidh.or.cr/docs/medidas/penales_se_01 .pdf>.

Penales Peruanos v Peru (Resolution of the Inter-American Court of Human Rights) Provisional Measures Requested by the Inter-American Commission on Human Rights Regarding Peru (27 January 1993) <https://www.corteidh.or.cr/docs/medidas/penales_se_02.pdf>.

Pietraroia v Uruguay (27 March 1981) No 44/1979, CCPR/C/OP/1.

Polay Campos v Peru (6 November 1997) CCPR/C/61/D/577/1994.

Polay Campos v Peru (10 March 2000) Report No 32/00 <https://cidh.oas.org/annualrep/99span/Inadmisible/Peru11048.htm>.

Polay Campos v Peru (20 March 2022) Report No 56/22 <https://www.oas.org/es/cidh/decisiones/2022/PEAD_1548-07_ES.PDF>.

Rieter E, *Preventing Irreparable Harm: Provisional Measures in International Human Rights Adjudication* (Antwerp, Intersentia 2010).

Roberts v Barbados (19 July 1994) CCPR/C/51/D/504/1992.

Rules of Procedure of the HRC (*OHCHR*, 4 January 2021) <https://tbinternet.ohchr.org/_layouts/15/treatybodyexternal/Download.aspx?symbolno=CCPR%2FC%2F3%2FRev.12&Lang=en>.

Ruiz Feases A, 'Sharpening the European Commission's tools: interim measures' (2020) 16 *European Competition Journal* 404.

Saidova v Tajikistan (8 July 2004) CCPR/C/81/D/964/2001.

Saleh and Carrero v Venezuela (Precautionary Measures) No 223–13 (2 March 2015).

Sanchez A, 'The Rebirth of Insurgency in Peru' (2003) 14 *Small Wars & Insurgencies* 185.

Sara and Others v Finland (23 March 1994) CCPR/C/50/D/431/1990.

Schemo DJ, 'A Born Revolutionary's Path to a Living 'Tomb' in Peru' *The New York Times* (New York, 4 January 1997) <https://www.nytimes.com/1997/01/04/world/a-born-revolutionary-s-path-to-a-living-tomb-in-peru.html>.

Setelich v Uruguay (28 October 1981) No 63/1979, CCPR/C/OP/1.

Soo Choi Y, 'The Peruvian Hostage Crisis: Brief Review of MRTA' (1997) 21 *International Journal of Comparative and Applied Criminal Justice* 33.

Spisso v Venezuela (17 March 2017) CCPR/C/119/D/2481/2014.

Steinert C, 'Who Is a Political Prisoner?' (2021) 6 *Journal of Global Security Studies.*

Subcommittee on Prevention of Torture and Other Cruel, Inhuman or Degrading Treatment or Punishment, 'General comment No. 1 (2024) on article 4 of the Optional Protocol (places of deprivation of liberty)' (4 July 2024) CAT/OP/GC/1.

Teferra ZM, 'Provisional Measures in International Human Rights Law: The Practice of the African Court on Human and Peoples' Rights' (2022) 6 *African Human Rights Yearbook* 28.

Trindade AC, 'The Evolution of provisional measures of protection under the case law of the Inter-American Court of Human Rights 1987–2002' (2003) 24 Human Rights Law Journal 162.

Tolipkhuzhaev v Uzbekistan (22 July 2009) CCPR/C/96/D/1280/2004.

UN General Assembly, 'Report of the Special Rapporteur on the question of torture and other cruel, inhuman or degrading treatment or punishment' (3 July 2001) A/56/156.

UN OHCHR, 'Reply to Questions Raised by Member States during the Interactive Dialogue at the 66th Session of the UN General Assembly' (*OHCHR*, 18 October 2011) <https://www.ohchr.org/sites/default/files/Documents/Issues/Torture/Reply_to_Questions_Raised_by_MStates_DialogueGA66.pdf>.

UN OHCHR, 'Immediate action needed to address conditions of detention in Latin America' (*OHCHR*, 22 February 2012) <https://www.ohchr.org/en/stories/2012/02/immediate-action-needed-address-conditions-detention-latin-america#:~:text=Citing%20a%20range%20of%20structural,in%20many%20prisons%20amount%20to>.

UN OHCHR, 'Informal guidance note by the secretariat for the States parties on procedures for the submission and consideration by treaty bodies of individual communications' (*OHCHR*, January 2017) <https://www.ohchr.org/sites/default/files/Documents/HRBodies/TB/NoteStatesParties.pdf>.

UN OHCHR, 'Guidance for Submitting an Individual Communication to the UN Treaty Bodies' (*OHCHR*, 2021) <https://www.ohchr.org/Documents/HRBodies/Gu

idance-note-for-complaints-form-E.docx#:~:text=The%20communication%20should%20be%20in,petitions%40ohchr.org>.

UN OHCHR, 'Non-discrimination: groups in vulnerable situations' (*OHCHR*, 2024) <https://www.ohchr.org/en/special-procedures/sr-health/non-discrimination-groups-vulnerable-situations>.

UN OCHCR, 'Status of Ratification Interactive Dashboard' (*OHCHR*, 2025) <https://indicators.ohchr.org/>.

van Alebeek R and Nollkaemper A, 'The Legal Status of Decisions by Human Rights Treaty Bodies in National Law' in Keller H and Ulfstein G (eds), *UN Human Rights Treaty Bodies: Law and Legitimacy* (Cambridge, Cambridge University Press 2012) 356–413.

Vandenhole W, *The Procedures Before the UN Human Rights Treaty Bodies: Divergence Or Convergence?* (Antwerpen, Intersentia 2004).

Van Baelen A and Burbano Herrera C, 'LGBTI Persons Deprived of Liberty: Over-represented, Extremely Vulnerable and De Jure Invisible' in Burbano Herrera C and Haeck Y (eds), *Human Rights Behind Bars: Tracing Vulnerability in Prison Populations Across Continents from a Multidisciplinary Perspective* (Cham, Springer Nature 2022) 173–202.

Vargas Más v Peru (26 October 2005) CCPR/C/85/D/1058/2002.

Weiss v Austria (24 October 2012) CCPR/C/106/D/1821/2008.

Young K, *The Law and Process of the UN Human Rights Committee* (Leiden, Brill 2021).

Zelaya Blanco v Nicaragua (20 July 1994) CCPR/C/51/D/328/1988.

PART 2

Prisons: Crisis and Structural Problems

CHAPTER 5

The COVID-19 Pandemic and Prison Policy in Latin America

María Luisa Romero and Soledad Sánchez Jeanney

1 Introduction

Beyond the public health emergency it unleashed, the COVID-19 pandemic exposed and exacerbated the vulnerabilities faced by the world's poorest and most marginalized people, including those deprived of liberty. In Latin America,[1] where penitentiary systems have suffered decades of abandonment and official neglect, the pandemic brought tragedy and unrest to prisons and posed unique challenges for governments, monitoring bodies, civil society, and international institutions. The pandemic also served both as a reminder and a warning that the region must prioritize human dignity and ensure that

1 In this chapter, by Latin America we refer to the 19 Spanish and Portuguese-speaking independent countries in the Americas. The Americas is composed of 35 independent states, 34 of which are members of the Organization of American States (Nicaragua is no longer a Member State as of November 2023). See: Organization of American States, 'Member States' (*OAS*, 1 January 2024) <https://www.oas.org/en/member_states/default.asp> accessed 12 April 2024; OAS Permanent Council Resolution CP/RES. 1234 (2466/23) (8 November 2023). The Latin America and Caribbean region, according to United Nations membership, is composed of 33 Member States, which are the 35 independent states of the Americas except for Canada and the United States. See: United Nations, 'Regional groups of Member States' (*UN Department for General Assembly and Conference Management*, 1 January 2024) https://www.un.org/dgacm/en/content/regional-groups accessed 12 April 2024. The Caribbean, according to CARICOM membership, is composed of 14 Member States that are independent States in the Americas, all of which speak languages other than Spanish or Portuguese. See: CARICOM, 'Member states and associate members' (*CARICOM*, 1 January 2024) <https://caricom.org/member-states-and-associate-members/> accessed 12 April 2024. The 19 Latin American countries are those leftover in the United Nations Latin America and Caribbean Region once the 14 CARICOM Member States that are independent States are excluded from the total of 33 States. Another way of seeing this is taking the 35 independent states in the Americas and excluding the 14 CARICOM independent States, Canada, and the United States. This means that Latin America, for the purposes of this chapter, is composed of the following 19 Spanish and Portuguese-speaking independent nations in the Americas: Argentina, Bolivia, Brazil, Chile, Colombia, Costa Rica, Cuba, Dominican Republic, Ecuador, El Salvador, Guatemala, Honduras, Mexico, Nicaragua, Panama, Paraguay, Peru, Uruguay and Venezuela.

© MARÍA LUISA ROMERO ET AL., 2026 | DOI:10.1163/9789004747739_006 persons deprived of liberty are not isolated and forgotten but are understood as inextricably linked to the well-being of society at large, not only from a security perspective but also from a health, social and moral one. In this sense, the pandemic presented a unique and historic opportunity for policymakers in Latin America to reassess and change course with respect to prisons and criminal justice, building on fragile but innovative policy experiments triggered by COVID-19. This chapter posits that the prison policies adopted by some countries in Latin America in response to the COVID-19 pandemic offer important lessons for governments and policymakers for much-needed prison reform in the region.

Since the beginning of the pandemic, international organizations and experts[2] highlighted the vulnerability of persons deprived of liberty around

---

2 See: António Guterres, 'We are all in this together: Human Rights COVID-19 Response and Recovery' (*United Nations*, 23 April 2020) <https://www.un.org/en/un-coronavirus-communications-team/we-are-all-together-human-rights-and-covid-19-response-and> accessed 12 April 2024; World Health Organization, 'UNODC, WHO, UNAIDS and OHCHR joint statement on COVID-19 in prisons and closed settings' (*WHO*, 13 May 2020) <https://www.who.int/news/item/13-05-2020-unodc-who-unaids-and-ohchr-joint-statement-on-covid-19-in-prisons-and-other-closed-settings/> accessed 12 April 2024; World Health Organization Regional Office for Europe, 'Preparedness, prevention, and control of COVID-19 in prisons and other places of detention: Interim Guidance' (*WHO Europe*, 15 March 2020) <https://www.who.int/europe/publications/i/item/WHO-EURO-2021-1405-41155-57257> accessed 12 April 2024; OHCHR and WHO, 'Interim Guidance – COVID-19: Focus on Persons Deprived of Their Liberty' (*Inter-Agency Standing Committee*, March 2020) <https://bangkok.ohchr.org/sites/default/files/documents/2024-07/final-iasc-interim-guidance-on-covid-19-focus-on-persons-deprived-of-their-liberty_0.pdf> accessed 12 April 2024; IACHR, 'IACHR concerned about specific risks faced by Persons Deprived of Liberty in the Americas during the COVID-19 pandemic' (*OAS*, 9 September 2020) <https://www.oas.org/en/iachr/media_center/PReleases/2020/212.asp> accessed 12 April 2024; IACHR, 'The IACHR urges States to guarantee the health and integrity of persons deprived of liberty and their families in the face of the COVID-19 pandemic' (*OAS*, 31 March 2020) <https://www.oas.org/en/iachr/media_center/PReleases/2020/066.asp> accessed 12 April 2024; IACHR, 'IACHR and OSRESCER Express Serious Concerns About the Human Rights Situation During the Response to the COVID-19 Pandemic in Nicaragua' (*OAS*, 8 April 2020) <https://www.oas.org/en/iachr/media_center/PReleases/2020/072.asp> accessed 12 April 2024; UN Subcommittee on Prevention of Torture and Other Cruel, Inhuman or Degrading Treatment or Punishment, 'Advice of the Subcommittee on Prevention of Torture to States Parties and National Preventive Mechanisms relating to the Coronavirus Pandemic' (25 March 2020) Working Paper CAT/OP/10 <https://tbinternet.ohchr.org/_layouts/15/treatybodyexternal/SessionDetails1.aspx?SessionID=2438&Lang=en> accessed 12 April 2024; IACtHR, 'COVID-19 y Derechos Humanos: Los problemas y desafíos deben ser abordados con perspectiva de derechos humanos y respetando las obligaciones internacionales' (*Corte IDH*, 9 April 2020) <https://www.corteidh.or.cr/tablas/alerta/comunicado/cp-27-2020.html> accessed 12 April 2024.

the world and made important recommendations to protect their health and human rights. These calls were particularly relevant in Latin America, where for decades local stakeholders and international watchdogs have called on governments to address the systemic weaknesses of the region's prison systems, often to no avail. However, the public health emergency led many governments in the region to implement a variety of policies to finally attempt to tackle some of these weaknesses. Perhaps most significantly, several Latin American countries attempted, through different methods, to directly address the long-standing problem of prison overcrowding. Yet, these efforts came late and faced significant challenges at the national level. The effectiveness of these measures in preventing COVID-19 transmission and related deaths is difficut to assess. At the same tine, they offer a glimmer of hope that governments in the region can and should take action to address the chronic problems prisons have historically faced.

This chapter is based on a policy paper with the same title published during the pandemic in 2021 by The Inter-American Dialogue[3] with recommendations for States and other relevant stakeholders. Based on the original paper, this chapter synthesizes, restructures and updates publicly available information, to adapt the content and adjust it to the objective of this book. While respecting the contextual and temporal framework of the original study, this review incorporates some new elements to enrich the analysis. It is important to clarify that the research is not based on a study of the region in exhaustive terms; rather, it uses the initiatives introduced in the analysis as illustrations of relevant regional responses.

The chapter's main objective is to reflect on the challenges and opportunities presented by the pandemic in the prison context to present takeaways and recommendations for States, individuals and organizations interested in pursuing prison reform in the region. The chapter begins by providing a brief overview of the challenges facing prisons in the region prior to COVID-19 and seeks to explain why the pandemic exacerbated these problems and deepened public health risks in the general population. It then outlines various policy measures implemented by several Latin American states during the first

3 The Inter-American Dialogue is a think tank in the field of international affairs headquartered in Washington D.C. It engages its network of global leaders to "foster democratic governance, prosperity and social equity in Latin America and the Caribbean" and works "to shape policy debate, devise solutions, and enhance cooperation with the Western Hemisphere". The Inter-American Dialogue, 'Our Mission' (*The Dialogue*, 1 January 2024) <https://thedialogue.org/> accessed 12 April 2024.

months of the COVID-19 pandemic in 2020, as well as some of the obstacles these policies faced.[4] The chapter concludes by sharing relevant takeaways with respect to the region's management of the COVID-19 pandemic in the context of Latin American prisons, to be taken into account as States construct more humane and secure prison systems.

2 Latin American Prisons and COVID-19, an Urgent New Challenge

2.1 *Background: Prisons in Latin America and Their Historical Challenges*

Prisons in Latin America are known for being overcrowded, unsanitary, chaotic, and violent, making the rehabilitation of persons deprived of liberty a tangible challenge.[5] International and local organizations have consistently documented these severe systemic weaknesses over the last several decades. For example, the Inter-American Commission on Human Rights (IACHR) has stressed the seriousness of prison overcrowding in the Americas for over 45 years.[6] The Inter-American Development Bank (IADB) highlighted in 2019 that the alarming growth of the prison population in Latin America and the Caribbean over the past 20 years "has collapsed the prison systems and is putting at risk the main objective of prisons: social reintegration of inmates".[7] With the COVID-19 pandemic, the pre-existing conditions that were already deemed to violate the human rights of people deprived of liberty in the region exacerbated inmates' vulnerability.

---

4 Unless otherwise noted, the information included spans the time period of March-July 2020.

5 For a recent summary on the general situation of prisons in Latin America and the Caribbean, see: Inter-American Development Bank, 'Dentro de las Prisiones de América Latina y el Caribe: una primera mirada al otro lado de las rejas' (*IDB*, September 2019) <https://publications.iadb.org/es/dentro-de-las-prisiones-de-america-latina-y-el-caribe-una-primera-mirada-al-otro-lado-de-las-rejas> accessed 12 April 2024. The Inter-American Development Bank has 26 borrowing member countries in Latin America and the Caribbean, which are the countries it refers to in its studies discussed in this chapter. The only Latin American country not included in those 26 countries is Cuba. See: Inter-American Development Bank, 'Borrowing member countries' (*IDB*, 1 January 2024) <https://www.iadb.org/en/who-we-are/how-we-are-organized/borrowing-member-countries> accessed 12 April 2024.

6 IACHR, '*Report on the Human Rights of Persons Deprived of Liberty in the Americas*' (*IACHR*, 31 December 2011) <https://www.oas.org/en/iachr/pdl/docs/pdf/PPL2011eng.pdf> para 157.

7 Inter-American Development Bank, 'Dentro de las Prisiones de América Latina y el Caribe' (n 5) 6 (Translation is ours).

In recent years, according to the IADB in 2019, Latin America and the Caribbean experienced a 120 percent growth in its prison population, compared to 24 percent worldwide.[8] South America led the trend in the region as of 2020, with a 175 percent increase.[9] The incarceration rate of women in the last decade in Latin America and the Caribbean also grew by 52 percent.[10] On average, in 2020, prisons in the region were operating at 144.2 percent capacity.[11] According to the IACHR, in many countries in the Americas the overcrowding problem is extreme, with over-capacity levels reaching more than 300 percent.[12] An IADB study released during COVID-19 found that around 58 percent of prisoners in Latin America and the Caribbean do not sleep in beds, a fact that illustrates the severity of this issue.[13]

The IACHR has noted that prison overcrowding is the foreseeable consequence of the following factors: a lack of adequate infrastructure, the implementation of repressive social control policies that resort to the deprivation of liberty as the first response to public security, the excessive use of pre-trial detention and deprivation of liberty as a criminal sanction, and the lack of a quick and efficient response by the court systems.[14] Regarding pre-trial detention, the World Prison Brief[15] reported in 2020 that its use increased in the

---

8 ibid 6.

9 Roy Walmsley, '*World Prison Population List* (*12th edition*)' (World Prison Brief, 6 November 2020) 2 <https://www.prisonstudies.org/sites/default/files/resources/downloads/wppl_12.pdf> accessed 12 April 2014.

10 Inter-American Development Bank, 'Dentro de las Prisiones de América Latina y el Caribe' (n 5) 13.

11 IACHR, 'IACHR concerned about specific risks faced by Persons Deprived of Liberty in the Americas during the COVID-19 pandemic' (*OAS*, 9 September 2020) <https://www.oas.org/en/iachr/media_center/PReleases/2020/212.asp> accessed 12 April 2024.

12 IACHR, 'The IACHR urges States to guarantee the health and integrity of persons deprived of liberty and their families in the face of the COVID-19 pandemic' (n 2).

13 Nathalie Alvarado and others, 'Las cárceles de América Latina y el Caribe ante la crisis sanitaria del COVID-19' 5 (*Inter-American Development Bank*, August 2020) <https://publications.iadb.org/publications/spanish/document/Las-carceles-de-America-Latina-y-el-Caribe-ante-la-crisis-sanitaria-del-COVID-19.pdf> accessed 12 April 2024.

14 IACHR, 'Report on the Human Rights of Persons Deprived of Liberty in the Americas' (n 6) para 451.

15 Unless otherwise noted, this chapter utilizes data from the World Prison Brief for its information on prison populations in different countries. The World Prison Brief is an online database that provides free access to information on prison systems around the world. It is hosted by the Institute for Crime & Justice Policy Research and Birkbeck College, University of London. According to its website, country information is updated monthly, using data largely derived from governmental or other official sources. The database also has 'highest to lowest' country lists, enabling country-by-country and regional comparisons to be made of prison population rates and totals, occupancy

Americas by 71 percent from 2000 to 2020, "with numbers more than trebling in Brazil, Paraguay and Venezuela and doubling in Argentina, Bolivia, Ecuador, El Salvador, Guatemala, Haiti, Nicaragua and Peru".[16] In Honduras, the Dominican Republic, Bolivia and Venezuela, more than half of the total prison population has not been sentenced.[17] In Paraguay, prisoners without a sentence constituted more than 70 percent of the prison population as of 2020.[18] The IACHR has singled out the use of pre-trial detention as one of the most serious and widespread problems affecting the human rights of persons deprived of liberty in the Americas.[19]

In addition to the inherent, practical problems that arise from overcrowding, prisons in the region suffer from widespread unsanitary conditions, including inadequate access to healthcare, hygienic services, drinking water and food. According to the United Nations Standard Minimum Rules for the Treatment of Prisoners (Nelson Mandela Rules), States owe a duty of care to prisoners that should be equivalent to the standards of health care that are available in the community.[20] However, the precariousness and lack of resources within prisons directly affect healthcare access and the quality of care that persons deprived of liberty receive. The IACHR has noted that the medical services provided in the region's prisons generally "do not meet minimum standards of care" and has highlighted several deficiencies such as insufficient and untrained medical personnel, as well as inadequate medicine, medical supplies and equipment.[21] The IACHR has also observed that food is

---

rates, and proportions of pre-trial/remand prisoners, female prisoners and foreign prisoners. Institute for Crime & Justice Policy Research and Birkbeck College, 'Welcome' (*World Prison Brief*, 2024) <https://www.prisonstudies.org/> accessed 12 April 2024.

16 Roy Walmsley, '*World Pre-trial/Remand Imprisonment List (4th edition)*' 2 (*World Prison Brief*, 4 February 2020) <https://www.prisonstudies.org/sites/default/files/resources/downloads/world_pre-trial_list_4th_edn_final.pdf> accessed 12 April 2014. This list clarifies that the data cited is provided "since about 2000".

17 ibid 6–8.

18 ibid 7.

19 IACHR, 'IACHR presents Report on Measures Aimed at Reducing the Use of Pretrial Detention' (*OAS*, 7 September 2017) <https://www.oas.org/en/iachr/media_center/PReleases/2017/136.asp> accessed 12 April 2024.

20 UN Office on Drugs and Crime (UNODC), 'The United Nations Standard Minimum rules for the treatment of prisoners (the Nelson Mandela Rules)' (17 December 2015) UN Resolution 70/175, Rule 24(1), 10. See also: UN Subcommittee on Prevention of Torture and Other Cruel, Inhuman or Degrading Treatment or Punishment, 'Advice of the Subcommittee on Prevention of Torture to States Parties and National Preventive Mechanisms relating to the Coronavirus Pandemic' (n 2) para 8.

21 IACHR, 'Report on the Human Rights of Persons Deprived of Liberty in the Americas' (n 6) paras 536–537.

not provided in appropriate conditions of quantity, quality and hygiene.[22] In a similar line, an IADB study released in 2020 during the pandemic revealed that 29 percent of the prison population in Latin America and the Caribbean does not receive medical care, 20 percent of prisoners do not have regular access to drinking water and only 37 percent have access to soap.[23]

Persons deprived of liberty, in part because so many come from socially disadvantaged segments of the community, are more susceptible to both communicable and noncommunicable diseases compared with people in the general population.[24] According to the World Health Organization (WHO), persons deprived of liberty "frequently face greater exposure to risks such as smoking, poor hygiene and weak immune defence due to stress, poor nutrition, or prevalence of coexisting diseases, such as bloodborne viruses, tuberculosis and drug use disorders".[25] Additionally, infectious diseases are more prevalent within correctional facilities.[26] For example, the IADB notes that tuberculosis in prisons in Latin America and the Caribbean is 81 times more prevalent than in the general population and that results are similar when analysing the incidence of HIV, hepatitis and syphilis.[27]

2.2 *COVID-19: An Urgent New Challenge for Latin American Prisons*

At the beginning of the COVID-19 pandemic, the two primary prevention measures recommended for the general population were handwashing and social distancing, which represented a challenge in the context of the endemic overcrowding and unsanitary conditions suffered by most Latin American

22 ibid para 476. For example, on a visit to a prison in El Salvador, the Rapporteur on the Rights of Persons Deprived of Liberty observed that the nutritional content and quality of the food were insufficient, almost entirely lacking in protein. Additionally, on a visit to a prison in the province of Buenos Aires, the Rapporteur found that prisoners in solitary confinement often lived without running water and had to eat with their hands.

23 Alvarado and others, 'Las cárceles de América Latina y el Caribe ante la crisis sanitaria del COVID-19' (n 13) 5.

24 See: UN Office on Drugs and Crime (UNODC) and WHO Regional Office for Europe, 'Good governance for prison health in the 21st century: A policy brief on the organization of prison health' vii (*UNODC*, 2013) <https://www.unodc.org/documents/hiv-aids/publications/Prisons_and_other_closed_settings/Good-governance-for-prison-health-in-the-21st-century.pdf> accessed 12 April 2024.

25 WHO Regional Office for Europe, 'Preparedness, prevention, and control of COVID-19 in prisons and other places of detention (n 2) 2.

26 Alvarado and others, 'Las cárceles de América Latina y el Caribe ante la crisis sanitaria del COVID-19' (n 13) 5.

27 Ibid. The IADB also notes, for example, that in Brazil, numbers for HIV inside prisons are 138 higher than for the general population.

prisons. As mentioned above, water is scarce in many prisons in Latin America and the Caribbean.[28] Basic hygiene products such as alcohol and hand sanitizer have been historically banned from prisons for security reasons.[29] In addition, prisons suffer from generally closed and poorly ventilated spaces that make them fertile ground for outbreaks of infection. Inadequate infrastructure[30] and lack of space due to institutions operating beyond their capacity add other complications that make isolation of the sick very difficult. It is therefore no surprise that viral epidemics have historically represented a threat in prison settings.[31]

Adding to these challenges, people deprived of liberty with COVID-19 symptoms may have avoided seeking medical attention for fear of being placed in isolation, as solitary confinement is usually a form of punishment in prisons.[32] Moreover, according to the IADB, in 2020 around 90,000 persons deprived of liberty in Latin America and the Caribbean were over the age of 65, constituting the most vulnerable age group for contracting the virus.[33] Older people in prisons also tend to suffer more frequently from chronic health conditions, like hypertension, asthma and diabetes, which increased the risk of serious complications from contracting COVID-19.[34]

Prisons during the COVID-19 pandemic also represented a public health risk beyond their walls. Physical and mental illness inside prisons can become a

28 Ibid.

29 See: Rita Rubin, 'The Challenge of Preventing COVID-19 Spread in Correctional Facilities' (2020) 323 JAMA 1760, doi:10.1001/jama.2020.5427; Michael Klein and others, 'The New Coronavirus and Enforcement of the New Separate System in Prisons' (2021) 33 Criminal Justice Policy Review 206, doi.org/10.1177/08874034211023572.

30 See, for example: IACHR, 'Report on the Human Rights of Persons Deprived of Liberty in the Americas' (n 6) para 468.

31 An article published in the JAMA Internal Medicine journal about COVID-19 in prisons and jails in the United States describes a Spanish influenza outbreak in San Quentin prison in California as follows: "Prior viral epidemics have wrought havoc in carceral settings. An account from San Quentin prison detailing the Spanish influenza of 1918 estimated that half of the 1900 prisoners contracted the disease during the first wave of the epidemic; sick calls increased from 150 to 700 daily." Laura Hawks and others, 'COVID-19 in Prisons and Jails in the United States' (2020) 180 JAMA Intern Med 1041, https://jamanetwork.com/journals/jamainternalmedicine/fullarticle/2765271.

32 See: Talha Burki, '*Prisons are 'in no way equipped' to deal with COVID-19*' (2020) 395 The Lancet 1411, doi.org/10.1016/S0140–6736(20)30984–3.

33 Alvarado and others, 'Las cárceles de América Latina y el Caribe ante la crisis sanitaria del COVID-19' (n 13) 5.

34 Equal Justice Initiative, 'Covid-19's Impact on People in Prison' (*EJI*, 21 August 2020) <https://eji.org/news/covid-19s-impact-on-people-in-prison/> accessed 12 April 2014.

burden on the public health-care system. Prisons are also subject to a constant flow of people. Even when family visits and prisoners' temporary day or night releases are suspended, prison officers and other staff are constantly oscillating between prisons and their communities,[35] which may pose significant health risks for the wider community. As stated by the WHO at the beginning of the pandemic, rapid transmission within prisons could have an amplifying effect, affecting countries' ability to control COVID-19 infection in the general population if strong prevention and control measures, adequate testing, treatment and care were not implemented in prisons and other places of detention.[36]

2.3 *Initial Impact of COVID-19 in Prisons in Latin America*

Assessing COVID-19's impact in Latin American prisons falls beyond the purview of this chapter. As will be developed below, this chapter recommends further study and assessment of COVID-19's impact in prisons in the region as well as more transparency from Latin American States regarding both the impact of the pandemic on the prison population and of the measures they implemented. However, a brief overview of reported cases, deaths and unrest can help illustrate the challenges faced by prison systems during the pandemic.

As the IACHR pointed out in 2020, there was a "failure to gather and report accurate data concerning the impact of the COVID-19 pandemic in the various prison systems".[37] Countries also varied in their degree and frequency of testing in prisons.[38] In September 2020, the IACHR reported that, by mid-August 2020, an estimated 138,522 prisoners had tested positive for COVID-19 and at least 1,504 had died of complications linked to the virus in the Americas.[39] However, the IACHR also warned that "actual figures could be significantly higher," given the lack of precise data.[40]

---

35 UNODC and WHO Regional Office for Europe, 'Good governance for prison health in the 21st century' (n 24) 3.

36 WHO Regional Office for Europe, 'Preparedness, prevention, and control of COVID-19 in prisons and other places of detention' (n 2) 1.

37 IACHR, 'IACHR concerned about specific risks faced by Persons Deprived of Liberty in the Americas during the COVID-19 pandemic' (*OAS*, 9 September 2020) <https://www.oas.org/en/iachr/media_center/PReleases/2020/212.asp> accessed 12 April 2024.

38 Ibid. The IACHR observed, for example, that in Brazil, only 64,536 persons deprived of liberty (less than 0,4 percent of the total prison population) had been tested for the virus by 3 September 2020 and that in Honduras, the State reported that only around 21 percent of the country prison population had been tested.

39 ibid.

40 ibid.

Alongside health challenges, since the early stages of COVID-19, violent uprisings related to the pandemic erupted in prisons across several Latin American States. The IACHR reported that riots broke out in protest against overcrowding, inadequate hygiene and the shortage of personal protective equipment to prevent COVID-19 transmission.[41] Prisons in Brazil, Venezuela, El Salvador, Colombia, Peru and Argentina witnessed riots and uprisings,[42] some resulting in large-scale escapes and violent confrontations with law enforcement, leading to hundreds of wounded and dozens of deaths.[43]

---

41 See: IACHR, 'The IACHR urges States to guarantee the health and integrity of persons deprived of liberty and their families in the face of the COVID-19 pandemic' (n 2).

42 For example: in March of 2020, riots and uprisings were recorded in the state of São Paulo in Brazil; in Zulia, Venezuela; in the San Roque prison in El Salvador; in La Modelo prison in the city of Bogotá, Colombia; in Trujillo, Perú; and in several prisons of Santa Fe, Argentina. See: Radio France Internationale, 'Brésil: évasions en masse de détenus suite aux mesures anti-coronavirus' *RFI* (Paris, 17 March 2020) <https://www.rfi.fr/fr/am%C3%A9riques/20200317-br%C3%A9sil-evasion-prison-semi-liberte-sao-paulo-corona virus-covid19> accessed 12 April 2024; Correo Del Sur, 'En vivo: Motín en la cárcel San Roque' *Correo Del Sur* (Sucre, 19 June 2020) <https://correodelsur.com/seguridad/20200619_en-vivo-motin-en-la-carcel-san-roque.html> accessed 12 April 2024; Redacción Judicial, 'Autoridades confirman 23 muertos tras motín en la cárcel La Modelo' *El Espectador* (Bogotá, 22 March 2020) <https://www.elespectador.com/judicial/autori dades-confirman-23-muertos-tras-motin-en-la-carcel-la-modelo-article-910653/> accessed 12 April 2024; IACHR, 'The IACHR urges States to guarantee the health and integrity of persons deprived of liberty and their families in the face of the COVID-19 pandemic' (n 2); Infobae, 'Motines en Santa fe: confirmaron cinco muertos por los incidentes en los penales de Coronda y Las Flores' (*Infobae*, 24 March 2020) <https://www.infobae.com/sociedad/policiales/2020/03/24/motines-en-carceles-confirmaron-que-son-tres-los-mue rtos-en-los-penales-de-corona-y-las-flores/> accessed 12 April 2024; *France24*, 'Al menos 17 muertos y nueve heridos deja motín en cárcel de Venezuela' *France24* (Caracas, 2 May 2020) <https://www.france24.com/es/20200502-al-menos-17-muertos-y-nueve -heridos-deja-mot%C3%ADn-en-c%C3%A1rcel-de-venezuela> accessed 12 April 2024.

43 In São Paulo, around 1,000 prisoners escaped following riots in several prisons, and in Venezuela, at least 84. Brazilian troops were deployed for the recapture, leading to violent confrontations; in Venezuela, reportedly ten prisoners were killed in the recapture efforts. In addition, in Trujillo, Peru, prisoners mutinied, resulting in 31 inmates injured. In Santa Fe, Argentina riots resulted in five prisoners being killed as well as another dozen wounded. In Los Llanos prison, in Venezuela, the confrontation reportedly resulted in 47 deaths and 75 persons wounded, including the director of the prison, who was stabbed in the back. See: Radio France Internationale, 'Brésil: évasions en masse de détenus suite aux mesures anti-coronavirus' *RFI* (Paris, 17 March 2020) <https://www. >rfi.fr/fr/am%C3%A9riques/20200317-br%C3%A9sil-evasion-prison-semi-liberte-sao -paulo-coronavirus-covid19> accessed 12 April 2024; AKE International, 'Latin America: Prison riots increase as COVID-19 spreads' (*AKEGroup*, 29 April 2020) <https://akegroup.com/2020/04/29/latin-america-prison-riots-increase-as-covid-19-spreads/> accessed 12 April 2024; IACHR, 'The IACHR urges States to guarantee the health and integrity of

Many Latin American prisons have historically experienced high levels of violence, making the riots, escapes, injuries, and deaths related to COVID-19 tragically unsurprising, though still deeply concerning. Moreover, there are numerous instances in Latin America of prisoners gaining control over internal prison security and management, including prisoners involved in organized crime, as has been noted by the IACHR and the United Nations Subcommittee on Prevention of Torture in countries such as Bolivia, Brazil, Guatemala, Colombia, Mexico, Honduras, Panama, Paraguay and more recently, Ecuador.[44] Some have argued that the pandemic increased the risk of "criminal

---

persons deprived of liberty and their families in the face of the COVID-19 pandemic' (n 2); Jorge Luis Pérez Valery, 'Se fugan 84 presos de cárcel en Venezuela; operación de recaptura deja al menos 10 fallecidos, dicen autoridades' *CNN Español* (Caracas, 19 March >2020) <https://cnnespanol.cnn.com/2020/03/19/alerta-10-abatidos-en-zulia-venezuela-tras-fuga-de-84-presos-informaron-autoridades>/> accessed 12 April 2024; Infobae, 'Motines en Santa fe: confirmaron cinco muertos por los incidentes en los penales de Coronda y Las Flores' (*Infobae*, 24 March 2020) <https://www.infobae.com/sociedad/policiales/2020/03/24/motines-en-carceles-confirmaron-que-son-tres-los-muertos-en-los-penales-de-corona-y-las-flores>/ accessed 12 April 2024; Tamara Taraciuk Broner, 'Decenas de muertos y heridos durante motín carcelario en Venezuela' (*Human Rights Watch*, 4 May 2020) <https://www.hrw.org/es/news/2020/05/04/decenas-de-muertos-y-heridos-durante-motin-carcelario-en-venezuela> accessed 12 April 2024; Observatorio Venezolano de Prisiones, '47 muertos y 75 heridos es la cifra extraoficial de víctimas por un motín en Cepella' (*Oveprisiones*, 2 May 2020) <https://oveprisiones.com/47-muertos-y-75-heridos-es-la-cifra-extraoficial-de-victimas-por-un-motin-en-cepella/> accessed 12 April >2024.

44 See, for example: IACHR, 'Report on the Human Rights of Persons Deprived of Liberty in the Americas' (n 6) paras 80–97; IACHR, 'Personas Privadas de Libertad en Ecuador' (*OAS*, 21 February 2022) <https://www.oas.org/es/cidh/informes/pdfs/Informe-PPL-Ecuador_VF.pdf> *accessed 12 April 2024*; UN Subcommittee on Prevention of Torture and Other Cruel, Inhuman or Degrading Treatment or Punishment, 'Visit to Mexico undertaken from 12 to 21 December 2016: observations and recommendations addressed to the State party' (20 September 2018) CAT/OP/MEX/2, para 84 <https://tbinternet.ohchr.org/_layouts/15/treatybodyexternal/Download.aspx?symbolno=CAT%2FOP%2FMEX%2F2&Lang=en>; UN Subcommittee on Prevention of Torture, 'Report on the visit of the Subcommittee on Prevention of Torture and other Cruel, Inhuman or Degrading Treatment of Punishment to Mexico' (31 May 2010) CAT/OP/MEX/1, paras 167 and 288 <https://tbinternet.ohchr.org/_layouts/15/treatybodyexternal/Download.aspx?symbolno=CAT%2FOP%2FMEX%2F1&Lang=en>; UN Subcommittee on Prevention of Torture, 'Visit to Brazil undertaken from 19 to 30 October 2015: observations and recommendations addressed to the State party' (16 February 2016) CAT/OP/BRA/3, para 42 <https://tbinternet.ohchr.org/_layouts/15/treatybodyexternal/Download.aspx?symbolno=CAT%2FOP%2FBRA%2F3&Lang=en>; UN Subcommittee on Prevention of Torture, 'Visit to the Plurinational State of Bolivia undertaken from 2 to 11 May 2017: observations and recommendations addressed to the State party' (24 July 2018) CAT/OP/BOL/3, para 39 <https://tbinternet.ohchr.org/_layouts/15/treatybodyexternal/Download.aspx?sym

opportunism",[45] as criminal organizations attempted to leverage the pandemic for concessions from prison authorities. Still, the fact remains that prisons in the region were put under heightened pressure and tension due to fear, uncertainty, and poor communication between authorities and those detained.[46] The combination of isolation in inhumane conditions, regular violations of fundamental human rights and the threat posed by the pandemic "[were] a dangerous recipe for acts of aggression and violent prison uprisings".[47]

3 COVID-19 and the Prison Policy Response in Latin America

Even before the COVID-19 pandemic, the unsanitary, underfunded and overcrowded prison systems for which Latin America is notorious, lacked the capacity, or the will—to implement even some of the most basic health prevention measures. However, since it became clear that the COVID-19 pandemic would not discriminate across borders or prison walls and given the ample and consistent advice from international organizations, authorities in different Latin American countries were forced to mobilize, albeit to different

bolno=CAT%2FOP%2FBOL%2F3&Lang=en>; UN Subcommittee on Prevention of Torture, 'Visit to Panama undertaken from 20 to 26 August 2017: observations and recommendations addressed to the State party' (31 July 2018) CAT/OP/PAN/1, para 71 <https://tbinternet.ohchr.org/_layouts/15/treatybodyexternal/Download.aspx?symbolno=CAT%2FOP%2FPAN%2F1&Lang=en>; UN Human Rights Office of the High Commissioner, 'Ecuador: UN torture prevention body remains seriously concerned by prison crisis after second visit' (*OHCHR*, 6 October 2022) <https://www.ohchr.org/en/press-releases/2022/10/ecuador-un-torture-prevention-body-remains-seriously-concerned-prison-crisis> accessed 12 April 2024.

45 See: AKE International, 'Latin America: Prison riots increase as COVID-19 spreads' (n 43). The argument presented in this paper regarding "criminal opportunism" is that "[i]n all too many countries, of which Brazil, El Salvador and Mexico are clear-cut examples, criminal organizations operate from within prisons with outside support. COVID-19 could embolden these groups to increase their demands to the state by threatening widespread riots, and they can gain leverage from inmates should the state be seen as reluctant to address what can be portrayed as a humanitarian request.".

46 See: Patricio Domínguez and Pedro Rodriguez Martinez, 'Pandemic and Prisons: What Are the Challenges for Latin American Governments?' (*Inter-American Development Bank*, 22 April 2020) <https://blogs.iadb.org/ideas-matter/en/pandemic-and-prisons-what-are-the-challenges-for-latin-american-governments/> accessed 12 April 2024.

47 See Yulia Vorobyeva and others, 'Can the Northern Triangle Contain a Prison Pandemic?' (*The Latin American Advisor*, 30 June 2020) <https://www.thedialogue.org/analysis/can-the-northern-triangle-contain-a-prison-pandemic/> accessed 12 April 2024 .

degrees and speeds, to try to avoid a foreseeable health and humanitarian disaster in their nations' prisons.

3.1 *Recommendations of International Human Rights Bodies*

In the midst of this critical situation, international bodies and experts gave prison authorities around the globe ample and detailed guidelines that reflected the general consensus on health, sanitary and other policy measures that needed to be prioritized.[48] In addition to the frontline sanitary measures, as well as the importance of providing accurate and complete information to people deprived of liberty and alternatives to guarantee their right to communication, the recommendations all emphasized the reduction of prison overcrowding.

Michelle Bachelet, then United Nations High Commissioner for Human Rights, called for urgent action in March 2020 to prevent COVID-19 "rampaging through places of detention", emphasizing the need to reduce the number of people in prison.[49] The UN's Subcommittee on Prevention of Tor-

48 See: WHO Regional Office for Europe, 'Preparedness, prevention, and control of COVID-19 in prisons and other places of detention' (n 2); OHCHR, 'Urgent action needed to prevent COVID-19 rampaging through places of detention – Bachelet' (*OHCHR*, 25 March 2020) <https://www.ohchr.org/en/statements/2020/03/urgent-action-needed-prevent-covid-19-rampaging-through-places-detention> accessed 12 April 2024; UN Subcommittee on Prevention of Torture and Other Cruel, Inhuman or Degrading Treatment or Punishment, 'Advice of the Subcommittee on Prevention of Torture to States Parties and National Preventive Mechanisms relating to the Coronavirus Pandemic' (n 2); OHCHR and WHO, 'Interim Guidance – COVID-19: Focus on Persons Deprived of Their Liberty' (n 2); IACHR, 'The IACHR urges States to guarantee the health and integrity of persons deprived of liberty and their families in the face of the COVID-19 pandemic' (n 2); IACtHR, 'COVID-19 y Derechos Humanos: Los problemas y desafíos deben ser abordados con perspectiva de derechos humanos y respetando las obligaciones internacionales' (*Corte IDH*, 9 April 2020) <https://www.corteidh.or.cr/tablas/alerta/comunicado/cp-27-2020.html> accessed 12 April 2024; Office of the United Nations High Commissioner for Human Rights – Regional Office for South America, 'COVID-19: Argumentos que justifican medidas para reducir la población privada de libertad' (*OHCHR's South America Regional Office*, April 2020) <https://www.pj.gov.py/descargas/ID2-701_covid_y_medidas_reduccion_personas_privadas_de_libertad_argumentos_y_estandares_internacionales_final_1.pdf> accessed 1 March 2021; World Health Organization, 'UNODC, WHO, UNAIDS and OHCHR joint statement on COVID-19 in prisons and closed settings' (*WHO*, 13 May 2020) <https://www.who.int/news/item/13-05-2020-unodc-who-unaids-and-ohchr-joint-statement-on-covid-19-in-prisons-and-other-closed-settings/> accessed 12 April 2024.

49 OHCHR, 'Urgent action needed to prevent COVID-19 rampaging through places of detention – Bachelet' (n 48).

ture and Other Cruel, Inhuman or Degrading Treatment or Punishment (SPT) also recommended taking measures to reduce prison populations "by implementing schemes of early, provisional or temporary release for those detainees for whom it is safe to do so".[50] The WHO pointed to the need for the "limitation of persons in pre-trial detention and implementation of non-custodial measures" to reduce the risk of spreading the virus in prisons.[51] The IACHR urged States in the Americas to reduce overcrowding as a necessary measure to contain the pandemic and the Inter-American Court of Human Rights emphasized the need for rational and orderly alternative measures to the deprivation of liberty.[52] The recommendations made it clear that States needed to implement strict health and control measures just as they would for the general population, but that in the context of prisons, these would likely be insufficient at best because of overcrowding and the other systemic challenges already mentioned above. To prevent potentially catastrophic consequences in prisons—and beyond—, States would have to take measures, some very basic, others more difficult, that were long overdue.

3.2 *Policy Responses to Address Critical Sanitation Deficiencies*

National authorities and prison systems in the region had to respond to the pandemic first and foremost by addressing obvious and critical long-standing sanitation deficiencies that had been structurally overlooked. Countries issued protocols and guidelines for the prevention and management of COVID-19, emphasizing measures to improve basic hygiene.[53] For example,

50 UN Subcommittee on Prevention of Torture and Other Cruel, Inhuman or Degrading Treatment or Punishment, 'Advice of the Subcommittee on Prevention of Torture to States Parties and National Preventive Mechanisms relating to the Coronavirus Pandemic' (n 2) para 9, points 2 and 3.

51 OHCHR and WHO, 'Interim Guidance – COVID-19: Focus on Persons Deprived of Their Liberty' (n 2) 3. See also: WHO, 'UNODC, WHO, UNAIDS and OHCHR joint statement on COVID-19 in prisons and closed settings' (n 48).

52 IACHR, 'The IACHR urges States to guarantee the health and integrity of persons deprived of liberty and their families in the face of the COVID-19 pandemic' (n 2); IACtHR, 'COVID-19 y Derechos Humanos: Los problemas y desafíos deben ser abordados con perspectiva de derechos humanos y respetando las obligaciones internacionales' (*OAS*, 9 April 2020) <https://www.corteidh.or.cr/tablas/alerta/comunicado/cp-27-2020.html> accessed 12 April 2024.

53 See, for example: Servicio Penitenciario Federal, 'Guía de actuación para la prevención y control del COVID-19 en el Servicio Penitenciario Federal' (25 March 2020) 11 <https://www.fiscales.gob.ar/wp-content/uploads/2020/03/Anexo-582020.pdf.pdf.pdf>; Gendarmería de Chile, 'Medidas con que Gendarmería enfrenta al coronavirus' <https://html.gendarmeria.gob.cl/doc/medidas.pdf> accessed 12 April 2024; Ministerio de Salud y Protección Social Bogotá, 'Lineamientos para control, prevención y manejo de casos

in Honduras, Colombia and Mexico, state health and security agencies established guidelines on cleaning and disinfection,[54] promoted education on hygiene[55] and planned dissemination campaigns to encourage prevention and healthy measures.[56] Some countries also attempted to address chronic sanitary deficiencies in prisons by increasing access to critical health needs

---

por COVID-19 para la población privada de la libertad-PPL en Colombia' (*Minsalud*, April 2020) <https://www.fiduprevisora.com.co/wp-content/uploads/2021/02/LINEAMIENTOS-PARA-CONTROL-PREVENCI%C3%93N-PPL.pdfhttps://www.minsalud.gov.co/Ministerio/Institucional/Procesos%20y%20procedimientos/GIPS10.pdf> accessed 12 April 2024; Ministerio de Gobernación Dirección General del Sistema Penitenciario, 'Se activan protocolos preventivos contra el Coronavirus' (*Gobierno de Guatemala*, 20 March 2020) <https://dgsp.gob.gt/se-activan-protocolos-preventivos-contra-el-coronaviru/> accessed 12 April 2024; Secretaría de Salud, 'Lineamientos para la prevención y manejo de COVID-19 en población privada de libertad' (*Gobierno de la República de Honduras*, 16 March 2020) <http://www.dgvmn.gob.hn/documents/COVID19/Lineamientos%20manejo%20ppl%20covid19.pdf> accessed 1 March 2021 (link is currently unavailable); Secretaría de Seguridad y Protección Ciudadana and others, 'Protocolo de actuación para la atención de COVID-19 al interior de centros federales de reinserción social (CEFERESOS)' (March 2020) <https://coronavirus.gob.mx/wp-content/uploads/2020/04/Protocolo_De_Actuacion_COVID-19_CEFERESOS.pdf> accessed 1 March 2021; Ministerio de Justicia, 'Acciones de prevención de covid-19' (*Gobierno Nacional de Paraguay*) <https://www.ministeriodejusticia.gov.py/institucion/acciones-de-prevencion-covid-19> accessed 1 March 2021 (link is currently unavailable); Instituto Nacional Penitenciario, 'Comunicado N. 05–2020-INPE' INPE dispone medidas preventivas para mitigar situaciones de contagio por coronavirus' (*Ministerio de Justicia y Derechos Humanos Perú*, 6 March 2020) <https://www.gob.pe/institucion/inpe/noticias/189620-comunicado-n-05-2020-inpe> accessed 12 April 2024.

54 Secretaría de Salud, 'Lineamientos para la prevención y manejo de COVID-19 en población privada de libertad' (n 53) 16.

55 Ministerio de Salud y Protección Social Bogotá, 'Lineamientos para control, prevención y manejo de casos por COVID-19 para la población privada de la libertad-PPL en Colombia' (n 53) 19.

56 Secretaría de Seguridad y Protección Ciudadana and others, 'Protocolo de actuación para la atención de COVID-19 al interior de centros federales de reinserción social (CEFERESOS)' (n 53).

such as water, electricity, and flu vaccines.[57] Governments also received donations from international organizations or through local charity.[58]

57 In Peru, for example, the government informed that water, electricity, and food rations were increased, and sanitary services and drainage systems were given maintenance. Instituto Nacional Penitenciario, '#PerúEstáEnNuestras- Manos' (*Twitter*, 28 March 2020) <https://twitter.com/INPEgob/status/1244075552702529536> accessed 12 April 2024. In Panama, the Minister of Government enacted a three-phase plan to combat potable water shortages in prisons. This plan consisted of enabling new tanks for transportation, opening new wells and taking surplus water from other prisons to those most in need. Vivian Jaén, 'Ministra de Gobierno: 'La falta de agua potable es una de las falencias más grandes del Sistema Penitenciario del país' *Mi Diario* (Panama, 27 July 2020) <https://www.midiario.com/nacionales/ministra-de-gobierno-la-falta-de-agua-potable-es-una-de-las-falencias-mas-grandes-del-sistema-penitenciario-del-pais/>. See also: Ministerio de Gobierno, 'Comunicado Medidas Temporales Contra el COVID-19 en el Sistema Penitenciario' (*República de Panamá*, 26 March 2020) <https://www.mingob.gob.pa/comunicado-medidas-temporales-contra-el-covid-19-en-el-sistema-penitenciario/>. In Guatemala, the Supreme Court ruled that emergency protocols – including the need to provide more drinking water and food services – were required to protect prisoners from the pandemic. Glenda Sanchez, 'CSJ ordena implementar 'protocolos específicos' por covid-19 en cárceles' *República* (Guatemala, 22 July 2020) <https://republica.gt/guatemala/2020-7-22-16-10-34-csj-ordena-implementar-protocolos-especificos-por-covid-19-en-carceles>. Similarly, in Paraguay, Panama, and Chile, the prison systems teamed up with their governments' Ministry of Health to protect the prison population from contracting influenza. Ministerio de Justicia, 'Continúa aplicación de vacunas contra la influenza en centros penitenciarios' (*Gobierno Nacional de Paraguay*, 18 June 2020) <https://www.ministeriodejusticia.gov.py/noticias/continua-aplicacion-de-vacunas-contra-la-influenza-en-centros-penitenciarios> (link is currently unavailable, last access in March 2021); Redacción de TVN Noticias, 'Privados de libertad reciben artículos de aseo' *TVN Noticias* (Panama, 17 April 2020) <https://www.tvn-2.com/nacionales/coronavirus-en-panama-privados-libertad-reciben-articulos-aseo-sistema-penitenciario_1_1188004.html>; Ministerio de Salud Chile, 'Ministros de Salud y Justicia implementan medidas de prevención por COVID-19 en ex Penitenciaria' (*Ministerio de Salud Chile*, 13 March 2020) <https://deis.minsal.cl/ministros-de-salud-y-justicia-implementan-medidas-de-prevencion-por-covid-19-en-ex-penitenciaria/> accessed 12 April 2024.

58 For example, in El Salvador, the International Committee of the Red Cross (ICRC) installed 103 water dispensers and donated more than 17,000 bars of soap, 100 gallons of chlorine, 140,300 purifying water tablets, 2,736 gallons of sodium hypochlorite, as well as gloves and sanitary towels across multiple prisons. In Honduras, the ICRC donated 19,000 masks, 40,000 globes and 500 gallons of disinfectant chlorine. In Nicaragua, the ICRC donated equipment that would help prison personnel, including plastic glasses, gloves and masks. Comité Internacional de la Cruz Roja, 'México y América Central: El CICR apoya a lugares de detención para prevenir y controlar la propagación de la COVID-19' (*ICRC*, 7 April 2020) <https://www.icrc.org/es/document/el-cicr-apoya-lugares-de-detencion-para-prevenir-y-controlar-la-propagacion-de-la-covid-19> accessed 12 April 2024. Additionally, in Argentina, Brazil, Chile, Uruguay and Paraguay, the ICRC donated

Some countries also involved their prison populations in the manufacturing of sanitary supplies to benefit prisons as well as society-at-large. In Brazil,[59] Paraguay,[60] Peru[61] and Guatemala,[62] persons deprived of liberty made face masks, providing an opportunity for work while contributing to their country's pandemic response.

---

machines and supplies for the production of masks and personal protective equipment, as well as cleaning, hygiene and sanitation products. Comité Internacional de la Cruz Roja, 'Brasil y Cono Sur; El CICR presta apoyo a los sistemas penitenciarios de la región en la lucha contra la pandemia' (*ICRC*, 14 May 2020) <https://www.icrc.org/es/document/brasil-y-cono-sur-el-cicr-presta-apoyo-los-sistemas-penitenciarios-de-la-region-para> accessed 12 April 2024. See also: Comité Internacional de la Cruz Roja, 'América Latina y el CICR en tiempos de COVID-19: así adaptamos nuestra acción' (*ICRC*, 23 April 2020) <https://www.icrc.org/es/document/america-latina-y-el-cicr-en-tiempos-de-covid-19-asi-adaptamos-nuestra-accion#atajoLima> accessed 12 April 2024.

59 In Brazil, women in detention manufactured face masks for prison and security officials. The secretary of Brazil's prison system championed these efforts as a way to help society with urgent pandemic equipment needs. Estúdio Folha, 'Detentas do Amazonas produzem mascaras' (*Estudio Folha*, 1 April 2020) <https://estudio.folha.uol.com.br/iniciativascontraocoronavirus/2020/04/1988630-detentas-do-amazonas-produzem-mascaras.shtml> accessed 12 April 2024.

60 In Paraguay, persons deprived of liberty partnered with a local trading company to manufacture masks, and as of 15 April 2020, roughly 3,500 masks were produced daily. Paraguay's prison system director described this partnership as an excellent opportunity to provide prisoners with work while also positively contributing to society's well-being. Ministerio de Justicia, 'COVID-19: PPL de cuatro penitenciarias elaboran 3,500 tapabocas por día' (*Gobierno Nacional de Paraguay*, 15 April 2020) <https://www.ministeriodejusticia.gov.py/noticias/covid-19-ppl-de-cuatro-penitenciarias-elaboran-3500-tapabocas-por-dia> accessed March 2021 (link is currently unavailable).

61 In Peru, as part of the program "Productive prisons", inmates produced for sale masks with traditional Cusco textile designs. Andina, 'Cárceles Productivas: internos del Cusco confeccionan mascarillas y mamelucos' (*Andina*, 12 June 2020) <https://andina.pe/agencia/noticia-carceles-productivas-internos-del-cusco-confeccionan-mascarillas-y-mamelucos-801277.aspx>.

62 In Guatemala, a former gang member in prison producing masks for front-line public servants was quoted as saying that "in addition to helping Guatemala, I am helping myself": AFP, 'Estoy aportando a Guatemala y me estoy ayudando a mi mismo': Ex pandilleros cosen mascarillas en la cárcel' *RPP Noticias* (Guatemala, 30 March 2020) <https://rpp.pe/mundo/actualidad/coronavirus-covid-19-estoy-aportando-a-guatemala-y-me-estoy-ayudando-a-mi-mismo-ex-pandilleros-cosen-mascarillas-en-la-carcel-noticia-1255102>. See also a similar testimony in Mexico: AFP, 'Covid-19 au Mexique: des detenus cousent des masques' *Le Journal de Montréal* (Montréal, 26 March 2020) <https://www.journaldemontreal.com/2020/03/26/covid-19-au-mexique--des-detenus-cousent-des-masques>.

3.3 *Policy Responses to Facilitate Safe Communication with the Outside World*

As soon as the first cases of COVID-19 reached Latin America, governments rushed to restrict or eliminate prison visits to mitigate disease transmission. In Latin American prisons, due to some of the systemic weaknesses already mentioned, visits not only constitute the main way to communicate and maintain contact with family; they are instrumental to the rehabilitation process and an important source of food, basic hygiene, and health supplies.[63] The suspension of visits threatened to bring a whole new set of challenges, including those related to mental health and the potential eruption of tension and violence.

Against this backdrop, several prison systems in Latin America turned to technology to connect prisoners with the outside world, some in ways never been attempted before. In several countries, authorities from different agencies issued recommendations regarding the importance of communication and technological tools for family contact, and made technology, such as videoconference calls, available as a guarantee of rights and also as a way of easing tensions and avoiding riots.[64] In an unprecedented move in Argentina,

63 In this sense, in its Advice regarding COVID-19 issued in March 2020, the UN Subcommittee for the Prevention of Torture called on Member States to the Optional Protocol on the Convention of Torture to enable families to continue providing detainees with necessary supplies of food and other supplies, "with due respect for necessary protective measures". UN Subcommittee on Prevention of Torture and Other Cruel, Inhuman or Degrading Treatment or Punishment, 'Advice of the Subcommittee on Prevention of Torture to States Parties and National Preventive Mechanisms relating to the Coronavirus Pandemic' (n 2).

64 In Argentina, for example, the Prison Ombudsman at the federal level declared telephone communication with family as fundamentally important, especially during the pandemic, and highlighted the need for all people deprived of liberty to be able to receive phone calls in their respective living sectors in addition to the videoconferencing opportunities that had already been established. In Paraguay, the Director of the Specialized Unit for Information and Communication Technologies explained that persons deprived of liberty may now feel accompanied by their relatives during the national quarantine through the use of technology. In Guatemala, the General Directorate of the Prison System indicated that videoconference calls would be implemented to make up for family visits during the quarantine and as a way to avoid riots. Francisco M. Mugnolo, 'Recomendación sobre el acceso a la comunicación de personas alojadas en el SPF' (*Procuración Penitenciaria de la Nación*, 2 June 2020) <https://www.ppn.gov.ar/index.php/institucional/noticias/2696-recomendacion-sobre-el-acceso-a-la-comunicacion-de-personas-alojadas-en-el-spf> accessed 12 April 2024; Ministerio de Justicia, 'PPL se comunican con familiares mediante videollamadas' (*Gobierno Nacional de Paraguay*, 28 March 2020) <https://www.ministeriodejusticia.gov.py/noticias/ppl-se-comunican-con-familiares-mediante-videollamadas> accessed March 2021 (link is currently unavail-

the Criminal Court of Cassation of Buenos Aires authorized all of the province's prisons to allow use of cell phones so prisoners could maintain contact with their families while visits remained restricted.[65] Reports in June 2020 from the province's Minister of Justice and Human Rights indicated that roughly 22,000 prisoners had registered cell phones since the Court's authorization.[66] At the same time, authorities made clear that restrictions would be in place to prevent potential criminal activity.[67]

Restrictions in prisons due to the pandemic also meant the suspension of many educational and outreach services for those deprived of liberty, which can be critical for the prison population, both for rehabilitation and mental health efforts. In some countries, authorities collaborated with universities to allow prisoners to remotely access cultural and artistic courses and other activities.[68]

---

able); Katerin Chumil, 'Coronavirus: videoconferencias podrían sustituir las visitas en las cárceles' *Prensa Libre* (Guatemala, 27 March 2020) <https://www.prensalibre.com/guatemala/justicia/coronavirus-videoconferencias-podrian-sustituir-las-visitas-en-las-carceles/> accessed 12 April 2024.

65 See: Microjuris–Al Día Argentina, 'La comunicación en tiempos de Coronavirus: Se autoriza el uso de teléfono celular a los internos, con el fin de mantener el vínculo familiar durante el periodo de vigencia del aislamiento social' (*Microjuris*, 14 April 2020) <https://aldiaargentina.microjuris.com/2020/04/14/la-comunicacion-en-tiempos-de-coronavirus-se-autoriza-el-uso-de-telefono-celular-a-los-internos-con-el-fin-de-mantener-el-vinculo-familiar-durante-el-periodo-de-vigencia-del-aislamiento-social/> accessed 12 April 2024.

66 Notas Periodismo Popular, 'El gobierno bonaerense planea construir 2 mil plazas en cárceles' (*Notas Periodismo Popular*, 18 June 2020) <https://www.notasperiodismopopular.com.ar/2020/06/18/el-gobierno-bonaerense-planea-construir-2-mil-plazas-en-carceles/> accessed 12 April 2024; Andrés Klipphan, 'Julio Alak: 'El Servicio Penitenciario Bonaerense es una deuda de la democracia' (*Infobae*, 18 June 2020) <https://www.infobae.com/politica/2020/06/18/julio-alak-el-servicio-penitenciario-bonaerense-es-una-deuda-de-la-democracia/> accessed 12 April 2024.

67 Infobae, 'Celulares en las cárceles: los presos tendrán permitido comunicarse por WhatsApp pero no podrán usar las redes sociales' (*Infobae*, 31 March 2020) <https://www.infobae.com/coronavirus/2020/03/31/celulares-en-las-carceles-bonaerenses-los-presos-tendran-permitido-comunicarse-por-whatsapp-pero-no-podran-usar-las-redes-sociales/> accessed 12 April 2024.

68 In Chile, for example, the Gendarmerie collaborated with the Universidad Católica de la Santisima Concepcion to allow 150 prisoners to remotely access cultural activities. See: Gendarmería de Chile, '#SomosReinserciónYSeguridadPública' (*Twitter*, 19 June 2020) <https://x.com/Gendarmeria_CL/status/1274046983242682369> accessed 12 April 2024. Similarly, prisons in Argentina partnered with the Universidad Nacional Villa Maria to offer a variety of remote artistic courses, such as theatre, chorus, and a literary workshop for prisoners. Redacción El Diario del centro del país, 'La UNVM dictará talleres virtuales artísticos para personas privadas de su libertad' *El Diario* (Argentina, 23 July 2020)

3.4 *Policy Responses to Reduce Prison Overcrowding*

Policy responses addressing sanitation and technology required effort and resources, but they were far less controversial and complex than measures to reduce the prison population, arguably the most critical in the context of prisons and COVID-19. For decades, international organizations, human rights advocates and criminal justice experts have pushed governments to implement policies to reduce the alarming levels of overcrowding in Latin America.[69] Yet, the region has yet to see coherent, consistent and effective efforts in this regard. For this reason, it was encouraging to observe the efforts taken by some nations at the beginning of the pandemic to reduce overcrowding.

Starting in March 2020, countries worldwide, including in Latin America, started processes aimed at reducing their prison populations through their judiciary, legislative, and executive branches.[70] In Latin America, these initiatives took various forms, including presidential pardons, executive decrees, emergency legislation, and directives from justice officials. The remainder of this section outlines several examples of national initiatives adopted in the region to reduce prison populations in the context of the pandemic, specifically in the following countries: Argentina, Bolivia, Brazil, Chile, Colombia, Costa Rica, Dominican Republic, Ecuador, Honduras, Mexico, Nicaragua, Panama and Peru. The section concludes by discussing legal and practical challenges that may have hindered the effectiveness of these measures.

3.4.1 Judicial Measures

Brazil's judiciary was among the first in the region to take actions to reduce the country's prison population. In March 2020, the National Justice Council issued extensive recommendations to federal judges aimed at reducing the prison population by adopting alternative measures.[71] The recommendations

<https://www.eldiariocba.com.ar/locales/2020/7/23/la-unvm-dictara-talleres-virtuales-artisticos-para-personas-privadas-de-su-libertad-25205.html> accessed 12 April 2024.

69 See, for example: IACHR, 'Report on the Human Rights of Persons Deprived of Liberty in the Americas' (n 6) paras 156–157.

70 See, for example: Human Rights Watch, 'Announced releases of Detainees in the Justice Systems Due to Covid-19' (*Human Rights Watch*, 22 May 2020) <https://www.hrw.org/sites/default/files/media_2020/05/announced_releases_detainees_covid19_1.pdf> accessed 12 April 2024.

71 National Council of Justice of Brazil, Recomendação N. 62 (17 March 2020); Instituto Latinoamericano de las Naciones Unidas para la Prevención del Delito y el Tratamiento del Delincuente (ILANUD), 'El Sistema Penitenciario ante la Encrucijada producto de la crisis provocada por el COVID-19' (April 2020) 20 https://cdn.sanity.io/files/6u5teakk/production/305d773e4871f4b7d7ab56d4306a20051b5056c3.pdf?dl= accessed 12 April 2024.

included reviewing pre-trial detention cases for those in overcrowded conditions, those who had exceeded 90 days in detention or those related to non-violent crimes, as well as early release, house arrest or alternative socio-educational measures for pregnant or breastfeeding women, minors and the elderly, among other risk groups.[72] Even before these recommendations were issued, there had already been similar responses at the state level in Brazil, in particular in the State of Minas Gerais. The Justice Tribunal also recommended house arrest for those in open and semi-open regimes and for those detained for not having paid alimony, as well as a review of pre-trial measures and an evaluation of alternatives to deprivation of liberty for those facing higher risk, such as persons over 60 and diabetics.[73]

In *Argentina*, courts at both the federal and state levels called on relevant judicial actors to adopt measures addressing overcrowding in the country's prisons.[74] In March, the President of the Supreme Court of Justice of the Province of Buenos Aires established that it was the responsibility of the competent magistrates to evaluate the adoption of alternative or mitigating measures in favour of the most vulnerable persons deprived of liberty in the context of COVID-19.[75] In early April 2020, the Federal Chamber of Criminal Cassation shared with judges in its jurisdiction the recommendations of the IACHR

72 National Council of Justice of Brazil, Recomendação N. 62 (17 March 2020); IACHR, 'The IACHR urges States to guarantee the health and integrity of persons deprived of liberty and their families in the face of the COVID-19 pandemic' (n 2).

73 Presidência and Secretaria Especial da Presidência e das Comissõesm Permanentes Brasil, Portaria Conjunta Nº 19/ PR-TJMG/2020 (16 March 2020) 2; ILANUD, 'El Sistema Penitenciario ante la Encrucijada producto de la crisis provocada por el COVID-19' (n 71) 20.

74 Centro de Información Judicial, 'Acordada 9/20 de la Cámara Federal de Casación Penal' (*Cámara Federal de Casación Penal*, 13 April 2020) 5–6 <https://www.cij.gov.ar/nota-37089-Acordada-9-20-de-la-C-mara-Federal-de-Casaci-n-Penal.html> accessed 12 April 2024. See also: Raúl A. Roust, 'Análisis jurisprudencial de las decisiones adoptadas en relación a la situación de las personas privadas de su libertad en la actual situación de pandemia (Covid-19)' (*Microjuris*, 30 April 2020) <https://aldiaargentina.microjuris.com/2020/05/14/analisis-jurisprudencial-de-las-decisiones-adoptadas-en-relacion-a-la-situacion-de-las-personas-privadas-de-su-libertad-en-la-actual-situacion-de-pandemia-covid-19/> accessed 12 April 2024.

75 Eduardo de Lázzari and Martin Daniel Lorat, 'Ref. Expte. N.: SDH-96–2020' (*Poder Judicial de la Provincia de Buenos Aires*, 25 March 2020) <http://www.scba.gov.ar/includes/descarga.asp?id=45344&n=Ver%20resoluci%F3n%2052-20.pdf> accessed 12 April 2024; Poder Judicial de la Provincia de Buenos Aires, 'COVID-19 (Coronavirus). Personas privadas de la libertad. Determinaciones en el marco de las medidas de aislamiento social y prevención de riesgos dispuestas por el Estado Nacional' (*SCBA*, 25 March 2020) <https://www.scba.gov.ar/institucional/nota.asp?expre=Personas%20privadas%20de%20la%20libertad&veradjuntos=no> accessed 12 April 2024.

regarding COVID-19 in the prison context,[76] including addressing overcrowding, reevaluating cases of pretrial detentions and evaluating the possibility of adopting alternative measures such as early release and house arrest.[77] The Federal Chamber then issued additional guidelines regarding applicable alternative measures,[78] recommending prioritizing, among other groups, people who had committed nonviolent crimes and were in pre-trail detention or close to serving their sentence, pregnant women and persons with higher health risks, such as the elderly and persons with disabilities.[79] The Court also emphasized "extreme prudence" in the application of these provisions in cases of serious crimes.[80]

In *Costa Rica*, starting in early April 2020, sentencing judges issued different "corrective measures" calling for the swift relocation or removal of prisoners suffering from preexisting conditions.[81] According to one judicial order, due to humanitarian reasons, prison authorities had to carry out evaluations of persons deprived of liberty whose health was at risk according to Ministry of Health guidelines and then the National Institute of Criminology had to expeditiously resolve each recommendation of relocation or release.[82] Based on the order, the Ministry of Justice issued instructions as to who qualified for release: those who were close to the end of their sentence and did not pose a risk to

76 IACHR, 'The IACHR urges States to guarantee the health and integrity of persons deprived of liberty and their families in the face of the COVID-19 pandemic' (n 2).

77 Centro de Información Judicial, 'Proveído de la Cámara Federal de Casación Penal' (*Cámara Federal de Casación Penal*, 2 April 2020) <https://www.cij.gov.ar/nota-37032-Prove-do-de-la-C-maraFederal-de-Casaci-n-Penal.html> accessed 12 April 2024.

78 Centro de Información Judicial, 'Acordada 9/20 de la Cámara Federal de Casación Penal' (n 74).

79 Centro de Información Judicial, 'Acordada 9/20 de la Cámara Federal de Casación Penal' (n 74) 10–11. See also: Ministerio Público Fiscal, 'Jurisprudencia de la Cámara Federal de Casación Penal-Sala de Feria-relacionada al COVID-19' (*República Argentina*, April 2020) 14 <https://www.fiscales.gob.ar/wp-content/uploads/2020/04/Informe_Jurisprudencia-CFCP_sala-feria-coivd_informe.pdf>.

80 Centro de Información Judicial, 'Acordada 9/20 de la Cámara Federal de Casación Penal' (n 74) 11 and 15.

81 Hulda Miranda, 'Jueces ordenan reubicar o sacar a presos con enfermedades de riesgo ante COVID-19' (*Semanario Universidad*, 6 April 2020) <https://semanariouniversidad.com/ultima-hora/jueces-ordenan-reubicar-o-sacar-a-presos-con-enfermedades-de-riesgo-ante-covid-19/> accessed 12 April 2024.

82 Ministerio de Justicia y Paz, 'Ministerio de Justicia y Paz acata orden de juzgado de ejecución de la pena sobre valoraciones extraordinarias por Covid-19' (*República de Costa Rica*, 22 April 2020) <https://www.mjp.go.cr/Comunicacion/Nota?nom=Ministerio-de-Justicia-y-Paz-acata-orden-de-Juzgado-de-Ejecucion-de-la-Pena-sobre-valoraciones-extraordinarias-por-Covid-19>.

themselves or a third party, those suffering from diseases, including chronic kidney failure, heart disease, autoimmune diseases, lung disease, cancer patients, multiple sclerosis and immunosuppressed patients, pregnant women or those with babies in intensive care and people over 65 years of age.[83] In addition to medical criteria, the Ministry determined that viable support outside prisons (understood as support from families or others) to those persons deprived of liberty who qualified for release would be "indispensable".[84]

In *Ecuador*, the National Court of Justice, making reference to the IACHR's recommendations, exhorted judges in the country to privilege non-custodial precautionary measures, especially in the case of minors and women.[85] Similarly, in *Peru*, the Supreme Court of Justice issued directives for criminal judges to address the situation of persons deprived of liberty to evaluate the modification of their legal status, including through the termination of pretrial detention.[86]

In the *Dominican Republic*, the Attorney General instructed prosecutors to request from judges, with urgency, alternative custodial measures for persons over the age of 60 and those with chronic or terminal illnesses.[87] Excluded

---

83 ibid.

84 ibid.

85 El Telégrafo, 'CNJ sugiere a jueces privilegiar medidas alternativas en lugar de la prisión' *El Telégrafo* (Ecuador, 12 April 2020) <https://www.eltelegrafo.com.ec/noticias/judicial/12/cnj-sugiere-jueces-privilegiar-medidas-alternativas-prision> accessed 12 April 2024; ILANUD, 'El Sistema Penitenciario ante la Encrucijada producto de la crisis provocada por el COVID-19' (n 71) 20.

86 Poder Judicial de Perú, Resolución administrativa No. 000138–2020-CE-PJ (7 May 2020). See also: Instituto de Estudios Jurídicos de Ejecución Penal, 'Emergencia carcelaria y pandemia en Argentina' (*INEJEP*, 2021) 42 <https://www.palermo.edu/Archivos_content/2020/derecho/mayo/documento-inejep/INEJEP-emergencia-carcelaria-y-pandemia-en-argentina.pdf> accessed 12 April 2024.

87 Procuraduría General de la República, 'Procuraduría solicita al CPJ habilitación jueces para conocer cambios provisionales en cumplimiento de penas de adultos mayores y enfermos riesgo Coronavirus' (*Gobierno de la República Dominicana*, 29 March 2020 <https://pgr.gob.do/procuraduria-solicita-al-cpj-habilitacion-jueces-para-conocer-cambios-provisionales-en-cumplimiento-de-penas-de-adultos-mayores-y-enfermos-riesgo-coronavirus/> accessed 12 April 2024; Procuraduría General de la República, 'Cambio provisional de prisión por coronavirus solo será solicitado en casos internos de más de 60 años y los que tengan registrados con enfermedades crónicas previo al estado de emergencia' (*Gobierno de la República Dominicana*, 31 March 2020) <https://pgr.gob.do/cambio-provisional-de-prision-por-coronavirus-solo-sera-solicitado-en-casos-internos-de-mas-de-60-anos-y-los-que-tengan-registrados-con-enfermedades-cronicas-previo-al-estado-de-emergencia/> accessed 12 April 2024. See also: ILANUD, 'El Sistema Penitenciario ante la Encrucijada producto de la crisis provocada por el COVID-19' (n 71) 21.

from the instruction were those who committed serious crimes of gender, sexual, or domestic violence or drug trafficking, among others.[88]

3.4.2 Legislative Measures

In *Chile*, the government passed a law on 17 April 2020 commuting prison sentences to house arrests with the objective of preventing the spread of coronavirus in prisons.[89] The general commutative pardon only applied to a select portion of the prison population – including men over the age of 60, women over the age of 55, women who were pregnant or had a child under 2, and those who were serving night incarceration sentences.[90] Only those who complied with strict sentencing requirements, for example, having served at least half their sentence and having a remaining 36 months or less of their term to serve, were eligible for this pardon.[91] The President of Chile clarified that the General Commutative Pardon Act did not confer impunity but instead modified or substituted existing prison sentences with alternative home confinement.[92] Additionally, the act would not apply to those incarcerated for serious crimes, including but not limited to torture, rape, femicide, migrant smuggling, terrorism, or crimes against humanity.[93] According to the President, these exclusions were meant to respect the victims of these crimes, "the main commitment of our Government and State will always be the victims of crime, but we also need to treat people deprived of their liberty humanely and protect their health and lives".[94]

Like Chile, *Mexico* also took legislative measures as a response to COVID-19. On 20 April 2020, the General Congress of Mexican States passed an Amnesty Law intended to reduce prison overcrowding by granting amnesty to persons

88 Procuraduría General de la República, 'Cambio provisional de prisión por coronavirus solo será solicitado en casos internos de más de 60 años' (n 87).

89 BCN Ley Chile, Ley 21228, Concede Indulto General Conmutativo a Causa de la Enfermedad COVID-19 en Chile, Ministerio de Justicia y Derechos Humanos (17 April 2020) <https://www.bcn.cl/leychile/navegar?idNorma=1144400>.

90 ibid Articles 2 and 3.

91 ibid.

92 Cristopher Ulloa, 'Piñera promulga ley de indulto conmutativo por Coronavirus en Chile' *CNN Español* (Chile, 16 April 2020) <https://cnnespanol.cnn.com/2020/04/16/pinera-promulga-ley-de-indulto-conmutativo-por-coronavirus-en-chile/>.

93 BCN Ley Chile, Ley 21228 (n 89) Article 15.

94 Chile Reports, 'President Piñera passed Pardon Act for COVID-19 to prevent large-scale contagion in prison facilities' (*Gobierno de Chile*, 16 April 2020) <https://chilereports.cl/en/news/2020/04/16/president-pi%C3%B1era-passes-pardon-act-for-covid-19-to-prevent-large-scale-contagion-in-prison-facilities> accessed March 2021 (link is currently unavailable).

serving pre-trial detention or sentences in the federal system.[95] The law was clear that eligibility was reserved for first-time offenders, provided they had committed specific offenses such as abortion, drug-related crimes, non-violent robbery and sedition.[96] In the case of indigenous people, any crime could qualify if the judicial proceeding did not follow due process or if the right to an interpreter was violated.[97] Similar to Chile, the Mexican law also excluded those committed for serious crimes.[98] As to the process to request amnesty, the law required that the Executive Branch create a special commission to evaluate each case, and established that the amnesty request would have to be made by the person deprived of liberty, a family member or a public human rights organization.[99] The commission would have up to four months to make its determination.

In *Honduras*, the National Congress issued Decree No. 36–2020, which reformed the Criminal Procedure Code, on 2 June 2020.[100] The decree cited in its introduction the recommendations issued by the human rights international bodies, particularly those of the IACHR that urged states to adopt measures to guarantee the health and safety of persons deprived of liberty and their families in the context of COVID-19.[101] Thus, the Honduran penal code reform allowed for persons detained who had not yet been convicted of a crime or were in vulnerable health groups to obtain house arrest during the pandemic. Eligibility for alternate pre-trial detention was not granted to those accused of crimes linked to drug trafficking, rape, arms trafficking, or who were related to criminal groups known as maras.[102]

3.4.3 Executive Branch Measures

In *Argentina*, the Federal Penitentiary Service promoted initiatives aimed at mitigating overcrowding, referencing the guidelines issued by the Federal Chamber of Criminal Cassation.[103] For example, a memorandum requested prison health units to analyse cases and submit to courts and tribunals a list

95 Congreso General de los Estados Unidos Mexicanos, Decreto por el que se expide la Ley de Amnistía (22 April 2020) Secretaría de Gobernación México (SEGOB).

96 ibid Article 1.

97 ibid Article 1, Section IV.

98 ibid Article 2.

99 ibid Article 3.

100 La Gaceta, Poder Legislativo Decreto No. 36–2020 (10 June 2020) República de Honduras.

101 ibid 9.

102 ibid 10.

103 See the section above under judicial measures.

a list of vulnerable groups by pathology, condition, and age, so judges could consider possible alternative measures to prison.[104]

In *Bolivia*, the interim government issued a presidential decree on 4 May 2020, which had to be previously approved by the Legislative Assembly, providing the benefit of amnesty (applying to pre-trial detainees) or pardon (applying to those convicted) for humanitarian reasons in the context of the national health emergency.[105] This decree referenced, as considerations for the reform, the recommendations issued by the WHO on preventive health measures and the IACHR on guidance for mitigating the spread of the virus in prison systems.[106] Presidential Decree N°4226 established eligibility for amnesty or pardon for persons deprived of liberty who met the following qualifications: those over the age of 58, with advanced or terminal chronic disease, with severe or serious disabilities, pregnant or lactating women and those who had under their sole care one or more sons or daughters under the age of six.[107] The benefits did not apply to repeat offenders and to those who were being investigated or had been convicted for a series of crimes, including homicide, rape, sexual assault against children, arms smuggling, terrorism and genocide. To qualify, persons deprived of liberty had to present an application to the public defender, the prison system had to provide a report for the evaluation, and the judge would make the final decision.[108]

In *Colombia*, in the context of the national emergency declared due to the pandemic, the instrument to facilitate prison population reduction was an Executive Legislative Decree, which has the force of law. Legislative Decree No. 546 of 14 April 2020 cited the recommendations of the IACHR, the United Nations High Commissioner for Human Rights and the WHO, stating that it was clear that the country's current overcrowding situation required urgent

104 República de Argentina, Poder Ejecutivo Nacional. Memorandum: Impartir Directivas respecto del Alerta Epidemiológica del Coronavirus – (COVID-19) (13 March 2020) <https://cnpt.gob.ar/2022/wp-content/uploads/2022/01/06_ME-2020-16932042-APN-DGRCSPF.pdf>; INEJEP, 'Emergencia carcelaria y pandemia en Argentina' (n 86) 18.

105 Paulo Cuiza, 'Dos condenados por narcotráfico, los primeros en beneficiarse con el indulto en Bolivia' (*La Razón*, 19 May 2020) <https://eju.tv/2020/05/dos-condenados-por-narcotrafico-los-primeros-en-beneficiarse-con-el-indulto-en-bolivia/> accessed 12 April 2024; Claudia Villeda and Juan J. Cusicanqui, 'La Asamblea Legislativa aprueba nuevo indulto y amnistía' (*La Razón*, 30 April 2020) <https://www.la-razon.com/nacional/2020/04/30/asamblea-legislativa-nuevo-indulto-amnistia/> (link is currently unavailable) accessed 12 April 2024.

106 Portal Jurídico Lexivox, Bolivia, Decreto Presidencial N. 4226 (4 May 2020) Considerando <https://www.lexivox.org/norms/BO-DP-N4226.xhtml>.

107 ibid Article 2.

108 ibid Articles 6 and 9.

and immediate action.[109] The decree allowed house arrest for persons over 60, pregnant women, and individuals with underlying diseases or disabilities, or who had served 40 percent of their sentence or were convicted of terms under five years, among others.[110] The Colombian decree also specifically excluded a long list of crimes, ranging from serious offenses such as forced disappearance and torture to lesser ones such as possession of hazardous substances or objects or firearms.[111]

In *Panama*, the Ministry of Government issued several decrees through which the President granted early releases to persons deprived of liberty and referring to the national emergency arising from the pandemic as a driver of the releases.[112]

In *Peru*, on 23 April 2020, the government issued Executive Decree No. 004–2020-JUS, which allowed the President to grant releases to benefit a prioritized group of inmates during the health emergency due to COVID-19.[113] This decree allowed releases through common presidential pardons, on humanitarian grounds, and through commutations of sentences.[114] To qualify for a pardon based on humanitarian reasons, the person had to suffer from a chronic disease that would increase their vulnerability to COVID-19 conta-

---

109 Ministerio de Justicia y de Derecho, Decreto Legislativo Número 546 (14 April 2020) República de Colombia <https://www.funcionpublica.gov.co/eva/gestornormativo/norma.php?i=112859>.

110 ibid Article 2.

111 Ministerio de Justicia y de Derecho, Decreto Legislativo Número 546 (n 109) Article 6.

112 República de Panamá, '253 privados de libertad han sido beneficiados con rebaja de pena' (*Ministerio de Gobierno*, 9 June 2020) <https://www.mingob.gob.pa/253-privados-de-libertad-han-sido-beneficiados-con-rebaja-de-pena/>; República de Panamá, Decreto Ejecutivo N. 265 (9 April 2020); República de Panamá, Decreto Ejecutivo N. 270 (13 April 2020) <https://vlex.com.pa/vid/decreto-ejecutivo-n-270-842826623>; República de Panamá, Decreto Ejecutivo N. 271 (20 April 2020)<https://vlex.com.pa/vid/decreto-ejecutivo-n-271-843715718>; República de Panamá, Decreto Ejecutivo N. 272 (28 April 2020) <https://vlex.com.pa/vid/decreto-ejecutivo-n-272-843996403>; República de Panamá, Decreto Ejecutivo N. 277 (3 June 2020) <https://www.gacetaoficial.gob.pa/pdfTemp/29038_A/GacetaNo_29038a_20200603.pdf>; República de Panamá, Decreto Ejecutivo N. 279 (8 June 2020) <https://www.gacetaoficial.gob.pa/pdfTemp/29042_B/GacetaNo_29042b_20200608.pdf>; República de Panamá, Decreto Ejecutivo N. 304 (4 August 2020) <https://www.gacetaoficial.gob.pa/pdfTemp/29083_B/GacetaNo_29083b_20200804.pdf>.

113 El Peruano, *Decreto Supremo No. 004–2020* que establece supuestos especiales para la evaluación y propuesta de recomendación de Gracias Presidenciales, y determina su procedimiento, en el marco de la emergencia sanitaria por COVID-19 (23 April 2020).

114 ibid Article 1.

gion.[115] For common pardons or commutation of sentences, the decree listed several conditions, including: being a mother with her child in prison, being pregnant, having six months left to complete the sentence imposed, and being over 60 years old.[116]

Nicaragua, unlike the rest of the countries reviewed in this chapter, did not have a specific policy response related to prison releases because of the pandemic, but it did rely on executive powers to release persons deprived of liberty during the same time period.[117] On 13 May 2020, the government granted 2,815 prisoners the legal benefit of family coexistence to release them from prison, citing Mother's Day as the motivation.[118] The news regarding the release did not mention COVID-19 but did emphasize the release of elderly prisoners with chronic illnesses.[119] These releases took place amid increased complaints of COVID-19 transmission in prisons, concerns raised by the families of political prisoners, and denunciations made by a top United States official.[120]

---

115 ibid Article 2.

116 ibid Article 3.

117 Specifically, Nicaragua released prisoners based on Article 60 of Law 473 of 2003, which is the country's Prison Regime legislation. Article 60 refers to the regime of family coexistence, the period immediately before completion of sentence, in which prisoners are allowed to live with their families. La Gaceta No. 222, Ley No. 473 Ley de Régimen Penitenciario y Ejecución de la Pena (21 November 2003) Presidente y Asamblea Nacional de la República de Nicaragua <http://legislacion.asamblea.gob.ni/normaweb.nsf/9e314815a08d4a6206257265005d21f9/493bad7a4c8167ce062587ab00638e02?OpenDocument>.

118 Europa Press, 'Nicaragua pone en libertad a 2,800 presos ante denuncias por un posible brote de coronavirus en las cárceles del país' (*Europa Press*, 13 May 2020) <https://www.europapress.es/internacional/noticia-nicaragua-pone-libertad-2800-presos-denuncias-posible-brote-coronavirus-carceles-pais-20200513225618.html> accessed 12 April 2024; El 19 Digital, 'Sistema Penitenciario Nacional entrega a 2,815 personas a sus Familias' (*El 19 Digital*, 13 May 2020) <https://www.el19digital.com/articulos/ver/titulo:103275-sistema-penitenciario-nacional-entrega-a-2815-personas-a-sus-familias> accessed 12 April 2024.

119 ibid.

120 Álvaro Navarro, 'Alto funcionario de Estados Unidos denuncia que el COVID-19 se esparce en las cárceles de Nicaragua' (*Artículo 66*, 12 May 2020) <https://www.articulo66.com/2020/05/12/alto-funcionario-departamento-estado-denuncia-covid-19-esperace-prisiones-nicaragua/> accessed 12 April 2024; Gabriela Selser, 'Nicaragua releases more than 2,800 inmates amid pandemic' *The Seattle Times* (Managua, 13 May 2020) <https://www.seattletimes.com/seattle-news/health/nicaragua-releases-more-than-2800-inmates-amid-pandemic/> accessed 12 April 2024.

3.5 *Results of Measures to Reduce the Prison Population*

While there is information about the initial policy measures taken in Latin America with the aim of reducing prison populations, the actual implementation process and results from such measures are difficult to assess. This is due to the limited official information as to the number of persons deprived of liberty released on the ground of humanitarian reasons due to COVID-19. A preliminary conclusion on the countries reviewed for this chapter is that, during the early pandemic, no country – except Nicaragua,[121] whose government never attributed its massive releases to the pandemic – released more than 10 percent of its prison population; most released less than 5 percent.[122] The conclusions from the June 2020 regional study "The Effects of Coronavirus in Prisons in Latin America" conducted by the *Sociedad de Criminología Latinoamericana* (*SOCLA*) and the *Centro de Estudios Latinoamericanos sobre Inseguridad y Violencia UNTREF* (*CELIV*) similarly point to the fact that although two out of every three prison systems in Latin America adopted measures such as early release or house arrest,[123] fewer than 2 percent of incarcerated people had obtained any release benefit.[124]

Further investigation is warranted into the limited number of prisoner releases in Latin American prisons, despite the numerous and diverse efforts

121 Nicaragua released around 6,000 prisoners between April and July of 2020: 1,700 in April; 2,815 in May and 1,605 in July. Nelly Alvarado, 'En esta Semana Santa más de 1,700 presos y presas regresan a sus hogares' (*Sistema Penitenciario Nacional*, 9 April 2020) <https://www.migob.gob.ni/penitenciario/en-esta-semana-santa-mas-de-1700-presos-y-presas-regresan-a-sus-hogares> accessed 12 April 2024; Europa Press, 'Nicaragua pone en libertad a 2,800 presos ante denuncias por un posible brote de coronavirus en las cárceles del país' (*Europa Press*, 13 May 2020) <https://www.europapress.es/internacional/noticia-nicaragua-pone-libertad-2800-presos-denuncias-posible-brote-coronavirus-carceles-pais-20200513225618.html>; El 19 Digital, 'Sistema Penitenciario Nacional entrega a 2,815 personas a sus Familias' (*El 19 Digital*, 13 May 2020) <https://www.el19digital.com/articulos/ver/titulo:103275-sistema-penitenciario-nacional-entrega-a-2815-personas-a-sus-familias> accessed 12 April 2024; Nelly Alvarado, '1,605 presos y presas regresan a sus hogares' (Sistema Penitenciario Nacional, 15 July 2020) <https://www.migob.gob.ni/penitenciario/1605-presos-y-presas-regresan-a-sus-hogares/> accessed 12 April 2024.

122 For a more detailed explanation on this, see: María L. Romero, Luisa Stalman and Azul H. Solá, 'The Covid-19 Pandemic and Prison Policy in Latin America' (*The Inter-American Dialogue*, April 2021) <https://www.thedialogue.org/wp-content/uploads/2021/04/The-Covid-19-Pandemic-and-Prison-Policy-.pdf> accessed 12 April 2024.

123 Marcelo Bergman and others, 'The Effect of Coronavirus in Prisons in Latin America' (*Sociedad de Criminología Latinoamericana* (*SOCLA*), 12 June 2020) 27 <https://criminologialatam.wordpress.com/2020/06/12/efectos-del-covid-19-carceles-de-latino-america/> accessed 12 April 2024.

124 ibid 28.

across the region to reduce overcrowding. One initial hypothesis suggests that most release efforts targeted a narrow segment of the prison demographic: individuals at highest risk of contracting illnesses or those who had not committed serious crimes and had already completed a significant portion of their sentences. Besides the enduring obstacle of political will, the factors delineated below may also have delayed and complicated efforts to reduce overcrowding, and therefore merit analysis for prospective prison reforms in the region.

3.6 *Challenges to Efforts to Reduce Prison Overcrowding*

3.6.1 Public Opposition to Prisoner Releases and Challenges in Courts

One challenge that is perhaps obvious, and at the same time unavoidable, is the unpopularity of mass prisoner releases. While international organizations, human rights activists and criminal justice experts recommending prison releases during the pandemic, there was also vocal opposition coming from various fronts, including defenders of victims' rights and those who saw this as a challenge to public security.[125] In some countries, this led to successful legal challenges in courts, as will be described below.

For example, after a civil association for victims' rights filed in court an "*amparo*"[126] in April 2020,[127] the Argentine Federal Chamber of Criminal Cas-

125 See, for example, in Argentina: Veronica Smink, 'Coronavirus en Argentina: por qué genera tanta polémica la decisión de sacar de la cárcel a algunos presos por riesgo a que contraigan el covid-19' *BBC News Mundo Argentina* (Argentina, 1 May 2020) <https://www.bbc.com/mundo/noticias-america-latina-52496655> accessed 12 April 2024.

126 The action of "amparo" in most legal systems in Latin America is a legal remedy for the protection of individual rights, particularly to provide swift and effective relief against unconstitutional or unlawful acts by public officials or institutions. In Argentina, the writ or action of "amparo" is established in its Constitution as a "prompt and expeditious" judicial measure that can be filed against public authorities or private individuals to protect rights recognized in the Constitution, treaties, or national law. Organization of American States, National Constitution of Argentina (1994) Article 43.

127 In April 2020, *Asociación Usina de Justicia*, a civil association for victims' rights filed an amparo against the recommendations and guidelines issued by the Federal Chamber of Criminal Appeals regarding possible alternative measures to imprisonment due to the COVID-19 pandemic. The Association argued that the directives issued by the Federal Chamber stripped judges of their independence when making considerations for prisoner releases. Additionally, the Association contended that prisoner releases would in no way prevent the spread of the virus because there was no indication that these prisoners would comply with the national quarantine, considering they were already incarcerated for breaking the law. The statement highlighted that measures to reduce population, rather than reduce overcrowding, promoted impunity. In it, the president of the association, Dana Cohen Agrest, declared "civil society is anguished over the massive

sation's recommendations and guidelines regarding prisoner release during the pandemic were declared unconstitutional by a lower court judge who reasoned that "the independence of the judge is absolute".[128] Similarly, the Buenos Aires Supreme Court revoked a habeas corpus that allowed house arrest during the pandemic for persons detained for minor offenses who exhibited higher health risks,[129] stating that it was up to individual judicial bodies to evaluate the requests from the persons deprived of liberty while considering the rights of victims.[130]

In Brazil, opposition to prison release efforts came from judges as well as from the Ministry of Justice. The then Minister of Justice made statements against the National Justice Council's recommendation to release prisoners in high-risk groups, in pretrial detention and those convicted of nonviolent crimes.[131] According to the report published by the *Sociedad de Criminología Latinoamericana*, since there was no centralized policy for releases, decisions were made at the local level and "some judges followed the criticism of the then-Minister".[132] For example, a judge denied a house arrest grant, reasoning

---

release of dangerous prisoners". Fabio Ferrer, 'Coronavirus en Argentina: presentaron un amparo contra las liberaciones de presos con la excusa del covid-19' (*Infobae*, 30 April 2020) <https://www.infobae.com/politica/2020/04/30/coronavirus-en-argentina-presentaron-un-amparo-contra-las-liberaciones-de-presos-con-la-excusa-del-covid-10/> accessed 12 April 2024.

128 Poder Judicial de la Nación, Juzgado Nacional en lo Criminal y Correccional, NRO. 37 (2 May 2020) 17.

129 Provincia de Buenos Aires Poder Judicial, *Habeas Corpus N.102.555* (8 April 2020). See also: Patricia Blanco, 'Coronavirus: beneficiarán con arresto domiciliario a más de 400 presos de la Provincia de Buenos Aires' (*Infobae*, 9 April 2020) <https://www.infobae.com/sociedad/policiales/2020/04/09/coronavirus-beneficiaran-con-arresto-domiciliario-a-mas-de-400-presos-de-la-provincia-de-buenos-aires/> accessed 12 April 2024.

130 Suprema Corte de Justicia Provincia de Buenos Aires, *P-133682-Q* (4 May 2020) <https://www.scba.gov.ar/includes/descarga.asp?id=45522&n=Ver%20sentencia%20(causa%20P133682).pdf>. See also: 0221, 'La Suprema Corte revocó el fallo que habilitó las prisiones domiciliarias por el covid-19' (*0221*, 11 May 2020) <https://www.0221.com.ar/nota/2020-5-11-12-42-0-la-suprema-corte-revoco-el-fallo-del-juez-platense-que-habilito-las-excarcelaciones> accessed 12 April 2024.

131 Bergman and others, 'The Effect of Coronavirus in Prisons in Latin America' (n 123) 37; UOL, 'Moro aprova manutenção da prisão de Gaddel: 'Coronavírus não é subterfúgio' (*UOL*, 30 March 2020) <https://noticias.uol.com.br/politica/ultimas-noticias/2020/03/30/moro-aprova-manutencao-da-prisao-de-geddel-coronavirus-nao-e-subterfugio.htm> accessed 12 April 2024. 0221, 'La Suprema Corte revocó el fallo que habilitó las prisiones domiciliarias por el covid-19' (*0221*, 11 May 2020) <https://www.0221.com.ar/nota/2020-5-11-12-42-0-la-suprema-corte-revoco-el-fallo-del-juez-platense-que-habilito-las-excarcelaciones> accessed 12 April 2024.

132 Bergman and others, 'The Effect of Coronavirus in Prisons in Latin America' (n 123) 37.

that of the approximately 7,780,000,000 inhabitants on Earth, only the three occupants of the international space station were not subject to contamination by the notorious coronavirus.[133]

3.6.2 Concerns over Impunity

In several Latin American countries, there were also concerns expressed by civil society, human rights advocates and policymakers that those convicted for crimes against humanity and other human rights abuses could take advantage of the extraordinary circumstances created by the pandemic to be released from prison.[134] In Guatemala, for example, civil society organizations denounced that the health crisis was being used to facilitate impunity both in adjudicated cases and in ongoing processes involving crimes against humanity.[135]

---

133 Poder Judiciário Tribunal de Justiça do Estado de São Paulo, Despacho, *Processo N° 2061058–72.2020.8.26.0000, Codigo N° 1033FB57* (1 April 2020) <https://www.estadao.com.br/blogs/blog/wp-content/uploads/sites/41/2020/04/2061058-7220208260000pdf pdf_010420200535.pdf?srsltid=AfmBOo037rx7afDGDM4O-lfrUeQr6oJHKT_siREKPyw1uroaLnaLgWGt>. This decision was reversed two months later by Judge Luiz Edson Fachin of the Federal Supreme Court, who stated that the decision reflected the judge's personal impressions on the subject, went against sanitary recommendations, and contradicted the guidelines outlined by the National Justice Council. However, soon after, on 31 May, another lower court judge, Otavia Rocha from the Sao Paulo Court of Justice, denied a request that would have granted house arrest to a prisoner with HIV on the basis that the risk of contagion is not sufficient for prisoner release. Tiago Angelo, 'Fachin reverte decisão que citou astronautas e príncipes para negar domiciliar' (*Consultor Jurídico*, 12 May 2020) <https://www.conjur.com.br/2020-mai-12/fachin-reverte-decisao-cita-astronautas-negar-domiciliar/> accessed 12 April 2024; Poder Judiciário Tribunal de Justiça do Estado de São Paulo, *Habeas Corpus N° 2101302–43.2020.8.26.0000, Codigo N° 10BEC9D9* (31 May 2020) 7–9; Migalhas, 'Negada domiciliar a réu com HIV base em decisão de que só astronautas estão livres do coronavírus' (*Migalhas*, 3 June 2020) <https://www.migalhas.com.br/quentes/328259/negada-domiciliar-a-reu-com-hiv-com-base-em-decisao-de-que-so-astronautas-estao-livres-do-coronavirus> accessed 12 April 2024. Translation is ours.

134 See, for example: Prensa Comunitaria KM169, 'En la emergencia del coronavirus militares condenados y en prisión preventiva pretenden salir de la cárcel' (*Prensa Comunitaria*, 17 April 2020) <https://prensacomunitar.medium.com/en-la-emergencia-del-coronavirus-militares-condenados-y-en-prisi%C3%B3n-preventiva-pretenden-salir-de-d598d4b1e0e6> accessed 12 April 2024; Jo-Marie Burt and Paulo Estrada, 'In Guatemala, COVID-19 Puts Justice on Hold, Emboldening Convicted War Criminals to Seek Their Freedom' (*International Justice Monitor*, 17 April 2020) <https://www.ijmonitor.org/2020/04/in-guatemala-covid-19-puts-justice-on-hold-emboldening-convicted-war-criminals-to-seek-their-freedom/> accessed 12 April 2024.

135 Prensa Comunitaria KM169, 'En la emergencia del coronavirus militares condenados y en prisión preventiva pretenden salir de la cárcel' (*Prensa Comunitaria*, 17 April 2020) <https://prensacomunitar.medium.com/en-la-emergencia-del-coronavirus-militares-condenados-y-en-prisi%C3%B3n-preventiva-pretenden-salir-de-d598d4b1e0e6>.

Some also expressed concerns that requests from high-profile prisoners, who were responsible for very serious crimes and enjoyed privileged living and sanitary conditions compared to the general prison population,[136] diverted attention and resources away from the primary objective of prison releases, which, as previously explained, was addressing overcrowding. In Chile, the Constitutional Court rejected a challenge of unconstitutionality to the Commutative Pardon Act[137] pushed by senators who alleged that the law was discriminatory because it excluded prisoners convicted of serious human rights crimes. A concurring opinion highlighted that the legal action had suspended "the entry into force and execution of the pardon law for days and eventually valuable weeks, subtracting days needed to save lives".[138] In addition to concerns regarding impunity for serious human rights crimes, there were also arguments put forth, for example in Honduras, that politicians were taking advantage of the opportunity created by the pandemic to pass controversial reforms to protect former officials from facing corruption or money laundering charges.[139]

3.6.3 Questions as to Whether Extraordinary Measures Passed Were Actually Effective

In June 2020, the then Minister of Justice of Colombia was reported to have said that since the Decree Law 546 of 2020[140] contained multiple exclusions and exceptions, more prisoners had been released through ordinary measures

136 See, for example: Prensa Comunitaria KM169, 'En la emergencia del coronavirus militares condenados y en prisión preventiva pretenden salir de la cárcel' (*Prensa Comunitaria*, 17 April 2020) <https://prensacomunitar.medium.com/en-la-emergencia-del-coronavirus-militares-condenados-y-en-prisi%C3%B3n-preventiva-pretenden-salir-de-d598d4b1e0e6>; Andrea Aguilar Córdoba, 'Polémica por ley que permitiría indulto a condenados por crímenes en dictadura chilena por el COVID-19' (*Agencia Anadolu*, 7 April 2020) <https://www.aa.com.tr/es/mundo/polémica-por-ley-que-permitiría-indulto-a-condenados-por-crímenes-en-dictadura-chilena-por-el-covid-19/1796077> accessed 12 April 2024.

137 See *section 3.4.2 supra* under Legislative Measures.

138 Tribunal Constitucional Chile, *Sentencia Rol 8574–2020* (16 April 2020) Boletín N° 13.358–070, concurring opinion of Justice Rodrigo Pica Flores, para 66 <https://www.pucv.cl/uuaa/site/docs/20200504/20200504135024/stc_rol_n___8574_2020.pdf>.

139 La Tribuna, 'Reforman polémico artículo 184 del Código Procesal Penal' *Diario La Tribuna* (Honduras, 25 April 2020) <https://www.latribuna.hn/2020/04/25/reforman-polemico-articulo-184-del-codigo-procesal-penal/> accessed March 2021 (link currently not available).

140 See *section 3.4.3 supra* under Executive Branch Measures.

than through the Decree that was passed responding to the pandemic.[141] An analysis published by a national newspaper focusing on whether the decree had worked to reduce overcrowding concluded, similarly, that there were so many crimes excluded that the measure was ineffective.[142] In Bolivia, the World Organization Against Torture expressed concern that the Presidential Decree of Amnesty and Pardon had "proven completely inefficient to reduce the concerning levels of overcrowding in Bolivian prisons" and requested that the decree be modified to allow for more flexibility.[143]

3.6.4 Reintegration Challenges

Life post-prison, with its related social and economic implications on the former prisoner and society in general, is an important consideration under normal conditions, and one that became more salient as release efforts increased in the early stages of the pandemic. As mentioned above, in Costa Rica, the Ministry of Justice determined that support to prisoners once they left prisons was an indispensable criterion for release.[144] In at least one country, Chile, it was reported that one hundred prisoners rejected the general pardon in April 2020 and decided to remain in prison facilities rather than serve their remaining sentences under house arrest.[145] According to unofficial

---

141 Gobierno de Colombia, "Esperamos seguir generando estrategias para solucionar la problemática del hacinamiento': Ministra Cabello' (*Minjusticia*, 3 June 2020) <https://www.minjusticia.gov.co/Sala-de-prensa/Paginas/esperamos-seguir-generando-estrategias-para-solucionar-la-problematica-del-hacinamiento-ministra-cabello.aspx> accessed 12 April 2024.

142 Ligia María Vargas Mendoza, '¿Sirvió el decreto para deshacinar las cárceles que expidió el Gobierno en la emergencia?' *El Espectador* (Bogotá, 23 September 2020) <https://www.elespectador.com/judicial/sirvio-el-decreto-para-deshacinar-las-carceles-que-expidio-el-gobierno-en-la-emergencia-article/> accessed 12 April 2024. See also *Section 3.4.3 supra* under Executive Branch Measures.

143 ANF, 'Organización Mundial contra la Tortura lamenta grave situación sanitaria en penales de Bolivia' (*Correo del Sur*, 27 July 2020) <https://correodelsur.com/sociedad/20200727_organizacion-mundial-contra-la-tortura-lamenta-grave-situacion-sanitaria-en-penales-de-bolivia.html> accessed 12 April 2024.

144 See *section 3.4.1 supra* under Judicial Measures.

145 Carlos Reyes, 'No quieren salir de la cárcel: Más de 100 reos rechazan indulto para abandonar penales por coronavirus' *La Tercera* (Chile, 27 April 2020) <https://www.latercera.com/la-tercera-pm/noticia/no-quieren-salir-de-la-carcel-mas-de-100-reos-rechazan-indulto-para-abandonar-penales-por-coronavirus/PNUDTSGGORBB7FZMUDJQPLCSMQ/> accessed 12 April 2024. See also: Patricio Domínguez and Pedro Rodriguez Martinez, 'Ideas to Safely Reduce Prison Populations during the Pandemic' (*Inter-American Development Bank*, 4 May 2020) <https://blogs.iadb.org/ideas-matter/en/ideas-to-safely-reduce-prison-populations-during-the-pandemic/> accessed 12 April 2024.

sources, some persons decided to remain in prison because they would have no home to return to, wihle others preferred to stay to retain jobs and benefits that would be unavailable outside.[146] This example in Chile, reflecting the absence of a post-prison support policy, illustrates a broader regional issue without material, psychological and social support, whether it comes from family—the government—or not-for-profit organizations—former prisoners often struggle to break the cycle of release and recidivism.[147]

4 Takeaways and Recommendations

The COVID-19 pandemic underscored the vulnerability of prisons to disease transmission, stemming from the confinement, poor sanitation, overcrowding and prevalence of health susceptibilities among inmates. It also highlighted states' longstanding failure to address even basic sanitary needs. At the same time, the pandemic revealed that governments did recognize the gravity of the threat and took measures to reduce overcrowding. These measures should be seriously considered beyond times of crisis and should prompt serious consideration of the urgent necessity to reassess prison policies post-pandemic.

Unfortunately, the post-pandemic reality shows that, despite States' efforts to reduce overcrowding during the pandemic, prison populations in countries in the region have continued growing, with few exceptions. In 2018,[148] the Latin American region had around 1.6 million of people deprived of liberty according to the World Prison Brief.[149] In the years after the pandemic, fig-

146 Reyes, 'No quieren salir de la cárcel: Más de 100 reos rechazan indulto para abandonar penales por coronavirus' (n 145).

147 See: UN Office on Drugs and Crime, *Introductory Handbook on the Prevention of Recidivism and the Social Reintegration of Offenders* (Vienna, United Nations 2012) 63–64.

148 The World Prison Brief contains information from 2018 and 2020 for most Latin American countries. Since the pandemic started in 2020, 2018 was used to calculate pre-pandemic prison population. See: Information available in World Prison Brief on Argentina, Bolivia, Brazil, Chile, Colombia, Costa Rica, Dominican Republic, Ecuador, El Salvador, Guatemala, Honduras, Mexico, Nicaragua, Panama, Paraguay, Peru, Uruguay and Venezuela. Cuba's most recent information before 2020 was from 2012. See: Institute for Crime & Justice Policy Research and Birkbeck College, 'South America' (*World Prison Brief*, 1 January 2024) <https://www.prisonstudies.org/map/south-america> accessed 12 April 2024.

149 In 2018, Argentina recorded 103,209 people deprived of liberty, Bolivia 18.368, Brazil 744,216, Chile 41,689, Colombia 118,513, Costa Rica 19,728, Dominican Republic 26,078, Ecuador 37,996, El Salvador 39,642, Guatemala 24,303, Honduras 20,505, Mexico 197,988, Nicaragua 20,918, Panama 16,561, Paraguay 14,696, Peru 87,995, Uruguay 10,233, and

ures[150] show that the region has reached an overall prison population of almost 1.9 million.[151] A few countries, Colombia,[152] Ecuador,[153] Costa Rica,[154] Guatemala,[155] and Honduras[156] recorded decreases in their prison population

Venezuela 46,915. In the case of Cuba, the last public numbers of prison population were registered in 2012: 57,337. Using the numbers listed here, in 2018 the region had 1,646,890 persons deprived of liberty. See: Institute for Crime & Justice Policy Research and Birkbeck College, 'Highest to Lowest – Prison Population Total' (*World Prison Brief*, 1 January 2024) < https://www.prisonstudies.org/highest-to-lowest/prison-population-total?field_region_taxonomy_tid=All> accessed 12 April 2024.

150 It is important to indicate that the post-pandemic figures of each Latin American state were taken from the "highest to lowest" list of the World Prison Brief, where the information is the most recent available but not necessarily all from the same date. For the purpose of this document, and in order to establish a regional number, the most recent information was considered. The data used for this chapter, came, for example, from 2020 in the case of Argentina, Brazil, Venezuela, Costa Rica, El Salvador and Honduras; from 2023 in the case of Bolivia, Colombia, Ecuador, Paraguay, Peru, Uruguay, Guatemala and Panama; and from the beginning of 2024 for Chile, Mexico and the Dominican Republic. According to the database of World Prison Brief, Nicaragua does not have public information for prison population after 2018 and in the case of Cuba, the last information is from the beginning of 2020. For this reason, for Nicaragua and Cuba, the figures were based on the last available data from 2018 and 2020.

151 In 2022, Argentina recorded 117,810 people under detention, Brazil 839,672, Venezuela 67,200, Costa Rica 17,829, El Salvador 71,000, and Honduras 19,619; in 2023, Bolivia had a prison population of 25,291, Colombia 101,622, Ecuador 30,804, Paraguay 17,006, Peru 94,502, Uruguay 14,965, Guatemala 23,361, and Panama 22,239; and, finally, in the beginning of 2024, Chile had 54,453 people in prisons, Mexico 232,684, and Dominican Republic 26,396. In the case of Cuba, the most recent information of prison population was registered in 2020: 90,000 people under detention; and in Nicaragua, the most recent data is from 2018: 20,918. Using the numbers available as of 2024 as detailed here, the region had 1,887,371 persons deprived of liberty. See: Institute for Crime & Justice Policy Research and Birkbeck College, 'Highest to Lowest – Prison Population Total' (n 149).

152 In 2018 Colombia had 118,513 people under detention; by the end of 2023, the population was 101,622. See: Colombia data in World Prison Brief, Institute for Crime & Justice Policy Research.

153 In 2018 Ecuador had a total of 37,996 people deprived of liberty; by the end of 2023, the population was 30,304. See: Ecuador data in World Prison Brief, Institute for Crime & Justice Policy Research.

154 In 2018 Costa Rica had 19,728 people deprived of liberty; by the end of 2022, the population was 17,829. See: Costa Rica data in World Prison Brief, Institute for Crime & Justice Policy Research.

155 In 2018 Guatemala had 24,303 people under detention; by the end of 2023 the population was 23,361. See: Guatemala data in World Prison Brief, Institute for Crime & Justice Policy Research.

156 In 2018 Honduras had 20,506 people deprived of liberty; by the end of 2022, the population was 19,619. See: Honduras data in World Prison Brief, Institute for Crime & Justice Policy Research.

in comparison with the pre-pandemic period (and it would be worthwhile to further study the reasons for this), while the rest of the Latin American states countries reflected increases.

In addition, crises in prison contexts in the region continue to exacerbate, as exemplified by two countries: Ecuador and El Salvador. Ecuador, which has faced structural problems in its prisons system for decades, has seen hundreds of inmates killed since 2021 due to intra-prison violence linked to organized crime.[157] In El Salvador, since 2022, authorities have adopted a state of emergency to fight gang violence,[158] which includes a policy of mass incarceration that has led the country to have the highest prison population rate in the world.[159] These cases serve to highlight the challenges resulting from countries' long-standing neglect of their prison system and of the use of incarceration policies to address public safety issues.

However, even in the current post-pandemic context, the experiences of the COVID-19 pandemic should prompt governments in the region to reconsider the laws, policies and practices that have led to such high levels of overcrowding and inhumane prisons in the first place. In particular, governments should analyse and derive lessons from the experience of countries attempting to reduce prison population during the pandemic. The efforts of the countries described in this chapter can provide valuable lessons for government authorities, policymakers, international human rights bodies and advocates. The pandemic opened a window of opportunity to foster a more humane and sensible discussion about prison conditions and respect for the human rights

157 See IACHR, 'Situation of Persons Who Are Deprived of Liberty in Ecuador' (*OAS*, 2022) 8 <https://www.oas.org/es/cidh/informes/pdfs/Informe-ppl-Ecuador_VF.pdf> accessed 12 April 2024; BBC News, 'Inmates Free 57 Ecuador prison guards after stand-off' *BBC News* (London, 2 September 2023) <https://www.bbc.com/news/world-latin-america-66691767> accessed 12 April 2024; Al Jazeera, 'Ecuador assesses toll of prison violence as 17 guards still held' *Al Jazeera* (Doha, 26 July 2023) <https://www.aljazeera.com/news/2023/7/26/ecuador-assesses-toll-of-prison-violence-as-17-guards-still-held> accessed 12 April 2024.

158 IACHR, 'CIDH urge a El Salvador implementar acciones en seguridad ciudadana de conformidad con los derechos humanos, incluyendo bajo el Régimen de Excepción' (*OAS*, 22 April 2022) <https://www.oas.org/es/CIDH/jsForm/?File=/es/cidh/prensa/comunicados/2022/082.asp> accessed 12 April 2024.

159 Karla Arévalo, 'El Salvador: país con la tasa de encarcelamiento más alta del mundo. Informe' (*Voz de América*, 31 March 2023) <https://www.vozdeamerica.com/a/el-salvador-el-pais-con-la-tasa-de-encarcelamiento-mas-alta-del-mundo/7030583.html> accessed 12 April 2024. Also, according to World Prison Brief Data, El Salvador has the highest prison population rate in the entire world, reaching 1,086 persons deprived of liberty per 100.000 of national population. See: Institute for Crime & Justice Policy Research and Birkbeck College, 'Highest to Lowest – Prison Population Total' (n 149).

of people deprived of liberty. The following section below offers some key takeaways, recommendations, and a suggested agenda for related research and policymaking.

4.1 *Prison Health Is Public Health*

The COVID-19 pandemic has underscored in vivid terms that prison health is public health and should be treated as such. Health is a human right and should extend to all people, without discrimination, including those who are incarcerated and who are therefore disproportionately vulnerable.[160] The COVID-19 pandemic highlighted that prison conditions in Latin America, such as overcrowding, limited access to hygiene products, poor ventilation, inadequate nutrition, and deteriorated infrastructure represent important challenges to public health. It also emphasized the possible public health costs of over-incarceration.

In the region, some governments responded to the threat of COVID-19 by implementing basic and health and sanitation measures. Countries addressed chronic problems of water shortages, increased food rations, and gave maintenance to sanitary and drainage systems. Cleaning supplies were distributed, spaces disinfected with the help of prisoners themselves, and vaccination programs strengthened. The importance of training and involving prisoners, personnel and family members in prevention, was emphasized. Moving forward, governments across the region should include prisons as a public health priority, using a human rights approach. Multiple challenges exist, such as lack of funding and human resources. However, clarifying the connection between prisons and public health is an essential step in the right direction. There is, in fact, a public health case for prison and criminal justice reform.

4.2 *States Can and Should Mobilize to Improve Prison Conditions*

Faced with the threat of COVID-19, several countries in the region pushed for initiatives to address some of the vulnerabilities in their prison systems. As the then-Chairman of the SPT, Sir Malcolm Evans, described in his 2020 address to the United Nations General Assembly, referring to nations across the globe:

> [W]e have seen States being able to do some positive things which they had previously said were impossible – such as dramatically reducing

160 See: UNODC, Nelson Mandela Rules (n 20) Rule 24: "The provision of health care for prisoners is a State responsibility. Prisoners should enjoy the same standards of health care that are available in the community and should have access to necessary health-care services free of charge without discrimination on the grounds of their legal status".

prison populations in order to reduce overcrowding, allowing phones and tablets in prisons in order to enhance communications with the outside world, for example.[161]

In the Latin American countries studied, initiatives to reduce overcrowding were diverse and came from all three branches of government. In an area in which prison administrators are too frequently left alone, the involvement of the legislative and judiciary branches in the search for viable responses to the pandemic in the prison context was refreshing. Efforts to reduce overcrowding through legislation, judicial guidelines, or executive orders were widespread throughout the region and the allowance of technology to compensate for the lack of human contact was innovative. The results and impact of the different measures taken by nations in Latin America deserve further study and analysis precisely because they could be replicated to improve prison conditions across the region, a need that remains pressing even without a pandemic.

4.3 *Countries Need to Seriously Rethink the Importance of Reducing Prison Overcrowding*

The COVID-19 pandemic highlighted what has been reiterated by criminal justice and human rights experts: overcrowding not only violates the rights of persons deprived of liberty but is also concerning from a public health perspective. In this context, COVID-19 serves as a reminder to government authorities and society in general that any criminal justice reform that seeks to reduce prison populations should have at its core those people who should not be in prison in the first place and those who have not been convicted of a crime. Vulnerable populations such as the elderly, children, pregnant women, and those in ill physical or mental health, should also be given due regard, like several of the measures to reduce prison population during the pandemic did.

There are a variety of alternative measures that States can have in place instead of prison sentences, such as community service for non-violent offenders, rehabilitation for drug-users, educational opportunities for children, restorative justice techniques, and therapeutic assistance. For sentenced

161 UN Subcommittee on Prevention of Torture and Other Cruel, Inhuman or Degrading Treatment or Punishment, 'Statement by Sir Malcolm Evans, Chairperson, 75th Session of the General Assembly, Third Committee, Item #72 (a)' (*Journal of the United Nations*, 15 October 2020) 4 <https://estatements.unmeetings.org/estatements/11.0030/20201015/EGUdH5dFYORS/d1FK59pxbkwf_en.pdf> accessed 12 April 2024.

prisoners who advance in their rehabilitation process through education, work, or other activities, options include nightly/weekend prison sentences and partial release to work or be at home with family. These opportunities also help prepare those deprived of liberty for the reintegration process. Also, similar to what several of the country initiatives during the pandemic included, States can consider early release for those above a certain age, who have completed most of their sentence, or who have abided by good behaviour during their time in prison.

The efforts of some countries in the region to release people from prison during the pandemic also raise the following considerations for governments:

- any programs that promote alternatives to prison should acknowledge that society should be informed and receive sensible explanations as to the importance of these measures; public perception can be key in shaping policy related to criminal justice and security;
- non-custodial measues should not be used to advance impunity for serious crimes such as human rights violations and public corruption;
- offering adequate opportunities for outgoing prisoners is essential to ensure a successful transition back into the community; and
- reliable information and data are required to design policies that are sustainable and effective.

4.4 *Technology Use Should Be Expanded to Complement Important Aspects of Prison Life*

Crises can and should spark innovation. Such has been the case of prison systems in the region that attempted to mitigate the worst effects of the restrictions on contact with the outside world by using technology to provide alternative means of communication. During the pandemic, people everywhere learned to use virtual means to communicate better with loved ones, study, work, and even exercise; technology was also used for medical and judicial purposes. These experiences also offer important lessons for places of deprivation of liberty. The right of people deprived of liberty to receive in-person visits should always be respected, but technology can aid tremendously in complementing the contacts that prisoners have with their families. In the specific case of those persons deprived of liberty who do not receive visits because they are foreigners or because their families live too far away, technology can help build important bridges for them to be in touch with their outside world.

Technology can also be beneficial and should be explored to alleviate other collateral consequences of confinement, such as the lack of effective and sufficient educational and rehabilitation programs as well as inadequate medical attention. Using technological alternatives such as video-calling or virtual courses to connect prisoners with education and vocational materials could greatly enhance rehabilitation efforts in prisons. Prisons in the region that partnered with universities to offer cultural activities to inmates provide good practices that should be analysed and possibly replicated. Similarly, the use of telemedicine can help treat prisoners who otherwise would not receive specialized health care in prisons.

Of course, like other changes implemented during the pandemic, technology also comes with its challenges. For one, virtual calls, distance learning, and telemedicine can never replace in-person contact in the prison context. Persons deprived of liberty, many of whom have lived marginalized lives, benefit especially from human interaction. Separately, technology is costly. In addition to the resources that governments need to invest to offer technological alternatives in prisons, it may be difficult for family members of persons deprived of liberty, given the significant levels of poverty amongst the prison population in Latin America, to have access to adequate equipment and internet to connect with their loved ones. However, governments would need to balance these considerations with the fact that many times prisons are remote, and it may also be expensive for families to travel to visit their loved ones.

Another concern from prison administrators regarding the use of technology to connect prisoners with the outside world is security. Hardware and other equipment can be vandalized and weaponized and cellular or digital connections have been used to coordinate criminal activity or to access pornography.

Policy makers and administrators need to be aware of all these considerations while at the same time acknowledging that in the pandemic, access to technology became more essential than ever, outside and inside prisons. If leveraged correctly, and accompanied by thoughtful and innovative policies, technology can complement existing practices and greatly improve living conditions in prisons while also contributing to the rehabilitation process of those deprived of liberty.

4.5 *Greater Transparency Is Needed about the Impact of Pandemic-Related Prison Policies*

Before the COVID-19 pandemic, several prison systems in the region were already marked by difficulty in the access to statistics and information and a lack of transparency. During the pandemic, which called for closer scrutiny of the system, there was a troubling lack of complete and updated data as well as underreporting from States regarding the impact of COVID-19 in prisons.

Transparency and consistent flow of information are essential for better management and oversight practices required during times of crisis and help alleviate possible tension and anxiety amongst prisoners and their families. Also, governments should be accountable to their citizens regarding the results of the different measures adopted.

4.6 *Further Research Is Needed for Policy Design/Making*

For real transformation to take place in prisons systems in Latin America, research and science need to inform public policies. More information and research are necessary regarding COVID-19's impact in prisons, including:

- *Accurate and complete information regarding impact of COVID-19 in prisons in Latin America, including the number of those infected and numbers of related deaths.* Public health experts, policy makers, criminal justice, and other relevant professionals can benefit from access to such detailed data to make recommendations that can more effectively address the specific challenges that were faced by each country and the region. Going forward, this information could help improve health in prisons and disease prevention as well as shape prison policy more generally.
- *Comparative analysis of the different measures taken by countries and their impact.* It is essential that countries analyse the implementation process and results of their policy solutions enacted and recommended during the pandemic, gaining insight into their effectiveness or shortcomings. For measures that attempted to reduce overcrowding, the information should include, for example, numbers of prisoners who were released, the method that was used, and recidivism rates among the relevant population, which will be important for guiding future efforts. To enhance the identification of best practices and lessons learned, comparative analyses should be conducted between countries. Due consideration should also be given to the differential impact that COVID-19 has had in particularly vulnerable groups within the general population deprived of liberty, such as women, children, and the elderly.

Regional cooperation, solidarity, and innovation will be key in assessing research and results as well as in establishing policy going forward. There must be greater information sharing and cooperation between Latin American countries regarding the impact of COVID-19 as well as for setting the priorities in the policy agenda. International bodies, such as the United Nations, and regional bodies such as the IAHCR have an important role to play in identifying best practices and in providing recommendations to States. Other regional institutions such as the IADB and more broadly the Organization of American States can help spearhead comparative research at the regional level and provide technical assistance to States.

5 Conclusion

COVID-19 made glaringly clear a reality that should be the starting point for a new type of reform: prisons and society are intrinsically interdependent and face shared risks as well as responsibilities. The lessons of COVID-19 offer Latin America a historic opportunity to reimagine its prison systems and relationships with individuals deprived of their liberty. The timing and circumstances are still present for a more humane and sensible discussion about prison conditions, respect for the human rights of people deprived of liberty and the urgent need to rethink prison policy. If a crisis as devastating as the COVID-19 pandemic does not provoke a positive paradigm shift in the region's approach to persons deprived of liberty, it is difficult to envision what will.

Acknowledgments

This chapter was originally published as a policy paper by the Inter-American Dialogue in April 2021. It was authored by María Luisa Romero with research support of Inter-American Dialogue staff Azul Hidalgo Solá and Luisa Stalman and it is available here: https://www.thedialogue.org/wp-content/uploads/2021/04/The-Covid-19-Pandemic-and-Prison-Policy-.pdf. In 2023, Soledad Sánchez Jeanney worked with Romero to update that paper for this publication. Stephanie Davie Vielman provided research and editorial support.

References

0221, 'La Suprema Corte revocó el fallo que habilitó las prisiones domiciliarias por el COVID-19' (*0221*, 11 May 2020) <https://www.0221.com.ar/nota/2020-5-11-12-42-0-la-suprema-corte-revoco-el-fallo-del-juez-platense-que-habilito-las-excarcelaciones>.
0221, 'La Suprema Corte revocó el fallo que habilitó las prisiones domiciliarias por el COVID-19' (*0221*, 11 May 2020) <https://www.0221.com.ar/nota/2020-5-11-12-42-0-la-suprema-corte-revoco-el-fallo-del-juez-platense-que-habilito-las-excarcelaciones>.
AFP, 'Estoy aportando a Guatemala y me estoy ayudando a mi mismo': Ex pandilleros cosen mascarillas en la cárcel' *RPP Noticias* (Guatemala, 30 March 2020) <https://

rpp.pe/mundo/actualidad/coronavirus-covid-19-estoy-aportando-a-guatemala-y-me-estoy-ayudando-a-mi-mismo-ex-pandilleros-cosen-mascarillas-en-la-carcel-noticia-1255102>.

AFP, 'Covid-19 au Mexique: des detenus cousent des masques' *Le Journal de Montréal* (Montréal, 26 March 2020) <https://www.journaldemontreal.com/2020/03/26/covid-19-au-mexique–des-detenus-cousent-des-masques>.

Aguilar Córdoba A, 'Polémica por ley que permitiría indulto a condenados por crímenes en dictadura chilena por el COVID-19' (*Agencia Anadolu*, 7 April 2020) <https://www.aa.com.tr/es/mundo/pol%c3%a9mica-por-ley-que-permitir%c3%ada-indulto-a-condenados-por-cr%c3%admenes-en-dictadura-chilena-por-el-covid-19/1796077>.

AKE International, 'Latin America: Prison riots increase as COVID-19 spreads' (*AKE Group*, 29 April 2020) <https://akegroup.com/2020/04/29/latin-america-prison-riots-increase-as-covid-19-spreads/>.

Al Jazeera, 'Ecuador assesses toll of prison violence as 17 guards still held' *Al Jazeera* (Doha, 26 July 2023) <https://www.aljazeera.com/news/2023/7/26/ecuador-assesses-toll-of-prison-violence-as-17-guards-still-held>.

Alvarado N, 'En esta Semana Santa más de 1,700 presos y presas regresan a sus hogares' (*Sistema Penitenciario Nacional*, 9 April 2020) <https://www.migob.gob.ni/penitenciario/en-esta-semana-santa-mas-de-1700-presos-y-presas-regresan-a-sus-hogares>.

Alvarado N, '1,605 presos y presas regresan a sus hogares' (Sistema Penitenciario Nacional, 15 July 2020) <https://www.migob.gob.ni/penitenciario/1605-presos-y-presas-regresan-a-sus-hogares/>.

Alvarado N and others, 'Las cárceles de América Latina y el Caribe ante la crisis sanitaria del COVID-19' 5 (*Inter-American Development Bank*, August 2020) <https://publications.iadb.org/publications/spanish/document/Las-carceles-de-America-Latina-y-el-Caribe-ante-la-crisis-sanitaria-del-COVID-19.pdf>.

Andina, 'Cárceles Productivas: internos del Cusco confeccionan mascarillas y mamelucos' (*Andina*, 12 June 2020) <https://andina.pe/agencia/noticia-carceles-productivas-internos-del-cusco-confeccionan-mascarillas-y-mamelucos-801277.aspx>.

ANF, 'Organización Mundial contra la Tortura lamenta grave situación sanitaria en penales de Bolivia' (*Correo del Sur*, 27 July 2020) <https://correodelsur.com/sociedad/20200727_organizacion-mundial-contra-la-tortura-lamenta-grave-situacion-sanitaria-en-penales-de-bolivia.html>.

Angelo T, 'Fachin reverte decisão que citou astronautas e príncipes para negar domiciliar' (*Consultor Jurídico*, 12 May 2020) <https://www.conjur.com.br/2020-mai-12/fachin-reverte-decisao-cita-astronautas-negar-domiciliar/>.

Arévalo K, 'El Salvador: país con la tasa de encarcelamiento más alta del mundo. Informe' (*Voz de América*, 31 March 2023) <https://www.vozdeamerica.com/a/el

-salvador-el-pais-con-la-tasa-de-encarcelamiento-mas-alta-del-mundo/7030583.html>.

BBC News, 'Inmates Free 57 Ecuador prison guards after stand-off' *BBC News* (London, 2 September 2023) <https://www.bbc.com/news/world-latin-america-66691767>.

BCN Ley Chile, Ley 21228, Concede Indulto General Conmutativo a Causa de la Enfermedad COVID-19 en Chile, Ministerio de Justicia y Derechos Humanos (17 April 2020).

Bergman M and others, 'The Effect of Coronavirus in Prisons in Latin America' (*Sociedad de Criminología Latinoamericana* (*SOCLA*), 12 June 2020) 27 <https://criminologialatam.wordpress.com/2020/06/12/efectos-del-covid-19-carceles-de-latino-america/>.

Blanco P, 'Coronavirus: beneficiarán con arresto domiciliario a más de 400 presos de la Provincia de Buenos Aires' (*Infobae*, 9 April 2020) <https://www.infobae.com/sociedad/policiales/2020/04/09/coronavirus-beneficiaran-con-arresto-domiciliario-a-mas-de-400-presos-de-la-provincia-de-buenos-aires/>.

Burki T, 'Prisons Are 'in no way equipped' to Deal with the COVID-19' (2020) 395 *The Lancet* 1411–1412.

Burt J and Estrada P, 'In Guatemala, COVID-19 Puts Justice on Hold, Emboldening Convicted War Criminals to Seek Their Freedom' (*International Justice Monitor*, 17 April 2020) <https://www.ijmonitor.org/2020/04/in-guatemala-covid-19-puts-justice-on-hold-emboldening-convicted-war-criminals-to-seek-their-freedom/>.

CARICOM, 'Member states and associate members' (*CARICOM*, 1 January 2024) <https://caricom.org/member-states-and-associate-members/>.

Chile Reports, 'President Piñera Passed Pardon Act for COVID-19 to Prevent Large-scale Contagion in Prison Facilities' (*Gobierno de Chile*, 16 April 2020) <https://chilereports.cl/en/news/2020/04/16/president-pi%C3%B1era-passes-pardon-act-for-covid-19-to-prevent-large-scale-contagion-in-prison-facilities&#> accessed March 2021 (link is currently unavailable).

Chumil K, 'Coronavirus: videoconferencias podrían sustituir las visitas en las cárceles' *Prensa Libre* (Guatemala, 27 March 2020) <https://www.prensalibre.com/guatemala/justicia/coronavirus-videoconferencias-podrian-sustituir-las-visitas-en-las-carceles/>.

Centro de Información Judicial, 'Proveído de la Cámara Federal de Casación Penal' (*Cámara Federal de Casación Penal*, 2 April 2020) <https://www.cij.gov.ar/nota-37032-Prove-do-de-la-C-maraFederal-de-Casaci-n-Penal.html>.

Centro de Información Judicial, 'Acordada 9/20 de la Cámara Federal de Casación Penal' (*Cámara Federal de Casación Penal*, 13 April 2020) 5–6 <https://www.cij.gov.ar/nota-37089-Acordada-9-20-de-la-C-mara-Federal-de-Casaci-n-Penal.html>.

Comité Internacional de la Cruz Roja, 'México y América Central: El CICR apoya a lugares de detención para prevenir y controlar la propagación de la COVID-19'

(*ICRC*, 7 April 2020) <https://www.icrc.org/es/document/el-cicr-apoya-lugares-de-detencion-para-prevenir-y-controlar-la-propagacion-de-la-covid-19>.

Comité Internacional de la Cruz Roja, 'Brasil y Cono Sur; El CICR presta apoyo a los sistemas penitenciarios de la región en la lucha contra la pandemia' (*ICRC*, 14 May 2020) <https://www.icrc.org/es/document/brasil-y-cono-sur-el-cicr-presta-apoyo-los-sistemas-penitenciarios-de-la-region-para>.

Comité Internacional de la Cruz Roja, 'América Latina y el CICR en tiempos de COVID-19: así adaptamos nuestra acción' (*ICRC*, 23 April 2020) <https://www.icrc.org/es/document/america-latina-y-el-cicr-en-tiempos-de-covid-19-asi-adaptamos-nuestra-accion#atajoLima>.

Congreso General de los Estados Unidos Mexicanos, Decreto por el que se expide la Ley de Amnistía (22 April 2020) Secretaría de Gobernación México (SEGOB).

Correo Del Sur, 'En vivo: Motín en la cárcel San Roque' *Correo Del Sur* (Sucre, 19 June 2020) <https://correodelsur.com/seguridad/20200619_en-vivo-motin-en-la-carcel-san-roque.html>.

Cuiza P, 'Dos condenados por narcotráfico, los primeros en beneficiarse con el indulto en Bolivia' (*La Razón*, 18 May 2020) <https://www.la-razon.com/nacional/2020/05/18/dos-condenados-por-narcotrafico-los-primeros-en-beneficiarse-con-el-indulto-en-bolivia/>.

de Lázzari E and Daniel Lorat M, 'Ref. Expte. N.: SDH-96–2020' (*Poder Judicial de la Provincia de Buenos Aires*, 25 March 2020) <http://www.scba.gov.ar/includes/descarga.asp?id=45344&n=Ver%20resoluci%F3n%2052-20.pdf>.

Domínguez P and Rodriguez Martinez P, 'Ideas to Safely Reduce Prison Populations during the Pandemic' (*Inter-American Development Bank*, 4 May 2020) <https://blogs.iadb.org/ideas-matter/en/ideas-to-safely-reduce-prison-populations-during-the-pandemic/>.

Domínguez P and Rodriguez Martinez P, 'Pandemic and Prisons: What Are the Challenges for Latin American Governments?' (*Inter-American Development Bank*, 22 April 2020) <https://blogs.iadb.org/ideas-matter/en/pandemic-and-prisons-what-are-the-challenges-for-latin-american-governments/>.

El 19 Digital, 'Sistema Penitenciario Nacional entrega a 2,815 personas a sus Familias' (*El 19 Digital*, 13 May 2020) <https://www.el19digital.com/articulos/ver/titulo:103275-sistema-penitenciario-nacional-entrega-a-2815-personas-a-sus-familias>.

El 19 Digital, 'Sistema Penitenciario Nacional entrega a 2,815 personas a sus Familias' (*El 19 Digital*, 13 May 2020) <https://www.el19digital.com/articulos/ver/titulo:103275-sistema-penitenciario-nacional-entrega-a-2815-personas-a-sus-familias>.

El Peruano, Decreto Supremo No. 004–2020 que establece supuestos especiales para la evaluación y propuesta de recomendación de Gracias Presidenciales, y determina su procedimiento, en el marco de la emergencia sanitaria por COVID-19 (23 April 2020).

El Telégrafo, 'CNJ sugiere a jueces privilegiar medidas alternativas en lugar de la prisión' *El Telégrafo* (Ecuador, 12 April 2020) <https://www.eltelegrafo.com.ec/noticias/judicial/12/cnj-sugiere-jueces-privilegiar-medidas-alternativas-prision>.

Estúdio Folha, 'Detentas do Amazonas produzem mascaras' (*Estudio Folha*, 1 April 2020) <https://estudio.folha.uol.com.br/iniciativascontraocoronavirus/2020/04/1988630-detentas-do-amazonas-produzem-mascaras.shtml>.

Europa Press, 'Nicaragua pone en libertad a 2,800 presos ante denuncias por un posible brote de coronavirus en las cárceles del país' (*Europa Press*, 13 May 2020) <https://www.europapress.es/internacional/noticia-nicaragua-pone-libertad-2800-presos-denuncias-posible-brote-coronavirus-carceles-pais-20200513225618.html>.

Europa Press, 'Nicaragua pone en libertad a 2,800 presos ante denuncias por un posible brote de coronavirus en las cárceles del país' (*Europa Press*, 13 May 2020) <https://www.europapress.es/internacional/noticia-nicaragua-pone-libertad-2800-presos-denuncias-posible-brote-coronavirus-carceles-pais-20200513225618.html>.

Equal Justice Initiative, 'Covid-19's Impact on People in Prison' (*EJI*, 21 August 2020) <https://eji.org/news/covid-19s-impact-on-people-in-prison/>.

Ferrer F, 'Coronavirus en Argentina: presentaron un amparo contra las liberaciones de presos con la excusa del COVID-19' (*Infobae*, 30 April 2020) <https://www.infobae.com/politica/2020/04/30/coronavirus-en-argentina-presentaron-un-amparo-contra-las-liberaciones-de-presos-con-la-excusa-del-covid-10/>.

France24, 'Al menos 17 muertos y nueve heridos deja motín en cárcel de Venezuela' *France24* (Caracas, 2 May 2020 <https://www.france24.com/es/20200502-al-menos-17-muertos-y-nueve-heridos-deja-mot%C3%ADn-en-c%C3%A1rcel-de-venezuela>.

Gendarmería de Chile, 'Medidas con que Gendarmería enfrenta al coronavirus' <https://html.gendarmeria.gob.cl/doc/medidas.pdf&#>.

Gendarmería de Chile, '#SomosReinserciónYSeguridadPública' (*Twitter*, 19 June 2020) <https://x.com/Gendarmeria_CL/status/1274046983242682369> accessed 12 April 2024.

Gobierno de Colombia, "Esperamos seguir generando estrategias para solucionar la problemática del hacinamiento': Ministra Cabello' (*Minjusticia*, 3 June 2020) <https://www.minjusticia.gov.co/Sala-de-prensa/Paginas/esperamos-seguir-generando-estrategias-para-solucionar-la-problematica-del-hacinamiento-ministra-cabello.aspx>.

Guterres A, 'We Are All in This Together: Human Rights COVID-19 Response and Recovery' (*United Nations*, 23 April 2020) <https://www.un.org/en/un-coronavirus-communications-team/we-are-all-together-human-rights-and-covid-19-response-and&#>.

Hawks L and others, 'COVID-19 in Prisons and Jails in the United States' (2020) 180 *JAMA Internal Medicine* 1041–1042.

Human Rights Watch, 'Announced releases of Detainees in the Justice Systems Due to Covid-19' (*Human Rights Watch*, 22 May 2020) <https://www.hrw.org/sites/default/files/media_2020/05/announced_releases_detainees_covid19_1.pdf>.

IACHR, 'IACHR and OSRESCER Express Serious Concerns About the Human Rights Situation During the Response to the COVID-19 Pandemic in Nicaragua' (*OAS*, 8 April 2020) <https://www.oas.org/en/iachr/media_center/PReleases/2020/072.asp>.

IACHR, 'IACHR presents Report on Measures Aimed at Reducing the Use of Pretrial Detention' (*OAS*, 7 September 2017) <https://www.oas.org/en/iachr/media_center/PReleases/2017/136.asp>.

IACHR, 'Report on the Human Rights of Persons Deprived of Liberty in the Americas' (*IACHR*, 31 December 2011) <https://www.oas.org/en/iachr/pdl/docs/pdf/PPL2011eng.pdf>.

IACHR, 'IACHR concerned about specific risks faced by Persons Deprived of Liberty in the Americas during the COVID-19 pandemic' (*OAS*, 9 September 2020) <https://www.oas.org/en/iachr/media_center/PReleases/2020/212.asp

IACHR, 'The IACHR urges States to guarantee the health and integrity of persons deprived of liberty and their families in the face of the COVID-19 pandemic' (*OAS*, 31 March 2020) <https://www.oas.org/en/iachr/media_center/PReleases/2020/066.asp>.

IACHR, 'The IACHR urges States to guarantee the health and integrity of persons deprived of liberty and their families in the face of the COVID-19 pandemic' (*OAS*, 31 March 2020) <https://www.oas.org/en/iachr/media_center/PReleases/2020/066.asp>.

IACHR, 'Personas Privadas de Libertad en Ecuador' (*OAS*, 21 February 2022) <https://www.oas.org/es/cidh/informes/pdfs/Informe-ppl-Ecuador_VF.pdf>.

IACtHR, 'COVID-19 y Derechos Humanos: Los problemas y desafíos deben ser abordados con perspectiva de derechos humanos y respetando las obligaciones internacionales' (*OAS*, 9 April 2020) <https://www.corteidh.or.cr/tablas/alerta/comunicado/cp-27-2020.html>.

IACHR, 'Situation of Persons Who Are Deprived of Liberty in Ecuador' (*OAS*, 2022) 8 <https://www.oas.org/es/cidh/informes/pdfs/Informe-ppl-Ecuador_VF.pdf>.

IACHR, 'CIDH urge a El Salvador implementar acciones en seguridad ciudadana de conformidad con los derechos humanos, incluyendo bajo el Régimen de Excepción' (*OAS*, 22 April 2022) <https://www.oas.org/es/cidh/jsForm/?File=/es/cidh/prensa/comunicados/2022/082.asp>.

IACtHR, 'COVID-19 y Derechos Humanos: Los problemas y desafíos deben ser abordados con perspectiva de derechos humanos y respetando las obligaciones internacionales' (*Corte IDH*, 9 April 2020) <https://www.corteidh.or.cr/tablas/alerta/comunicado/cp-27-2020.html&#>.

IACtHR, 'COVID-19 y Derechos Humanos: Los problemas y desafíos deben ser abordados con perspectiva de derechos humanos y respetando las obligaciones internacionales' (*Corte IDH*, 9 April 2020) <https://www.corteidh.or.cr/tablas/alerta/comunicado/cp-27-2020.html>.

ILANUD, 'El Sistema Penitenciario ante la Encrucijada producto de la crisis provocada por el COVID-19' (April 2020) <https://cdn.sanity.io/files/6u5teakk/production/305d773e4871f4b7d7ab56d4306a20051b5056c3.pdf?dl=&>.

Infobae, 'Motines en Santa fe: confirmaron cinco muertos por los incidentes en los penales de Coronda y Las Flores' (*Infobae*, 24 March 2020) <https://www.infobae.com/sociedad/policiales/2020/03/24/motines-en-carceles-confirmaron-que-son-tres-los-muertos-en-los-penales-de-corona-y-las-flores/>.

Infobae, 'Motines en Santa fe: confirmaron cinco muertos por los incidentes en los penales de Coronda y Las Flores' (*Infobae*, 24 March 2020) <https://www.infobae.com/sociedad/policiales/2020/03/24/motines-en-carceles-confirmaron-que-son-tres-los-muertos-en-los-penales-de-corona-y-las-flores/.

Infobae, 'Celulares en las cárceles: los presos tendrán permitido comunicarse por WhatsApp pero no podrán usar las redes sociales' (*Infobae*, 31 March 2020) <https://www.infobae.com/coronavirus/2020/03/31/celulares-en-las-carceles-bonaerenses-los-presos-tendran-permitido-comunicarse-por-whatsapp-pero-no-podran-usar-las-redes-sociales/>.

Institute for Crime & Justice Policy Research and Birkbeck College, 'South America' (*World Prison Brief*, 1 January 2024) <https://www.prisonstudies.org/map/south-america>.

Institute for Crime & Justice Policy Research and Birkbeck College, 'Highes to Lowest – Prison Population Total' (*World Prison Brief*, 1 January 2024) <https://www.prisonstudies.org/highest-to-lowest/prison-population-total?field_region_taxonomy_tid=All>.

Instituto de Estudios Jurídicos de Ejecución Penal, 'Emergencia carcelaria y pandemia en Argentina' (*INEJEP*, 2021) 42 <https://www.palermo.edu/Archivos_content/2020/derecho/mayo/documento-inejep/INEJEP-emergencia-carcelaria-y-pandemia-en-argentina.pdf>.

Instituto Nacional Penitenciario, '#PerúEstáEnNuestras- Manos' (*Twitter*, 28 March 2020) <https://twitter.com/INPEgob/status/1244075552702529536>.

Inter-American Development Bank, 'Dentro de las Prisiones de América Latina y el Caribe: una primera mirada al otro lado de las rejas' (*BID*, 2019) <https://publications.iadb.org/es/dentro-de-las-prisiones-de-america-latina-y-el-caribe-una-primera-mirada-al-otro-lado-de-las-rejas>.

Inter-American Development Bank, 'Borrowing member countries' (*IDB*, 1 January 2024) <https://www.iadb.org/en/who-we-are/how-we-are-organized/borrowing-member-countries>.

Jaén V, 'Ministra de Gobierno: 'La falta de agua potable es una de las falencias más grandes del Sistema Penitenciario del país' *Mi Diario* (Panama, 27 July 2020) <https://www.midiario.com/nacionales/ministra-de-gobierno-la-falta-de-agua-potable-es-una-de-las-falencias-mas-grandes-del-sistema-penitenciario-del-pais/>.

Klein M and others, 'The New Coronavirus and Enforcement of the New Separate System in Prisons' (2021) 33 *Criminal Justice Policy Review* 206–230.

Klipphan A, 'Julio Alak: 'El Servicio Penitenciario Bonaerense es una deuda de la democracia' (*Infobae*, 18 June 2020) <https://www.infobae.com/politica/2020/06/18/julio-alak-el-servicio-penitenciario-bonaerense-es-una-deuda-de-la-democracia/>.

La Gaceta, Poder Legislativo Decreto No. 36–2020 (10 June 2020) República de Honduras.

La Gaceta No. 222, Ley No. 473 Ley de Régimen Penitenciario y Ejecución de la Pena (21 November 2003) Presidente y Asamblea Nacional de la República de Nicaragua.

La Tribuna, 'Reforman polémico artículo 184 del Código Procesal Penal' *Diario La Tribuna* (Honduras, 25 April 2020) <https://www.latribuna.hn/2020/04/25/reforman-polemico-articulo-184-del-codigo-procesal-penal/>.

Ligia María Vargas Mendoza, '¿Sirvió el decreto para deshacinar las cárceles que expidió el Gobierno en la emergencia?' *El Espectador* (Bogotá, 23 September 2020) <https://www.elespectador.com/judicial/sirvio-el-decreto-para-deshacinar-las-carceles-que-expidio-el-gobierno-en-la-emergencia-article/>.

Microjuris–Al Día Argentina, 'La comunicación en tiempos de Coronavirus: Se autoriza el uso de teléfono celular a los internos, con el fin de mantener el vínculo familiar durante el periodo de vigencia del aislamiento social' (*Microjuris*, 14 April 2020) <https://aldiaargentina.microjuris.com/2020/04/14/la-comunicacion-en-tiempos-de-coronavirus-se-autoriza-el-uso-de-telefono-celular-a-los-internos-con-el-fin-de-mantener-el-vinculo-familiar-durante-el-periodo-de-vigencia-del-aislamiento-social/>.

Migalhas, 'Negada domiciliar a réu com HIV base em decisão de que só astronautas estão livres do coronavírus' (*Migalhas*, 3 June 2020) <https://www.migalhas.com.br/quentes/328259/negada-domiciliar-a-reu-com-hiv-com-base-em-decisao-de-que-so-astronautas-estao-livres-do-coronavirus>.

Ministerio de Gobernación Dirección General del Sistema Penitenciario, 'Se activan protocolos preventivos contra el Coronavirus' (*Gobierno de Guatemala*, 20 March 2020) <https://dgsp.gob.gt/se-activan-protocolos-preventivos-contra-el-coronaviru/>.

Ministerio de Gobierno, 'Comunicado Medidas Temporales Contra el COVID-19 en el Sistema Penitenciario' (*República de Panamá*, 26 March 2020) <https://www.mingob.gob.pa/comunicado-medidas-temporales-contra-el-covid-19-en-el-sistema-penitenciario/>.

Ministerio de Justicia, 'Continúa aplicación de vacunas contra la influenza en centros penitenciarios' (*Gobierno Nacional de Paraguay*, 18 June 2020) <https://www.ministeriodejusticia.gov.py/noticias/continua-aplicacion-de-vacunas-contra-la-influenza-en-centros-penitenciarios>.

Ministerio de Justicia, 'Acciones de prevención de covid-19' (*Gobierno Nacional de Paraguay*) <https://www.ministeriodejusticia.gov.py/institucion/acciones-de-prevencion-covid-19>.

Ministerio de Justicia, 'COVID-19: PPL de cuatro penitenciarias elaboran 3,500 tapabocas por día' (*Gobierno Nacional de Paraguay*, 15 April 2020) <https://www.ministeriodejusticia.gov.py/noticias/covid-19-ppl-de-cuatro-penitenciarias-elaboran-3500-tapabocas-por-dia>.

Ministerio de Justicia, 'PPL se comunican con familiares mediante videollamadas' (*Gobierno Nacional de Paraguay*, 28 March 2020) <https://www.ministeriodejusticia.gov.py/noticias/ppl-se-comunican-con-familiares-mediante-videollamadas>.

Ministerio de Justicia y de Derecho, Decreto Legislativo Número 546 (14 April 2020) República de Colombia.

Ministerio de Justicia y Paz, 'Ministerio de Justicia y Paz acata orden de juzgado de ejecución de la pena sobre valoraciones extraordinarias por Covid-19' (*República de Costa Rica*, 22 April 2020) <https://www.mjp.go.cr/Comunicacion/Nota?nom=Ministerio-de-Justicia-y-Paz-acata-orden-de-Juzgado-de-Ejecucion-de-la-Pena-sobre-valoraciones-extraordinarias-por-Covid-19>.

Ministerio de Salud Chile, 'Ministros de Salud y Justicia implementan medidas de prevención por COVID-19 en ex Penitenciaria' (*Ministerio de Salud Chile*, 13 March 2020) <https://deis.minsal.cl/ministros-de-salud-y-justicia-implementan-medidas-de-prevencion-por-covid-19-en-ex-penitenciaria/>.

Ministerio de Salud y Protección Social Bogotá, 'Lineamientos para control, prevención y manejo de casos por COVID-19 para la población privada de la libertad-PPL en Colombia' (*Minsalud*, April 2020) <https://www.fiduprevisora.com.co/wp-content/uploads/2021/02/LINEAMIENTOS-PARA-CONTROL-PREVENCI%C3%93N-PPL.pdf>.

Ministerio Público Fiscal, 'Jurisprudencia de la Cámara Federal de Casación Penal-Sala de Feria-relacionada al COVID-19' (*República Argentina*, April 2020) 14 <https://www.fiscales.gob.ar/wp-content/uploads/2020/04/Informe_Jurisprudencia-CFCP_sala-feria-coivd_informe.pdf>.

Miranda H, 'Jueces ordenan reubicar o sacar a presos con enfermedades de riesgo ante COVID-19' (*Semanario Universidad*, 6 April 2020) <https://semanariouniversi

dad.com/ultima-hora/jueces-ordenan-reubicar-o-sacar-a-presos-con-enfermedades-de-riesgo-ante-covid-19/>.

Mugnolo FM, 'Recomendación sobre el acceso a la comunicación de personas alojadas en el SPF' (*Procuración Penitenciaria de la Nación*, 2 June 2020) <https://www.ppn.gov.ar/index.php/institucional/noticias/2696-recomendacion-sobre-el-acceso-a-la-comunicacion-de-personas-alojadas-en-el-spf>.

National Council of Justice of Brazil, Recomendação N. 62 (17 March 2020).

Navarro A, 'Alto funcionario de Estados Unidos denuncia que el COVID-19 se esparce en las cárceles de Nicaragua' (*Artículo 66*, 12 May 2020) <https://www.articulo66.com/2020/05/12/alto-funcionario-departamento-estado-denuncia-covid-19-esperace-prisiones-nicaragua/>.

Notas Periodismo Popular, 'El gobierno bonaerense planea construir 2 mil plazas en cárceles' (*Notas Periodismo Popular*, 18 June 2020) <https://www.notasperiodismopopular.com.ar/2020/06/18/el-gobierno-bonaerense-planea-construir-2-mil-plazas-en-carceles/>.

OAS Permanent Council Resolution CP/RES. 1234 (2466/23) (8 November 2023).

Observatorio Venezolano de Prisiones, '47 muertos y 75 heridos es la cifra extraoficial de víctimas por un motín en Cepella' (*Oveprisiones*, 2 May 2020) <https://oveprisiones.com/47-muertos-y-75-heridos-es-la-cifra-extraoficial-de-victimas-por-un-motin-en-cepella/>.

Office of the United Nations High Commissioner for Human Rights – Regional Office for South America, 'COVID-19: Argumentos que justifican medidas para reducir la población privada de libertad' (*OHCHR's South America Regional Office*, April 2020) <https://www.pj.gov.py/descargas/ID2-701_covid_y_medidas_reduccion_personas_privadas_de_libertad_argumentos_y_estandares_internacionales_final_1.pdf>.

OHCHR, 'Urgent action needed to prevent COVID-19 rampaging through places of detention – Bachelet' (*OHCHR*, 25 March 2020) <https://www.ohchr.org/en/statements/2020/03/urgent-action-needed-prevent-covid-19-rampaging-through-places-detention>.

OHCHR and WHO, 'Interim Guidance – COVID-19: Focus on Persons Deprived of Their Liberty' (*Inter-Agency Standing Committee*, March 2020) <https://interagencystandingcommittee.org/sites/default/files/migrated/2020-11/IASC%20Interim%20Guidance%20on%20COVID-19%20-%20Focus%20on%20Persons%20Deprived%20of%20Their%20Liberty_0.pdf>.

Organization of American States, 'Member States' (*OAS*, 1 January 2024) <https://www.oas.org/en/member_states/default.asp>.

Organization of American States, National Constitution of Argentina (1994).

Poder Judicial de la Provincia de Buenos Aires, 'COVID-19 (Coronavirus). Personas privadas de la libertad. Determinaciones en el marco de las medidas de aislamiento social y prevención de riesgos dispuestas por el Estado Nacional' (*SCBA*,

25 March 2020) <https://www.scba.gov.ar/institucional/nota.asp?expre=Personas%20privadas%20de%20la%20libertad&veradjuntos=no>.

Poder Judicial de la Nación, Juzgado Nacional en lo Criminal y Correccional, NRO. 37 (2 May 2020).

Poder Judicial de Perú, Resolución administrativa No. 000138–2020-CE-PJ (7 May 2020).

Poder Judiciário Tribunal de Justiça do Estado de São Paulo, *Habeas Corpus N° 2101302–43.2020.8.26.0000, Codigo N° 10BEC9D9* (31 May 2020).

Portal Jurídico Lexivox, Bolivia, Decreto Presidencial N. 4226 (4 May 2020) Considerando.

Prensa Comunitaria KM169, 'En la emergencia del coronavirus militares condenados y en prisión preventiva pretenden salir de la cárcel' (*Prensa Comunitaria*, 17 April 2020) <https://prensacomunitar.medium.com/en-la-emergencia-del-coronavirus-militares-condenados-y-en-prisi%C3%B3n-preventiva-pretenden-salir-de-d598d4b1e0e6>.

Presidência and Secretaria Especial da Presidência e das Comissõesm Permanentes Brasil, Portaria Conjunta N° 19/ PR-TJMG/2020 (16 March 2020).

Procuraduría General de la República, 'Procuraduría solicita al CPJ habilitación jueces para conocer cambios provisionales en cumplimiento de penas de adultos mayores y enfermos riesgo Coronavirus' (*Gobierno de la República Dominicana*, 29 March 2020 <https://pgr.gob.do/procuraduria-solicita-al-cpj-habilitacion-jueces-para-conocer-cambios-provisionales-en-cumplimiento-de-penas-de-adultos-mayores-y-enfermos-riesgo-coronavirus/>.

Procuraduría General de la República, 'Cambio provisional de prisión por coronavirus solo será solicitado en casos internos de más de 60 años y los que tengan registrados con enfermedades crónicas previo al estado de emergencia' (*Gobierno de la República Dominicana*, 31 March 2020) <https://pgr.gob.do/cambio-provisional-de-prision-por-coronavirus-solo-sera-solicitado-en-casos-internos-de-mas-de-60-anos-y-los-que-tengan-registrados-con-enfermedades-cronicas-previo-al-estado-de-emergencia/>.

Provincia de Buenos Aires Poder Judicial, *Habeas Corpus N.102.555* (8 April 2020).

Radio France Internationale, 'Brésil: évasions en masse de détenus suite aux mesures anti-coronavirus' *Radio France Internationale* (Paris, 17 March 2020) <https://www.rfi.fr/fr/am%C3%A9riques/20200317-br%C3%A9sil-evasion-prison-semi-liberte-sao-paulo-coronavirus-covid19>.

Redacción Judicial, 'Autoridades confirman 23 muertos tras motín en la cárcel La Modelo' *El Espectador* (Bogotá, 22 March 2020) <https://www.elespectador.com/judicial/autoridades-confirman-23-muertos-tras-motin-en-la-carcel-la-modelo-article-910653/>.

Redacción de TVN Noticias, 'Privados de libertad reciben artículos de aseo' *TVN Noticias* (Panama, 17 April 2020) <https://www.tvn-2.com/nacionales/coronavirus-en-panama-privados-libertad-reciben-articulos-aseo-sistema-penitenciario_1_1188004.html>.

Redacción El Diario del centro del país, 'La UNVM dictará talleres virtuales artísticos para personas privadas de su libertad' *El Diario* (Argentina, 23 July 2020) <https://www.eldiariocba.com.ar/locales/2020/7/23/la-unvm-dictara-talleres-virtuales-artisticos-para-personas-privadas-de-su-libertad-25205.html>

República de Argentina, Poder Ejecutivo Nacional. Memorandum: Impartir Directivas respecto del Alerta Epidemiológica del Coronavirus – (COVID-19) (13 March 2020).

República de Panamá, '253 privados de libertad han sido beneficiados con rebaja de pena' (*Ministerio de Gobierno*, 9 June 2020) <https://www.mingob.gob.pa/253-privados-de-libertad-han-sido-beneficiados-con-rebaja-de-pena/>.

República de Panamá, Decreto Ejecutivo N. 265 (9 April 2020).

República de Panamá, Decreto Ejecutivo N. 270 (13 April 2020).

República de Panamá, Decreto Ejecutivo N. 271 (20 April 2020).

República de Panamá, Decreto Ejecutivo N. 272 (28 April 2020).

República de Panamá, Decreto Ejecutivo N. 277 (3 June 2020).

República de Panamá, Decreto Ejecutivo N. 279 (8 June 2020).

República de Panamá, Decreto Ejecutivo N. 304 (4 August 2020).

Reyes C, 'No quieren salir de la cárcel: Más de 100 reos rechazan indulto para abandonar penales por coronavirus' *La Tercera* (Chile, 27 April 2020) <https://www.latercera.com/la-tercera-pm/noticia/no-quieren-salir-de-la-carcel-mas-de-100-reos-rechazan-indulto-para-abandonar-penales-por-coronavirus/PNUDTSGGORBB7FZMUDJQPLCSMQ/>.

Romero LM, Stalman L, and Solá AH, 'The Covid-19 Pandemic and Prison Policy in Latin America' (*The Inter-American Dialogue*, April 2021) <https://www.thedialogue.org/wp-content/uploads/2021/04/The-Covid-19-Pandemic-and-Prison-Policy-.pdf>.

Roust RA, 'Análisis jurisprudencial de las decisiones adoptadas en relación a la situación de las personas privadas de su libertad en la actual situación de pandemia (Covid-19)' (*Microjuris*, 30 April 2020) <https://aldiaargentina.microjuris.com/2020/05/14/analisis-jurisprudencial-de-las-decisiones-adoptadas-en-relacion-a-la-situacion-de-las-personas-privadas-de-su-libertad-en-la-actual-situacion-de-pandemia-covid-19/>.

Rubin R, 'The Challenge of Preventing COVID-19 Spread in Correctional Facilities' (2020) 323 *JAMA* 1760–1761.

Sanchez G, 'CSJ ordena implementar 'protocolos específicos' por covid-19 en cárceles' *República* (Guatemala, 22 July 2020) <https://republica.gt/guatemala/2020-7-22

-16-10-34-csj-ordena-implementar-protocolos-especificos-por-covid-19-en-carceles>.

Secretaría de Salud, 'Lineamientos para la prevención y manejo de COVID-19 en población privada de libertad' (*Gobierno de la República de Honduras*, 16 March 2020) <http://www.dgvmn.gob.hn/documents/COVID19/Lineamientos%20manejo%20ppl%20covid19.pdf>.

Secretaría de Seguridad y Protección Ciudadana and others, 'Protocolo de actuación para la atención de COVID-19 al interior de centros federales de reinserción social (CEFERESOS)' (March 2020) <https://coronavirus.gob.mx/wp-content/uploads/2020/04/Protocolo_De_Actuacion_COVID-19_CEFERESOS.pdf>.

Selser G, 'Nicaragua releases more than 2,800 inmates amid pandemic' *The Seattle Times* (Managua, 13 May 2020) <https://www.seattletimes.com/seattle-news/health/nicaragua-releases-more-than-2800-inmates-amid-pandemic/>.

Servicio Penitenciario Federal, 'Guía de actuación para la prevención y control del COVID-19 en el Servicio Penitenciario Federal' (25 March 2020) <https://www.fiscales.gob.ar/wp-content/uploads/2020/03/Anexo-582020.pdf.pdf.pdf>.

Smink V, 'Coronavirus en Argentina: porqué genera tanta polémica la decisión de sacar de la cárcel a algunos presos por riesgo a que contraigan el covid-19' *BBC News Mundo Argentina* (Argentina, 1 May 2020) <https://www.bbc.com/mundo/noticias-america-latina-52496655>.

Suprema Corte de Justicia Provincia de Buenos Aires, *P-133682-Q* (4 May 2020).

Taraciuk Broner T, 'Decenas de muertos y heridos durante motín carcelario en Venezuela' (*Human Rights Watch*, 4 May 2020) <https://www.hrw.org/es/news/2020/05/04/decenas-de-muertos-y-heridos-durante-motin-carcelario-en-venezuela>.

The Inter-American Dialogue, 'Our Mission' (*The Dialogue*, 1 January 2024) <https://thedialogue.org/>.

Tribunal Constitucional Chile, *Sentencia Rol 8574–2020* (16 April 2020) Boletín N° 13.358–070, concurring opinion of Justice Rodrigo Pica Flores.

Ulloa C, 'Piñera promulga ley de indulto conmutativo por Coronavirus en Chile' *CNN Español* (Chile, 16 April 2020) <https://cnnespanol.cnn.com/2020/04/16/pinera-promulga-ley-de-indulto-conmutativo-por-coronavirus-en-chile/>.

United Nations, 'Regional groups of Member States' (*UN Department for General Assembly and Conference Management*, 1 January 2024) <https://www.un.org/dgacm/en/content/regional-groups&#>.

UN Human Rights Office of the High Commissioner, 'Ecuador: UN torture prevention body remains seriously concerned by prison crisis after second visit' (*OHCHR*, 6 October 2022) <https://www.ohchr.org/en/press-releases/2022/10/ecuador-un-torture-prevention-body-remains-seriously-concerned-prison-crisis>.

UN Subcommittee on Prevention of Torture and Other Cruel, Inhuman or Degrading Treatment or Punishment, 'Visit to Mexico undertaken from 12 to 21 December 2016: observations and recommendations addressed to the State party' (20 September 2018) CAT/OP/MEX/2 <https://tbinternet.ohchr.org/_layouts/15/treatybodyexternal/Download.aspx?symbolno=CAT%2FOP%2FMEX%2F2&Lang=en>.

UN Subcommittee on Prevention of Torture, 'Report on the visit of the Subcommittee on Prevention of Torture and other Cruel, Inhuman or Degrading Treatment of Punishment to Mexico' (31 May 2010) CAT/OP/MEX/1 <https://tbinternet.ohchr.org/_layouts/15/treatybodyexternal/Download.aspx?symbolno=CAT%2FOP%2FMEX%2F1&Lang=en>.

UN Subcommittee on Prevention of Torture, 'Visit to Brazil undertaken from 19 to 30 October 2015: observations and recommendations addressed to the State party' (16 February 2016) CAT/OP/BRA/3 <https://tbinternet.ohchr.org/_layouts/15/treatybodyexternal/Download.aspx?symbolno=CAT%2FOP%2FBRA%2F3&Lang=en>.

UN Subcommittee on Prevention of Torture, 'Visit to the Plurinational State of Bolivia undertaken from 2 to 11 May 2017: observations and recommendations addressed to the State party' (24 July 2018) CAT/OP/BOL/3 <https://tbinternet.ohchr.org/_layouts/15/treatybodyexternal/Download.aspx?symbolno=CAT%2FOP%2FBOL%2F3&Lang=en>.

UN Subcommittee on Prevention of Torture, 'Visit to Panama undertaken from 20 to 26 August 2017: observations and recommendations addressed to the State party' (31 July 2018) CAT/OP/PAN/1 <https://tbinternet.ohchr.org/_layouts/15/treatybodyexternal/Download.aspx?symbolno=cat%2FOP%2FPAN%2F1&Lang=en>.

UN Subcommittee on Prevention of Torture and Other Cruel, Inhuman or Degrading Treatment or Punishment, 'Advice of the Subcommittee on Prevention of Torture to States Parties and National Preventive Mechanisms relating to the Coronavirus Pandemic' (25 March 2020) Working Paper CAT/OP/10 <https://tbinternet.ohchr.org/_layouts/15/treatybodyexternal/SessionDetails1.aspx?SessionID=2438&Lang=en&#>.

UN Subcommittee on Prevention of Torture and Other Cruel, Inhuman or Degrading Treatment or Punishment, 'Statement by Sir Malcolm Evans, Chairperson, 75th Session of the General Assembly, Third Committee, Item #72 (a)' (*Journal of the United Nations*, 15 October 2020) <https://estatements.unmeetings.org/estatements/11.0030/20201015/EGUdH5dFYORS/d1FK59pxbkwf_en.pdf>.

UN Office on Drugs and Crime (UNODC) and World Health Organization Regional Office for Europe, 'Good governance for prison health in the 21st century: A policy brief on the organization of prison health' (*UNODC*, 2013) <https://www.unodc.org/documents/hiv-aids/publications/Prisons_and_other_closed_settings/Good-governance-for-prison-health-in-the-21st-century.pdf>.

UN Office on Drugs and Crime, *Introductory Handbook on the Prevention of Recidivism and the Social Reintegration of Offenders* (Vienna, United Nations 2012).

UOL, 'Moro aprova manutenção da prisão de Gaddel: Coronavírus não é subterfúgio' (*UOL*, 30 March 2020) <https://noticias.uol.com.br/politica/ultimas-noticias/2020/03/30/moro-aprova-manutencao-da-prisao-de-geddel-coronavirus-nao-e-subterfugio.htm>.

Valery JLP, 'Se fugan 84 presos de cárcel en Venezuela; operación de recaptura deja al menos 10 fallecidos, dicen autoridades' *CNN Español* (Caracas, 19 March 2020) <https://cnnespanol.cnn.com/2020/03/19/alerta-10-abatidos-en-zulia-venezuela-tras-fuga-de-84-presos-informaron-autoridades/>.

Vorobyeva Y and others, 'Can the Northern Triangle Contain a Prison Pandemic?' (*The Latin American Advisor*, 30 June 2020) <https://www.thedialogue.org/analysis/can-the-northern-triangle-contain-a-prison-pandemic/>.

Villeda C and Cusicanqui JJ, 'La Asamblea Legislativa aprueba nuevo indulto y amnistía' (*La Razón*, 30 April 2020) <https://www.la-razon.com/nacional/2020/04/30/asamblea-legislativa-nuevo-indulto-amnistia/>.

Walmsley R, 'World Prison Population List (12th edition)' (World Prison Brief, 6 November 2020) <https://www.prisonstudies.org/sites/default/files/resources/downloads/wppl_12.pdf>.

Walmsley R, 'World Pre-trial/Remand Imprisonment List (4th edition)' (*World Prison Brief*, 4 February 2020) <https://www.prisonstudies.org/sites/default/files/resources/downloads/world_pre-trial_list_4th_edn_final.pdf>.

World Health Organization, 'UNODC, WHO, UNAIDS and OHCHR joint statement on COVID-19 in prisons and closed settings' (*WHO*, 13 May 2020) <https://www.who.int/news/item/13-05-2020-unodc-who-unaids-and-ohchr-joint-statement-on-covid-19-in-prisons-and-other-closed-settings/>.

World Health Organization Regional Office for Europe, 'Preparedness, prevention, and control of COVID-19 in prisons and other places of detention: Interim Guidance' (*WHO Europe*, 15 March 2020) <https://www.who.int/europe/publications/i/item/WHO-EURO-2021-1405-41155-57257>.

CHAPTER 6

Addressing the Impact and Response to the COVID-19 Pandemic in Latin American Prisons

Lucia Nuñovero Cisneros and José Luis Pérez Guadalupe

1 Latin American Prisons: Structural Challenges and Context*

Since the 1990s, evidence has shown an accelerated increase of incarceration rates and penitentiary population in Latin America within a context of expanded punishment, criminalization and growing exclusion and inequality.[1] Additionally, overcrowding resulting from limited prison infrastructure made it very difficult to classify or provide security and rehabilitation to inmates, instead it rather fostered violence and degrading treatment in prisons from the region.[2]

Dammert and Zúñiga[3] showed that prison population expansion in Latin America was even more accentuated in facilities situated in main cities, maximal security prisons and in semi-open establishments. This research also revealed abuse, poor living conditions, and difficulties for surveillance and security as well exacerbated problems of criminal contagion, recidivism, and violence, with gangs charging quotas for access to proper accommodation, basic utensils, and food in prisons. It also provided evidence on the scarcity of resources allocated to treatment, health, and food; and the epidemiological risks and impact on physical and mental health of inmates and officials.

---

* This research was funded by the Centro de Investigación, Capacitación y Asesoría Jurídica at the Pontificia Universidad Católica del Perú. (CICAJ-PUCP).

1 Elias Carranza, *Justicia penal y sobrepoblación penitenciaria: respuestas posibles* (Siglo XXI 2001); Elias Carranza, 'Criminalidad, criminalización, y cárcel en la globalización, en américa latina y en los países de altos ingresos' (2009) 1 Revista digital de ciencias penales de Costa Rica 481; Elias Carranza, 'Situación Penitenciaria en América Latina y el Caribe, ¿Qué hacer?' (2012) 8 Anuario de Derechos Humanos 31.

2 Elias Carranza, *Política criminal y penitenciaria en América Latina y el Caribe* (San José, 2003).

3 Lucia Dammert and Liza Zúñiga, 'La cárcel: problemas y desafíos para las Américas' (*FLACSO Chile*, 2008) <https://flacso.cl/biblioteca/product/la-carcel-problemas-y-desafios-para-las-americas/> accessed 15 January 2024.

Indeed, many prisons in Latin America failed to provide physicians, medications, or data records for epidemiological monitoring.

The critical situation of Latin American prisons has been related to structural issues such as racialization, penal selectivity, or the criminalization of poverty, and served as a context for studying inmate self-organization and prison violence.[4] Regarding structural issues, prison population growth has long time ago been related to economic adjustment processes in Latin America, especially in countries with a developed welfare state, such as Chile, and also to severe anti-drug policies applied during the 90s in the Andean countries.[5] More recently, Hathazy and Müller have discussed factors aggravating incarceration rates such as unemployment, authoritarianism, and socioeconomical transformations experienced in the region.[6] However, even though Carranza and Iturralde[7] argued that incarceration rates and overcrowding were a consequence of neoliberal policies from the 90s, the last 15 years have proven that moderate or leftist governments in Latin America also maintained the tendency to imprisonment and punitive policies, as Ariza and Iturralde have rightly pointed out.[8]

More recent studies have shown that even though prison population expanded over 140% between 2000 and 2018 in the region, these problems were even more serious in countries such as Ecuador, Paraguay, Venezuela, Peru and Brazil. Following the international literature,[9] the rise of the prison

4 Chloé Constant, *Pensar las cárceles de América Latina* (Lima, IFEA 2016).

5 Jorge Núñez Vega, 'Hipertrofia represiva: la cuestión carcelaria en América Latina' (2005) 12 Quórum, Revista de pensamiento iberoamericano 140.

6 Paul Hathazy and Markus-Michael Müller, 'The rebirth of the prison in Latin America: Determinants, regimes and social effects' (2016) 65 Crime, Law and Social Change 113; Máximo Sozzo, *Postneoliberalismo y penalidad en América del Sur Buenos Aires* (Clacso 2016) 189–283.

7 Carranza, 'Situación Penitenciaria en América Latina y el Caribe, ¿Qué hacer?' (n 1); Manuel Iturralde, 'O governo neoliberal de la inseguranca social na America Latina; semelhanzas e diferencias con o Norte Global' in Vera Malaguti (ed), *Loic Wacquant ea questao penal no capitalism neoliberal* (Revam 2012) 169–191.

8 Libardo Ariza and Manuel Iturralde, 'Las prisiones y las transformaciones del campo del control del crimen en Colombia' in Libardo Ariza, Manuel Iturralde and Leon Tamayo (eds), *Cárceles, Derecho y Sociedad. Aproximaciones al mundo penitenciario en Colombia* (Bogotá, Universidad de los Andes 2021) 23–53.

9 Sonja Snacken, Kristel Beyens and Hilde Tubex, 'Changing prison population in Western countries: Fate of policy' (1998) 3 European Journal of Crime, Criminal Law and Criminal Justice 18; John F. Pffaf, 'The Micro and Macro Causes of Prison Growth' (2012) 28 Georgia State University Law Review 1237; José Cid Moliné, 'El incremento de la población reclusa en España entre 1996–2006: Diagnóstico y remedios' (2008) 2 Revista Española de Investigación Criminológica 23; Ignacio Gonzáles Sánchez, 'Aumento de presos y código penal. Una

population in Latin America is linked to pre-trial detention rates, the lack of implementing alternatives to prison, and the extended length of sentences for crimes such as drug trafficking.[10] On the other hand, prison overcrowding more recently ceased to be a problem in countries who invested in prison infrastructure such as Chile or Mexico.[11] Also, Soares and Naitomi have found, analysing the cases of countries like Chili, that government effectiveness reduced prison overcrowding, in spite of economic or criminal factors. In other words, recent data shows that even if incarceration rates increase, by promoting the construction of prisons, alternative policies or community programs for prisoners, Latin American countries could deal more effectively with current crises at their penitentiary systems.[12]

On the other hand, regarding social dynamics and informal organizations, mass incarceration in Latin American prisons has been characterized in terms of lack of control on the part of the authorities, due to insufficient staff and inmate organizations who provide goods and self-governance, fluid communication with street criminality, and violence in terms of riots, violent deaths and get-aways as a consequence of overpopulation and poor living conditions.[13]

This characterization provides an extreme appraisal of Latin American prisons, such as the one described by Darke and Karam in Brazil,[14] where anti-

---

explicación insuficiente' (2011) 13 Revista Electrónica de Ciencia penal y Criminología 1, 14–15; Alfred Blumstein, 'Bringing Down the U.S. Prison Population' (2011) 91 The Prison Journal Supplement 12, 18.

10 Lucia Nuñovero Cisneros, 'Factores de aumento de la población penitenciaria en el Perú, medidas alternativas y vigilancia electrónica' (2017) 37 Estudios Penales y Criminológicos 369; Marcelo Bergman and Elena Azaloa, 'Cárceles de México: Cuadros de una crisis' (2007) 1 Revista Latinoamericana de Seguridad Ciudadana 74, 79; Astrid Arrarás and Emily Bello-Pardo, 'General trends of prisons in the Americas' in Jonathan D. Rosen and Marten W. Brienen (eds), *Prisons in the Americas in the twenty-first century: A human dumping ground* (Lexington Books 2015) 1–13; Marcelo Bergman and Gustavo Fondevilla, *Prisons and Crime in Latin America* (Cambridge, Cambridge University Press 2021).

11 Lucia Nuñovero Cisneros, 'Cárceles en América Latina 2000–2018. Tendencias y desafíos' (2019) 50 Cuaderno de Trabajo PUCP 1.

12 Rodrigo R. Soares and Joana Naritomi, 'Understanding high crime rates in Latin America. The Role of Social and Policy Factors' in Rafael Di Tella, Sebastien Edwards and Ernesto Schargrodsky (eds), *The Economics of Crime* (University of Chicago Press 2010) 19–55; Katherine E. Limoncelli, Jeff Mellow and Chongmin Na, 'Determinants of intercountry prison incarceration rates and overcrowding in Latin America and the Caribbean' (2020) 30 International Criminal Justice Review 10.

13 Arrarás and Bello-Pardo, 'General trends of prisons in the Americas' (n 10).

14 Sacha Darke and Chris Garces, 'Surviving in the new mass carceral zone' (2017) 229 Prison Service Journal 2; Chris Garces, Tomas Martin and Sacha Darke, 'Informal prison dynamics in Africa and Latin America' (2013) 91 Criminal Justice Matters 26.

drug legislation accounts for almost 60% of inmates and many studies show the scarcity of personnel and resources, as well as the impossibility of controlling a lot of Brazilian overcrowded prisons where gangs such as the PCC and Commando Vermelho control prison spaces and provide quasi-legal forms of self-government.[15] Self-government of inmates as a threat to prison management was first described in the region by Pérez Guadalupe in the Lurigancho prison during terrorism times in the nineties in Peru, and more recently by Cerbini in Bolivia and Antillano in Venezuelan prisons.[16] This extra-legal form of government provided by groups of inmates and prison gangs has been identified up to the point of providing a label for Latin American Prisons,[17] given the reduced governance capacities of some highly overcrowded penitentiary institutions.

Finally, Pérez Guadalupe, Cavallaro and Nuñovero recently expanded this discussion, providing a distinction between prison governance and inmate organization management styles for the region[18] beyond the aforementioned 'Abdicated Management' or self-government of inmates and the 'Authoritarian Management' in which the institutional government is strong and there is no possibility of dialogue with inmates.[19] Thus, an 'Apparent Management' style is proposed for Latin American prisons where a co-government exists between a weak and corrupt institution and criminal organizations that end

---

15 Karina Biondi, *Sharing this walk: An ethnography of prison life and the PCC in Brazil* (Chapel Hill, UNC Press Books 2016); Camila Caldeira Nunes Dias and Fernando A. Salla, 'Formal and informal controls and punishment: The production of order in the prisons of São Paulo' (2017) 229 Prison Service Journal 19.

16 José L. Pérez Guadalupe, *Faites y atorrantes: una etnografía del penal de Lurigancho* (Lima, Pontificia Universidad Teológica 1994); José L. Pérez Guadalupe, *La construcción social de la realidad carcelaria* (Lima, Pontificia Universidad Católica del Perú 2000); Francesca Cerbini, *La casa de jabón: etnografía de una cárcel boliviana* (Universidad Complutense de Madrid 2011); Andrés Antillano, 'When prisoners make the prison self-rule in Venezuelans prisons' (2017) 229 The Prison Service Journal 26; Julienne Weegels, 'Prisoner self-governance and survival in a Nicaraguan city police jail' (2017) 229 Prison Service Journal 15.

17 David Skarbek, 'Covenants without the sword? Comparing prison self-governance globally' (2016) 110 American Political Science Review 845.

18 José L. Pérez Guadalupe, James Cavallaro and Lucia Nuñovero Cisneros, 'Towards a governance model of ungovernable prisons: How recognition of inmate organizations, dialogue, and mutual respect can transform violent prisons in Latin America' (2021) 70 Catholic University of Washington Law Review 367.

19 Julie de Dardel and Ola Soderstrom, 'The Rise and Fall of Supermax: How the US prison model and ultra punitive penal policy travelled to Colombia' (2015) Université de Neuchatel Maison d'analyse de processus sociaux Working paper 3.

up ruling the prison under the shadows.[20] A more balanced 'Prison Governance' style is also found in Lurigancho Prison in Peru, whereby dialogue with inmates organizations contributes to peaceful coexistence, improving services and prison order.

This context provided several challenges for Latin American countries when dealing with the Covid-19 pandemic in prisons. The aim of this chapter is to analyse a variety of policies implemented in these countries to tackle the pandemic effects in prisons. Although it has not been enough argued in recent literature, penitentiary systems are highly diverse and were also differently impacted by COVID-19 policies. In the first part, prison statistics will show prison populations and overcrowding variations during the COVID-19 years in Latin American countries. Through a review of literature and interviews with experts, the effects of COVID-19 pandemic and the responses implemented in the specific cases of countries such as Mexico, Colombia, Peru, Chile, Brazil and Argentina will also be analysed. The second part will provide a broad discussion of the lessons to be drawn from these critical years, in terms of common issues to be tackled and aspects to be highlighted for a more effective response to Latin American penitentiary systems challenges.

2 Aggravating Critical Scenarios in Latin America

By the beginning of the COVID-19 pandemic, specialists warned of the risk regarding Latin American prisons due to their poor sanitary conditions, food scarcity and overcrowding, which made isolation impossible and resulted in inmates accumulating untreated health conditions while barely having access to proper health services.[21]

Nevertheless, according to available prison statistics, in countries such as Bolivia (+37%), Uruguay (14%), Paraguay (10%) and Panama (9%), prison population continued to increase largely during the COVID-19 pandemic (see variation between years 2020–2022 on Table 6.1), even if most of them were

20 Julienne Weegels, Ramiro Gual and Olga Espinoza, 'Compartiendo el poder: Experiencias de cogobierno entre reclusos y autoridades en las cárceles latinoamericanas' in Norberto Hernández Jiménez (ed), *Temas Criminológicos Latinoamericanos* (Bogotá, Tirant lo Blanch 2021) 321–370; Jennifer E. Peirce, 'Provós, Representantes, Agentes: The Evolution of Prison Governance Arrangements in the Dominican Republic's Prison Reform Process' in Máximo Sozzo (ed), *Prisons, Inmates and Governance in Latin America* (Cham, Springer International Publishing 2022) 93–126.

21 Talha Burki, 'Prisons are no way equipped to deal with COVID-19' (2020) 395 The lancet 1411.

countries where the prison population did not exceed 25,000 inmates nationwide.

On the other hand, very moderate increases or no increases in the number of inmates were evidenced in countries with the largest prison population such as Argentina (+7%), Mexico (+4%), and Brazil (+3%) with the exception of Colombia. Other countries from the region showing significant prison population increases during the previous decades made efforts to reduce or keep this growth at the lowest level during the pandemic: such is the case in Ecuador, Guatemala and Honduras and Peru. As shown in the table above,

TABLE 6.1 Variations of prison population in Latin America 2010–2022

COUNTRY	2010	2012	2014	2016	2018	2020	2022*	VAR 2010–2022	VAR COVID-19 2020–2022
Ecuador	11,800	21,080	25,902	26,421	37,996	39,251	31,245	165%	-20%
Nicaragua	6,500	9,168	10,569	14,675	20,918	-	-	-	-
Paraguay	6,197	7,916	10,949	13,607	14,696	13,821	15,151	144%	10%
Guatemala	11,148	15,013	18,425	21,031	24,303	25,538	24,570	120%	-4%
Bolivia	9,406	14,272	14,220	16,038	18,368	18,260	25,000	166%	37%
Peru	45,464	58,019	70,276	79,644	87,995	92,195	87,466	92%	-5%
Honduras	11,846	12,095	16,331	17,253	20,506	21,675	19,619	65%	-9%
Brazil	496,251	548,003	622,202	722,120	744,216	811,707	835,643	68%	3%
Argentina	65,095	66,484	75,769	92,161	103,209	106,559	114,074	75%	7%
Panama	12,293	14,468	15,208	15,690	16,561	17,967	19,545	59%	9%
Uruguay	8,700	9,418	9,542	10,561	10,233	11,755	13,402	54%	14%
El Salvador	24,662	27,033	36,334	36,824	39,642	37,190	36,663	49%	-2%
Costa Rica	12,110	15,600	18,263	17,889	19,728	19,226	15,345	27%	-20%
Colombia	84,444	113,884	113,623	118,532	118,513	97,414	97,486	15%	-18%
Mexico	219,027	239,089	255,638	217,868	197,988	214,231	223,416	2%	4%
Venezuela	40,825	45,224	51,256	54,738	46,915	37,543	33,558	-17%	-10%
Chile	54,628	51,882	45,501	43,603	41,689	39,884	39,299	-28%	-1%

SOURCE: WORLD PRISONS BRIEF
*HISTORICAL REPORTED BETWEEN FEBRUARY 2022 AND AUGUST 2023

countries that were able to reduce their prison population by 2022 were Costa Rica (-20%), Ecuador (-20%), Colombia (-18%),[22] Venezuela (-10%), Honduras (-9%), Peru (-5%), Guatemala (-4%), El Salvador (-2%) and Chile (-1%), although most of them reached very moderate effects in this regard.

In terms of prison occupancy or inmate population over housing capacity, most countries implemented policies to reduce overcrowding during the pandemic, depending on the severity of the problem. Thus, as shown in Table 6.2. in terms of percentage points, the most significant reduction in prison overcrowding can be observed in Bolivia (-94), El Salvador (-79), Colombia (-22) and Peru (-20), although it has been suggested this could represent in some cases the effect of relocating inmates outside the penitentiary system. In most countries, the proportion of inmates without a sentence remained at the same levels or decreased during the pandemic. However, countries like Costa Rica and Chile, although showing good results in terms of reducing prison population, had increased the proportion of pre-trial prisoners during COVID-19. The proportion of women incarcerated in the region either decreased or remained the same during this period, and even decreased significatively in countries such as Brazil, Paraguay, Panama and Chile.

The subsequent analysis of Colombian, Chilian, Argentinian, Mexican and Peruvian prisons in times of COVID-19 through the lenses of experts and spe-

TABLE 6.2 Variation in prison occupancy, percentages of pre-trial inmates and women in Latin America prisons in the context of COVID-19

	Prison occupancy			Pre-trial inmates			Women		
Country	**2019**	**2022***	**VAR COVID-19**	**2019**	**2022***	**VAR COVID-19**	**2019**	**2022***	**VAR COVID-19**
Bolivia	364%	270%	-94	70%	65%	-15	8%	8%	0
Guatemala	358%	293%	9	48%	49%	1	11%	11%	0
Peru	232%	212%	-20	39%	37%	-2	6%	5%	-1
El Salvador	215%	136%	-79	28%	23%	-5	8%	7%	-1
Honduras	194%	204%	10	53%	54%	1	6%	6%	0

22 This general number might not reflect in countries like Colombia, where more than overall population reduction, inmates were relocated in detention centers outside the penitentiary system.

TABLE 6.2 Variation in prison occupancy, percentages of pre-trial inmates and women (*cont.*)

	Prison occupancy			Pre-trial inmates			Women		
Country	2019	2022*	VAR COVID-19	2019	2022*	VAR COVID-19	2019	2022*	VAR COVID-19
Nicaragua	178%	178%	0	21%	21%	0	5%	5%	0
Brazil	168%	147%	-12	33%	30%	-3	7%	5%	-2
Venezuela	154%	143%	-21	63%	63%	0	5%	6%	1
Colombia	153%	119%	-22	34%	25%	-9	7%	7%	0
Paraguay	143%	160%	12	78%	70%	-8	7%	5%	-2
Ecuador	140%	133%	-5	3. 4%	37%	3	7%	7%	0
Costa Rica	139%	120%	-14	13%	To%	7	5%	4%	-1
Argentina	124%	113%	-9	45%	45%	0	5%	4%	-1
Panama	111%	134%	21	44%	37%	-7	7%	5%	-2
Uruguay	104%	131%	26	77%	22%	-55	5%	5%	0
Chili	103%	91%	-12	33%	37%	5	9%	7%	-2
Mexico	94%	103%	9	39%	42%	3	5%	6%	1

SOURCE: WORLD PRISONS BRIEF, FEBRUARY
*HISTORICAL REPORTED BETWEEN FEBRUARY 2022 AND AUGUST 2023

cialized literature accounts for various aspects, some similarities and also divergences in terms of policing over the structural problems of our penitentiary systems.

2.1 *Colombia*

Colombia has registered critical levels of prison overcrowding in the last decades, with occurrences of escapes, violence, and lack of control from the authorities,[23] especially between 2014 and 2016 and in prisons such as "La Guajira" where overcrowding reached almost 500%. The Constitutional Court

23 Ruby S. Jaramillo Marín and Diego F. Cruz Palomo, 'La insuficiencia de las medidas adoptadas para la población privada de la libertad en Colombia con ocasión de la pandemia de la enfermedad por Coronavirus' (2020) 19 Opinión Jurídica 151; Manuel Iturralde, Nicolás Santamaria and Juan P. Uribe, 'COVID-19 y la crisis estructural de las prisiones en Colombia' (*Friedrich Ebert Stiftung*, 2020) <https://library.fes.de/pdf-files/bueros/kolumbien/17264.pdf> accessed 15 January 2024.

declared an Unconstitutional State of Affairs in Colombian prisons through resolution T-153 from 1998 and reaffirmed it through resolutions T-388 from 2013 and T-762 from 2015. In 2016, the Constitutional Court pronounced against undignified conditions of detention in overcrowded Colombian prisons, referring to inmates having a very poor diet, using containers as latrines and not accessing proper health services.[24] Thus, before the pandemic, the precarious conditions of Colombian prisons and health services were very well established and known, as well as the risks they represented for spreading an infectious disease through populations and communities.[25] Furthermore, although the number of riots related to the imprisonment of armed groups decreased since the beginning of the 1990s, in recent years incidents such as jailbreaks, indiscipline and strikes were reported in Colombian prisons.

2.1.1 The Impact of COVID-19

At the beginning of April 2020, 3 cases were confirmed in the Villavicencio City Prison Center, including one of a 78-year-old inmate who became the first victim of COVID-19 in prison a few days later. Regarding the Colombian penitentiary system main branch supervised by National Penitentiary (INPEC), recent research showed that between April and October 2020, the government identified 16,804 cases in prisons after applying 41,754 RT-PCR s. The figures at that time accounted 136 deaths in prisons, 63% of them of inmates aged 60 years or older.[26]

By March, several riots were reported involving 12 prisons when prisoners demanded better conditions and preventive measures; the most violent occurred in "La Modelo" Prison in Bogotá involving the death of 23 inmates, and damages to prison infrastructure.[27] The pandemic affected population in prisons with higher levels of overcrowding; also, liberation policies left

24 Luis Botero-Luis and Santiago Forero Cardozo, 'COVID-19 una pandemia que reveló las dificultades que afrontan las mujeres colombianas' (2020) 22 Univ. Estud Bogotá 11.

25 Iturralde, Santamaria and Uribe, 'COVID-19 y la crisis estructural de las prisiones en Colombia' (n 23); Victor H. Piñeros-Baez, 'COVID-19 en prisión. Una aproximación a la tendencia epidemiológica en Colombia' (2021) 23 Rev. Salud Pública 1; Ingrid T. Gómez, Claudia R. Llerena and Angie P. Zabaleta, 'Tuberculosis y tuberculosis farmacorresistente en personas privadas de la libertad' (2015) 17 Rev Salud Pública 97–105.

26 Victor H. Piñeros-Báez, 'Public health responses for the management of COVID-19 in detention centers. Literature review' (2020) 22 Revista de Salud Pública 238.

27 Jaramillo Marín and Cruz Palomo, 'La insuficiencia de las medidas adoptadas para la población privada de la libertad en Colombia con ocasión de la pandemia de la enfermedad por Coronavirus' (n 23); Piñeros-Báez, 'Public health responses for the management of COVID-19 in detention centers. Literature review' (n 26).

excluded larger groups of inmates associated with drug crimes.[28] Additionally, it impacted women when family support and visits were affected by COVID-19 policies, and still by 2022 some women had not seen their children for more than 2 years.

Some data was provided in a timely and detailed manner, nevertheless the Constitutional Court requested the penitentiary system in December 2021 to report coverage and vaccination schemes. Instruments such as the 'Guidelines for control, prevention and management of COVID-19 cases' were adopted and specific protocols were established, with the difficulty that two institutions oversee prison management: the INPEC and the USPEC. Measures were insufficient and delayed, originating riots and protests, especially because overcrowding, limited access to water, and similar conditions of many prisons made it very difficult to isolate infected inmates or promote hygiene.[29] Even if a state of emergency was declared in prisons, the judicial system has currently open investigations into the use of force during the march riots.[30]

The government issued the Decree 546–2020 in April, making it possible to replace the custodial sentence or pretrial detention with home arrest in cases of greater vulnerability to COVID-19.[31] There was also a larger number of releases carried out by the courts and by the prohibition of new entrances to prison.[32] Finally, reducing overcrowding in the Colombian case promoted by the Constitutional Court's resolution fostered ever harder conditions of detention for inmates who were relocated in Police units or transitory detention centres, as highlighted in the sentence SU122/22 of the Constitutional Court of Colombia.

---

28 Botero-Luis and Forero Cardozo, 'COVID-19 una pandemia que reveló las dificultades que afrontan las mujeres colombianas' (n 24).

29 Botero-Luis and Forero Cardozo, 'COVID-19 una pandemia que reveló las dificultades que afrontan las mujeres colombianas' (n 24); Iturralde, Santamaria and Uribe, 'COVID-19 y la crisis estructural de las prisiones en Colombia' (n 23).

30 Norberto Hernández Jiménez, María C. Rodríguez Borrero and Valeria Echeverry Rodríguez, 'La paradoja del uso racional de la fuerza. Cárceles colombianas en tiempos de COVID-19' (2021) 78 Estudios de Derecho 273.

31 Iturralde, Santamaria and Uribe, 'COVID-19 y la crisis estructural de las prisiones en Colombia' (n 23); Jaramillo Marín and Cruz Palomo, 'La insuficiencia de las medidas adoptadas para la población privada de la libertad en Colombia con ocasión de la pandemia de la enfermedad por Coronavirus' (n 23).

32 Hernández Jiménez, Rodríguez Borrero and Echeverry Rodríguez, 'La paradoja del uso racional de la fuerza. Cárceles colombianas en tiempos de COVID-19' (n 30); Iturralde, Santamaria and Uribe, 'COVID-19 y la crisis estructural de las prisiones en Colombia' (n 23).

2.2 *Brazil*

Brazil's critical panorama involves more than 800,000 inmates, an infrastructure deficit, and lack of water provision and services, particularly in states such as São Paolo, Rio Grande do Sul, Minas Gerais and Rio de Janeiro. In general, overcrowding rose above 200% before the pandemic, and although there are some good practices and well managed prisons, human rights mechanisms, organizations, and researchers have shown severe health and sanitary problems affecting Brazilian prison population.[33] In 2017 and 2018, large massacres occurred in northern prisons, and then in 2019 several deaths were registered after violent riots in prisons where gangs and organizations such as Comando Vermelho and Primero Comando do Capital maintain control over prisoners.[34] This situation affecting human rights led to a pronouncement of the Supreme Court in 2015 declaring the Brazilian prison system unconstitutional and requiring alternative measures to be formulated to reduce overcrowding.

2.2.1 The Impact of COVID-19

Between 2020 and 2021, an approximate of 2,200 deaths were registered per year (more than the average of 2,000 deaths registered in previous years), however 70% of them (higher percentage than in previous years) were related to health causes. The National Council of Justice reported in August 2020 that 106 inmates have died because of COVID-19,[35] testing less than 5% of the prison population. This number reveals an underreported account of deaths,[36] despite the existence of an official website for COVID-19 in prisons. Uprisings and breaks occurred in prisons such as Mongaguá in São Paolo; peaceful protests or movements channelled the discontent of inmates, their families and staff asking for measures regarding COVID-19. There was not too much transparency about the vaccination process either. According to interviews, measures delivered involved suspending visits and projects with the outside community, cleaning, and providing masks. However, they were difficult to implement due to the lack of infrastructure and

33 Vanessa A. de Barros and Carolyne Reis Barros, 'Reflexões sobre a casa dos mortos em tempos de pandemia: as prisões brasileiras' (2020) 28 Caderno De Administração 95.

34 Biondi, *Sharing this walk: An ethnography of prison life and the PCC in Brazil* (n 15); Sacha Darke, *Conviviality and Survival: Co-Producing Brazilian Prison Order* (London, Palgrave Macmillan 2018).

35 Lina Barbieri, 'Necropolítica e gestão prisional durante a pandemia no Brasi' (2020) 28 Boletim IBCCRIM 2.

36 Conselho Nacional de justicia Relatório de Monitoramento da Covid-19 e da Recomedacao 62/CNJ nos Sistemas Penitenciário e de Medidas Socioeducativas II (2020) CNJ-PNUD-DEPEN.

adequate (unsanitary) cells as vulnerable groups ended up being housed in dark cells or worse conditions. After some months, the administration reopened visits and access to projects, with activities organized remotely. Prison personnel were considered a priority group for vaccination and the ministry promoted the use of videoconferences between inmates and family members.

Regarding policies, the National Council of Justice gave some recommendations about releasing inmates at risk (despite the resistance of many judges) and required contingency plans to be built and monitored by an observatory in each state, regarding testing, vaccines and serious cases.[37] Also, the Superior Court of Justice dictated a double account of penalty when undergone in overcrowded cells and the liberation of pregnant women or women with children. Some states got better results implementing sanitary, vaccination, or oxygen provision measures, despite the enormous difficulties faced in overcrowded prisons all over the country.[38] Prison population was reduced by about 10% in 2020 but immediately continued to grow and reached 800,000 inmates in 2021. Experts point out that this is in part due to the punitive culture of the country and to the impoverishment and criminality expansion generated by the context of COVID-19.

2.3 *Chili*

The year 2010 was critical for the penitentiary system in Chili, when the incarceration rate rose to 310 per 100,000 inhabitants, almost the highest in Latin America at the time. After some policies focused on prison infrastructure, by February 2020, Chilean prisons housed almost 43,000 inmates, without showing a significative problem regarding general overcrowding.[39] However, a study made by the National Institute of Human Rights showed that 50% of Chilian prisons were overcrowded, including emblematic cases such as Limache prison with 189% of overcrowding and Talca Women's Penitentiary Center with 277% of overcrowding.[40] Shortage of beds, heating, toilets, water,

37 Conselho Nacional de justicia Orientacao Técnica, Orientacao conjunta sobre a atualizacao dos protocolos de prevencao da Covid-19 em espacos de privacao de liberdade, 2021.

38 Vanessa Barros, Carolyn Reis-Barros and Thaís Máximo, 'Trabalhar nas prisoes em tempos de pandemia: Questoes para reflexao' in Ludmila de Vasconcelos and others (eds), *Janelas da Pandemia* (Belo Horizonte, Editora Instituto DH 2020).

39 Fiscalía Judicial Corte Suprema, 'Situación recintos penitenciarios en pandemia COVID-19' (2020).

40 Litigación Estructural para América del Sur (Leasur), 'Informe de condiciones carcelarias. Situación de las cárceles en Chile 2019' (*LEASUR*, 2019).

and health personnel were verified by the Judicial Prosecutor of the Supreme Court in 2017.[41] Nevertheless, in recent years, riots nor breaks have been recorded in Chilian prisons.

2.3.1 The Impact of COVID-19

On March 28, the first case in prisons was confirmed at Puente Alto prison, followed by outbreaks in Santiago city prisons and other regions. Official records showed that by the end of December 2020, 2,223 inmates and 1,823 guards were infected nationwide, and also 17 inmates and 2 officials deceased because of the virus.[42] By February 2022, deaths increased to 36 inmates and 5 officials according to the Gendarmerie of Chile.[43]

In March 2020, violent protests occurred at the Santiago 1 facility, regarding lack of sanitary supplies and poor hygienic conditions. Gendarmerie officials and Carabineros put down the uprising which left injured inmates but no fatalities. Similar events occurred in Puente Alto prison, carrying transfer of inmates to other prisons. The government was accused of excesses when controlling these riots and of contributing to the virus spread through transfers.[44] On the other hand, the pandemic affected vulnerable groups such as women with children who rejected the pardon benefices to keep working in prisons, ensuring a better quality of life than outside.

At the beginning of the pandemic, NGOs, human rights and civil society organizations manifested against the lack of timely and transparent information from the part of the authorities, highlighting inmates' psychological needs, and provided assistance to inmates and their families.[45] An informative

41 Julián del Rio Lohan and Juan Valenzuela Embry, 'Coronavirus y Hacinamiento: La crisis que dejó al descubierto el COVID-19 en las cárceles chilenas, Memoria para optar por el título de periodista' (Undergraduate Thesis, Universidad de Chile 2020); Ángela Peralta Jordán, 'Cárcel y Pandemia. Profundización de una crisis permanente. El caso chileno' (2021) 36 Universitas 84.

42 Catalina Droppelmann Roepke, 'Responding to the coronavirus crisis in Chile' (2022) 253 Prison Service Journal 52.

43 Gendarmería de Chile, 'Plan de Acción de Gendarmería para enfrentar Coronavirus' (*Gendarmeria de Chile*, 2020) <https://www.gendarmeria.gob.cl/corona_2020.html> accessed 1 July 2023 (link is currently unavailable).

44 del Rio Lohan and Valenzuela Embry, 'Coronavirus y Hacinamiento: La crisis que dejó al descubierto el COVID-19 en las cárceles chilenas, Memoria para optar por el título de periodista' (n 41); Peralta Jordán, 'Cárcel y Pandemia. Profundización de una crisis permanente. El caso chileno' (n 41).

45 Centro de estudios justicia y Sociedad, 'Datos en Perspectiva Coronavirus y la cuarentena carcelaria' (*Pontificia Universidad Católica de Chile*, 2020) <https://justiciaysociedad.uc.cl/wp-content/uploads/2021/12/Datos-en-perspectiva-2-coronavirus-carcel-final.pdf>

service was then provided by the Gendarmerie, publishing updated data on infected people, deaths, vaccinations, as well as instructions related to the pandemic. The Ministry of Health and actors such as universities and the Medical College contributed to a better response in Chilean prisons. A protocol was issued with isolation and protection measures since February 2020 and later the Ministry of Justice launched the "Justice Takes Care of You" Plan for establishments. Likewise, schedules arrangements and stress reducing policies were implemented.[46] The suspension of rehabilitation activities and delays in implementing video calls were resented by the population, with the return of family visits in December. By July 2020, 5,800 *tests* had been carried out, covering 14% of officials and 7% of inmates.

Chilean government issued early on the Law N°21228 regulating a general commutative pardon, that essentially transformed prison sentences into house arrest when related to minor crimes and groups at higher risk of mortality. An estimate of 1,600 inmates were released by June, and another 1,600 through conditional releases and 2,500 in total after judges dictated house arrests.[47]

2.4 *Argentina*

According to the data, the incarcerated population in Argentina rose above 100,000 inmates even before COVID-19, including detainees at police stations and police centres. Although this has been a structural problem for several decades, the situation worsened in 2015, and the Nation's Penitentiary Prosecutor and the Provincial Memory Commission reported serious limitations regarding sanitary conditions, particularly in Buenos Aires prisons. Protests, collective habeas corpus and hunger strikes occurred in 2016 in reaction to the modification of the Criminal Execution Law, and the process of pacification involved opening a dialogue between the government, the Judiciary, the academy and inmates' representatives.[48]

---

accessed 15 January 2024; Peralta Jordán, 'Cárcel y Pandemia. Profundización de una crisis permanente. El caso chileno' (n 41); del Rio Lohan and Valenzuela Embry, 'Coronavirus y Hacinamiento: La crisis que dejó al descubierto el COVID-19 en las cárceles chilenas, Memoria para optar por el título de periodista' (n 41).

46 ibid; Droppelmann Roepke, 'Responding to the coronavirus crisis in Chile' (n 42).

47 Fiscalía Judicial Corte Suprema, 'Situación recintos penitenciarios en pandemia COVID-19' (n 39); Lina Marmolejo and others, 'Responding to COVID-19 in Latin American prisons: the cases of Argentina, Chile, Colombia, and Mexico' (2020) 15 Victims & Offenders 1062.

48 Gabriel I. Anitua, 'Emergencia penitenciaria y emergencia sanitaria. Propuestas para mitigar las violaciones de de rechos humanos en las cárceles argentinas' (2020) 19

2.4.1 The Impact of COVID-19

Official data and information on COVID-19 was not available in Argentina, particularly at Buenos Aires prison services. Therefore, underreported occurrences and reduced capacity for testing explain the lack of credibility of figures showing 3,070 inmates infected globally by December 2020. With alternative records, the Provincial Memory Commission estimated 178 deaths by 2020 and denounced that by March 2021 only 345 swab tests were applied in the Province of Buenos Aires.

By the end of March, violent riots were registered in the La Coronda and Las Flores prisons at Santa Fé, related to the restrictions on visits and liberation policies, involving the death of 5 inmates.[49] Globally, the National Committee for the Prevention of Torture registered 90 protests in 2020, all of them related to overcrowding and urgent measures regarding COVID-19. These reactions were not all violent, and included peaceful hunger strikes, collective habeas corpus requests, and activism from human rights organizations, civil society, and academia.[50] Despite the authority's opacity and the extremely punitive media context, organizations and civil society provided data to the public opinion. Epidemiological measures involved directives for case detection and informative talks, a dissemination campaign, and the creation of crisis committees.[51] Early in March, the Nation's Penitentiary Prosecutor requested the Ministry of Justice to regulate access to mobile telephones[52] and the Ministry of Health published some "Recommendations for the attention and health care access for people in the context of confinement and their workers

Revista Critica Penal y Poder 157; Centro de estudios legales y sociales, 'COVID-19 y sobrepoblación carcelaria' (*CELS*, 2020) <https://www.cels.org.ar/web/publicaciones/covid-19-y-sobrepoblacion-carcelaria/> accessed 15 January 2024; Centro de estudios de ejecución penal, 'Privación de libertad en tiempos de COVID-19' (*CEEP*, 2020) <http://www.derecho.uba.ar/institucional/pdf/2020-ceep-documento-covid.pdf> accessed 15 January 2024; Instituto De Estudios Jurídicos De Ejecución Penal, 'Emergencia carcelaria y pandemia en Argentina' (*INEJEP*, 2020) <https://www.pensamientopenal.com.ar/system/files/2021/03/miscelaneas49000.pdf> accessed 15 January 2024.

49 Anitua, 'Emergencia penitenciaria y emergencia sanitaria. Propuestas para mitigar las violaciones de de rechos humanos en las cárceles argentinas' (n 48).

50 Centro de estudios de ejecución penal, 'Privación de libertad en tiempos de COVID-19' (n 48); Paula D. Franco, 'Representaciones del conflicto del Penal de Villa Devoto' (2020) 6 Actas de Periodimo y Comunicación 1.

51 Instituto De Estudios Jurídicos De Ejecución Penal, 'Emergencia carcelaria y pandemia en Argentina' (n 48).

52 Centro de estudios legales y sociales, 'COVID-19 y sobrepoblación carcelaria' (n 48).

in the framework of the pandemic". A violent uprising at Devoto Prison led to the opening of a dialogue roundtable between delegates, civil society and authorities, reaching agreements in terms of liberations of high-risk groups, improving conditions and suspending inmate transfers.[53]

Government discourse implied transferring responsibility to the Judicial who issued recommendations regarding vulnerable groups and alternative measures such as house arrest, liberations, and habeas corpus impacting prison population, for the first time in more than a decade in Argentina. At Buenos Aires, the Attorney General issued house arrest directives to public defenders in cases of vulnerable groups and The Criminal Cassation Court issued the same recommendation, even though it was limited afterwards by the Supreme Court of the Province.[54] Some studies have reported between 800 and 3,500 inmates, although the data is not clear[55] and the trend shows a quick return to increasing prison population. These measures, however, did focus on vulnerable population, and registers of women in federal prisons fell from 1,170 in March 2019 to 709 in May 2020.[56]

2.5 *Mexico*

Incarceration rates and prison overcrowding were reduced prior to the pandemic after the implementation of procedural reforms in Mexico.[57] However, according to the Decentralized Administration for Prevention and Social Readaptation, by January 2020, overcrowding was present in 37% of Mexican prisons, and infrastructure problems attained 70% of them. Pre-trial detention and lack of security personnel and treatment were reported by Human Rights mechanisms. In 2016 a study found that 30% of inmates did not have access to water, 25% had to pay for it and 30% did not have access to medicines.[58]

---

53 Centro de estudios de ejecución penal, 'Privación de libertad en tiempos de COVID-19' (n 48); Franco, 'Representaciones del conflicto del Penal de Villa Devoto' (n 50).

54 Gustavo A. Arocena, 'COVID-19 y Cárceles argentinas' in Maximiliano Raijman and Ricardo Erizan (eds), *El derecho argentino frente a la pandemia y post-pandemia COVID-19* (Córdoba, Universidad Nacional de Córdoba 2020) 285–322; Instituto De Estudios Jurídicos De Ejecución Penal, 'Emergencia carcelaria y pandemia en Argentina' (n 48); Franco, 'Representaciones del conflicto del Penal de Villa Devoto' (n 50).

55 Centro de estudios legales y sociales, 'COVID-19 y sobrepoblación carcelaria' (n 48).

56 Instituto De Estudios Jurídicos De Ejecución Penal, 'Emergencia carcelaria y pandemia en Argentina' (n 48).

57 Marmolejo and others, 'Responding to COVID-19 in Latin American prisons: the cases of Argentina, Chile, Colombia, and Mexico' (n 47).

58 Dirección general de investigación estratégica, 'Medidas de prevención y control del COVID-19 en los centros penitenciarios' (México CDMX, Instituto Belisario Domínguez,

Violent deaths that appear as suicides, riots, and lack of disciplinary sanctions are part of a larger problem of the Mexican penitentiary system. According to the Prison Observatory, between 2010 and 2019, 121 prisons breaks were registered in Mexico. The larger number of prison breaks was registered in the state of Sinaloa, the land of "El Chapo".

2.5.1 The Impact of COVID-19

On April 15, two outbreaks were registered in Yucatán and the State of Mexico. By June 2020, 75 confirmed cases and 5 deaths were reported, casting suspicions on the real numbers offered to public opinion. By September 2020, 315 deaths were confirmed including inmates and prison staff[59] and as of May 2021, 23 incidents including violent riots and escapes were identified, some of them resulting in injuries and deaths, triggered by the suspension of cultural and academic activities and restrictive policies for visits. The Human Rights commission found deficiencies in care provision for women and minors in 30 prisons, and deficiencies in care provision for vulnerable groups. The closure of schools during the pandemic impacted women with children, even though they were allowed to visit their mothers once a month. In centres such as Marta, housing inmates with HIV and LGBTIQ+ population, overcrowding made impossible physical distancing, access to hygiene and cleaning. Lack of information provided by the State also explain why 717% more complaints regarding inmates' right to health were registered in 2020 in comparison to 2019.[60]

In March 2020, the United Nations Office on Drugs and Crime (UNODC) and the Pan-American Health Organization released "COVID-19 Special Standards for Mexico", and on April 7 the Federal Government presented the Action Protocol for COVID care in Federal Penitentiary Centers, which were the basis

Senado de la República, 2020); Alberto Espejel Espinoza, 'El COVID-19 y la población carcelaria en México' (2020) 6 Cuaderno Jurídico y Político 56.

59 Angel A. Salas, '(Sobre)vivir la COVID-19. Experiencias de encierro en centro penitenciario de la ciudad de México' (2020) 50 Revista de Bioética y Derecho 149–166.

60 Comisión Nacional de los Derechos Humanos, 'Comunicado de prensa DGC/139/2020' (*CNDH*, 2020) <https://www.cndh.org.mx/sites/default/files/documentos/2020-04/Com_2020_139.pdf> accessed 15 January 2024; Comisión Nacional de los Derechos Humanos, 'Posicionamiento de la CNDH sobre el Informe del Departamento de Estado Norteamericano "México 2020 Reporte de los Derechos Humanos"' (*CNDH*, 2021) <https://www.cndh.org.mx/sites/default/files/documentos/2021-04/Posicionamiento_CNDH_reporte_Departamento_Estado_EU.pdf> accessed 15 January 2024.

for each state government protocols for prisons.[61] Work and education activities were suspended, and staff schedules were adapted, requiring new hires and relocations. Main problems detected by the CNDH were the lack of basic medical infrastructure and ambulances, and the lack of testing in certain prisons. Good practices such as controlling temperature, cleaning, and distributing hygiene material in certain prisons were also known, considering that right before the COVID-19 pandemic, there was an outbreak of measles in Mexican prisons.

At the policy level in April 2020, the President promoted an Amnesty Legislation for people at high-risk, quickly approved by the Senate. This law targeted indigenous people, women and defendants for committing offences without violence[62] and relaunched judicial activities previously paralyzed due to a lack of technological infrastructure.[63] At the federal level, some entities also promoted the release of the vulnerable population and an estimate of 4,000 inmates benefited from early release, including 2,700 in the State of Mexico through the application of electronic bracelets. Still, liberation policies had a very moderate impact and the prison population continued to grow during 2021.

2.6 *Peru*

The Peruvian prison population has expanded largely over the last years, reaching one of the highest prison rates in South America. Overcrowding rose to 140% over the system capacity by February 2020, and even more than 400% in prisons like Callao or Cañete; characterized by severe sanitary problems and limited capacities to provide rehabilitation. In 2018, the UN Subcommittee on Prevention of Torture highlighted the State's underperformance for allocating human resources, services, and materials to provide health care in prisons. Regarding the population of inmates affected by chronic or infectious diseases such as TBC, HIV/AIDS, and psychiatric conditions who remain often untreated,[64] the Constitutional Court declared the unconstitu-

---

61 Dirección general de investigación estratégica, 'Medidas de prevención y control del COVID-19 en los centros penitenciarios' (n 58); Espejel Espinoza, 'El COVID-19 y la población carcelaria en México' (n 58).

62 Marisol L. Garcia, 'La política criminal, en la amnistía otorgada por el gobierno federal en tiempos de COVID-19' (2021) 65 Revista Jurídica Jalisciense 209–235; Espejel Espinoza, 'El COVID-19 y la población carcelaria en México' (n 58).

63 Alberto M. Orozco Ravelo, 'La COVID-19 y la justicia de ejecución de sanciones penales' (2020) Caso Jalisco 131.

64 José L. Pérez Guadalupe and Lucia Nuñovero Cisneros, 'Ejecución de la Pena privativa de libertad en el Perú y Derechos Humanos' in Sofia Galván and others (eds), *Ejecución*

tional state of affairs in Peruvian prisons in 2020. On the other hand, the 2012 reform involved organized dialogue with inmates, followed by a considerable decrease in violent deaths, prison breaks and riots until nowadays.[65]

2.6.1 The Impact of COVID-19

By the middle of March 2020, 5 inmates from a northern prison presented symptoms of COVID-19 at the same time a riot occurred, the first of many to explode all over the country. In April 2020, testing started to be seriously implemented by authorities[66] and by February 2021, 453 inmates and 53 prison officers were reported to be deceased in Peru as a result of the COVID-19 pandemic.[67]

On the other hand, between February and November 2020, 18 riots and 14 brawls were reported in Peruvian prisons.[68] The most violent fights occurred during March and April, such as the Trujillo uprising that left 3 inmates deceased and the Castro Castro riot which left 9 inmates deceased. In May 2020, the Inter-American Commission on Human Rights condemned acts of violence in Peruvian prisons, at the same time various peaceful protests took place, including 500 prison workers protesting at the Lurigancho prison.[69]

Penal y Sistema Carcelario (Bogotá, Fundación Konrad Adenauer KAS, Centro de Estudios de Justicia de Américas CEJA -Ed, Tirant Lo Blanch 2021) 375–396.

65 Guadalupe, Cavallaro and Nuñovero Cisneros, 'Towards a governance model of ungovernable prisons: How recognition of inmate organizations, dialogue, and mutual respect can transform violent prisons in Latin America' (n 18).

66 Andrey Sindeev and Blanca M. Martinez-Alvarez, 'Características clínico-epidemiológicas de los reclusos infectados y fallecidos por COVID-19 según datos del INPE' (2022) 24 Revista Española de Sanidad Penitenciaria 16.

67 Lucia Nuñovero Cisneros, 'Vacunar en las cárceles' *El Comercio* (Peru, 12 February 2021) <https://elcomercio.pe/opinion/colaboradores/vacunar-en-las-carceles-por-lucia-nunovero-vacunacion-carceles-penales-covid-19-noticia/> accessed 15 February 2024.

68 Gustavo Ytokazy, 'Peruvian Prison reforms and the Covid-19 outbreak' (2021) 34 Asian Journal of Latin American Studies 99–127; Guadalupe, Cavallaro and Nuñovero Cisneros, 'Towards a governance model of ungovernable prisons: How recognition of inmate organizations, dialogue, and mutual respect can transform violent prisons in Latin America' (n 18).

69 José L. Pérez Guadalupe and Lucia Nuñovero Cisneros, 'Condenados a una pena privativa de salud. La crisis carcelaria en tiempos de coronavirus' (2020) in Carlos Meléndez, *Pandemonio: hospitales colapsados, una economía en recesión, cárceles amotinadas y millones de peruanos esperando un bono que nunca llegará* (Crisol 2020) 109–145; Lucce Bracco and others, 'Resistiendo a la COVID-19 y levantando las voces desde el encierro: análisis de cartas públicas de mujeres recluidas en prisiones de Lima' (2022) 12 Oñati Socio Legal Series 1.

Measures implemented by the government included restricting the entry of visitors and making budget transfers to improve health and food conditions in Peruvian prisons. Overcrowding made social distancing impossible, and the Constitutional Court and the Ombudsman proposed pardons and prison benefits to reduce prison population. The internal organization of inmates contributed to preventing riots in prisons such as Lurigancho.[70]

After several weeks marked by disagreements between authorities and changes at the National Penitentiary Council,[71] pardon mechanisms for populations at risk were decreed, while judicial directives and emergency legislation in June allowed conversion of penalties, house arrests, and the use of electronic surveillance. Between March and July 2020, 7,570 inmates were released, only 5% because of pardon mechanisms and 81% due to judicial decisions.[72] Flexibility in liberation measures continued to reduce prison population in 2021.

3 Final Remarks: What Worked and What Did Not?

After discussing the main health and security impacts as well as relevant policies and measures implemented by these countries, according to interviews and literature, some cross-cutting aspects emerge requiring further discussion to improve policies and responsiveness from governments.

3.1 *Access to Information Matters*

Transparency on penitentiary issues in countries of the region continues to be a problem, affecting credibility of figures provided by the authorities.[73] In the context of COVID-19, it aggravated the conflict and uncertainty within inmates, families and communities. Some countries were able to revert the

70 Guadalupe, Cavallaro and Nuñovero Cisneros, 'Towards a governance model of ungovernable prisons: How recognition of inmate organizations, dialogue, and mutual respect can transform violent prisons in Latin America' (n 18).

71 Pérez Guadalupe and Nuñovero Cisneros, 'Condenados a una pena privativa de salud. La crisis carcelaria en tiempos de coronavirus' (n 69).

72 Ytokazy, 'Peruvian Prison reforms and the Covid-19 outbreak' (n 68); Guadalupe, Cavallaro and Nuñovero Cisneros, 'Towards a governance model of ungovernable prisons: How recognition of inmate organizations, dialogue, and mutual respect can transform violent prisons in Latin America' (n 18).

73 Diana Mateus, 'Hacinamiento Carcelario y Covid-19 en América Latina' (*Fiedrich Ebert Stiftung*, 2020) <https://library.fes.de/pdf-files/bueros/la-seguridad/16288.pdf> accessed 15 February 2024.

situation and generate good practices. The Chilean case stands out, providing a web constantly updated with numbers of deaths, infections, protocols, and implementing direct communication channels with inmates' relatives.

3.2 *Measures as Recipes to Be Adapted to a Challenging Context*

Preventive and responsive measures were identical, following the recommendations of international organizations[74] and introduced quickly in some countries through protocols, which involved the use of masks, the isolation of those infected, visit restrictions, staff reduction, suspension of educational activities and labour, educational campaigns, distribution of hygiene kits, tests, and so on.[75] However, the challenge was not to prescribe measures, but to adapt them to overcrowded prisons devoid of services, staff and minimal conditions, many of which exist in Latin America. For instance, visit limitations in many prisons restricted inmates' access to minimum elements for survival, which worsened the situation in many contexts.[76] Criticisms given on the Guide issued by UNODC Mexico echo the reality of what these countries faced during the pandemic. The kinds of Protocols that describe a top-down reality, presenting merely recommendations from international organizations on ideal situations, without considering that distancing or hand washing were impossible in some cases, fail to provide practical approaches and recommendations adapted to reality such as coordinating with delegates and inmates' organizations.[77]

---

74 We refer, for example, to the publication on March 15 of the Provisional Guide "Preparation, prevention and control of Covid-19 in prisons and other places of detention" of the World Health Organization. WHO, 'Preparation, prevention and control of Covid-19 in prisons and other places of detention' (*WHO*, 15 March 2020) <https://iris.who.int/bitstream/handle/10665/336525/WHO-EURO-2020-1405-41155-55954-eng.pdf> accessed 15 January 2024.

75 Marmolejo and others, 'Responding to COVID-19 in Latin American prisons: the cases of Argentina, Chile, Colombia, and Mexico' (n 47); SOCLA-CELIV, 'Los efectos del coronavirus en las cárceles de Latinoamérica' (*Criminología Latam*, 2020) <https://criminologialatam.wordpress.com/2020/06/12/efectos-del-covid-19-carceles-de-latino-america/> accessed 15 January 2024.

76 Dirección general de investigación estratégica, 'Medidas de prevención y control del COVID-19 en los centros penitenciarios' (n 58); Garcia, 'La política criminal, en la amnistía otorgada por el gobierno federal en tiempos de COVID-19' (n 62).

77 Garcia, 'La política criminal, en la amnistía otorgada por el gobierno federal en tiempos de COVID-19' (n 62); Pérez Guadalupe and Lucia Nuñovero Cisneros, 'Ejecución de la Pena privativa de libertad en el Perú y Derechos Humanos' (n 64).

3.3 *Testing in Prisons and Management of Incidents*

Testing varied within the region, with a tendency to be scarce,[78] particularly in cases such as Mexico or Argentina where entire wards wherein inmates showed symptoms were isolated without testing. Poor management of incidents, as well as early deceases protocols unimplemented in countries like Argentina or Peru, played a role in triggering many of the most violent riots that the region experienced during the pandemic.

However, security and governance problems that occurred during the pandemic in countries such as Colombia, Peru, Chili, Mexico and Argentina were glimpsed early on, considering that by March 2020, the Inter-American Commission on Human Rights urged the State members to adopt measures to face contagion and reduce overcrowding in detention centres, as well as to guarantee the necessary measures to comply with prevention measures in the areas of food, health, sanitation and to maintain order and safety to avoid riots and violent uprisings.[79]

3.4 *Lack of Planification and Use of Force*

In April 2020, the High Commissioner for Human Rights expressed its concern about the excessive use of force against incarcerated people as shown in the Argentinian, Colombian, Chilean and Peruvian cases in particular. Most violent riots – leaving injuries and deaths – occurred at the beginning of the pandemic and involved demands related to preventive measures and conditions. Violent riots occurred at the most overcrowded and understocked prisons. Lack of clarity in protocols, little transparency and restrictions on the contact with the outside world contributed to discontent of inmates and staff. The suspension of judicial processes in many countries also aggravated the uncertainty experienced by the inmates during these years.

3.5 *Communication with Relatives*

One of the policies that contributed the most to mitigate these conflicts during the pandemic, consisted in liberalizing communications between inmates and their families, through videoconferences or the controlled use of cell phones.

---

78 Banco Interamericano de Desarrollo, 'Las cárceles de América Latina y el caribe ante la crisis sanitaria del COVID-19' (*BID*, 2020) <https://publications.iadb.org/es/las-carceles-de-america-latina-y-el-caribe-ante-la-crisis-sanitaria-del-covid-19> accessed 15 January 2024.

79 Jaramillo Marín and Cruz Palomo, 'La insuficiencia de las medidas adoptadas para la población privada de la libertad en Colombia con ocasión de la pandemia de la enfermedad por Coronavirus' (n 23).

TABLE 6.3 Main impacts and COVID-19 prison policies in selected countries

COVID impact		**Relevant policies and measures**	
Epidemiological	**Security**	**Relevant measures**	**Release**
		Colombia	
– Updated but partial public data. – 16,800 infected and 136 deaths as of October 2020. – Women without visits from their children for a long time.	– More than 12 riots. – Riot in Bogotá leaves 23 dead and more than 80 injured (March 21). – Overcrowding and outbreaks of violence in Temporary Detention Centers.	– Use of irregular force in the mutiny of March 21. –Massive although delayed application of *tests.* –Vaccination moderately prioritized. –Establishment of protocols and application of measures in April-June.	– Decree replacing sentences (1000 inmates). – Ordinary judicial release mechanisms (20,000 inmates).
		Chili	
– Public data updated somewhat late. – 2,223 infected detainees and 17 deaths as of December 2020. – Women in the role of caring for children who are more precarious in the labour market.	– Riot in Santiago 1 on March 19 leaves 25 injured. – Riots and protests in Puente Alto leave 26 injured. – Demonstrations in Colina and Roncagua. – Transfers generated contagion and misrule.	– Transparency of information and communication with family members. – Articulation with other actors, particularly in the health sector.	– Commutative pardon (1,600 inmates as of June). – Variation of preventive detention (2,500 inmates). – Conditional release (1,500 inmates).

TABLE 6.3 Main impacts and COVID-19 prison policies in selected countries (*cont.*)

COVID impact		**Relevant policies and measures**	
Epidemiological	**Security**	**Relevant measures**	**Release**
		– Early purchase of supplies, but delays in the implementation of video calls, use of telephones, and return of reintegration activities. – Protocols and testing with certain limitations.	
	Argentina		
– Data scarcely published. Underrecord. – 3,070 infected detainees and 178 deaths as of December 2020. – Population of elderly inmates for federal crimes.	– 90 protests in 2020. – Riots in Santa Fe in March left 5 dead. – Riots in April in Buenos Aires such as Villa Devoto and other prisons, involving deaths, injuries and transfers. – Hunger strikes and demonstrations. – Punitive media debate.	– Limited testing and early vaccination of the elderly. Late coverage to remote locations. – Participation of civil society and organizations. – Crisis Committees and Dialogue Tables. – Use of cell phones in Buenos Aires and video conference systems. – Educational infrastructure was used for isolation.	– Transfer of the responsibility of the Executive and Legislative Power to the Judicial Power. – The Judiciary recommended alternative measures for risk groups (elderly adults, women with children), as well as attention to cases of inmates in jail in risk groups. (Decrease in overpopulation from 13% to 2% in SPF and 2% in SPB).

TABLE 6.3 Main impacts and COVID-19 prison policies in selected countries (*cont.*)

COVID impact		**Relevant policies and measures**	
Epidemiological	**Security**	**Relevant measures**	**Release**
	Brazil		
– Official data with underreporting. –30,467 confirmed cases and 184 deaths including prison staff as of August 2020.	– Peaceful protests.	– Limited application of sanitary measures, testing and vaccination. – Participation of civil society and organizations.	– Transfer of the responsibility of the Executive and Legislative Power to the Judicial Power. – The Judiciary issued recommendations for alternative measures for risk groups, despite the resistance of many judges. (32 thousand people were released, a 10% decrease that was not sustained over time)
	Mexico		
– Official data with little credibility. Under record. – 4,405 confirmed cases and 315 deaths including prison personnel as of December 2020.	– 23 incidents of violence resulting in injuries and deaths. –Punitive media debate.	– Demands for information and complaints exacerbated protests and anguish.	– Law of Amnesty for people at risk, aimed at indigenous people, women, people in situations of poverty or vulnerability.

TABLE 6.3 Main impacts and COVID-19 prison policies in selected countries (*cont.*)

COVID impact		**Relevant policies and measures**	
Epidemiological	**Security**	**Relevant measures**	**Release**
– Population of women with minor children and overcrowded population with HIV and LGBTI.		– Inspectorates and CNDH reports detected lax implementation of measures as good practices. – Lack of testing in many establishments. – Forecast of ambulances and transfer of family for burial in CDMX. – Prioritized vaccination for older adults.	– 250 people released at a later date and 2,487 requests as of June. – Release for humanitarian reasons in federal entities (3,984 inmates). – Relocation of maximum-security inmates.
	Peru		
–Official data published late. –37,103 infected and 445 deceased by October 2020. – Population of women with children convicted of serious crimes.	– 18 riots and 14 brawls as of November 2020, particularly in March and April in more overcrowded prisons.	– Early visit restrictions and isolation protocols. – Transfers to former prisons. – Internal organization of the detainees prevented violent riots.	– Conversion of light sentences, remission of sentences, electronic surveillance and review of preventive detention.
	The Trujillo mutiny left 3 deaths and 17 injured and the Castro Castro mutiny left 9 dead and 65 injured.	– Support of the Armed Forces for security. – Use of force questioned in the Castro Castro mutiny.	– Variations and other releases by the Judiciary (81% of the 7,600 inmates released).

TABLE 6.3 Main impacts and COVID-19 prison policies in selected countries (*cont.*)

COVID impact		**Relevant policies and measures**	
Epidemiological	**Security**	**Relevant measures**	**Release**
	– Workers' protests. – Punitiveness of the Executive.	– Clashes and lack of leadership between authorities.	– Pardon to risk groups (5% of those released).

SOURCE: JARAMILLO AND CRUZ, 2020; BOTERO-LUIS AND FORERO, 2022; PIÑEROS-BAEZ, 2021; HERNÁNDEZ, 2021; ITURRALDE, SANTAMARÍA AND URIBE; BARBIERI, 2020; CONSELHO NACIONAL DE JUSTICIA RELATÓRIO DE MONITORAMENTO DA COVID-19, 2020; CONSELHO NACIONAL DE JUSTICIA ORIENTACAO TÉCNICA, 2021; LUDMILA DE VASCONCELOS AND OTHERS, 2020; DROPPELMANN, 2022; GENDARMERÍA DE CHILE, 2022; MARMOLEJO AND OTHERS, 2020; ANITUA, 2020; INSTITUTO DE ESTUDIOS JURÍDICOS DE EJECUCIÓN PENAL, 2020; CENTRO DE ESTUDIOS DE EJECUCIÓN PENAL, 2020; DIRECCIÓN GENERAL DE INVESTIGACIÓN ESTRATÉGICA,2020; ESPEJEL, 2020; COMISIÓN NACIONAL DE LOS DERECHOS HUMANOS, 2021; SALAS, 2020; GARCÍA, 2021; YTOKAZY, 2021; SINDEEV AND MARTÍNEZ-ALVAREZ, 2022; PÉREZ GUADALUPE AND NUÑOVERO CISNEROS, 2020.

Likewise, measures such as the round tables established with relatives and civil society such as the ones that took place in Argentina, or the provision of ambulances to transport families to burials in Mexico City, contributed to defusing the situation. Civil society involvement was positive, reinforcing alternative mechanisms and pushing inmates claims to resolutions.

3.6 *Releasing from the Executive and from the Judiciary*

Mechanisms offered by the executive did not obtain results as extensive as expected. Substitution mechanisms in Colombia, commutative pardon in Chile, the humanitarian pardon in Peru, as well as the amnesty law in Mexico were quite modest, in the best of cases reaching about two or three thousand inmates to be released. The prison population decreased in some countries where the Judiciary contributed by issuing directives or activating release mechanisms including suspensive and conditional modalities as well as house arrests. Public defenders and prosecutors have played a role in these massive releases in a context marked by retributive tendencies and governments reluctance to dictate these kinds of policies.

Acknowledgements

This work was funded by the Centro de Investigación, Capacitación y Asesoría Jurídica at the Pontificia Universidad Católica del Perú (CICAJ-PUCP).

References

Anitua GI, 'Emergencia penitenciaria y emergencia sanitaria. Propuestas para mitigar las violaciones de de rechos humanos en las cárceles argentinas' (2020) 19 *Revista Critica Penal y Poder* 157–166.

Antillano A, 'When Prisoners Make the Prison Self-Rule in Venezuelans Prisons' (2017) 229 *The Prison Service Journal* 26–30.

Arocena GA, 'COVID-19 y Cárceles argentinas' in Raijman M and Erizan R (eds), *El derecho argentino frente a la pandemia y post-pandemia COVID-19* (Córdoba, Universidad Nacional de Córdoba 2020) 285–322.

Ariza L and Iturralde M, 'Las prisiones y las transformaciones del campo del control del crimen en Colombia' in Ariza L, Iturralde M and Tamayo L (eds), *Cárceles, Derecho y Sociedad. Aproximaciones al mundo penitenciario en Colombia* (Bogotá, Universidad de los Andes 2021) 23–53.

Arrarás A and Bello-Pardo E, 'General Trends of Prisons in the Americas' in Rosen JD and Brienen MW (eds), *Prisons in the Americas in the Twenty-First Century: A Human Dumping Ground* (Lexington Books 2015) 1–13

Banco Interamericano de Desarrollo, 'Las cárceles de América Latina y el caribe ante la crisis sanitaria del COVID-19' (*BID*, 2020) <https://publications.iadb.org/es/las-carceles-de-america-latina-y-el-caribe-ante-la-crisis-sanitaria-del-covid-19>.

Barbieri L, 'Necropolítica e gestão prisional durante a pandemia no Brasi' (2020) 28 *Boletim IBCCRIM* 2–3.

Barros V, Reis-Barros C and Máximo T, 'Trabalhar nas prisoes em tempos de pandemia: Questoes para reflexao' in de Vasconcelos L and others (eds), *Janelas da Pandemia* (Belo Horizonte, Editora Instituto DH 2020).

Bergman M and Fondevilla G, *Prisons and Crime in Latin America* (Cambridge, Cambridge University Press 2021).

Bergman M and Azaloa E, 'Cárceles de México: Cuadros de una crisis' (2007) 1 *Revista Latinoamericana de Seguridad Ciudadana* 74–87.

Biondi K, *Sharing This Walk: An Ethnography of Prison Life and the PCC in Brazil* (Chapel Hill, UNC Press Books 2016).

Blumstein A, 'Bringing Down the U.S. Prison Population' (2011) 91 *The Prison Journal Supplement* 12–26.

Botero-Luis L and Forero Cardozo S, 'COVID-19 una pandemia que reveló las dificultades que afrontan las mujeres colombianas' (2020) 22 *Univ. Estud Bogotá* 11–32.

Bracco L and others, 'Resistiendo a la COVID-19 y levantando las voces desde el encierro: análisis de cartas públicas de mujeres recluidas en prisiones de Lima' (2022) 12 *Oñati Socio Legal Series* 1–19.

Burki T, 'Prisons Are No Way Equipped to Deal with COVID-19' (2020) 395 *The lancet* 1411–1412.

Caldeira Nunes Dias C and Salla FA, 'Formal and Informal Controls and Punishment: The Production of Order in the Prisons of São Paulo' (2017) 229 *Prison Service Journal* 19–22.

Carranza E, *Justicia penal y sobrepoblación penitenciaria: respuestas posibles* (Siglo XXI 2001).

Carranza E, *Política criminal y penitenciaria en América Latina y el Caribe* (San José, 2003).

Carranza E, 'Criminalidad, criminalización, y cárcel en la globalización, en américa latina y en los países de altos ingresos' (2009) 1 *Revista digital de ciencias penales de Costa Rica* 481–496.

Carranza E, 'Situación Penitenciaria en América Latina y el Caribe, ¿Qué hacer?' (2012) 8 *Anuario de Derechos Humanos* 31–66.

Centro de estudios de ejecución penal, 'Privación de libertad en tiempos de COVID-19' (*CEEP*, 2020) <http://www.derecho.uba.ar/institucional/pdf/2020-ceep-documento-covid.pdf>.

Centro de estudios justicia y Sociedad, 'Datos en Perspectiva Coronavirus y la cuarentena carcelaria' (*Pontificia Universidad Católica de Chile*, 2020) <https://justiciaysociedad.uc.cl/wp-content/uploads/2021/12/Datos-en-perspectiva-2-coronavirus-carcel-final.pdf>.

Centro de estudios legales y sociales, 'COVID-19 y sobrepoblación carcelaria' (*CELS*, 2020) <https://www.cels.org.ar/web/publicaciones/covid-19-y-sobrepoblacion-carcelaria/>.

Cerbini F, *La casa de jabón: etnografía de una cárcel boliviana* (Universidad Complutense de Madrid 2011).

Cid Moliné J, 'El incremento de la población reclusa en España entre 1996 – 2006: Diagnóstico y remedios' (2008) 2 *Revista Española de Investigación Criminológica* 23–24.

Comisión Nacional de los Derechos Humanos, 'Comunicado de prensa DGC/139/2020' (*CNDH*, 2020) <https://www.cndh.org.mx/sites/default/files/documentos/2020-04/Com_2020_139.pdf>.

Comisión Nacional de los Derechos Humanos, 'Posicionamiento de la CNDH sobre el Informe del Departamento de Estado Norteamericano "México 2020 Reporte de los Derechos Humanos"' (*CNDH*, 2021) <https://www.cndh.org.mx/sites/default/fil

es/documentos/2021-04/Posicionamiento_CNDH_reporte_Departamento_Estado_EU.pdf>.

Conselho Nacional de justicia Relatório de Monitoramento da Covid-19 e da Recomedacao 62/CNJCNJ nos Sistemas Penitenciário e de Medidas Socioeducativas II (2020) CNJ- PNUD-DEPEN.

Constant C, *Pensar las cárceles de América Latina* (Lima, IFEA 2016).

Darke S, *Convivality and Survival: Co-Producing Brazilian Prison Order* (London, Palgrave Macmillan 2018).

Darke S and Garces C, 'Surviving in the New Mass Carceral Zone' (2017) 229 *Prison Service Journal* 2–9.

Dammert L and Zúñiga L, 'La cárcel: problemas y desafíos para las Américas' (*FLACSO Chile*, 2008) <https://flacso.cl/biblioteca/product/la-carcel-problemas-y-desafios-para-las-americas/>.

de Barros VA and Reis Barros C, 'Reflexões sobre a casa dos mortos em tempos de pandemia: as prisões brasileiras' (2020) 28 *Caderno De Administração* 95–99.

de Dardel J and Soderstrom O, 'The Rise and Fall of Supermax: How the US Prison Model and Ultra Punitive Penal Policy Travelled to Colombia' (2015) Université de Neuchatel Maison d'analyse de processus sociaux Working paper 3.

del Rio Lohan J and Valenzuela Embry J, 'Coronavirus y Hacinamiento: La crisis que dejó al descubierto el COVID-19 en las cárceles chilenas, Memoria para optar por el título de periodista' (Undergraduate Thesis, Universidad de Chile 2020).

Dirección general de investigación estratégica, 'Medidas de prevención y control del COVID-19 en los centros penitenciarios' (México CDMX, Instituto Belisario Domínguez, Senado de la República, 2020).

Droppelmann Roepke C, 'Responding to the Coronavirus Crisis in Chile' (2022) 253 *Prison Service Journal* 52–57.

Espejel Espinoza A, 'El COVID-19 y la población carcelaria en México' (2020) 6 *Cuaderno Jurídico y Político* 56–68.

Fiscalía Judicial Corte Suprema, 'Situación recintos penitenciarios en pandemia COVID-19' (2020).

Franco PD, 'Representaciones del conflicto del Penal de Villa Devoto' (2020) 6 *Actas de Periodimo y Comunicación* 1–14.

Garces C, Martin T and Darke S, 'Informal Prison Dynamics in Africa and Latin America' (2013) 91 *Criminal Justice Matters* 26–27.

Garcia ML, 'La política criminal, en la amnistía otorgada por el gobierno federal en tiempos de COVID-19' (2021) 65 *Revista Jurídica Jalisciense* 209–235.

Gendarmería de Chile, 'Plan de Acción de Gendarmería para enfrentar Coronavirus' (*Gendarmeria de Chile*, 2020) <https://www.gendarmeria.gob.cl/corona_2020.html>.

Gómez IT, Llerena CR and Zabaleta AP, 'Tuberculosis y tuberculosis farmacorresistente en personas privadas de la libertad' (2015) 17 *Rev Salud Pública* 97–105.

Gonzáles Sánchez I, 'Aumento de presos y código penal. Una explicación insuficiente' (2011) 13 *Revista Electrónica de Ciencia penal y Criminología* 1–22.

Guadalupe JL, Cavallaro J and Nuñovero Cisneros L, 'Towards a Governance Model of Ungovernable Prisons: How Recognition of Inmate Organizations, Dialogue, and Mutual Respect Can Transform Violent Prisons in Latin America' (2021) 70 *Catholic University of Washington Law Review* 367–419.

Hathazy and Müller M, 'The Rebirth of the Prison in Latin America: Determinants, Regimes and Social Effects' (2016) 65 *Crime, Law and Social Change* 113–135.

Hernández Jiménez N, Rodríguez Borrero MC and Echeverry Rodríguez V, 'La paradoja del uso racional de la fuerza. Cárceles colombianas en tiempos de COVID-19' (2021) 78 *Estudios de Derecho* 273–296.

Instituto De Estudios Jurídicos De Ejecución Penal, 'Emergencia carcelaria y pandemia en Argentina' (*INEJEP*, 2020) <https://www.pensamientopenal.com.ar/system/files/2021/03/miscelaneas49000.pdf>.

Iturralde M, 'O Governo Neoliberal de La Inseguranca Social Na America Latina; Semelhanzas E Diferencias Con O Norte Global' in Malaguti V (ed), *Loic Wacquant ea questao penal no capitalism neoliberal* (Revam 2012) 169–191.

Jaramillo Marín RS and Cruz Palomo DF, 'La insuficiencia de las medidas adoptadas para la población privada de la libertad en Colombia con ocasión de la pandemia de la enfermedad por Coronavirus' (2020) 19 *Opinión Jurídica* 151–161.

Limoncelli KE, Mellow J and Na C, 'Determinants of Intercountry Prison Incarceration Rates and Overcrowding in Latin America and the Caribbean' (2020) 30 *International Criminal Justice Review* 10–29.

Litigación Estructural para América del Sur (Leasur), 'Informe de condiciones carcelarias. Situación de las cárceles en Chile 2019' (*LEASUR*, 2019).

Marmolejo L and others, 'Responding to COVID-19 in Latin American Prisons: The Cases of Argentina, Chile, Colombia, and Mexico' (2020) 15 *Victims & Offenders* 1062–1085.

Mateus D, 'Hacinamiento Carcelario y Covid-19 en América Latina' (*Fiedrich Ebert Stiftung*, 2020) <https://library.fes.de/pdf-files/bueros/la-seguridad/16288.pdf>.

Nuñovero Cisneros L, 'Factores de aumento de la población penitenciaria en el Perú, medidas alternativas y vigilancia electrónica' (2017) 37 *Estudios Penales y Criminológicos* 369–390.

Nuñovero Cisneros L, 'Cárceles en América Latina 2000–2018. Tendencias y desafíos' (2019) 50 *Cuaderno de Trabajo PUCP* 1–29.

Nuñovero Cisneros L, 'Vacunar en las cárceles' *El Comercio* (Peru, 12 February 2021) <https://elcomercio.pe/opinion/colaboradores/vacunar-en-las-carceles-por-lucia-nunovero-vacunacion-carceles-penales-covid-19-noticia/>.

Núñez Vega J, 'Hipertrofia represiva: la cuestión carcelaria en América Latina' (2005) 12 *Quórum, Revista de pensamiento iberoamericano* 140–155.

Orozco Ravelo AM, 'La COVID-19 y la justicia de ejecución de sanciones penales' (2020) *Caso Jalisco* 131–137.

Peirce JE, 'Provós, Representantes, Agentes: the Evolution of Prison Governance Arrangements in the Dominican Republic's Prison Reform Process' in Sozzo M (ed), *Prisons, Inmates and Governance in Latin America* (Cham, Springer International Publishing 2022) 93–126.

Peralta Jordán Á, 'Cárcel y Pandemia. Profundización de una crisis permanente. El caso chileno' (2021) 36 *Universitas* 84–98.

Pérez Guadalupe JL, *Faites y atorrantes: una etnografía del penal de Lurigancho* (Lima, Pontificia Universidad Teológica 1994).

Pérez Guadalupe JL, *La construcción social de la realidad carcelaria* (Lima, Pontificia Universidad Católica del Perú 2000).

Pérez Guadalupe JL and Nuñovero Cisneros L, 'Condenados a una pena privativa de salud. La crisis carcelaria en tiempos de coronavirus' in Meléndez C (eds), *Pandemonio: hospitales colapsados, una economía en recesión, cárceles amotinadas y millones de peruanos esperando un bono que nunca llegará* (Crisol 2020) 109–145.

Pérez Guadalupe JL and Nuñovero Cisneros L, 'Ejecución de la Pena privativa de libertad en el Perú y Derechos Humanos' in Galván S and others (eds), *Ejecución Penal y Sistema Carcelario* (Bogotá, Fundación Konrad Adenauer KAS, Centro de Estudios de Justicia de Américas CEJA -Ed, Tirant Lo Blanch 2021) 375–396.

Pffaf JF, 'The Micro and Macro Causes of Prison Growth' (2012) 28 *Georgia State University Law Review* 1237–1271.

Piñeros-Báez VH, 'Public Health Responses for the Management of COVID-19 in Detention Centers. Literature Review' (2020) 22 *Revista de Salud Pública* 238–245.

Piñeros-Baez VH, 'COVID-19 en prisión. Una aproximación a la tendencia epidemiológica en Colombia' (2021) 23 Rev. Salud Pública 1–8.

Salas AA, '(Sobre)vivir la COVID-19. Experiencias de encierro en centro penitenciario de la ciudad de México' (2020) 50 *Revista de Bioética y Derecho* 149–166.

Sindeev A and Martinez-Alvarez BM, 'Características clínico-epidemiológicas de los reclusos infectados y fallecidos por COVID-19 según datos del INPE' (2022) 24 *Revista Española de Sanidad Penitenciaria* 16–24.

Skarbek D, 'Covenants without the Sword? Comparing Prison Self-Governance Globally' (2016) 110 *American Political Science Review* 845–862.

Snacken S, Beyens K and Tubex H, 'Changing Prison Population in Western Countries: Fate of Policy' (1998) 3 *European Journal of Crime, Criminal Law and Criminal Justice* 18–53.

Soares RR and Naritomi J, 'Understanding High Crime Rates in Latin America. the Role of Social and Policy Factors' in Di Tella R, Edwards S and Schargrodsky E (eds), *The Economics of Crime* (University of Chicago Press 2010) 19–55.

SOCLA-CELIV, 'Los efectos del coronavirus en las cárceles de Latinoamérica' (*Criminología Latam*, 2020) <https://criminologialatam.wordpress.com/2020/06/12/efectos-del-covid-19-carceles-de-latino-america/>.

Sozzo M, *Postneoliberalismo y penalidad en América del Sur Buenos Aires* (Clacso 2016)

Weegels J, 'Prisoner Self-Governance and Survival in a Nicaraguan City Police Jail' (2017) 229 *Prison Service Journal* 15–18.

Weegels J, Gual R and Espinoza O, 'Compartiendo el poder: Experiencias de cogobierno entre reclusos y autoridades en las cárceles latinoamericanas' in Hernández Jiménez N (ed), *Temas Criminológicos Latinoamericanos* (Bogotá, Tirant lo Blanch 2021) 321–370.

WHO, 'Preparation, prevention and control of Covid-19 in prisons and other places of detention' (*WHO*, 15 March 2020) <https://iris.who.int/bitstream/handle/10665/336525/WHO-EURO-2020-1405-41155-55954-eng.pdf>.

Ytokazy G, 'Peruvian Prison Reforms and the Covid-19 Outbreak' (2021) 34 *Asian Journal of Latin American Studies* 99–127.

CHAPTER 7

A Lost Critical Juncture: COVID-19 in Brazilian Prisons

Maíra Rocha Machado and Natalia Pires de Vasconcelos

1 Introduction

The COVID-19 pandemic was an unprecedented crisis in Brazil. According to official reports, the virus infected over 36 million people and caused the deaths of close to 700,000 people by the end of 2022,[1] though these numbers could be greatly underestimated as many of the Bolsonaro era's anti-science governmental measures might have led to even higher levels of morbidity and mortality.[2]

The pandemic paralyzed the country and suspended normality for the institutional life of most public organizations. Efficiently confronting the pandemic required social isolation, testing, changes in the habits of the population as a whole, and an intense debate between public authorities about how to care for the sick while preventing new cases.[3] These recommendations were even more urgent in prison settings[4] given the imminent risk of contagion to confined people, and especially pressing in overcrowded prison sys-

1 See Brazil's official pandemic statistics at: https://covid.saude.gov.br/

2 Elize Massard de Fonseca and others, 'Political discourse, denialism and leadership failure in Brazil's response to COVID-19' (2021) 16 Global public health 1251; Gabriela Lotta and others, 'Community health workers reveal COVID-19 disaster in Brazil' (2020) 396 The Lancet 365; Lucas Ferrante and others, 'How Brazil's President turned the country into a global epicenter of COVID-19' (2021) 42 Journal of Public Health Policy 439.

3 Lorena G. Barberia and others, 'Brazil needs a coordinated and cooperative approach to tackle COVID-19' (2021) 27 Nature Medicine 1133.

4 UN Subcommittee on Prevention of Torture and Other Cruel, Inhuman or Degrading Treatment or Punishment, 'Advice of the Subcommittee on Prevention of Torture to States Parties and National Preventive Mechanisms relating to the Coronavirus Pandemic' (*OHCHR*, 2020) <https://www.ohchr.org/sites/default/files/Documents/HRBodies/OPCAT/AdviceStatePartiesCoronavirusPandemic2020.pdf> accessed 8 December 2023; World Health Organization, 'UNODC, WHO, UNAIDS and OHCHR joint statement on COVID-19 in prisons and other closed settings' (*WHO*, 2020) <https://www.who.int/news/item/13-05-2020-unodc-who-unaids-and-ohchr-joint-statement-on-covid-19-in-prisons-and-other-closed-set accessed 8 December 2023.

tems such as the Brazilian one. Brazil had in 2020, and still has in 2023, the third largest prison population in the world:[5] around 700,000 people are incarcerated in state and federal prisons, with an average occupancy level in 2020 of 150% (a minimum of 80% occupancy level in the state of Amapá and a maximum of 340% in the state of Roraima), and an average pre-trial detention rate of 30% (a minimum of 14% in Rondonia and a maximum of 51.7% in Bahia).[6]

In this chapter, we argue that the pandemic, as a moment of crisis, was also an opportunity to challenge and reform Brazilian incarceration practices. Since the 1990s, judges throughout Brazil have ruled in favour of virtually any claim brought by members of the general public that invokes the right to health as grounds for challenging state practices.[7] The right to health was enacted as a fundamental and constitutional right in 1988, and its 30-year case law allows for its protection regardless of organizational or budgetary restrictions.[8]

The judicial tendency to protect the right to health over other rights became particularly acute during the pandemic, when the judicial system not only changed its proceedings to match the needs of isolation and remote work (such as suspending proceedings, deferring deadlines, and switching in-person hearings to virtual), but also worked to guarantee the protection of different constitutional rights to strengthen the constitutional right to health. Courts, to name a few examples, extended procedural and contractual deadlines, guaranteed the right to housing by suspending evictions, secured states'

---

5 Institute for Crime & Justice Policy Research and Birkbeck College, 'Highest to Lowest – Prison Population Total' (*World Prison Brief*, 2024) <https://www.prisonstudies.org/highest-to-lowest/prison-population-total?field_region_taxonomy_tid=All> accessed 29 January 2024.

6 There are, however, serious inconsistencies over the current number of people in prisons in Brazil. As per SISDEPEN, the federal authority in charge of overseeing the entire prison system, there was an estimated number of 667,641 people incarcerated in December 2020; and 669,916 in December 2021. Ministério da justiça e Segurança Pública, 'Painéis Dinâmicos' (*Secretaria Nacional de Políticas Penais*, 2023) <https://www.gov.br/senappen/pt-br/servicos/sisdepen/paineis-anteriores> accessed 8 December 2023. Independent accounts by academic researchers and civil society (*Forum de Segurança Pública*), show, yet other numbers: 753,966 by December 2020, and 815,165 by December 2021. See: Acervo Digital do Fórum Brasileiro de Segurança Pública 'Anuario 16' (FBSP, 2023) <https://publicacoes.forumseguranca.org.br/items/4f923d12-3cb2-4a24-9b63-e41789581d30> accessed 22 September 2025.

7 Octávio L. Motta Ferraz, *Health as a Human Right. The politics and judicialisation of health in Brazil* (Cambridge, Cambridge University Press 2021).

[illegible]ibid; Daniel W. L. Wang, 'Right to health litigation in Brazil: the problem and the institu-[illegible]ponses' (2015) 15 Human Rights Law Review 617.

tacle to changing decision-making practices in criminal law. The last section concludes this chapter and introduces new challenges and a research agenda.

2 Crisis and Institutional Change

The analysis of crisis as an opportune moment for change is a particularly important topic in historical neoinstitutionalism thought. Although what has come to be called historical neoinstitutionalism does not consist of a uniform and completely integrated theoretical body, the works that are organized within it are especially concerned with explaining the relations between institutions – considered here as "official and unofficial procedures, protocols, norms and conventions" inherent to the organizational structures of a political community, a political economy, and political action.[13] Associated with the socioeconomic structure and the collection of ideas and beliefs prevalent in a political community, institutions would have the ability to explain individual and collective action over time.

Institutions could affect the behaviour and action of individuals, either because they act as more or less efficient stabilizers of the uncertainties associated with individual and collective behaviour, or because they determine the worldview of agents through "moral and cognitive models that allow the interpretation of action".[14] This effect of institutions occurs especially because of their perennial and stable nature, which generally prevents sudden changes of course in individuals' actions while conditioning future choices, making the content and form of new actions dependent on the trajectory of past actions (trajectory dependence or path dependence). One of the main concerns of this theoretical body is to explain precisely the moments of change that "break" or weaken the path dependence and perenniality of institutions. The key concept, in this case, is that of "critical juncture".

Capoccia and Kelemen[15] explain that most of the life of political institutions is marked by long periods of stability, in which only very gradual changes occur, highly dependent on the trajectory of past decisions. Occasionally, however, institutions undergo major and profound changes. These dramatic changes are caused by moments of critical juncture – relatively short and

13 Peter A. Hall and Rosemary C. R. Taylor, 'The three versions of neo-institutionalism' (2003) 58 Lua Nova 193.
14 Hall and Taylor, 'The three versions of neo-institutionalism' (n 13).
15 Giovanni Capoccia and Daniel R. Kelemen, 'The study of critical junctures: Theory, narrative, and counterfactuals in historical institutionalism' (2007) 59 World Politics 341.

contingent periods in which a set of factors allows the suspension of structural influences (economic, organizational, ideological) and the weight of past ways on political action, allowing new forms of decision-making. These moments expand the list of possible choices for political agents with power, and the consequences of these choices are perceived as contingent and momentary, potentially giving rise to new moments of stability and path dependence.[16]

Soifer[17] proposes analysing moments of critical juncture from the characterization of permissive and productive conditions, necessary and sufficient for an institutional change to occur. Determining the presence of these conditions would allow us to distinguish moments of critical juncture from historical moments that favour the status quo. Permissive conditions are those factors or conditions that increase the power of agency and contingent action, allowing the adoption of paths divergent from those adopted in the past. These conditions mark the duration of the critical junctures because they suspend or detach the network of relations that stabilizes social relations and, thus, open a window of opportunity for change. Political and economic crises are clear examples of permissive conditions, as exogenous shocks, moments of rupture, and times of instability that demand contingent responses from agents, opening space for agency. Crises, however, are a necessary but not sufficient condition for change. They open this window of opportunity, but other factors need to be present for institutional change to occur and a new moment of path dependence to emerge.

Soifer calls these other factors productive conditions. These occur in the context of permissive conditions and are also necessary, but not sufficient, to bring about institutional change. They need the context created by the permissive conditions to produce these reform effects, but they give shape to the institutional result that emerges from the moment of juncture.

In a same moment of crisis, for example, countries undergo different forms of institutional change because of different productive conditions. The stock of economic and political ideas at a given critical moment is an example of a productive condition. In the case studied by Soifer, the collapse of export markets that followed the crisis of 1929 and the Second World War (permissive condition) would have put an end to an era of economic policies directed exclusively at the export of primary goods. However, the response by Latin American countries – the adoption of economic policies of import substitu-

16 ibid 343

17 Hillel D. Soifer, 'The Causal Logic of Critical Junctures' (2012) 45 Comparative Political Studies 1572.

tion (result) – would have been possible only because of the emergence of a set of influential ideas supported by economists in the Economic Commission for Latin America and the Caribbean – ECLAC (productive condition). These two factors, economic crisis and new ideas about economic policy, acted in a pre-crisis context (characterized by an already-mobilized working class and the presence of small entrepreneurs) and generated a regional institutional change: the adoption of import substitution policies until the mid-1970s.

The pre-crisis context is also a relevant variable. As a critical antecedent, this variable does not cause permissive conditions, which behave like an exogenous shock, but acts on the viability and content of productive conditions. In the example, the substitution of imports as a viable economic policy, beyond its formulation on paper, would occur only if countries in the region had a large and mobilized class of workers and small producers capable of reversing their productive potential in the direction of such a policy.

In this chapter, we apply this theoretical framework in an attempt to shed light on an empirical and theoretical problem: why has the COVID-19 pandemic not altered incarceration practices within the Brazilian criminal justice system? This question clearly shows some of the assumptions we intend to discuss in the next sections.

The first is that the COVID-19 pandemic can be seen as an external shock to criminal-justice practices. We discuss below how the pandemic can be considered a permissive condition that allows for contingent and individual action, suspending institutional normality. The second is that Brazil's criminal justice system has come under pressure from this "external shock" but has not changed significantly during the pandemic. Some of the immediate responses to the pandemic permitted different decisions about who should be incarcerated. But these permissible decisions, at a time of contingency, were not taken, largely because the rationality that characterizes practices within the criminal legal system did not shift to become a productive condition for institutional change.

3 Permissive Conditions: The COVID-19 Pandemic

The COVID-19 pandemic can be considered a crisis and a permissive condition for change. Characterizing the pandemic as a crisis is appropriate not only because the health crisis was an exogenous and large event. It is a crisis because it has affected and still affects in different ways health systems and criminal legal systems worldwide, with specific consequences in carceral settings.

3.1 *Inside Prisons: Crisis and Prison Systems*

Inside prisons, the pandemic functions as a permissive condition by exposing the inadequacies and indignities of the criminal justice system and suspending the "institutional normality" of prison functioning. Brazil has a prison population of around 700,000 people, the third largest in the world. Most of the people incarcerated (67%) are identified as black and brown, young, and coming from the most vulnerable socioeconomic strata of society.[18]

Before the pandemic, most of the prison system did not meet the minimum legal standards for healthcare delivery. In addition to overcrowding, only 63% of the country's prison units had medical clinics available for incarcerated people, and less than 60% of these clinics had specific spaces for healthcare, such as vaccination and suture rooms, testing facilities, and x-rays. In addition, most health services within the prison system were provided by nursing assistants since most units did not have a doctor or nurse present every day.[19] Given the lack of staff and structure, most health services needed to be provided outside prisons, which involves the organization of police escorts to hospitals, a scarce resource for prison units.[20]

Added to the lack of health services and overcrowding are the unsanitary and unsafe conditions of many prisons in the country: windowless cells filled with people huddled in hot, humid spaces with little air circulation and incoming sunlight. In some units, there might be a constant lack of water and power or even sanitation. For these reasons, diseases such as tuberculosis and HIV/AIDS are more prevalent within the prison population than outside prisons. Violence is also part of daily prison life, not only from prison officers and the police but also among imprisoned people, inside and outside the context of rebellions.[21]

18 Poliana S. Ferreira and others, 'Black Population and Prison in Brazil: Impacts Of Covid' (2020) 4 Afro Cebrap: Informative Racial Inequalities and Covid-19 1.

19 ibid.

20 Marden M. Soares Filho and Paula M. Gomes Bueno, 'Demography, vulnerabilities and the right to health of the Brazilian prison population' (2016) 21 Science & Collective Health 1999; Luiz H. Fernandes, 'The need to improve health care in prisons' (2014) 48 Journal of Public Health 275.

21 Global Health Justice Partnership, 'Responding to the justice and rights implications of the COVID-19 pandemic' (*GHJP*, 2021) <https://law.yale.edu/ghjp/projects/infectious-disease-and-justice/covid-19> accessed 31 May 2021; Harnoldo C. Coelho and others, 'HIV prevalence and risk factors in a Brazilian penitentiary' (2007) 23 Cadernos de Saúde Pública 2197; Yiran E. Liu and others, 'All-cause and cause-specific mortality during and following incarceration in Brazil: A retrospective cohort study' (2021) 18 PLoS Medicine 1; Camilla N. Dias and Fernando Salla, 'Organized Crime in Brazilian Prisons: The Example of the PCC' (2013) 2 International Journal of Criminology and Sociology 397.

The COVID-19 pandemic, therefore, comes to a prison system that, in its state of "institutional normalcy", was already long affected by a lack of basic infrastructure, overcrowding, violence, and racism. Since the first COVID-19 cases were recorded in April 2020 in the states of Pará and Rio de Janeiro, the virus spread throughout the prison system: all 26 states recorded confirmed cases and deaths. The National Penitentiary Department reports, as of 22 October 2022 (the last date the panel was updated), 67,367 "detected" cases, 33,559 suspected cases, and 293 deaths.[22] The National Council of Justice presents a grimmer scenario, registering 108,358 cases and 661 deaths.[23] Numbers from both sources are certainly underestimated as they rely on reports submitted by state officials who do not update information regularly or even properly report deaths or confirmed cases caused by COVID-19.[24]

The health crisis suspended the "normality" of prison functioning by forcing correctional departments to create and implement new protocols and procedures to minimally protect employees and people incarcerated from COVID-19 infection, as well as isolate and treat confirmed cases. There was, however, no single, coordinated administrative response to the pandemic in Brazil's prisons.[25] The federal government issued recommendations and guidelines for its own prison facilities, but it was up to state officials to implement them and even request additional federal funding. There is also a general lack of transparency and information not only for COVID-19 cases among incarcerated people and prison staff, but also for the measures adopted by each correctional facility.[26]

---

22 See: Ministério da justiça e Segurança Pública, 'Painel de Monitoramento dos Sistemas Prisionais' (*Secretaria Nacional de Políticas Penais*, 2023) <https://www.gov.br/senappen/pt-br/assuntos/acoes-contra-pandemia/painel-de-monitoramento-dos-sistemas-prisionais> accessed 19 September 2023.

23 See: CNJ, 'Covid-19 no Sistema Prisional' (*CNJ*, 2022) <https://www.cnj.jus.br/wp-content/uploads/2022/04/boletim-covid-19-marco2022.pdf> accessed 8 December 2023.

24 Check out the work of Infovirus, mapping the delay in updating information on numbers of cases and deaths in the prison system and the lack of transparency of DEPEN and state administrations on the subject. Infovirus, 'Homepage' (*Covidnaprisoes*, 2021) https://www.instagram.com/infovirusprisoes/ accessed 22 September 2025.

25 Natalia P. de Vasconcelos and others, 'Covid-19 and Prisons in Latin America. Global Health Justice Partnership' (*Yale Law and Public Health Schools*, 2022) <https://law.yale.edu/sites/default/files/area/center/ghjp/documents/brazilcolombia_commentary_final.pdf> accessed 29 January 2024

26 Camila Prando and Rafael Godoi, 'The management of data on the pandemic in prisons: a comparison between the concealment practices of the prison administration departments of RJ and D' (2020) Dilemmas: Journal of Conflict Studies and Social Control 1.

A response commonly adopted (though in an uncoordinated way) to the pandemic was the lockdown of correctional units, preventing access by outside people except for essential personnel and law enforcement. That meant that family members, lawyers, human rights advocates, and non-essential staff (such as teachers, priests, and social workers) were kept out of prison walls and allowed very little contact with people incarcerated inside.

The Brazilian prison system, as many others in the world, depends on different stakeholders and state and non-state actors to maintain its operations.[27] It is a space that is formed by and operates at the junction of the executive, legislative, and judicial powers, but it is also heavily reliant on families and civil society. Families are especially central to this policy as they ensure that incarcerated people have access to many essentials, such as hygiene items, medicines, and clothing, while providing emotional care and support generally not offered by state prison management.[28] Even more importantly, family members are one of the main sources of food through the delivery of what is known as "jumbo", a food package that complements the often-insufficient and non-nutritious food offered by the state. Public defenders, lawyers, and civil society organizations were also barred from entering correctional spaces, greatly affecting their capacity to review and control correctional staff and law enforcement activities. Reports of increased violence and torture, combined with the denial of healthcare access, were notified by human-rights organizations in the scarce moments they could communicate with incarcerated people.[29]

27 Sandro Cabral and Maria F. Santos, 'Accountability Mechanisms in Public Services: Activating New Dynamics in a Prison System' (2018) 21 International Public Management Journal 795.

28 Rafael Godoi and others, 'Epistemopolitics of the São Paulo prison device: reflecting on experiences of research-intervention with the Prison Pastoral' (2020) 7 Journal of Empirical Studies in Law 143–158. See also: National Agenda for Decarcerating, 'O que defendemos' (*Pelo Desencarceramento e Desmilitarização*, 2021) <https://desencarceramento.org.br/> accessed 27 May 2021.

29 de Vasconcelos and others, 'Covid-19 and Prisons in Latin America. Global Health Justice Partnership' (n 25). See also: Pastoral Carcerária, 'Questionário sobre Coronavírus nas Prisões Revela que Situação no Cárcere está muito pior um ano após o início da Pandemia' (*Pastoral Carcerária*, 19 April 2021) <https://carceraria.org.br/combate-e-prevencao-a-tortura/questionario-sobre-coronavirus-nas-prisoes-revela-que-situacao-no-carcere-esta-muito-pior-um-ano-apos-o-inicio-da-pandemia> accessed 8 December 2023; Pastoral Carcerária, 'Denúncias de violação de direitos no sistema prisional aumentaram 82% durante a pandemia, segundo Pastoral' (*Pastoral Carcerária*, 7 April 2021) <https://carceraria.org.br/combate-e-prevencao-a-tortura/denuncias-de-violacao-de-direitos-no-sistema-prisional-aumentaram-82-durante-a-pandemia-segundo-pastoral> accessed 8 December 2023.

3.2 *Outside the Prison: Crisis and the Justice System*

Outside prison walls, the health crisis suspended institutional normality for the organization and operation of the health and the justice systems. In healthcare services, elective care was postponed, the number of staff for non-urgent or non-COVID-19-related treatment was drastically reduced, and hospital staff and resources were redirected to deal directly with the pandemic.[30] Indeed, these decisions are to be expected even in a health system facing an epidemic. But the speed at which the virus spread and the severity of COVID-19 infections, coupled with the inefficient and negligent actions of Bolsonaro's government, made the scenario even more urgent and dependent on the contingent action of state bureaucracies.[31]

In the justice system, all in-person activities were suspended for more than a year, procedural deadlines were extended or suspended, and, in the criminal law sphere, pre-trial hearings were suspended or held by videoconference, making judges and appellate courts further removed from contact with incarcerated people.

Most of the judicial system acted in favour of effective and science-based measures to confront the crisis. Judges and courts, for example, including the Supreme Federal Court, mediated federative conflicts between states and the federal government[32] to ensure that responses to the pandemic could be implemented by states and municipalities even in the face of constant attacks by Bolsonaro.[33] A few members of the judicial system, however, did endorse Bolsonaro's agenda and determined the provision of unproven, early treatments such as hydroxychloroquine,[34] or granted individual injunctions for COVID-19 hospitalization, breaching policy protocols and healthcare triage guidelines.[35]

---

30 Massard de Fonseca and others, 'Political discourse, denialism and leadership failure in Brazil's response to COVID-19' (n 2).

31 ibid.

32 de Vasconcelos and Arguelhes, 'Covid-19, federalismo e descentralização no STF: reorientação ou ajuste pontual?' (n 9).

33 Camila L. Asano and others, 'Bulletin Rights in the Pandemic No. 3' (*Center for Research in Sanitary Law*, 2020) <https://cepedisa.fsp.usp.br/wp-content/uploads/2023/02/03boletimcovid_PT_05.pdf> accessed 22 September 2025.

34 Court of Justice of Santa Catarina, 'Use of chloroquine against Covid, judge says, is consensual decision between doctor and patient' (*TJSC*, 2021) <https://www.tjsc.jus.br/web/imprensa/-/uso-de-cloroquina-contra-covid-diz-juiz-e-decisao-consensual-entre-medico-e-paciente?inheritRedirect=true> accessed 31 May 2021.

35 Dhiego Maia, 'STJ suspende liminares que determinavam internações em UTI para Covid em Cuiabá' *Folha de S. Paulo* (Gonçalves, 17 April 2021) <https://www1.folha.uol.com.br/equilibrioesaude/2021/04/stj-suspende-liminares-que-determinavam-internacoes-em-u

Judicial interference with the country's public-health policy has been a trend long before the pandemic. Thousands of individual lawsuits are filed every year requiring services and treatments often not offered by the country's universal healthcare policy. The vast majority of these lawsuits are decided in favour of patients, regardless of the safety and cost-effectiveness of treatments, challenging healthcare policy priority-setting provisions while also expanding the scope of the country's constitutional right to health.[36]

The pandemic also brought before the judicial system as public-health questions problems that, before the health crisis, would not have been formulated as legal demands for the right to health. Claims for a safe and healthy workplace,[37] for suspending evictions,[38] and for access to better prison conditions, early release, house arrest, and probation/parole[39] were topics framed through the language of access to health and the constitutional right to health, forcing judges and courts to think about the impact of the pandemic on different spheres of life and, especially, about the needs and dignity of vulnerable populations.

4 Crisis Response: Recommendation 62

Against this backdrop, Recommendation 62 of the National Council of Justice was published on March 17, 2020, containing several measures directed to courts to prevent the spread of COVID-19 within the correctional system. Articles 4 and 5 stand out, listing what the National Council of Justice recommended as hypotheses for the reassessment of pre-trial detention and for

---

ti-para-covid-em-cuiaba.shtml> accessed 8 December 2023; Lucas Janone, 'Justice suspends decrees on restrictive measures against Covid-19 in Rio' *CNN Brasil* (Rio de Janeiro, 5 May 2021) <https://www.cnnbrasil.com.br/nacional/2021/05/05/justica-suspende-decretos-sobre-medidas-restritivas-contra-covid-19-no-rio> accessed 28 May 2021.

36 Motta Ferraz, *Health as a Human Right* (n 7); João Biehl and others, 'Between the court and the clinic: lawsuits for medicines and the right to health in Brazil' (2012) 14 Health and Human Rights Journal 1.

37 Maia, 'STJ suspende liminares que determinavam internações em UTI para Covid em Cuiabá' (n 35).

38 Firpo and Tavolari, 'Políticas de moradia em momentos de crise: a centralidade do aluguel' (n 9).

39 Natalia P. de Vasconcelos, Maira R. Machado and Daniel W. L. Wang, 'COVID-19 in prisons: a study of habeas corpus decisions by the São Paulo Court of Justice' (2020) 54 Revista de Administração Pública 1472; Natalia P. de Vasconcelos, Maira R. Machado and Henrique Y. J. Wang, 'Pandemia Só das Grades para Fora: os Habeas Corpus Julgados pelo Tribunal de Justiça de São Paulo' (2020) 17 Revista Direito Público 541.

Article 4 – To recommend investigating judges to consider the following measures in order to reduce the epidemiological risks and in light of the virus spread at each location:

I – To reconsider pre-trial detention, in accordance with Article 316 of the Criminal Procedure Code, with preference to:
a) pregnant women, lactating women, mothers or people caring for under-12 child or disabled person, elderly people, native Brazilians, people with disability, people in risk group*;
b) People detained in institutions running at above full capacity, without dedicated health care professionals, under an interdiction order, with cautionary measures determined by an international jurisdictional body, or with facilities conducive to the new coronavirus spread;
c) Preventive detentions that surpassed the 90-day period or that are related to crimes that involve violence or the threat of violence against a person [...]

Article 5 – To recommend correctional judges to consider the following measures in order to reduce the epidemiological risks and in light of the virus spread at each location:
I – Early release from closed and semi-closed prison following the Supreme Court binding precedent 56, particularly in relation to:
a) pregnant women, lactating women, mothers or people caring for under-12 child or disabled person, elderly people, native Brazilians, people with disability, people in risk group*;
b) People detained in institutions running at above full capacity, without dedicated health care professionals, under an interdiction order, with cautionary measures determined by an international jurisdictional body, or with facilities conducive to the new coronavirus spread; [...]
III – House arrest for people serving sentence in open and semi-closed prison, under the conditions to be defined by the correctional judge.
IV – House arrest for people with confirmed or suspected Covid-19 diagnosis according to medical report, if adequate space for isolation is not available at the facility [...]

FIGURE 7.1 CNJ Recommendation 62/2020
SOURCE: RECOMMENDATION 62 OF THE NATIONAL COUNCIL OF JUSTICE. AUTHORS' CLIPPINGS. According to the Recommendation, the health-risk group included the elderly, pregnant women, and people with chronic, immunosuppressive, respiratory and other pre-existing comorbidities that may lead to a worsening of the general state of health from the contagion, with special attention to diabetes, tuberculosis, kidney diseases, HIV and co-infections.

granting early release, house arrest, or changes from fully closed to semi-open incarceration regimes (Figure 7.1). These hypotheses were not created by the National Council of Justice. Recommendation 62 builds on criminal procedure norms and Supreme Court precedents that provided basic guidelines for guaranteeing the rights of incarcerated people. However, the Recommendation expands these norms' original scope to specifically protect people in risk groups and detained in precarious and unsafe spaces.

Recommendation 62 is not only a response to the pandemic, but also part of a longer and previous effort by groups within the judicial system, especially from the National Council of Justice, academia, and civil society, to make living conditions in prison a relevant and decisive variable in judicial decisions.[40]

In Brazil, the 1988 Constitution bans cruel punishment, the death penalty, and life-long sentences. However, this has not prevented judicial practices and the concrete functioning of correctional institutions from accepting and coexisting with the possibility of these forms of punishment in practice. One thing is the punishment determined by law, another is the punishment imposed in individual sentences, and yet another is the punishment actually lived by the person who has been sentenced.

The French historian André Zysberg, in a study of punitive practices in the Ancien Régime, offers an eloquent image for this reflection. The study analyses the penalty of galleys between the 17th and 18th centuries, a time before the emergence of modern criminal law and prison sentences as we know them. The galleys were ships that mostly relied on oars for propulsion. Individuals serving a criminal sentence were sent to forced labour as oarsmen. The author reports that being sentenced to the galleys "represented, at once, a torture, a corporal punishment and a mode of social exclusion and confinement".[41] Situated just below the death penalty on the scale of punishments, the duration of a sentence could vary between 3, 5, 7, or 10 years or could be for life. However, Zysberg points out that even when the duration of time was fixed, being sent to the galleys functioned almost like a death sentence due to the high number of deaths caused by the "poor quality of life and the exces-

40 Maíra R. Machado, 'Quando o estado de coisas é inconstitucional: sobre o lugar do Poder Judiciário no problema carcerário' (2020) 7 Journal of Constitutional Investigations 631. See also: National Agenda for Decarcerating, 'O que defendemos' (n 28).

41 André Zysberg, 'Histoire des galères, bagnes et prisons en France de l'Ancien Régime' in Jacques-Guy Petit (ed), *La Prison, Le Bagne et l'Histoire* (Geneva, Librairie des Méridiens 1984) 69.

sive duration of the campaigns"[42] and due to the systematic disregard of the stipulated maximum sentence time. As the author explains, "the bravest and most independent judges occasionally protested against this abuse of royal power, saying that it mocked their sentences as it meant the same thing sentencing a man to the galleys for 3 years or for life".[43]

This passage offers three relevant points. It reveals that death and the risk of death are often accepted as effects – very likely, in many cases – of other types of punishments prescribed by law and imposed by courts. In this view, the commitment to enforce the sentence that has been determined by the court requires judicial autonomy in the face of political/executive power: it is necessary to protest in order to enforce the terms of the sentence, i.e., the exact number of years prescribed. But Zysberg's passage also shows that even in the face of the broad knowledge that life in the galleys can result in death, illness, and mutilation, the judicial sentence itself continued to indicate only what the formal law prescribed as if reality: rowing for 3, 5, 7 or 10 years.[44] Zysberg's passage about the galleys in the Ancient Regime illustrates well the workings of the Brazilian criminal justice.[45] The punishment to be lived or experienced does not participate in the decision-making processes that determine punishment. As we will argue below, the indifference to life, and the disconnect between the judicial decision and the concrete experience that each person will face in the course of their sentences, are constitutive parts of how the Brazilian criminal justice system works.

By looking at the lived punishment, this chapter treats the experiences of pre-trial detention or final sentences indistinctly and, thus, highlights how the characteristics of the imprisoned person and the environment where they will or already live their sentences participate in the decision-making process. Looking at the lived experience of punishment involves understanding the biographical elements that characterize an individual sentence (the medical,

42 ibid 74.

43 ibid 69.

44 ibid 74. It also reports that, among those sentenced to the galleys, only mutilated and sick people remained in the harbor, crammed into old vessels or sent to hospitals.

45 Galley was established at the Philippine Ordinations, the legal corpus that governed most of Brazilian colonial life, and was maintained in the Criminal Code of the Brazilian Empire (1830). As the historian Silvia Lara clarifies, when these low-board vessels and oars ceased to exist "the penalty came to mean forced labor in public works by shackle – an iron ring with chain, attached to the leg". Silvia Lara, *Ordenações filipinas, Livro V* (São Paulo, Companhia das Letras 1999) 495. It is in this modality that the galley appears in the Criminal Code of 1830 (Articles 44 and 45). In the Penal Code of the Brazilian Republic (1890), the galley is finally removed from criminal law legislation.

biological, psychic, affective, and family histories, past and present, of those incarcerated) and institutional elements (the prison architecture, its human resources, the medical and legal-assistance services available, how people incarcerated will contact family members or be visited, the dynamics of their disciplinary regime) – in sum, the conditions that circumvent and guide their lived experience in prison.

The Brazilian criminal law dogmatics, up to Recommendation 62, rarely encouraged or favoured that the lived punishment factored into decisions about the entry into and exit from Brazilian prisons. Some characteristics of our criminal justice system contributed to this state of affairs.

First, in the context of judicial decisions made in cases of *flagrante delicto*, the person allegedly caught by the police is rarely considered, even when they are present before the judicial authority. The judicial reasoning focuses on whether it is possible to "guarantee public order" without detaining the person accused, which involves the judge exclusively determining the legality of police work.[46] The environment where the accused will be sent for their pre-trial detention is not even mentioned as a relevant part of the pre-trial decision process.

Second, at the final sentencing, the framework of Brazilian criminal law requires that the accused be checked for their criminal history, previous "social conduct", and overall "personality"[47] – categories that supposedly function as combined indicators of biographical factors[48] but that miss the social and economic conditions that affect and often greatly explain incarcerated people's biographies. Moreover, Brazilian legislation hardly considers the environment where the person will be sent. Judges are limited to determining the incarceration regime (full or "closed" incarceration, partial or "semi-open" incarceration, or "open" regimes like probation), a decision constrained by the amount of time one has been sentenced to serve.[49] The existence of correc-

46 Manuela A. Valença and Felipe Da Silva Freitas, 'The right to life and the ideal of social defense in decisions of the STJ in the context of the Covid-19 pandemic' (2020) 17 Revista Direito Público 570.

47 Article 59 of the Brazilian Penal Code establishes that "[t]he judge, taking into account the defendant's guiltiness, criminal history, social conduct, personality, motives, circumstances, and consequences of the crime, as well as the victim's behavior, shall establish a sentence as necessary and sufficient for the reproach and prevention of the crime".

48 Maira R. Machado, 'Entre a lei e o juiz: os processos decisórios na definição das penas' (2016) 126 Brazilian Journal of Criminal Sciences 181.

49 Brazilian Penal Code, Articles 33 to 42 and 59, III. As the *next section* will show, before the sentence, the ideas about punishment that constitute the core of decision-making practices focus on retribution and deterrence (Penal Code, Article 59). After that, with the beginning of the sentence's enforcement, this rationale is replaced by an idea of the

tional organizations that can receive or supervise people under each regime is not part of the decision, much less the concrete conditions of prison life in these establishments.[50]

Finally, the rules that regulate decisions during the sentence's enforcement, including the possibilities of early release and parole/probation, establish other barriers to considering the lived punishment: the prison management will assess the "conduct" of an incarcerated person, verifying the presence of disciplinary faults in the prison records.[51] The conditions of life in prison, among other factors that characterize the lived punishment, are not taken into account in the decision for early release unless the defence expressly requests it.

Some efforts have partially challenged this normative-institutional arrangement that largely excludes the lived punishment from decision-making processes. Among them is, for example, a Supreme Court decision that recognized "the unconstitutional state of affairs" of the Brazilian prison system.[52] In this acclaimed case, however, the Supreme Court denied requests that sought to precisely make the "dramatic picture" of prison conditions part of the sentencing decision.[53] Another main precedent, also from the Supreme Court, allowed for pregnant and lactating women, as well as mothers or people caring for children under 12 or disabled persons, to be released from pre-trial deten-

---

"harmonious social integration of the convict" and the purpose of punishment legally changes (Prison Law, Article 1). This split between different moments of the Brazilian criminal procedure and what they mean in terms of the purposes of punishment within the criminal legal system operates at three levels: at the normative level (the Penal Code *versus* the Prison Law), at the procedural level (procedural moment of knowing the crime and its appropriate punishment *versus* the sentence's enforcement) and at the punishment justification level (retribution and deterrence *versus* prison rehabilitation).

50 As an exception, the Supreme Court published, in 2016, the Binding Precedent 56 establishing that a person cannot be imprisoned in a more burdensome regime than what they were originally sentenced to due to the lack of an adequate penal establishment to serve their sentences.

51 Prison Law, Articles 39, 50, 112, *caput* and para 1.

52 See the decisions by the Brazilian Supreme Federal Court in the ADPF 347 case, available in Portuguese here: Supremo Tribunal Federal, 'Home' (*STF*, 2024) <https://portal.stf.jus.br/processos/detalhe.asp?incidente=4783560> accessed 29 January 2024.

53 Brazilian Federal Supreme Court (Plenary) Precautionary Measure in the Plea of Non-compliance with Fundamental Precept 347 (19 February 2016) Rapporteur: Mr Marco Aurélio; Machado, 'Quando o estado de coisas é inconstitucional: sobre o lugar do Poder Judiciário no problema carcerário' (n 41).

tion or sent to house arrest.[54] The case, however, does not take prison conditions intrinsically as part sentences but allows the judicial system to screen and protect only this specific group and only as long as they have not committed violent crimes.

In this context, when Recommendation 62 was issued by the National Council of Justice recommending judges to consider prison conditions as an essential part of sentencing, it was both "the most strategic document edited by the CNJ [National Council of Justice]" and also the target of several attacks, including from within the Supreme Federal Court, which contributed to mitigating its effects.[55]

Still, it is possible to observe something that is not negligible in the approval of a document with that type of content. In the face of an unprecedented health crisis, Recommendation 62 states verbatim that the decision-making process regarding the entry and exit of people in all of the country's correctional facilities needs to consider aspects of both the person and the environment where the person is being sent. Recommendation 62 shows that there is no way to prevent the virus's spread without placing the lived punishment at the forefront of the decision-making process.

The judiciary, however, remained resistant to this idea. Research conducted by the authors of this chapter and their co-authors assessed 6,771 decisions of one of the main state courts in the country, the São Paulo state Court of Appeal, in habeas petitions. The decisions were issued in the first two months of the pandemic and revealed that Recommendation 62 was not a driver for de-incarceration. Almost 90% of all habeas were rejected, and of the 54% of decisions that cite Recommendation 62, 90% of them were also rejected (Figure 7.2).[56]

The statistical analysis of these decisions pointed to an even worse scenario: Recommendation 62 was also correlated with habeas rejection,[57] indicat-

54 Brazilian Federal Supreme Court (2nd Class) Habeas Corpus 143.641/SP (9 October 2018) Rapporteur: Mr Lewandowski; Eloisa M. Almeida and others, *For Freedom: The Story of Collective Habeas Corpus for Mothers & Children* (São Paulo, Alana Institute 2019).

55 Manuela A. Valença and Felipe Da Silva Freitas, 'The right to life and the ideal of social defense in decisions of the STJ in the context of the Covid-19 pandemic' (2020) 17 Revista Direito Público 570, 576 and 580.

56 de Vasconcelos, Machado and Wang, 'COVID-19 in prisons: a study of habeas corpus decisions by the São Paulo Court of Justice' (n 39); de Vasconcelos, Machado and Wang, 'Pandemia Só das Grades para Fora: os Habeas Corpus Julgados pelo Tribunal de Justiça de São Paulo' (n 39).

57 de Vasconcelos, Machado and Wang, 'Pandemia Só das Grades para Fora: os Habeas Corpus Julgados pelo Tribunal de Justiça de São Paulo' (n 39).

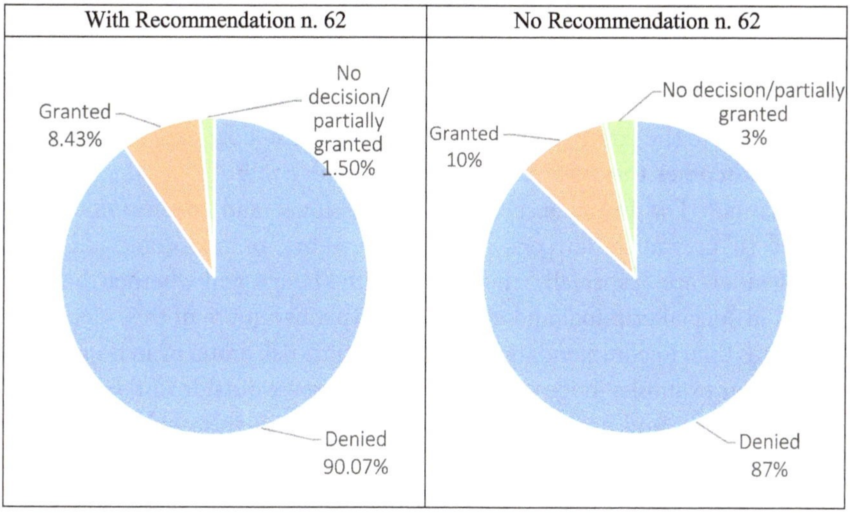

FIGURE 7.2 Habeas corpus decisions and citations to Recommendation 62, São Paulo state Court of Appeal
SOURCE: DE VASCONCELOS, MACHADO & WANG, 2020

ing that judges would invoke the recommendation to counter it when arguing for its non-application or the absence of any normative force.

The qualitative study of the court's reasoning from a representative and random sample of 371 cases revealed that among the few decisions where habeas relief was granted (21 cases out of 371), there is only one case in which Recommendation 62 was decisive. The decision authorized the house arrest of a person convicted of drug trafficking, serving time in a semi-open regime in an overcrowded establishment "for humanitarian reasons established by the National Council of Justice".[58]

Among the decisions of the sample involving elderly people (23 of 371 cases), only one request was granted. This was the case of a 72-year-old person with diabetes and other illnesses who had already served most of his sentence.[59] In the remaining 22 cases, the grounds for habeas denial (i) diverged, questioned, or opposed the terms of Recommendation 62; (ii) limited themselves to indicating that the denials were due to the need for "guaranteeing the public order" or "protecting society"; and, finally, (iii) required the defence to produce evidence on prisons conditions, information that the court itself

58 de Vasconcelos, Machado and Wang, 'COVID-19 in prisons: a study of habeas corpus decisions by the São Paulo Court of Justice' (n 39).

59 de Vasconcelos, Machado and Wang, 'COVID-19 in prisons: a study of habeas corpus decisions by the São Paulo Court of Justice' (n 39).

would be in a better position to discover,[60] especially considering prison lockdowns.

On the other hand, the study of the universe of decisions found that variables linked to the court itself and the judiciary were more explanatory of the habeas outcomes than variables linked to prison conditions or the health of defendants.[61] For instance, a judges' professional and institutional background (if previously lawyers, public prosecutors, or trial court judges[62]), their gender, and, especially, their time on the bench and whether they had served in special criminal and civil courts explained more of their decisions' outcomes than Recommendation 62 or the health-risk group of an imprisoned person. For example, judges who came from careers outside of the judiciary, such as lawyers and prosecutors, were more likely to grant habeas petitions than judges who had been judges for most of their careers. Another finding indicated that habeas petitions in which the person incarcerated was female had a higher probability of being granted, but female judges tended to reject more habeas petitions than male judges. Magistrates' time on the bench also mattered, a variable that was correlated with a higher probability of deferral, provided that the magistrate had not gone through special criminal and civil courts, which are traditionally known for more conservative positions.

Similar results were found for other courts. Hartmann et al.[63] analysed more than 900 habeas petitions filed before the Supreme Federal Court and the Superior Court of Justice between March and May 2020, and concluded that the pandemic had little effect on judicial reasoning or case outcomes. As in the case of São Paulo, the two courts granted very few habeas petitions in 2020–5.23% for the Supreme Court and 5.24% for the Superior Court of Justice. The Supreme Federal Court's rate was lower than the one recorded for the same period in 2019, when the Court granted 8.05% of its habeas petitions, while the Superior Court of Justice[64] kept its rate of granting stable from

60 ibid.

61 de Vasconcelos, Machado and Wang, 'Pandemia Só das Grades para Fora: os Habeas Corpus Julgados pelo Tribunal de Justiça de São Paulo' (n 39).

62 The Brazilian Constitution guarantees that at least one-fifth of all state courts of appeal' judges are selected among members of the Brazilian Bar Association and the Public Prosecutor's Office, while four-fifths of the seats are filled by trial court judges.

63 Ivar A. Hartmann and others, 'How Do the Brazilian Supreme Court and Superior Court of Justice Decide Habeas Corpus Writs during the COVID-19 Pandemic? A Census and Sample Based Analysis' (*FGV Direito Rio*, 2020 <https://papers.ssrn.com/sol3/papers.cfm?abstract_id=3659624> accessed 28 May 2021, http://dx.doi.org/10.2139/ssrn.3659624.

64 It is worth recognizing that among the few favorable habeas decisions is the Superior Court of Justice's decision to the collective *habeas* petition 568.693. In this case, the court

one year to the other. Habeas petitions registered by the Supreme Federal Court as related to the pandemic had lower approval rates than those not explicitly related: while habeas cases not registered as COVID-19-related had an approval rate of 5.76%, those that mentioned the pandemic had one of 4.02%.

Looking specifically at the reasoning for granting and not granting release, the authors find that the pandemic or prison conditions were mostly not considered in the judicial reasoning of these two courts. Within a 5-point scale, where 0 marks a case in which the pandemic is "absolutely not fundamental to the decision" and 5 marks a case in which the pandemic is "very fundamental to the decision", the study finds an average relevance of only 1.24% in granted cases and 1.39% in denied cases – percentages not statistically different from each other.

These empirical findings suggest that, if the pandemic has created conditions for institutional reform, with Recommendation 62 being a strong guideline toward de-incarceration, something inherent to the way judges conceive of criminal law has more force and explanatory power over their decisions.

5 Productive Conditions: Modern Penal Rationality

If permissive conditions relax or suspend institutional constraints, productive conditions require us to turn our attention to the ideas that gain support and can lead an institution and its actors to reorganize its processes in a certain perennial way. By looking at how judicial organizations in Brazil conceive of criminal law, punishment, and incarceration, it is possible to recognize the wide diffusion and crystallization, since the eighteenth century, of a set of ideas named "negative theories of punishment". These are the common denominators of all theories of retribution, deterrence, rehabilitation (or resocialization), and denunciation: they all rely on an obligation to punish,

used Recommendation 62 to grant pre-trial release to all people who had already been given pre-trial release conditioned on bail, but who had remained incarcerated due to lack of payment. The Court extended the effects of this decision to the entire national territory, following a request made by the Espirito Santo State Public Defender's Office See: Superior Tribunal de Justiça, 'Habeas Corpus N° 568.693' (*STJ*, 2020) <https://www.stj.jus.br/sites/portalp/SiteAssets/documentos/noticias/14102020%20HC-568.693.pdf> accessed 8 December 2023. We thank Reviewers 1 and 2 for suggesting to add this case.

on the valorisation of suffering and social exclusion, on the idea of prison as a sanction par excellence, and the demerit of alternatives to punishment.[65]

The theory of modern criminal rationality is built from and around the realization that negative theories of punishment constitute a "cognitive obstacle" to the reconstruction and innovation of criminal law.[66] Margarida Garcia and Richard Dubé[67] also point out that this set of ideas forms the "identity and self-description through which the [criminal legal] system and its actors conceive how criminal law functions, its 'identity', its 'singularity' (...)". The weight and scope of negative theories in the way of thinking, acting, and deciding criminal cases helps to explain why attempts to reform punitive practices have failed over the last two centuries. Neither the critique of prisons as punishment, which arose at the very inception of prisons, nor civil society's open and constant condemnation of the abuses and inhumane practices of our criminal legal system, could transform current punitive practices.[68] For Garcia and Dubé, what prevents us from embarking on a transformative reform is not the absence of "new ideas", but the absence of new, positive theories of punishment that can ground decision-making alternatives with the same institutional stability that we have observed in the case of negative theories.

The touchstone of positive theories, as elaborated below, is to establish a relationship of frank opposition to the idea that social exclusion and suffering can protect society. It is, therefore, a question of developing "alternative ideas that can support [...] ways of resolving conflicts that actively seek to protect society through measures that also protect the social inclusion of people who violate the laws, their social ties, and the conditions favourable to the re-establishment of social peace".[69]

---

65 The "points of cohesion" of negative theories of punishment – also called "conventional theories of punishment" are found in: Margarida Garcia and others (eds), *A Racionalidade Penal Moderna: Reflexões Teóricas e Explorações Empíricas Desde o sul* (São Paulo, Editora Almedina 2020) 60–73.

66 On the two decades of modern penal rationality theory, see the theory's author, describing its trajectory: Pires, 'Posfácio: Nascimento e desenvolvimento de uma teoria e seus problemas de pesquisa' (n 11).

67 Margarida Garcia and Richard Dubé, 'Criminal law reform: an idea whose time has come' in Julie Desrosiers, Margarida Garcia and Marie-Ève Sylvestre (eds), *Criminal Law Reform in Canada: Challenges and Opportunities* (Cowansville, Éditions Yvon Blais 2017) 3–35.

68 On the "enigma" of repetitive criticism of prison, see: Pires, 'Posfácio: Nascimento e desenvolvimento de uma teoria e seus problemas de pesquisa' (n 11) 310.

69 Garcia and Dubé, 'Criminal law reform: an idea whose time has come' (n 67) 18–19.

This reflection provides theoretical clues on the productive conditions that can lead to change within the criminal legal system: in the field of criminal law and punishment, reform requires that we break the link between society's protection and social exclusion, a link that arises from the imposition of suffering. This requires placing the person, and their social and economic background, not only in the field of vision but in the foreground of decision-making processes.

However, negative theories of punishment that make up modern penal rationality block this possibility in different ways. It is possible to say that the person who is an "object" of penal intervention enters the field of vision of modern penal rationality at the beginning of the nineteenth century, when prisons became a preferred form of penalty, and, above all, with the emergence of positivist criminology at the end of that century. This combination of punitive theories and practices gives the contours of prison rehabilitation theory. Until then, theories of retribution and deterrence, developed in the second half of the eighteenth century, were limited to observing the person who breaks the law as a person "provided with free will", who only adds to the punishment equation the extent of their moral responsibility and culpability.

Until then, the penalty is due for the crime. With the theory of prison rehabilitation, this "punishment-crime" equation is complexified, encompassing some characteristics of the person, particularly those that allow the identification of "pathologies" (biological, psychological, and/or social).[70] As a result, new ideas are added to the equation, such as the goal of "treating" the imprisoned person, promoting their "regeneration," "recovery," and "re-education." In other words, the advent of rehabilitation theories offers new reasons and ways of punishing but continues to value imprisonment and social exclusion with suffering as the way to rehabilitation, remaining closely linked to theories of retribution and deterrence. Modern penal rationality did and continues to focus on a form of rehabilitation theory that combines a criminalizing reading of behaviours with a medicalizing and pathologizing reading of people.

---

70 Mariana Raupp, 'La distinction école classique/école positive et la rationalité pénale moderne: une réflexion à partir du regard des sciences sociales sur la réforme pénale de 1984 au Brésil' in Richard Dubé, Margarida Garcia and Maira R. Machado (eds), *A racionalidade penal moderna : reflexões teóricas e explorações empíricas* (São Paulo, Editora Almedina 2020) 146–170. Maira R. Machado, 'The person-object of criminal intervention: first notes on the reception of positivist criminology in Brazil' (2005) 1 Revista Direito GV 79.

These ideas entered Brazilian criminal law through several mechanisms that favour the "disappearance" of the concrete person in decision-making processes when determining one's incarceration or release. This is accomplished through argumentative barriers that, by categorizing, generalizing, omitting, and filtering, eliminate biographical components indispensable to reforming the criminal legal system. In current judicial decisions, concrete people disappear to make way for "traffickers", "criminals", "dangerous individuals", etc.[71]

This is especially clear in the decisions analysed by De Vasconcelos, Machado and Wang[72] during the pandemic. Habeas denials in cases where there is an accusation of drug trafficking, for example – which make up 120 of the 245 decisions in the sample of decisions that contained any information on the type of crime – are centred on arguments related to the protection of the "orderly and honest community" in the face of a crime that does not even involve violence or serious threat.[73] Mentions of the "gravity" of a crime and how that justified the prison sentence, provisional or definitive, as a way to "guarantee public order" and "protect society", are also recurrent in the decisions and reinforce this perspective.[74]

This form of modern penal rationality prevented the pandemic, and Recommendation 62, from producing institutional change. Even if permissive conditions were present, productive conditions for a critical juncture required a substrate of new ideas on punishment and criminal legal practices towards incarceration that, despite existing, are still marginal within the practices of the Brazilian judicial system. Considerations on how punishment is lived have been formally separated from criminal law decision-making, as the individual and environmental factors that will shape experiences in prisons and jail are deemed irrelevant. During the pandemic, these factors persisted as separate and legally irrelevant elements from what was considered within judicial deci-

71 Various surveys have drawn attention, in different ways, to this point. See, for example, the research of Poliana Ferreira (2019) on the "de-racialization" of judicial processes (2019), of Luisa Ferreira (2021) regarding the crime of theft, and of Maíra R. Machado *et al* (2018) on drug trafficking.

72 de Vasconcelos, Machado and Wang, 'COVID-19 in prisons: a study of habeas corpus decisions by the São Paulo Court of Justice' (n 39); de Vasconcelos, Machado and Wang, 'Pandemia Só das Grades para Fora: os Habeas Corpus Julgados pelo Tribunal de Justiça de São Paulo' (n 39).

73 de Vasconcelos, Machado and Wang, 'COVID-19 in prisons: a study of habeas corpus decisions by the São Paulo Court of Justice' (n 39).

74 ibid.

sions, as their decision practices were and are entrenched in the organizational culture that constitutes the Brazilian criminal legal system.

6 Final Considerations

For historical neo-institutionalism, institutional reform can be explained by moments of critical juncture, where permissive and productive conditions alter entrenched institutional practices. As we have seen, the COVID-19 pandemic offered permissive conditions for criminal justice reform, suspending the normality of processes and the functioning of institutions in the criminal legal system. Recommendation 62 advised judges to de-incarcerate the prison population in situations of health risk, expanding the scope of previously existent criminal law norms and precedents. This contingent measure, which sought to meet health policy requirements during a pandemic, is also one of the results of a long intellectual and political process that tried to insert the conditions of the lived punishment into judicial decision-making.

The pandemic could have become a turning point, enabling a shift away from a culture of mass violation of the rights of incarcerated people, a window of opportunity to challenge entrenched judicial practices. What the empirical findings suggest is that institutional change did not occur. We argue that the pandemic, and its effects on the criminal legal system, such as the enactment of Recommendation 62, were not accompanied by productive conditions of reform. This is a lost critical juncture for the criminal legal system given the strength of modern criminal rationality. By favouring the "disappearance" of the concrete person from decision-making processes that determine punishment and incarceration, the modern penal rationality functions as an obstacle to considering the effects of prison life on the health and well-being of incarcerated people. Through the lens of historical neo-institutionalism, we argued that this legal rationality is an entrenched institutional culture, a set of ideas about which elements are relevant to correct legal violations and punish individuals, that excludes considerations about the humanity and the suffering of those who are incarcerated.

This chapter, thus, opens an agenda to investigate the causes of the criminal legal system's incapacity to change. We argue that combining the theoretical-methodological framework of historical neo-institutionalism and the theory of modern penal rationality offers fruitful explanatory avenues to understand criminal legal institutions and study conditions of reform. With historical neo-institutionalism, it is possible to look at the inter and intra-power dynamics – the constraints, the alignments, the fissures – in different historical moments, allowing comparisons and, with them, identifying institutional patterns over time. Modern penal rationality magnifies the perceptions and justifications for criminal law, addressing the "backbone" of incarceration practices and punishment: the crystallized ideas that legitimize and shape the distribution of suffering and social exclusion as a necessary result of current judicial practices.

The pandemic's effects on the criminal legal system are still recent and understudied. Now that more time has passed since the first confirmed cases, an agenda for understanding what happened inside and outside prison walls, and how that connects to criminal law and the work of courts, becomes central and pressing. This chapter focused on the empirical evidence we have so far, relying almost exclusively on habeas decisions. To understand how much the pandemic affected incarceration practices, new work should focus on whether correctional judges granted early release or house arrest outside of habeas cases, whether prison administration improved or even marginally changed its structures and practices, and, especially, whether alternatives to how criminal punishment is currently envisioned penetrated other spaces of political and judicial action not yet reflected in case law.

Acknowledgments

The authors greatly appreciate the reading and suggestions of Thomas Kadri, Matheus de Barros, Muriel Aronis, and Diego Werneck Arguelhes, as well as the precious comments of reviewers from *Direito e Práxis*. A first version of this chapter was published in Portuguese in 2021 at *Revista Direito e Práxis*. The journal kindly allowed us to republish an updated version and English version of the original work.[75]

References

Acervo Digital do Fórum Brasileiro de Segurança Pública 'Anuario 16' (*FBSP*, 2023) https://publicacoes.forumseguranca.org.br/items/4f923d12-3cb2-4a24-9b63-e41789581d30>.

75 See the original paper at: Maira R. Machado and Natalia P. de Vasconcelos, 'Uma conjuntura crítica perdida: a COVID-19 nas prisões brasileiras' (2021) 12 Revista Direito e Práxis 2015.

Almeida EM and others, *For Freedom: The Story of Collective Habeas Corpus for Mothers & Children* (São Paulo, Alana Institute 2019).

Asano CL and others, 'Bulletin Rights in the Pandemic No. 3' (*Center for Research in Sanitary Law*, 2020) https://cepedisa.fsp.usp.br/wp-content/uploads/2023/02/03boletimcovid_PT_05.pdf>.

Barberia and others LG, 'Brazil Needs a Coordinated and Cooperative Approach to Tackle COVID-19' (2021) 27 *Nature Medicine* 1133–1134.

Biehl J and others, 'Between the Court and the Clinic: Lawsuits for Medicines and the Right to Health in Brazil' (2012) 14 *Health and Human Rights Journal* 1–17.

Brazilian Federal Supreme Court (Plenary) Precautionary Measure in the Plea of Noncompliance with Fundamental Precept 347 (19 February 2016) Rapporteur: Mr Marco Aurélio.

Brazilian Federal Supreme Court (2nd Class) Habeas Corpus 143.641/SP (9 October 2018) Rapporteur: Mr Lewandowski.

Cabral S and Santos MF, 'Accountability Mechanisms in Public Services: Activating New Dynamics in a Prison System' (2018) 21 *International Public Management Journal* 795–821.

Capoccia G and Kelemen RD, 'The Study of Critical Junctures: Theory, Narrative, and Counterfactuals in Historical Institutionalism' (2007) 59 *World Politics* 341–369.

CNJ, 'Covid-19 no Sistema Prisional' (*CNJ*, 2022) <https://www.cnj.jus.br/wp-content/uploads/2022/04/boletim-covid-19-marco2022.pdf>.

Coelho HC and others, 'HIV Prevalence and Risk Factors in a Brazilian Penitentiary' (2007) 23 *Cadernos de Saúde Pública* 2197–2204.

Court of Justice of Santa Catarina, 'Use of chloroquine against Covid, judge says, is consensual decision between doctor and patient' (*TJSC*, 2021) <https://www.tjsc.jus.br/web/imprensa/-/uso-de-cloroquina-contra-covid-diz-juiz-e-decisao-consensual-entre-medico-e-paciente?inheritRedirect=true>.

Dallalana Quintans MT and others, 'Despejos e luta pelo direito à moradia na pandemia: resistências femininas na experiência da Ocupação Novo Horizonte' (2022) 13 *Revista Direito e Práxis* 1897–1916.

de Vasconcelos NP and Arguelhes DW, 'Covid-19, federalismo e descentralização no STF: reorientação ou ajuste pontual?' in Machado LM (ed), *Legado de uma Pandemia: 26 Vozes Conversam Sobre os Aprendizados Para Política Pública* (Rio de Janeiro, Autografia 2021) 191–207.

de Vasconcelos NP, Machado MR, and Wang DWL, 'COVID-19 in Prisons: A Study of Habeas Corpus Decisions by the São Paulo Court of Justice' (2020) 54 *Revista de Administração Pública* 1472–1485.

de Vasconcelos NP, Machado MR, and Wang HYJ, 'Pandemia Só das Grades para Fora: os Habeas Corpus Julgados pelo Tribunal de Justiça de São Paulo' (2020) 17 *Revista Direito Público* 541–569.

de Vasconcelos NP and others, 'Covid-19 and Prisons in Latin America. Global Health Justice Partnership' (*Yale Law and Public Health Schools*, 2022) <https://law.yale.edu/sites/default/files/area/center/ghjp/documents/brazilcolombia_commentary_final.pdf>.

Dias CN and Salla F, 'Organized Crime in Brazilian Prisons: The Example of the PCC' (2013) 2 *International Journal of Criminology and Sociology* 397–408.

Fernandes LH, 'The Need to Improve Health Care in Prisons' (2014) 48 *Journal of Public Health* 275–283.

Ferreira PS and others, 'Black Population and Prison in Brazil: Impacts Of Covid' (2020) 4 *Afro Cebrap: Informative Racial Inequalities and Covid-19* 1–35.

Ferrante L and others, 'How Brazil's President Turned the Country into a Global Epicenter of COVID-19' (2021) 42 *Journal of Public Health Policy* 439–451.

Firpo SP and Tavolari BMD, 'Políticas de moradia em momentos de crise: a centralidade do aluguel' in Machado LM (ed), *Legado de uma Pandemia: 26 Vozes Conversam Sobre os Aprendizados Para Política Pública* (Rio de Janeiro, Autografia 2021) 54–69.

Garcia M and Dubé R, 'Criminal Law Reform: an Idea Whose Time Has Come' in Desrosiers J, Garcia M, and Sylvestre M-E (eds), *Criminal Law Reform in Canada: Challenges and Opportunities* (Cowansville, Éditions Yvon Blais 2017) 3–35.

Garcia M and others (eds), *A Racionalidade Penal Moderna: Reflexões Teóricas e Explorações Empíricas Desde o sul* (São Paulo, Editora Almedina 2020).

Global Health Justice Partnership, 'Responding to the justice and rights implications of the COVID-19 pandemic' (*GHJP*, 2021) <https://law.yale.edu/ghjp/projects/infectious-disease-and-justice/covid-19>.

Godoi R and others, 'Epistemopolitics of the São Paulo Prison Device: Reflecting on Experiences of Research-Intervention with the Prison Pastoral' (2020) 7 *Journal of Empirical Studies in Law* 143–158.

Hall PA and Taylor RCR, 'The Three Versions of Neo-Institutionalism' (2003) 58 *Lua Nova* 193–223.

Hartmann IA and others, 'How Do the Brazilian Supreme Court and Superior Court of Justice Decide Habeas Corpus Writs during the COVID-19 Pandemic? A Census and Sample Based Analysis' (*FGV Direito Rio*, 2020 <https://papers.ssrn.com/sol3/papers.cfm?abstract_id=3659624> http://dx.doi.org/10.2139/ssrn.3659624.

Infovirus, 'Homepage' (*Covidnaprisoes*, 2021) https://www.instagram.com/infovirusprisoes/>.

Institute for Crime & Justice Policy Research and Birkbeck College, 'Highest to Lowest – Prison Population Total' (*World Prison Brief*, 2024) <https://www.prisonstudies.org/highest-to-lowest/prison-population-total?field_region_taxonomy_tid=All>.

Janone L, 'Justice suspends decrees on restrictive measures against Covid-19 in Rio' *CNN Brasil* (Rio de Janeiro, 5 May 2021) <https://www.cnnbrasil.com.br/nacional/

2021/05/05/justica-suspende-decretos-sobre-medidas-restritivas-contra-covid-19-no-rio>.

Lara S, *Ordenações filipinas, Livro V* (São Paulo, Companhia das Letras 1999).

Liu YE and others, 'All-Cause and Cause-Specific Mortality during and Following Incarceration in Brazil: A Retrospective Cohort Study' (2021) 18 *PLoS Medicine* 1–20.

Lotta G and others, 'Community Health Workers Reveal COVID-19 Disaster in Brazil' (2020) 396 The Lancet 365–366.

Luisa M.A. Ferreira. *Penas Iguais para Crimes Iguais? Estudo sobre igualdade e proporcionalidade na aplicação da lei penal* (São Paulo: Tirant Lo Blanch, 2021).

Machado MR, 'The Person-Object of Criminal Intervention: First Notes on the Reception of Positivist Criminology in Brazil' (2005) 1 *Revista Direito GV* 79–90.

Machado MR, 'Entre a lei e o juiz: os processos decisórios na definição das penas' (2016) 126 *Brazilian Journal of Criminal Sciences* 181–222.

Machado MR, 'Quando o estado de coisas é inconstitucional: sobre o lugar do Poder Judiciário no problema carcerário' (2020) 7 *Journal of Constitutional Investigations* 631–664.

Maia D, 'STJ suspende liminares que determinavam internações em UTI para Covid em Cuiabá' *Folha de S. Paulo* (Gonçalves, 17 April 2021) <https://www1.folha.uol.com.br/equilibrioesaude/2021/04/stj-suspende-liminares-que-determinavam-internacoes-em-uti-para-covid-em-cuiaba.shtml>.

Maíra R. Machado et al. *Penas alternativas para pequenos traficantes: os argumentos do TJSP na engrenagem do superencarceramento* (Revista Brasileira de Políticas Públicas, v. 8, n. 1, 2018, p. 604–629).

Massard de Fonseca E and others, 'Political Discourse, Denialism and Leadership Failure in Brazil's Response to COVID-19' (2021) 16 *Global public health* 1251–1266.

Ministério da justiça e Segurança Pública, 'Painéis Dinâmicos' (*Secretaria Nacional de Políticas Penais*, 2023) <https://www.gov.br/senappen/pt-br/servicos/sisdepen/paineis-anteriores>.

Ministério da justiça e Segurança Pública, 'Painel de Monitoramento dos Sistemas Prisionais' (*Secretaria Nacional de Políticas Penais*, 2023) <https://www.gov.br/senappen/pt-br/assuntos/acoes-contra-pandemia/painel-de-monitoramento-dos-sistemas-prisionais>.

Motta Ferraz OL, *Health as a Human Right. The politics and judicialisation of health in Brazil* (Cambridge, Cambridge University Press 2021).

National Agenda for Decarcerating, 'O que defendemos' (*Pelo Desencarceramento e Desmilitarização*, 2021) <https://desencarceramento.org.br/>.

Pastoral Carcerária, 'Denúncias de violação de direitos no sistema prisional aumentaram 82% durante a pandemia, segundo Pastoral' (*Pastoral Carcerária*, 7 April 2021) <https://carceraria.org.br/combate-e-prevencao-a-tortura/denuncias-de-vio

lacao-de-direitos-no-sistema-prisional-aumentaram-82-durante-a-pandemia-segundo-pastoral>

Pastoral Carcerária, 'Questionário sobre Coronavírus nas Prisões Revela que Situação no Cárcere está muito pior um ano após o início da Pandemia' (*Pastoral Carcerária*, 19 April 2021) <https://carceraria.org.br/combate-e-prevencao-a-tortura/questionario-sobre-coronavirus-nas-prisoes-revela-que-situacao-no-carcere-esta-muito-pior-um-ano-apos-o-inicio-da-pandemia>.

Pires AP, 'Critical Reflections on the Sociology of Punishment from the Work of Tom Daems' (2013) 37 *Déviance et Société* 131–153.

Pires AP, 'Posfácio: Nascimento E Desenvolvimento de Uma Teoria E Seus Problemas de Pesquisa' in Dubé R, Garcia M, and Machado MR (eds), *A Racionalidade Penal Moderna: Reflexões Teóricas e Explorações Empíricas Desde o sul* (São Paulo, Editora Almedina 2020) 295–328.

Poliana da Silva Ferreira. *A responsabilização da polícia que mata: um estudo de caso sobre o tratamento jurídico das abordagens policiais com resultado morte* (Master's dissertation in Law, São Paulo Law School, Fundação Getulio Vargas, 2019).

Prando C and Godoi R, 'The Management of Data on the Pandemic in Prisons: A Comparison between the Concealment Practices of the Prison Administration Departments of RJ and D' (2020) *Dilemmas: Journal of Conflict Studies and Social Control* 1–15.

Raupp M, 'La distinction école classique/école positive et la rationalité pénale moderne: une réflexion à partir du regard des sciences sociales sur la réforme pénale de 1984 au Brésil' in Dubé R, Garcia M, and Machado MR (eds), *A racionalidade penal moderna : reflexões teóricas e explorações empíricas* (São Paulo, Editora Almedina 2020) 146–170.

Soares Filho MM and Gomes Bueno PM, 'Demography, Vulnerabilities and the Right to Health of the Brazilian Prison Population' (2016) 21 *Science & Collective Health* 1999–2010.

Soifer HD, 'The Causal Logic of Critical Junctures' (2012) 45 *Comparative Political Studies* 1572–1597.

Superior Tribunal de Justiça, 'Habeas Corpus N° 568.693' (*STJ*, 2020) https://www.stj.jus.br/sites/portalp/SiteAssets/documentos/noticias/14102020%20HC-568.693.pdf>.

Supremo Tribunal Federal, 'Home' (STF, 2024) <https://portal.stf.jus.br/processos/detalhe.asp?incidente=4783560>.

UN Subcommittee on Prevention of Torture and Other Cruel, Inhuman or Degrading Treatment or Punishment, 'Advice of the Subcommittee on Prevention of Torture to States Parties and National Preventive Mechanisms relating to the Coronavirus Pandemic' (*OHCHR*, 2020) <https://www.ohchr.org/sites/default/files/Documents/HRBodies/OPCAT/AdviceStatePartiesCoronavirusPandemic2020.pdf>.

Valença MA and Da Silva Freitas F, 'The Right to Life and the Ideal of Social Defense in Decisions of the STJ in the Context of the Covid-19 Pandemic' (2020) 17 *Revista Direito Público* 570–595.

Wang DWL, 'Right to Health Litigation in Brazil: The Problem and the Institutional Responses' (2015) 15 *Human Rights Law Review* 617–641.

World Health Organization, 'UNODC, WHO, UNAIDS and OHCHR joint statement on COVID-19 in prisons and other closed settings' (*WHO*, 2020) <https://www.who.int/news/item/13-05-2020-unodc-who-unaids-and-ohchr-joint-statement-on-covid-19-in-prisons-and-other-closed-settings>.

Zysberg A, 'Histoire des galères, bagnes et prisons en France de l'Ancien Régime' in Petit J-G (ed), *La Prison, Le Bagne et l'Histoire* (Geneva, Librairie des Méridiens 1984) 69.

CHAPTER 8

Two Emergency Regimes: Prison, Judicial Intervention, and the COVID-19 Pandemic in Colombia

Libardo Ariza and Mario Torres

1 Introduction

The COVID-19 pandemic represented a rapid change in how prison authorities, governments, and courts addressed the prison crisis in Colombia. In the prison system, the Human Rights crisis has gone through decades with almost inexistent social improvement despite the numerous judicial rulings, particularly those of Colombia's Constitutional Court.[1] With the arrival of the COVID-19 pandemic, it was evident to both the courts and the government that fast intervention in the prison system was needed. Deficiencies in health access and overcrowding made prisons a source of contagion. The pandemic could threaten the health and lives of more than 120,000 people imprisoned in Colombia at the time.[2]

Two specific measures were taken in response to the COVID-19 pandemic to modify some social dynamics in the prison context. Firstly, the pandemic highlighted the profound shortcomings in prisoner healthcare services. This situation worsened in the face of such a public health event due to the immense deficiencies in the facilities' prevention, infrastructure, and services. Consequently, the Colombian government adopted health care protocols within prisons.[3] These protocols included predictable measures such as the use of masks, separation of incarcerated people who contracted COVID-19, efforts to improve ventilation and illumination, protocols for care of primary symptoms, and for the disposal of bodies of people who died. As shall be seen

1 The judicial interventions made by the Colombian Constitutional Court will be discussed in detail in *Section 2* of this chapter. See, for example: Constitutional Court of Colombia, *Judgement T-388/2013* (28 June 2013) P.P. Maria Victoria Calle.

2 Mario A. Torres Gómez, 'Estándares Internacionales Para La Garantía Del Derecho a La Salud de La Población Privada de La Libertad' in Libardo Ariza, Manuel Iturralde and Fernando León Tamayo (eds), *Cárcel, Derecho y Sociedad: Aproximaciones al Mundo Penitenciario En Colombia* (Bogotá, Ediciones Uniandes 2021) 355–380.

3 Ministry of Health and Social Protection, Resolution 843 of 2020.

later, these protocols were highly insufficient. In practice, they were only a formality in front of the immense sanitation and health care deficiencies in most Colombian prisons.

The COVID-19 pandemic led to a suspension of family visits to the prison.[4] Other types of external contact, like those with civil organizations and people outside the prison, were limited. Throughout this chapter, it will be argued that the restriction of visits is a drastic measure, especially in Latin American prisons, where family members perform essential functions such as providing food, medicine, and other basic necessities that are not provided by the state.[5] Simultaneously, restrictions on prison visits have created penitentiary systems that are farther from the public eye, closing the institutions and making them less monitored by civil society because of the physical inability to enter many of the prison facilities.

This chapter analyses the judicial intervention in the Colombian prison crisis in the context of COVID-19 through the response that both the government and the Colombian Constitutional Court carried out to intervene. In this way, the text hopes to understand how judicial intervention has led incarcerated persons to suffer violence and institutional abandonment during the pandemic within Colombian prisons. The chapter begins by studying Colombia's Constitutional Court response to the prison system's structural human rights crisis before the COVID-19 pandemic, through the 'Unconstitutional State of Affairs' doctrine. Then, it describes how the pandemic affected prisons, making some contributions on how the Colombian government and courts have intervened regarding the COVID-19 pandemic, from 2020 to 2022. In the last section, the chapter introduces the definition of 'punitive constitutionalism', defined as a process of constitutional intervention whose result generates that imprisoned people find themselves in the space of indefinite helplessness, abandoning people in uncertainty and fear. Then, the chapter analyses the theoretical significance of the Unconstitutional State of Affairs as a doctrine that, in practice, protects the penal institutions and preserves the suffering and uncertainty of those who are incarcerated in subhuman conditions in a context with simultaneous emergencies, in which the prison crisis is aggravated and complemented by the pandemic crisis. The duration of the

4 Ministry of Health and Social Protection, Resolution 313 of 2021.

5 Carol I. Abunza, Giovanny Paredes, Paola Bustos and Mónica A. Mendoza Molina, *Familia y privación de la libertad en Colombia* (Bogota, Universidad del Rosario 2016); Libardo Ariza and Carolina Á. Botero, 'En el corazón del Buen Pastor. La apropiación del discurso de los derechos humanos en el contexto penitenciario colombiano' (2015) 1 Antipoda. Revista de Antropología y Arqueología 45–64, https://doi.org/10.7440/antipoda23.2015.03.

COVID-19 pandemic is not exact, so this text analyses the pandemic period between March 1, 2021 and April 30, 2022, when some of the health emergency measures were lifted and vaccination programs started to become available in prisons.[6]

2 The Unconstitutional State of Affairs in Colombian Prisons

To analyse the meaning of confinement in Colombian prisons during the pandemic, it is relevant to address the context of constitutional intervention inside Colombian prisons prior to that period. The judicial intervention of Colombia's Constitutional Court has been essential in shaping the prison experience and creating a narrative of Human Rights violations in the prison system over the last two decades. The work of the Constitutional Court has been profound, to the point that it currently has a Special Following Room dedicated to following up on the prison crisis.

In this context, the most relevant doctrine used by the Constitutional Court is the 'Unconstitutional State of Affairs', created to attend to structural cases requiring broad constitutional remedies. This doctrine allows the Constitutional Court to oblige public policies to the other branches of government when specific requirements of a systematic violation of human rights are met. In this way, the Constitutional Court can compel the adoption of general remedies of a structural nature. The requirements established by the Constitutional Court to declare an Unconstitutional State of Affairs are three as follows. First, there is a massive and recurrent violation of the fundamental rights of a certain population. Second, such violation is not because of specific circumstances but due to general lack of compliance of certain authorities with their legal and constitutional obligations. Third, because of such non-compliance, individual *tutelas* are insufficient to overcome the massive violation of human rights.[7]

Initially, the doctrine of the Unconstitutional State of Affairs has allowed an opportunity for litigation within the prison system, which has found in the *Tutela* a way to denounce, or at least protest, before the judges the subhuman conditions in which they live. Decades before the pandemic, in 1998, because

6 Presidency of the Republic of Colombia, Decree 655/2022.

7 Josefina Q. Lyons, Angélica M. N. Monterroza and Malka I. Meza, 'La figura del estado de cosas inconstitucionales como mecanismo de protección de los derechos fundamentales de la población vulnerable en Colombia' (2011) 3 Revista Jurídica Mario Alario D'Filippo 69.

of a massive filing of *tutelas* by incarcerated persons, the Constitutional Court issued Judgement T-153 of 1998.[8] In that verdict, it declared the Unconstitutional State of Affairs in the Colombian penitentiary system for the first time. This first ruling concentrates its efforts on explaining how the crisis is sustained by the then 40% overcrowding, so its response was mainly focused on compelling remedies to the national government to invest in the construction of more prisons.[9] According to the Constitutional Court, the prison human rights crisis is mainly an issue of occupancy, overcrowding and infrastructure, not a problem of human rights violations and the impossibility of compliance with basic imprisonment conditions. With this framing of the problem, the solution to the prison crisis is arithmetical: construct more prisons to cope with the demand of inmates. The violations of human rights are of course mentioned, but remedies do not address any of the concerns about contextual human rights violations in prisons.

The legal remedy in this ruling allowed the construction of more prison capacity during the following ten years. According to INPEC statistics on prison capacity, prison capacity doubled from 35,000 to around 70,000 occupancy places,[10] but at the same time prison population tripled from approximately 40,000 inmates to 120,000 inmates in Colombian prisons. The overcrowding problem worsened during the following years because of the disproportionate increase in the prison population, and the aging of the infrastructure made the prison crisis even worse than in 1998.

Subsequently, as a result of several *tutelas* filed jointly by incarcerated people and Legal Clinics, in Judgement T-388 of 2013,[11] the Unconstitutional State of Affairs was again declared. On this occasion, the Court developed a comprehensive analysis of criminal policy problems, describing it as '*reactive,*

---

8 Constitutional Court of Colombia, *Judgment T-153/1998* (28 April 1998) M.P. Eduardo Cifuentes Muñoz.

9 Rafael A. Angel, 'Desarrollo Del Sistema Penitenciario y Carcelario Colombiano Entre 1995 y 2010' (*Instituto Rosarista de Accion Social*, 2011) <https://editorial.urosario.edu.co/pageflip/acceso-abierto/desarrollo-del-sistema-penitenciario.pdf> accessed 5 February 2024; Libardo Ariza, 'The Economic and Social Rights of Prisoners and Constitutional Court Intervention in the Penitentiary System in Colombia' in Daniel Bonilla Maldonado (ed), *Constitutionalism of the Global South: The Activist Tribunals of India, South Africa, and Colombia* (Cambridge, Cambridge University Press 2013) 129–162.

10 The term 'occupancy places' does not mean any significant construction of common areas to complement the growth in beds, it just means construction of beds in the same infrastructure. See: Libardo Ariza and Mario A. Torres, 'Definiendo el hacinamiento: estándares normativos y perspectivas judiciales sobre el espacio penitenciario' (2019) 21 Revista Estudios Socio Jurídicos 227.

11 Constitutional Court of Colombia, *Judgement T-388/2013* (n 1).

populist, unreflective, volatile, incoherent and subordinated to security policy'. Although the Court acknowledged that the efforts in the creation of infrastructure were mostly successful, it concluded that this had been an insufficient strategy because it took away attention from other problems, such as resocialization, health care, potable water, and access to justice. In this ruling, the Court issued orders to coordinate criminal policy, implemented structure, process, and result parameters. The most important remedy in this ruling is the order of application of a 'decreasing balance rule'. According to this rule, a person can only enter an overcrowded prison

> if, and only if, (i) the number of people entering is equal to or less than the number of people leaving the detention facility during the previous week, for whatever reason (…), and (ii) the number of people in the establishment has been constantly decreasing, in accordance with expectations and expected projections.[12]

The decreasing balance rule implies maintaining and progressively reducing the number of people in the prison system until there is no overcrowding. It is important to note that this particular remedy changes the framing of the problem but essentially sees the prison crisis as a problem of modernization of the penitentiary system, not as a human rights issue that requires immediate remedies to stop the suffering of those inside the prison walls.

A few months after this judgment, the Constitutional Court issued Judgement T-762 of 2015,[13] which recapitulates the crisis in the prison system. In this ruling, the Court uses a series of different remedies to address the prison situation: it establishes specific orders for overcoming each problem, defining compliance indicators, attributions, and competencies to follow up on compliance with the issued orders. With this information, the Court ordered the creation of a Special Room to monitor the prison situation, including entities of the Presidency of the Republic, entities of the penitentiary sector, and a union of civil society organizations.

One of the most important effects of implementing Judgement T-388 of 2013 was the transference of the problem from prisons to police stations and other transitory detention centres. Faced with the prisons' refusal to receive more people following the application of the decreasing balance rule, the police stations began to receive the detained population that could not be

12 ibid. Own translation.

13 Constitutional Court of Colombia, *Judgment T-762/2015* (16 December 2015) M.P. Maria Victoria Correa.

sent to prisons. Quickly, police stations became overcrowded, and, in some extreme cases, detainees were chained in public parks in front of police stations. Two rulings demonstrate this problem: Judgement T-151/2016, which for the first time analyses the problem, and a second, more relevant verdict: Judgement SU-122/2022. This ruling extends the declaration of an Unconstitutional State of Affairs to police stations and transitory detention centres, recognizing that the Court's orders have created the undesired effect of extending the problem to other spaces instead of solving the underlying problem.

This overcrowding of police stations is one of the most significant transformations in Colombian prison dynamics in the last three years. By December 2020, in the middle of the pandemic and approximately seven months after its start, police stations and Immediate Reaction Units (URI)[14] were overcrowded at over 200% of their capacity (see Table 8.1).[15] In 2023, at least one year after the pandemic, the overcrowding of temporary detention stations in districts such as Bogotá reached overcrowding of more than 400% of their capacity.[16]

TABLE 8.1 Capacity and overcrowding of police stations and URIS in Colombia

Type of centre	Capacity	Total incarcerated people	Overpopulation	Overcrowding
Police stations	5,831	17,477	11,646	200%
URI	1,292	1,834	542	42%
Total:		**19.311**		

SOURCE: DEFENSORÍA DEL PUEBLO, CITED IN JUDGMENT SU 122/2022, CONSTITUTIONAL COURT OF COLOMBIA, M.P DIANA FAJARDO RIVERA, CRISTINA PARDO AND JOSÉ REYES

14 The Immediate Reaction Units (URI) are small transitory detention cellblocks distributed in different small police stations in order to transport captured people from these detention centres to a prison after 36 hours. Nonetheless, these spaces in the last years have been used as permanent detention centres in which people are incarcerated for months.

15 Constitutional Court of Colombia, *Judgment SU-122/2022* (31 March 2022) M.P. Diana Fajardo Rivera, Cristina Pardo and José Reyes, para 511.

16 Maria N. García Vargas, 'Hacinamiento en estaciones de policía en Bogotá superan el 900% de ocupación' (*Radio Nacional de Colombia*, June 2023. <https://www.radionacional.co/actualidad/hacinamiento-estaciones-de-policia-en-bogota-superan-el-900-de-ocupacion> accessed 5 February 2024 .

These temporary detention spaces do not have the infrastructure or personnel conditions to receive people for more than 36 hours. However, given the refusal of prisons to receive people during and after the pandemic, these temporary detention centres have become permanent spaces of detention. Being imprisoned in a temporary place also seriously limits some rights such as the right to visits, access to recreation spaces, access to spaces to redeem sentences through study or work, access to decent sanitary spaces and access to water, among others. At the same time, these temporary detention spaces are controlled by the National Police of Colombia, not by a penitentiary institution such as the National Penitentiary and Prison Institute (INPEC). Consequently, the control and surveillance that civil organizations can carry out regarding possible human rights violations within police stations is significantly more difficult to achieve.[17]

3 The Pandemic Gets to the Prison

On March 18, 2020, Colombia woke up to the news of a riot in the country's largest prison: La Picota, in Bogotá.[18] At that moment, the enormous Third Generation prison[19] locked 9,488 people in a space designed for the confinement of 6,000. Bent by overcrowding, the vast prison complex that sprawls imposingly on the slopes of the town of Usme saw its fragile but stable internal social order threatened. The news received little attention, even though it foretold the events a few days later in La Modelo Prison, in Bogotá. The fear of the pandemic covered the prison system with an even denser halo of terrifying death expectance that, together with the intensification of isolation

17 The National Police of Colombia is a civil institution with a complex record of human rights violations. For example, on 9 September 2020, citizen Javier Ordonez was arrested for a minor crime and subsequently murdered in a temporary detention centre in Bogotá. The event unleashed intense violent protests in Bogotá, where on the first day 10 protesters were murdered with fire weapons by the National Police and 56 Immediate Attention Centres (small police stations) were burned by protesters amid the confrontations. See: Daniel Pardo, 'Policía en Colombia: ¿por qué la muerte de Javier Ordóñez desató una violencia inédita en Bogotá?' *BBC News* (Bogotá, 12 September 2020) <https://www.bbc.com/mundo/noticias-america-latina-54125522> accessed 5 February 2024.

18 Juan M. Vargas Ovalle, 'Incendio en la cárcel La Picota de Bogotá tras un intento de motín' *RCN Radio* (Bogotá, 17 March 2020) <https://www.rcnradio.com/bogota/incendio-en-la-carcel-la-picota-de-bogota-tras-un-intento-de-motin> accessed 5 February 2024.

19 According to an informal classification made by the National Penitenciary and Carcerary Institute of Colombia (INPEC), a third generation prison (ERON) means a prison constructed in the last twenty years.

caused by the restriction of visits to the prison, broke the internal social order. This restriction, intended as a measure to contain COVID-19 and the poor sanitary conditions in the prison, triggered the protest, which the prison guards strongly repressed.

The functioning of Colombian prisons largely depends on the families of the inmates. Amid the scarcity of the local penitentiary world, the food, clean clothes, and mattresses entered into the prisons by families of the prisoners are vital as a mechanism for adapting to confinement.[20] This, of course, without mentioning the affective and emotional support. A suspension of visits also becomes a drastic interruption of access to food, clothing, and toiletries, worsening the inmates' precarious living conditions. The threat of the pandemic and famine turned the prison experience into a punitive nightmare, a prison dystopia of isolation, scarcity, and fear of dying from contagion. The fear of the plague took over the penitentiary world:

> It was not the idea of prison that managed to stop those unfortunate people, but the certainty that everyone had that a prison sentence was equivalent to a death sentence, due to the excessive mortality that was observed in the municipal jail. That apprehension was certainly not unfounded. For obvious reasons, the plague was fiercest among all those who lived in groups: soldiers, religious or prisoners. Well, despite the isolation of certain detainees, a prison is a community and this is proven by the fact that in our municipal jail the guards paid their tribute to the disease as much as the prisoners. From the highest point of view of the plague, everyone, from the director to the last detainee, was condemned and, perhaps for the first time, impartial justice reigned in the prison.[21]

Despite the foreseeable impact that the suspension of visits would have on the prison system, it was the first measure adopted by the Colombian government to try to contain the rapid expansion of the virus within the penitentiary and prison system. The Italian authorities had done the same by suspending the entry of visitors to all prisons, which unleashed riots in 27 prisons in the coun-

---

20 Abunza, Paredes, Bustos and Mendoza Molina, *Familia y privación de la libertad en Colombia* (n 5).

21 Albert Camus, *The Plague* (England, Penguin Books).

try,[22] resulting in six deaths, looting of infirmaries, and panic inside the walls.[23] The explosion of the mutiny precedes the outbreak of the prison plague. This measure of closing the prisons walls to any external contact was equally incoherent, creating new problems or weakening the institutions that control human rights abuses within the prison system. For example, as a result of measures to isolate the prison population, it became much more difficult for any human rights organizations or government human rights agencies to enter prisons and detention centres.[24] Likewise, the measures to completely isolate the prison were incoherent with the penitentiary reality: While the incarcerated people were denied any extraordinary mechanism to leave the prison, the guards, administrative staff and health personnel continued entering and leaving the prison. As a result, the measures were disproportionate and in practice, had no effect in stopping contagion within prisons.

For the prison population, exposure to contagion of any disease is a latent risk. Facing illness is a daily occurrence in prisons. Outbreaks vary from mumps, rubella, and flu. The inhabitants of the populous prison city are exposed to more significant risks of contracting diseases such as HIV, hepatitis, and tuberculosis.[25] Even in systems with better infrastructure and services than the local prisons, it has been calculated that the prevalence rate of tuberculosis is 81 times higher than that of those outside them.[26] Prisons are

22 Lina Aristizábal, 'Cárceles y coronavirus: motines en Italia y presos a las casas en Irán' *France24* (Asia-Pacific, 9 March 2020) <https://www.france24.com/es/20200309-carceles-coronavirus-italia-motines-iran-presos> accessed 5 February 2024.

23 Spain decided to isolate the nearly eight thousand inmates who are held in twelve prisons in Madrid, Alava and La Rioja, areas considered to have 'significant transmission'. See: Óscar López Fonseca, 'Interior aísla 12 cárceles con más de 8.000 presos para evitar la expansión del coronavirus' *El País* (Madrid, 10 March 2020) <https://elpais.com/espana/2020-03-10/interior-aisla-a-mas-de-8000-presos-de-12-carceles-para-evitar-la-expansion-de-coronavirus.html> accessed 5 February 2024.

24 There was no direct order in the law to stop the visits from government control agencies like the Defensoría del Pueblo. Nonetheless, in practice there was a significant reduction in the visits and control of these government agencies over the prison system. For other human rights organisations, the prison system was mostly closed based on public health reasons.

25 Libardo Ariza, Manuel Iturralde and others, 'Indicadores de Derechos Humanos en el Sistema Penitenciario y Carcelario' (*Ministerio de Justicia y del Derecho de Colombia and Agencia Alemana para la Cooperación Internacional* (GIZ), 2017) <https://prisiones.uniandes.edu.co/images/Publicaciones/LineaBaseDDHH_2_compressed.pdf> accessed 5 February 2024.

26 Gen Sander, 'Preventing infectious diseases in prisons: A public health and human rights imperative' (*Penal Reform International*, 23 October 2015) <https://www.penalreform

places of contagion, overflowing with diseases that in the free world have been contained or are uncommon.

The prevention and mitigation measures recommended for the free population – washing hands, avoiding crowds, reducing social interactions, and reporting cases that present symptoms – seemed cynical in a prison world facing insurmountable challenges. Many prisons in the country do not have a stable potable water supply. The high rates of overcrowding – in some establishments 350 %, such as Riohacha, and in others 540 %, as in Florencia, Caqueta[27] – make it impossible to avoid contact and the accumulation of bodies in a closed place. Access to the services provided by the Intramural Primary Care Units[28] is excessively restricted. In fact, medical care is approximately thirty times lower than that offered to the general population.[29] Additionally, there is a significant under-reporting of mandatory notification events – those diseases with pandemic potential, such as SARS – and in practice, medical examinations are not performed before admission.

The anguish and uncertainty of the imprisoned person, constantly waiting for death or freedom as the only way to escape the suffering and violence of the penitentiary world, reached unimaginable intensity levels when the virus knocked on the prison doors. With no possibility of escape, no access to protection measures, crammed into a cell, and without any link with the outside world, terror took over the prisons, and soon death would roam the courtyards under the hum of the guard's bullets and the smoke from the charred mats. Not even in this context the release of incarcerated people was seriously considered as a remedy to avoid contagion, violence, and death. It was lockdown at any cost.

The Colombian government promulgated Legislative Decree 546 of 2020, 'whose main measure was to replace the prison sentence and preventive detention with measures of prison and house arrest in favour of the incarcerated population who had a higher level of risk in case of being infected by the virus'. The approach of the decree was widely criticized to the extent that it seemed to be more concerned with the possible effects that the releases would have on crime rates, than in preventing rapid growth of the pandemic within

.org/blog/preventing-infectious-diseases-in-prisons-a-public-health/> accessed 5 February 2024.

27 INPEC, 'Boletines Estadísticos' (*INPEC*, January 2020) <https://www.inpec.gov.co/estadisticas/-/document_library/TWBuJQCWH6KV/view/49294> accessed 5 February 2024.

28 "Intramural Care Services" is the primary health system provided by the prison infrastructure.

29 Ariza, Iturralde and others, 'Indicadores de Derechos Humanos en el Sistema Penitenciario y Carcelario' (n 25).

the penitentiary and prison system.[30] It was based on the potential danger that detained people posed and on the risk to public safety that their eventual release would have, rather than on the risk of contagion and death for the inhabitants of the penitentiary system.

Therefore, although this decree was issued based on suspending the normal functioning of the rule of law that produces the declaration of a state of emergency, its regulatory design did not seek to create a political scenario that would allow release from prison as a measure of political exception. The fundamental answer was to disaggregate people from the penitentiary system and avoid their potential death from contagion. It was not to stop their suffering but to administer it and to manage the release process that would allow the release of those people who were not a threat to the conservation of a social world believed to be peaceful. In this coexistence of two states of suspension of the normative order, such as the state of emergency and the Unconstitutional State of Affairs, the political decision to which the government and the judges agreed was that the prison doors must be locked at all costs and that only few could cross them to avoid being abandoned to the possibility of death.

The prison is located at the intersection between the state of emergency and the Unconstitutional State of Affairs and, in this space of confluence of two exceptional legal situations, each one with its characteristics and temporal scope, the imprisoned person is kept outside the protection and is exposed to the two situations of violence that it tries to avoid: the pandemic and the prison violence. This kind of dual and juxtaposed exceptionality does nothing but reaffirm the penitentiary world's inclusion as a factuality in the broader scheme of normality that the legal system tries to achieve.

Much of the criticism of Decree 546 focused on showing the problems of legislative technique that hindered it and the contradictory effects it would entail once it was put into operation by the procedural machinery. This '*curious release decree*'[31] created a complex arrangement that was, difficult to understand. At the same time, it was seen as favourable in some matters but restrict-

30 Manuel Iturralde, Nicolás Santamaría and Juan P. Uribe, 'El coronavirus en las cárceles colombianas. Análisis y propuestas de solución más allá de la coyuntura' (*Friedich Ebert Stiftung and Grupo de Prisiones Facultad de Derecho de la Universidad de Los Andes*, 2020) <https://derecho.uniandes.edu.co/sites/default/files/coronavirus-en-carceles-colombianas.pdf> accessed 5 February 2024.

31 Yesid Reyes Alvarado, 'El curioso decreto sobre excarcelación' *El Espectador* (Bogotá, 21 April 2020) <https://www.elespectador.com/opinion/columnistas/yesid-reyes-alvarado/el-curioso-decreto-sobre-excarcelacion-column-915579/> accessed 5 February 2024; Diego F. Cruz Palomo and Ruby S. Jaramillo Marín, 'La Insuficiencia De Las Medidas Adoptadas Para La población Privada De La Libertad En Colombia Con ocasión De La

ive in others, limiting the possibilities of accessing the substantive and procedural emergency arrangements to prevent the pandemic from spreading.[32]

Furthermore, the emergency release decision had to be subjected to the normal penal procedural rituals. Since review and approval were in the hands of the sentencing judges, it was expected that the release process would only cover a few people at a slow pace and that its impact on the prison world would surely have an impact when it was too late.[33] However, when the legislative decree reached the Constitutional Court for its constitutionality control, they avoided analysing 'whether the measure of home detention due to the pandemic has served fully or not, nor defining its degree of ineffectiveness or its "convenience"'[34] because it considers that this would be a political judgment unrelated to the material evaluation that it should assume in the control of the legislative decrees issued within the framework of the declaration of a state of exception.

But something unexpected happened. As Table 8.2 shows, only 825 incarcerated people accessed transitory domiciliary detention through the special

TABLE 8.2 Types of release for incarcerated people

Type of release	Total
Transitory domiciliary detention. Special procedure, Decree 546	825
Freedom, ordinary procedure	10,260
Domiciliary detention, ordinary procedure	7,597
Total releases	18,682

SOURCE: COLOMBIA'S CONSTITUTIONAL COURT, JUDGMENT C-255 DE 2020

Pandemia De La Enfermedad Por Coronavirus' (2020) 19 Opinión Jurídica 151, https://doi.org/10.22395/ojum.v19n40a7.

32 As Reyes explained: "In relation to people who are already serving a sentence, it is more benevolent in that it authorizes serving a sentence at home for those who have served 40% of it, instead of the 50% enshrined in the Code. Criminal, but it is more restrictive in relation to the crimes for which this benefit can be applied, not only because it increased by more than 20 the list of those for which it is not applicable, but because it limits house arrest to those who have been sentenced to sanctions not exceeding five years. In comparison, the Code allows it for crimes with minimum sentences of eight years". Alvarado, 'El curioso decreto sobre excarcelación' (n 31). Own translation .

33 Iturralde, Santamaría and Uribe, 'El coronavirus en las cárceles colombianas. Análisis y propuestas de solución más allá de la coyuntura' (n 30).

34 Constitutional Court of Colombia, *Judgment C-255/2020* (23 July 2020) M.P. Diana Fajardo Rivera.

procedure, while almost 18,000 people overcame their situation thanks to the ordinary procedure. Thus, paradoxically, and despite the exceptional regimes that the state of emergency and the Unconstitutional State of Affairs entailed, the overcoming of punitivism, produced and maintained by the constitutional discourse on the penitentiary crisis, was overcome through the usual routine of judges for the execution of sentences and security measures. This meant that the normal legal state offered a way to leave the penitentiary world, and this seriously questions the effectiveness of the paraphernalia around the Unconstitutional State of Affairs and the declarations of exceptionality. The normality that develops amid the exceptionality that states of emergency entail is the custodian of the key that opens the threshold to overcome the evils of punitive constitutionalism. The prison machine's daily, routine, anonymous, and silent gears determine who can leave its entrails.

The coexistence of the Unconstitutional State of Affairs and the emergency state of the pandemic in prison makes this a potentially unliveable, unbearable space. Regardless, the tens of thousands of people who did not manage to cross the threshold that was opened for a brief period must resist. The Court normalizes the exceptionality by allowing those 825 people who managed to cross the prison doors to confine themselves to their homes, like most of the free citizens during the pandemic confinement. They remained in home detention as a form of disaggregation of the penitentiary world and to overcome their legal punitivism. The few detained people who accessed the temporary home detention created by the emergency legislation did not have to return to prison immediately once it ceased to apply since

> It may be the case that the effects of the pandemic, combined with the conditions of the Unconstitutional State of Affairs, have had an impact in such a way that the centres or places of confinement, by the time of return, have less capacity to guarantee dignified and adequate conditions for the incarcerated population.[35]

It would be disproportionate, the Court explains:

> To subject people to a situation that seriously affects their human rights, to safeguard citizen security and other injured legal rights, other than life, personal integrity, training, and sexual integrity or others of the same rank.[36]

35 Constitutional Court of Colombia, *Judgment C-255/2020* (n 34). Own translation.

36 Constitutional Court of Colombia, *Judgment C-255/2020* (n 34). Own translation.

Consequently, the Court establishes that at the end of the six months of temporary domiciliary detention '*(the person) may not be detained again in the place where he was, if an outbreak of COVID-19 occurs within it, unless can it be detained guaranteed a special place that minimizes the possible risk of contagion*'. In practice, it leaves it to the discretion of the sentencing judges to decide whether a person should return to prison or not, but it does not order direct releases of the few people who managed to leave prison. According to the interpretation of the Constitutional Court, public security considerations can be prioritized over the right to health and personal integrity of incarcerated people.

The possibility of directly releasing people as a legal remedy to solve the severe violation of human rights has been implemented in other jurisdictions, such as the U.S prisons, with relative success in solving overcrowding and inhumane detention conditions with immediate effect.[37] In contrast, in Colombia, the release of people has been proposed before and during the pandemic. It has been systematically denied by the Constitutional Court, declaring that

> In a state of affairs contrary to the current constitutional order, such as the one the penitentiary and prison system is currently going through, people do not acquire a subjective constitutional right to be released, but rather to have criminal and prison policies designed and implemented that are favourable to freedom and sustainable over time (…).[38]

The criminal policy designs in place before and during the pandemic were mainly aimed at creating a criminal policy system that maintained the exclusion and suffering of incarcerated people, the inhumane conditions of confinement, and left the solution of the penitentiary crisis to the slow advance of ordinary procedural justice.

4 Prisons, Pandemic and Simultaneity of Emergencies

In this last part of the chapter we want to offer a reflection on the meaning of confinement and its relationship with judicial intervention. This section

37 US Supreme Court, *Brown v Plata* (2011) No 09–12; Jonathan Simon, *Mass Incarceration on Trial: A Remarkable Court Decision and the Future of Prisons in America* (New York, The New Press 2011).

38 Constitutional Court of Colombia, *Judgment T-388/2013* (n 1). Own translation.

explores the term 'punitive constitutionalism' as a way of describing the experience that the imprisoned person suffers as a consequence of the remedies that the Courts adopt in the simultaneity between the Unconstitutional State of Affairs and the State of Emergency produced by the pandemic. In the context of prisons, punitive constitutionalism is a process of constitutional intervention in which the courts create punitive remedies looking to improve the prison experience, when in fact the result of those remedies causes people to find themselves in a space of indefinite helplessness, immersing subjects in a space of uncertainty and fear.[39] The judicial interventions described in this chapter are a good example of punitive constitutionalism. The remedies designed by the Constitutional Court aim to protect the rights of people deprived of liberty and defend constitutional principles within the penitentiary space. However, in practice, this is an empty punitive promise[40] that produces the opposite effect: abandoning in confinement those people who suffer human rights violations.

This abandonment towards death, as a central feature of punitive constitutionalism, not only clashes with the historical pillars that support the apparatus of safeguards that protect the person against the excesses of the State's punitive power, but the virulence of this encounter makes it stagger and crack. In this sense, the judicial decisions that respond to structural penitentiary violence in the form of the declaration of an Unconstitutional State of Affairs, with its progressive and programmatic temporal approaches that suspend the imprisoned person in a world of guarantees without guarantees and sacrifice them while they wait for that imagined future that is a prison that respects the Constitution, weaken one of the bastions of guarantees: the prohibition of being subjected to cruel, inhuman and degrading treatment. As Ferrajoli points out,

> In this expanded version, guaranteeism comes to be configured as the other side of constitutionalism, given that its effectiveness depends on it: All constitutionally established fundamental rights require laws of action that introduce relative guarantees, prohibitions, and obligations that correspond to them. Thus, constitutional democracy, in its various

39 Shadd Maruna, 'Re-entry as a rite of passage' (2011) 1 Punishment & Society 3.

40 Bojan Bugarič, 'The False Promise of Constitutionalism' (2023) 117 AJIL Unbound 263, doi:10.1017/aju.2023.44.

> dimensions and levels, comes to be configured as a legal construction entirely composed of guarantees and guarantee institutions.[41]

The crack that the Unconstitutional State of Affairs and the state of emergency open in the historical structure of guaranteeism is as deep as it is silent. It is profound because it allows and accepts that the imprisoned person goes through a systematic violation of their rights, renouncing decisive protection of the person. In the wake of the Unconstitutional State of Affairs, the confinement machine does not stop adding people to the penitentiary world nor stops producing violations that must be endured by these people, who are the object of retribution. At the same time, it is silent because while the systems of constitutional intervention are being perfected, the unexpected effects of the application of the remedies are faced. The violation of rights spreads like a punitive pandemic throughout the institutional scheme of confinement, leaving behind an endless count of bodies stained by the rigours of the penitentiary world.

This is precisely what happened with the application of the decreasing balance rule by some local judges, which, in its effects, produced congestion at police stations and transitory detention centres, given the decision of the Superior Court of the Judicial District of Medellín, which exempted/suspended the application of the decreasing balance rule to allow the flow of imprisoned people to continue through the thresholds that communicate the different worlds of confinement.[42] The Constitutional Court's Monitoring Room created a complex scheme that sought to address

> The need to allow the entrance of people who remain in transitory detention centres in precarious conditions to establishments, despite the fact that, by virtue of the decisions of criminal judges in their respective processes, they should be confined in penitentiary and prison establishments.[43]

41 Luigi Ferrajoli, 'Garantismo penal' (2010) 32 Isonomía – Revista de Teoría y Filosofía del Derecho 209, 210.

42 Norberto Hernández Jimenez and Cristina Aranguren Páez, 'Comentario a la sentencia SU-122 de 2022' (2022) 18 Nuevo Foro Penal 181.

43 Constitutional Court of Colombia, Auto 110 de 2019, M.P. Gloria Stella Ortiz. Own translation.

In other words, in the case of Medellín, this meant that detained people were moved from the police stations to Bellavista Prison[44] in a fluid manner, without interruption or jams, thanks to '*the integration of the principle of proportionality to the rule of decreasing balance*'.[45]

When the Court affirms the malleable nature of the judicial remedies and accepts that the decreasing balancing rule can be modified, it indicates to the local judge that he will decide whether to apply it or not and to guide his decision based on the principle of proportionality. In this exercise, the consideration is carried out by studying places of confinement, their characteristics, the degree of indignity they contain, and how they affect the rights of the people who are detained there. This consideration is to decide which new people cannot be added, where they must remain, and to which place they cannot be moved. Ultimately, and despite the sophisticated paraphernalia of this kind of punitive constitutionalism, it is an administrative issue. A pro-security position replaces the counter-majoritarian position of the Court.

Despite the Court's technical effort to explain what a strict proportionality test is and how it should be applied in this case, the decision to keep people crowded in a transitional detention centre or in prison itself becomes a choice about degrees of pain, suffering, and inevitable violence:

> Therefore, the judge must assess whether the purpose pursued with the application of the decreasing balance rule, that is, the protection of the rights of inmates housed in prisons and penitentiaries, is a constitutional good of greater relevance than the constitutional value sacrificed. In this case, the fundamental rights of people who are detained in URIs (provisional detention centres) and police stations in precarious conditions.[46]

Ultimately, it is a displacement of the focus of constitutionalism, of moving the detained person within the confinement apparatus based on an unclear gradation of scales of suffering.[47]

44 Bellavista Prison is the biggest prison in the Medellin district.

45 Constitutional Court of Colombia, Auto 110 de 2019 (n 44). Own translation.

46 While this balancing is possible, theoretically, between detention centres subject to the information system resulting from the creation of the technical detention standards and the baseline of indicators, when it is a temporary detention centre that is not covered by the outline of the judgment T-762/2015, this consideration is done based on the penitentiary system that covers the most remote places from the Unconstitutional State of Affairs. Own translation.

47 For this reason, "what was ordered in Auto 110 of 2019, on the weighing of the application of the rule of decreasing balance and the introduction of prioritization criteria for peni-

The Unconstitutional State of Affairs condemns prison violence, pronounces it in its decisions, and avoids separating the subject who suffers it from the world of confinement. It keeps detainees in the punitivism of insurmountable suffering. By keeping them suspended in a space and time of suffering, the violence they suffer is perpetuated as a result of the case's legal framing from the point of view of progressivity, which makes the person's pain invisible by focusing on the stabilization of the 'prison population'.[48] In this reading of the relationship between punitive power and personal dignity, the historical efforts of the tradition of penal guarantees, which creates a system of individual safeguards as a limit to the excesses of the State's punitive power, are transformed into future goals that an institutional unlocking effort must achieve. The *pro homine* principle fades in the temporality imposed by the practice of punitive constitutionalism.

In this sense, the Unconstitutional State of Affairs destroys the system of individual safeguards against punitive power that defends criminal guarantees *'aimed at minimizing the violence of punitive intervention through its submission to strict limits imposed to protect the rights of the person'*.[49] Sotomayor and Tamayo point out that different discourses, shaped in specific historical contexts, promote the expansion of criminal law and the silent dismantling of the hard structure of penal guarantees. In their opinion, *'the political discourses that have acquired the greatest relevance in favouring the exacerbated growth of current criminal law are, above all, the risk society, Human Rights, and social defence'*.[50]

Paradoxically, the constitutional doctrine of the Unconstitutional State of Affairs should be understood as a way of reading the punitive power of the State that is based on its improvement, on the rhetorical search of limiting. From the point of view of the protection of the incarcerated person, it allows the application of cruel, inhuman and degrading treatment, abandoning the person to the violence of the penitentiary system. Despite ensuring, time and time again, that it is a *pro homine* speech, in its political effects, it is a *pro carceris* speech. The statements are as repeated as they are well-known and

---

tentiary and prison establishments, due to the greater impact on the human dignity of the inmates, does not really introduce any guarantee of the fundamental rights of incarcerated people". Own translation. Grupo de Estudios Penales Universidad EAFIT, 'Editorial' (2019) 15 Nuevo Foro Penal 15–16.

48 Luigi Ferrajoli, *Derecho y razón. Teoría del garantismo penal* (Madrid, Trotta 2011).

49 Juan O. Sotomayor Acosta, '¿El derecho penal garantista en retirada?' (2008) 21 Revista Penal 148. Own translation.

50 Juan O. Sotomayor Acosta, 'La 'nueva cuestión penal' y los retos de una ciencia penal garantista' (2014) 10 Nuevo Foro Penal 177, 179. Own translation.

range from the reaffirmation of resocialization as a function of punishment to the dignity of the imprisoned person as the limit of the punitive power of the State. When these statements are implemented by punitive constitutionalism, prison oppression is denounced. Still, its irremediable nature is accepted, and the tragedy is assumed, displacing its solution to an uncertain future under the formula of structural reform.

Hence, this constitutionalism recognizes prison violence in all of its manifestations. It tells prisoners that their suffering is real, that the violation of rights exists, and that what happens to them is true. It recomposes the internal logic of constitutional discourse and elevates it to an unprecedented level of sophistication and refinement. In doing so, it distances the constitutional discourse from the subject it is called to protect, creating an intelligibility gap that intensifies by virtue of the transmutation effect of legal language. In this sense, punitive constitutionalism is symbolic violence deployed through jurisprudence that naturalizes and legitimizes human suffering within the prison.[51]

Thus, punitive constitutionalism reminds us that criminal law is minimal and should work as an *ultima ratio* and in a residual manner. Prisoners should not be forced to endure cruel, inhuman, and degrading treatments and punishments. In short, prisons should respect the principles that define a Social State of Law. The jurisprudence's acceptance of the inevitable nature of human suffering implies that, in theory, none of this should be happening. Therefore, they translate it into the structure of progressivity to represent prison violence as a passing moment, as an instant that will disappear by simply closing our eyes to this temporary episode within the long history of prison modernization, accepting the inevitable nature of the tragedy.

When safeguards blur amid this hyper-justified construction of what continues to be a state of affairs that constitutionalism seeks to tame but against which it bends to accept its autonomy, it creates a fictitious legal description of the penitentiary world that trivializes the violence that the subjects who live there suffer. Thus, punitive constitutionalism attempts

> above all to capture the relationship between the two worlds and collapse it into an always spectacular relationship, by which fact and law, exception and norm, can only be located in a zone of indistinction. The

51 Pierre Bourdieu, 'The Force of Law: Toward a Sociology of the Juridical Field' (1987) 38 Hastings Law Journal 805.

> legal description of the world is a falsification of life, an impoverishment.[52]

The Unconstitutional State of Affairs is a projection that prevents the collapse of a legally created world, ordered in its claim to normative completeness, which is overlayed on the factual world of the penitentiary experience. This is why the experiences that make up the world of confinement are unconstitutional as they deny the validity of the legal order and threaten to destroy it in their encounter with the world of rights. Under the Unconstitutional State of Affairs doctrine, the factual and legal aspects are confused. The legal constitutional decision in this space of indistinction that results from this clash. This declaration creates the sacrificial moment of the prisoner who is legally protected and simultaneously abandoned to the violence and latency of death that runs through the penitentiary world.

For this reason, the need to maintain the effectiveness of the law requires the courts to demand the radical transformation of that factual world of the prison that opposes and resists it, but at the same time demands its conservation and the perpetuation of its validity in that sector of the legal system that is imposed on the prisoner as a transgressor: the execution of the sentence and the materiality of the penitentiary world. The *ius puniendi*'s symbolic structure remains intact despite its factuality being opposed to the political constitution. This is why the imprisoned person cannot be released, to the extent that the decision that disaggregates him from the penitentiary world as a rite of passage that overcomes the punitivism in which he lies would mean sacrificing not only the validity of the norm as an end to the sentence, but also the abstract protection of public security. The release is a rite of passage that can only be decided within the framework of the routine operation of the penitentiary machine.

An incarcerated person cannot be released to wander incognito, like a spectre of violence and danger, across the streets of the free world. Thus, the non-effectiveness of the Constitution, characteristic of the world of confinement, is compensated by the defence of the validity of the norm as the end of the punishment expressed in its effective materiality through imprisonment.

52 Thanos Zartaloudis, 'Violence Without Law? On Pure Violence as a Destituent Power' in Brendan Moran and Carlo Salzani (eds), *Towards the Critique of Violence – Walter Benjamin and Giorgio Agamben* (London, Bloomsbury Press 2015) 171.

5 Conclusion

In its sophistication, punitive constitutionalism creates an ideal punitive world that allows it to approach the infamy of the penitentiary world and name it to restore its own internal order to the violence it cannot contain. In its encounter with the fact of confinement, punitive constitutionalism declares that the penitentiary world exists in the realm of things, that its deployment opposes the constitutional order and that it must be corrected progressively, that the penitentiary machine must be reformed, that society should spare any effort or resources in this task, so that, one day, the rights of prisoners are respected. This constitutionalism will declare that the penitentiary world is a state of affairs that confronts and denies the constitutional order, declaring unconstitutional the prison crisis as a whole, including this legal doctrine to suspend the prison system in a state of permanent reform under the rhythm of progressiveness.

Despite the enormous symbolic power that comes with the declaration of an unconstitutional state of affairs, the material conditions of existence of the imprisoned person will not change significantly. The unconstitutional state of affairs doctrine seeks to restore the constitutional order disturbed by the imperfection of the penitentiary system as a condition that prisoners do not suffer its violence. In this context, inmates only enjoy the constitutionally required minimum rights; therefore, it will not interrupt the prison's operation nor allow those whom it has been captured to escape from its interior. Under these conditions, the prison system is made to remain in permanent crisis, like trying to repair a faulty moving train that does not stop picking up passengers to crowd them into its cars, waiting to reach an unknown destination in its perpetual motion.

References

Abunza CI, Paredes G, Bustos P, and Mendoza Molina MA, *Familia y privación de la libertad en Colombia* (Bogota, Universidad del Rosario 2016).

Angel RA, 'Desarrollo Del Sistema Penitenciario y Carcelario Colombiano Entre 1995 y 2010' (*Instituto Rosarista de Accion Social*, 2011) <https://editorial.urosario.edu.co/pageflip/acceso-abierto/desarrollo-del-sistema-penitenciario.pdf>.

Aristizábal L, 'Cárceles y coronavirus: motines en Italia y presos a las casas en Irán' *France24* (Asia-Pacific, 9 March 2020) <https://www.france24.com/es/20200309-carceles-coronavirus-italia-motines-iran-presos>.

Ariza L, 'The Economic and Social Rights of Prisoners and Constitutional Court Intervention in the Penitentiary System in Colombia' in Daniel Bonilla Maldonado (ed), *Constitutionalism of the Global South: The Activist Tribunals of India, South Africa, and Colombia* (Cambridge, Cambridge University Press 2013) 129–162.

Ariza L and Botero CA, 'En el corazón del Buen Pastor. La apropiación del discurso de los derechos humanos en el contexto penitenciario colombiano' (2015) 1 Antipoda. *Revista de Antropología y Arqueología* 45–64. https://doi.org/10.7440/antipoda23.2015.03.

Ariza L and Iturralde M and others, 'Indicadores de Derechos Humanos en el Sistema Penitenciario y Carcelario' (*Ministerio de Justicia y del Derecho de Colombia and Agencia Alemana para la Cooperación Internacional* (GIZ), 2017) <https://prisiones.uniandes.edu.co/images/Publicaciones/LineaBaseDDHH_2_compressed.pdf>.

Ariza L and Torres MA, 'Definiendo el hacinamiento: estándares normativos y perspectivas judiciales sobre el espacio penitenciario' (2019) 21 *Revista Estudios Socio Jurídicos* 227–258.

Bourdieu P, 'The Force of Law: Toward a Sociology of the Juridical Field' (1987) 38 *Hastings Law Journal* 805–853.

Bugarič B, 'The False Promise of Constitutionalism' (2023) 117 *AJIL Unbound* 263–268, doi:10.1017/aju.2023.44.

Camus A, *The Plague* (England, Penguin Books).

Constitutional Court of Colombia, *Judgment T-153/1998* (28 April 1998) M.P. Eduardo Cifuentes Muñoz.

Constitutional Court of Colombia, *Judgment T-388/2013* (28 June 2013) P.P. Maria Victoria Calle.

Constitutional Court of Colombia, *Judgment T-762/2015* (16 December 2015) M.P. Maria Victoria Correa.

Constitutional Court of Colombia, Auto 110 de 2019, M.P. Gloria Stella Ortiz.

Constitutional Court of Colombia, *Judgment C-255/2020* (23 July 2020) M.P. Diana Fajardo Rivera.

Constitutional Court of Colombia, *Judgment SU-122/2022* (31 March 2022) M.P. Diana Fajardo Rivera, Cristina Pardo and José Reyes.

Cruz Palomo DF and Jaramillo Marín RS, 'La Insuficiencia De Las Medidas Adoptadas Para La población Privada De La Libertad En Colombia Con ocasión De La Pandemia De La Enfermedad Por Coronavirus' (2020) 19 *Opinión Jurídica* 151–161. https://doi.org/10.22395/ojum.v19n40a7.

Ferrajoli L, 'Garantismo penal' (2010) 32 *Isonomía – Revista de Teoría y Filosofía del Derecho* 209–211.

Ferrajoli L, *Derecho y razón. Teoría del garantismo penal* (Madrid, Trotta 2011).

García Vargas MN, 'Hacinamiento en estaciones de policía en Bogotá superan el 900% de ocupación' (*Radio Nacional de Colombia*, June 2023. <https://www.radio

nacional.co/actualidad/hacinamiento-estaciones-de-policia-en-bogota-superan-el-900-de-ocupacion>.

Grupo de Estudios Penales Universidad EAFIT, 'Editorial' (2019) 15 Nuevo Foro Penal.

Hernández Jimenez N and Aranguren Páez C, 'Comentario a la sentencia SU-122 de 2022' (2022) 18 *Nuevo Foro Penal* 181–194.

INPEC, 'Boletines Estadísticos' (*INPEC*, January 2020) <https://www.inpec.gov.co/estadisticas/-/document_library/TWBuJQCWH6KV/view/49294>.

Iturralde M, Santamaría N, and Uribe JP, 'El coronavirus en las cárceles colombianas. Análisis y propuestas de solución más allá de la coyuntura' (*Friedich Ebert Stiftung and Grupo de Prisiones Facultad de Derecho de la Universidad de Los Andes*, 2020) <https://derecho.uniandes.edu.co/sites/default/files/coronavirus-en-carceles-colombianas.pdf>.

López Fonseca Ó, 'Interior aísla 12 cárceles con más de 8.000 presos para evitar la expansión del coronavirus' *El País* (Madrid, 10 March 2020) <https://elpais.com/espana/2020-03-10/interior-aisla-a-mas-de-8000-presos-de-12-carceles-para-evitar-la-expansion-de-coronavirus.html>.

Lyons JQ, Monterroza AMN, and Meza MI, 'La figura del estado de cosas inconstitucionales como mecanismo de protección de los derechos fundamentales de la población vulnerable en Colombia' (2011) 3 *Revista Jurídica Mario Alario D'Filippo* 69–80.

Maruna S, 'Re-entry as a rite of passage' (2011) 1 *Punishment & Society* 3–28.

Ministry of Health and Social Protection, Resolution 843 of 2020.

Ministry of Health and Social Protection, Resolution 313 of 2021.

Pardo D, 'Policía en Colombia: ¿por qué la muerte de Javier Ordóñez desató una violencia inédita en Bogotá?' *BBC News* (Bogotá, 12 September 2020) <https://www.bbc.com/mundo/noticias-america-latina-54125522>.

Presidency of the Republic of Colombia, Decree 655/2022.

Reyes Alvarado Y, 'El curioso decreto sobre excarcelación' *El Espectador* (Bogotá, 21 April 2020) <https://www.elespectador.com/opinion/columnistas/yesid-reyes-alvarado/el-curioso-decreto-sobre-excarcelacion-column-915579/>.

Sander G, 'Preventing infectious diseases in prisons: A public health and human rights imperative' (*Penal Reform International*, 23 October 2015) <https://www.penalreform.org/blog/preventing-infectious-diseases-in-prisons-a-public-health/>.

Simon J, *Mass Incarceration on Trial: A Remarkable Court Decision and the Future of Prisons in America* (New York, The New Press 2011).

Sotomayor Acosta JO, '¿El derecho penal garantista en retirada?' (2008) 21 *Revista Penal* 148–164.

Sotomayor Acosta JO, 'La 'nueva cuestión penal' y los retos de una ciencia penal garantista' (2014) 10 *Nuevo Foro Penal* 177–194.

Torres Gómez MA, 'Estándares Internacionales Para La Garantía Del Derecho a La Salud de La Población Privada de La Libertad' in Ariza L, Iturralde M, and León Tamayo F (eds), *Cárcel, Derecho y Sociedad: Aproximaciones al Mundo Penitenciario En Colombia* (Bogotá, Ediciones Uniandes 2021) 355–380.

US Supreme Court, *Brown v Plata* (2011) No 09–12.

Vargas Ovalle JM, 'Incendio en la cárcel La Picota de Bogotá tras un intento de motín' *RCN Radio* (Bogotá, 17 March 2020) <https://www.rcnradio.com/bogota/incendio-en-la-carcel-la-picota-de-bogota-tras-un-intento-de-motin>.

Zartaloudis T, 'Violence Without Law? On Pure Violence as a Destituent Power' in Moran B and Salzani C (eds), *Towards the Critique of Violence – Walter Benjamin and Giorgio Agamben* (London, Bloomsbury Press 2015) 169–186.

CHAPTER 9

Concluding Remarks: The Need to Fundamentally Rethink Who Is Imprisoned, Why, and under What Conditions

Yves Haeck and Clara Burbano Herrera

Many Latin American prisons have historically experienced terrible conditions including overcrowding, lack of health services, unsanitary and unsafe conditions. Some persons deprived of liberty are crammed in hot, humid spaces with little air circulation and incoming sunlight, while others are confined in very cold areas without proper clothing. In some units, there might be a constant lack of water, power or even sanitation. For these reasons, diseases such as tuberculosis are more prevalent among the prison population than they are outside. Within this deplorable context, family members assume a pivotal role, often being the main source of food, hygiene products, medicines and clothing, as well as providing emotional care and support that is generally not offered by the state prison administration. Violence is also part of daily prison life, perpetuated not only by prison officers and the police, but also by those imprisoned, both within and outside of the context of prison riots. Moreover, there are numerous instances in Latin America of prisoners gaining control over internal prison security and management, including prisoners involved in organized crime, as has been noted by the Inter-American Commission on Human Rights (IACHR) and the United Nations Subcommittee on Prevention of Torture. These dynamics have afflicted countries such as Bolivia, Brazil, Guatemala, Colombia, Mexico, Honduras, Panama, Paraguay and more recently, Ecuador.

In this context, certain individuals deprived of their liberty are disproportionately affected by deplorable prison conditions. As is the case beyond prison walls, individuals' experiences are shaped by their economic, social, cultural, and racial backgrounds. The intersection of these factors determines whether imprisonment constitutes a relatively privileged experience for a minority or an extreme hardship for the majority.

The objective of this volume is to contribute to the existing body of literature on the structural factors underlying the deplorable conditions experienced by individuals deprived of their liberty in Latin America. This collection has brought together distinguished scholars from various countries, each with

 DOI:10.1163/9789004747739_010

extensive expertise in the field. Employing a range of theoretical frameworks including "negative theories of punishment" (*Machado and Pires*) and "experimental constitutionalism" (*Ariza and Torres*) the contributors have provided a critical examination of the persistent deficiencies in prison conditions, despite ongoing efforts to improve them, including during the COVID-19 pandemic. The chapters within this volume have addressed a wide array of issues, including the experiences of incarcerated women, the sexual and reproductive health rights of female prisoners, the use of urgent measures to prevent human rights violations in detention facilities, and the impact of the COVID-19 pandemic on prison systems. In particular, the authors have analyzed how Latin American authorities have sought to reduce prison populations and enhance detention conditions through judicial, legislative, and executive initiatives. These measures include the reassessment of pre-trial detention practices, the implementation of alternative sentencing mechanisms such as early release and house arrest, and the granting of presidential pardons.

The subsequent lines will underscore some of the most critical issues explored by the contributors to this volume.

1 The Human Rights Approach to Prison: The Need to Fundamentally Rethink Who Is Imprisoned, Why, and under What Conditions

1.1 *The Relationship between Poverty and Disease*

The authors highlight that individuals deprived of liberty are disproportionately drawn from socioeconomically disadvantaged backgrounds, making them more vulnerable to both communicable and non-communicable diseases when compared to the general population.[1] Research indicates a strong correlation between poverty and the prevalence of disease among individuals deprived of their liberty. Incarcerated individuals frequently experience heightened exposure to risk factors such as smoking, inadequate hygiene, and weakened immune defences due to stress, poor nutrition, and coexisting health conditions, including bloodborne viruses, tuberculosis, and drug use

1 UN Office on Drugs and Crime (UNODC) and WHO Regional Office for Europe, 'Good governance for prison health in the 21st century: A policy brief on the organization of prison health' (*UNODC*, 2013) vii <https://www.unodc.org/documents/hiv-aids/publications/Prisons_and_other_closed_settings/Good-governance-for-prison-health-in-the-21st-century.pdf> accessed 12 April 2024.

disorders.[2] Consequently, infectious diseases are significantly more prevalent in correctional facilities. For instance, data from the Inter-American Development Bank (IADB) reveal that the prevalence of tuberculosis in prisons across Latin America and the Caribbean is 81 times higher than in the general population. Similar trends are observed regarding the incidence of HIV, hepatitis, and syphilis. (*Romero, Sanchez, Ariza, Torres*).

1.2 *The Relationship between Women from Marginalized Backgrounds and Punishment*

The authors have emphasized the disproportionate impact of drug and abortion laws on the incarceration of women. The analysis highlights that these legal frameworks do not impact all women equally; rather, they disproportionately affect women from marginalized backgrounds that are characterized by poverty, social inequality, low levels of education, and precarious employment, often within the informal economy. Additionally, many of these incarcerated women have experienced physical abuse and/or sexual violence. A considerable proportion are mothers – often single mothers – who frequently serve as primary caregivers for children, the elderly, or individuals with disabilities (*Youngers, Giacomello, Cruz; Martínez Romero, Sánchez, Ariza, Torres*). Machado argues that processes for the admission and release of people from state facilities need to take into account both individual and environmental factors related to the incarcerated person Analyzing the lived experience of punishment requires an examination of the biographical elements that shape an individual's sentence, including their medical, biological, psychological, emotional, and familial circumstances, both past and present. Additionally, institutional factors play a crucial role, such as prison architecture, the availability and quality of human resources, medical and legal assistance services, opportunities for maintaining contact with family members, visitation policies, and the structure of the disciplinary regime. Collectively, these factors shape and influence an individual's lived experience within the prison system.

---

2 WHO Regional Office for Europe, 'Preparedness, prevention, and control of COVID-19 in prisons and other places of detention' (*WHO*, 2021) 2 <https://iris.who.int/bitstream/handle/10665/339830/WHO-EURO-2021-1405-41155-57257-eng.pdf?sequence=1> accessed 12 April 2024.

2 The COVID-19 Pandemic Revealed and Exacerbated Policy Failures Affecting the Most Marginalized Persons in Society

The book has also addressed the novel coronavirus (COVID-19) pandemic, which has posed unprecedented challenges on a global scale, revealing and exacerbating policy failures affecting the most marginalised communities, including those deprived of their liberty. Many countries worldwide, including in Latin America, started processes aimed at reducing their prison populations through their judicial, legislative, and/or executive branches after COVID-19 was declared a pandemic in 2020. In Latin America, these initiatives took various forms, including presidential pardons, executive decrees, emergency legislation, and directives from justice officials. In general, states implemented three types of measures: i) policy responses to address critical sanitation deficiencies; ii) policy responses to facilitate safe communication with the outside world; and iii) policy responses to reduce prison overcrowding. The authors have explained that the prison policies implemented during this period offer important lessons to governments and policymakers for much-needed prison reform in the region.

2.1 *Alternative Sentencing Measures for Non-Violent Offenders*

Several alternative measures to incarceration exist which states can implement, particularly for non-violent offenders. These include community service, rehabilitation programs for individuals with substance use disorders, educational initiatives for juvenile offenders, restorative justice practices, and therapeutic interventions. Additionally, incarcerated individuals who demonstrate progress in their rehabilitation through education, employment, or other constructive activities may benefit from alternative sentencing arrangements, such as weekend or nightly imprisonment, as well as partial release for work or family reintegration. These measures not only contribute to rehabilitation, but also facilitate smoother reintegration into society. Furthermore, as seen in various national initiatives during the COVID-19 pandemic, states may consider early release policies for incarcerated individuals above a certain age, those who have completed the majority of their sentence, or who have demonstrated good behaviour during their incarceration. Nevertheless, it is important to note that these alternatives to imprisonment should not be used to facilitate impunity for serious crimes, such as human rights violations and public corruption.

2.2 *The Need to Regulate the Use of Force*

Since the early stages of the COVID-19 outbreak, alongside health challenges, violent uprisings related to the pandemic erupted in prisons across several Latin American countries. These riots broke out in protest against overcrowding, inadequate hygiene and the shortage of personal protective equipment to prevent COVID-19 transmission. Prisons in Brazil, Venezuela, El Salvador, Colombia, Peru and Argentina witnessed riots and uprisings, some resulting in large-scale escapes and violent confrontations with law enforcement, leading to hundreds of wounded and dozens of deaths. These incidents underscore the need to regulate the use of force. In the context of prisons, the use of force is to be regarded as the exception and must be employed solely as a last resort. The circumstances that may legitimately justify the use of force are strictly delineated. To prevent any abuse, recourse to force must respect the principles of legality, necessity and proportionality. Monitoring procedures must also be implemented, and those responsible for abuse must be held accountable. Prison staff and any others responsible for maintaining order, such as special forces who can be deployed in cases of mutiny or other serious incidents, must receive comprehensive training in the risks associated with the use of force and the legal framework that authorizes their intervention.

2.3 *More Information and Transparency Is Needed*

The general lack of transparency and information not only for COVID-19 cases among people deprived of liberty and prison staff, but also for the measures adopted by each correctional facility has been highlighted throughout this volume. The authors recommend further study and assessment of COVID-19's impact in prisons within the region. Furthermore, any programs that promote alternatives to prison should acknowledge that society should be informed and receive sensible explanations as to the importance of these measures; public perception can be key in shaping policy related to criminal justice and security. Moreover, a constant flow of information and data are required to design policies that are the most sustainable and effective.

3 Challenges

3.1 *Specific Alternatives to Incarceration Can Lead to a Multitude of Challenges*

The most prevalent gender-specific alternatives to incarceration employed in Latin America, and used during the COVID-19, are house arrest and electronic monitoring, which are frequently implemented together. While these measures may initially seem beneficial, they often pose significant challenges for individuals from disadvantaged backgrounds. Moreover, it is important to acknowledge that not all persons deprived of liberty have a home to return to, either due to having a lack of stable housing prior to imprisonment or because they have been abandoned by their families as a result of the stigma and discrimination frequently associated with the incarceration, particularly for women. Similarly, the effectiveness of electronic monitoring is contingent upon the individual having both a residence and family support, as the stringent conditions often imposed can serve to prevent those wearing an ankle monitor from securing employment (*Youngers, Giacomello, Cruz; Romero, Sánchez, Ariza, Torres*). In this context, it is relevant to highlight the situation in Chile, where, in April 2020, it was reported that one hundred prisoners rejected a general pardon and opted to remain in prison facilities rather than serve the remainder of their sentences under house arrest. According to unofficial sources, some individuals chose to remain incarcerated due to the absence of a home to which they could return, while others preferred imprisonment because their release would result in the loss of employment and benefits available to them within the prison system, but that would not be accessible otherwise. This Chilean case exemplifies the absence of a comprehensive post-incarceration reintegration policy and reflects a broader, systemic challenge in the region. Without adequate material, psychological, and social support – whether from family, the government, or non-profit organizations – former prisoners often face significant difficulties in successfully reintegrating into society, thereby increasing the risk of recidivism (*Romero and Garcia*).

3.2 *Countries Need to Critically Reassess the Importance of Reducing Prison Overcrowding*

Prison overcrowding not only violates the rights of individuals deprived of their liberty, but also poses significant public health risks. Overcrowded conditions exacerbate issues such as poor medical care, sanitation, and the spread of infectious diseases. Moreover, overcrowding undermines rehabilitation efforts and increases the likelihood of recidivism, as individuals are often released in worse conditions than when they entered. To address this, states must prioritize reducing overcrowding through judicial reforms and the development of effective alternatives to incarceration. This approach would not only safeguard human rights, but also contribute to better long-term social and public health outcomes.

3.3 *The Increasing Issue of Overcrowding in Latin American Prisons*

Post-pandemic analyses indicate that, despite governmental efforts to mitigate overcrowding during the health crisis, prison populations in many Latin

American countries have continued to rise, with only a few exceptions. According to the World Prison Brief, in 2018, approximately 1.6 million individuals were incarcerated across the region. By 2022, this number had increased to nearly 1.9 million. Notably, Colombia, Ecuador, Costa Rica, Guatemala, and Honduras experienced reductions in their prison populations compared to the pre-pandemic period. Investigating the underlying causes of these declines would be a valuable avenue for further research. However, the majority of Latin American states have recorded an overall increase in incarceration rates.

3.4 *Public Resistance to Prisoner Releases and Judicial Challenges*

In certain countries, particularly Brazil, significant resistance to efforts aimed at reducing prison populations was evident among judicial authorities and governmental officials. Opposition came not only from members of the judiciary, but also from the Ministry of Justice. The then Minister of Justice publicly opposed the National Justice Council's recommendation to release prisoners from high-risk groups, those in pre-trial detention, and individuals convicted of non-violent offenses.

3.5 *The Primacy of In-Person Visits and the Role of Technology*

The right of incarcerated individuals to receive in-person visits must be upheld at all times. However, technological advancements can serve as a valuable supplement in facilitating contact between prisoners and their families. Despite its benefits, the implementation of such technology remains costly. Governments must allocate substantial resources to develop and maintain technological solutions within correctional facilities. Additionally, given the high levels of poverty prevalent among the families of incarcerated individuals in Latin America, access to appropriate digital devices and reliable internet connections presents a significant barrier. Similarly, telemedicine offers a promising avenue for addressing the medical needs of prisoners who might otherwise lack access to specialized healthcare services within correctional institutions.

3.6 *The Role of International Human Rights Bodies and Organizations*

International cooperation and solidarity are essential for the assessment and dissemination of research findings on prison conditions. International institutions, such as the United Nations, and regional entities, including the IACHR, play a pivotal role in identifying best practices and issuing recommendations to states. Additionally, these organizations are instrumental in holding states accountable for violations of the rights of incarcerated individuals. Furthermore, regional institutions such as the Inter-American Development Bank and the Organization of American States (OAS) can facilitate comparative research and provide technical assistance to national governments.

4 Final Considerations

This volume has examined the complex and often contradictory realities surrounding incarceration, decarceration, and penal reform across Latin America, with a particular emphasis on gender-specific alternatives, post-pandemic developments, and systemic challenges. As the contributions have collectively demonstrated, measures such as house arrest and electronic monitoring, while presented as humane alternatives to imprisonment, frequently replicate or exacerbate existing inequalities when implemented without the necessary material and social support. The Chilean case, in which individuals rejected early release due to precarious living conditions or fear of losing prison-based employment, exemplifies the urgent need for comprehensive reintegration strategies that extend beyond the prison gate. At the same time, the persistence, and in many cases escalation, of prison overcrowding despite the global health crisis highlights the limited effectiveness of temporary or reactive measures. Structural reform remains hindered by political resistance, institutional inertia, and public scepticism toward decarceration initiatives. Although technological solutions and international cooperation offer promising avenues for progress, their potential is constrained by deep-rooted socio-economic disparities and insufficient investment.

Taken together, the chapters in this volume underscore the pressing need for a paradigm shift in how Latin American states approach criminal justice. Meaningful reform must go beyond punitive responses and engage with the broader socio-political conditions that produce incarceration. This includes addressing poverty, inequality, gender-based discrimination, and the social stigma attached to criminalisation. As editors, we hope that the insights presented here contribute to a more nuanced understanding of these issues and encourage sustained dialogue and action both within the region and in global discussions on justice reform.

References

UN Office on Drugs and Crime (UNODC) and *WHO* Regional Office for Europe, 'Good governance for prison health in the 21st century: A policy brief on the organization of prison health' (*UNODC*, 2013) <https://www.unodc.org/documents/hiv-aids/publications/Prisons_and_other_closed_settings/Good-governance-for-prison-health-in-the-21st-century.pdf>.

WHO Regional Office for Europe, 'Preparedness, prevention, and control of COVID-19 in prisons and other places of detention' (*WHO*, 2021) <https://iris.who.int/bitstream/handle/10665/339830/WHO-EURO-2021-1405-41155-57257-eng.pdf?sequence=1>.

Index

www.ingramcontent.com/pod-product-compliance
Lightning Source LLC
Chambersburg PA
CBHW071247230926
51849CB00001B/264
9789004747722